HIPPOCRENE CO...

W9-BKE-990

RUSSIAN-ENGLISH/ ENGLISH-RUSSIAN DICTIONARY

RUSSIAN-ENGLISH/ ENGLISH-RUSSIAN DICTIONARY

Oleg & Ksana Beniukh

HIPPOCRENE BOOKS, INC.
New York

Second printing, 1995

Copyright © 1993 by Oleg & Ksana Beniukh.

For information, address:
Hippocrene Books
171 Madison Avenue
New York, NY 10016

ISBN 0-7818-0132-X

Printed in the United States of America.

CONTENTS
ОГЛАВЛЕНИЕ

page
стр.

RUSSIAN-ENGLISH DICTIONARY
РУССКО-АНГЛИЙСКИЙ СЛОВАРЬ

ENGLISH-RUSSIAN DICTIONARY
АНГЛО-РУССКИЙ СЛОВАРЬ

THE RUSSIAN ALPHABET —
РУССКИЙ АЛФАВИТ

Аа	Ии	Рр	Шш
Бб	Йй	Сс	Щщ
Вв	Кк	Тт	ъ
Гг	Лл	Уу	ы
Дд	Мм	Фф	ь
Ее, Ёё	Нн	Хх	Ээ
Жж	Оо	Цц	Юю
Зз	Пп	Чч	Яя

THE ENGLISH ALPHABET —
АНГЛИЙСКИЙ АЛФАВИТ

Aa	Gg	Mm	Tt
Bb	Hh	Nn	Uu
Cc	Ii	Oo	Vv
Dd	Jj	Pp	Ww
Ee	Kk	Qq	Xx
Ff	Ll	Rr	Yy
		Ss	Zz

RUSSIAN-ENGLISH
DICTIONARY
РУССКО-АНГЛИЙСКИЙ
СЛОВАРЬ

Preface

This dictionary has been designed as a clear, convenient and concise reference book. It can be used both by those who speak fluent Russian and those who have just acquainted themselves with the Russian alphabet. It will be of interest and value to students of Russian, tourists, visitors to conferences, businessmen, and others, who may simply want to understand Russian menus, theatre programmes, street-signs, notices, etc. The dictionary contains over 7 000 vocabulary entries, alphabetically arranged and supplied with the basic grammatical information. The verbs are given in the imperfective aspect, which is normally treated as the basic form of the simple verb.

This dictionary's innovative feature is the transliteration of every Russian word and expression, which the users will find most helpful. For this purpose the Editors have chosen the Library of Congress transliteration system, it being the least confusing while providing the necessary pronunciation guides.

LIST OF ABBREVIATIONS

abbr.	abbreviation
adj.	adjective
adv.	adverb
coll.	colloquial
comp.	comparative
conj.	conjunction
electr.	electrical
f.	feminine
fig.	figurative
gram.	grammar
indecl.	indeclinable
interj.	interjection
m.	masculine
med.	medicine
mus.	musical
n.	neuter
num.	numeral
obs.	obsolete
paren.	parenthesis
part.	participle
phot.	photography
pl.	plural
pred.	predicate
prep.	preposition
pron.	pronoun
sl.	slang

smb.	somebody
smth.	something

TRANSLITERATION GUIDE

а — a	к — k	х — kh
б — b	л — l	ц — ts
в — v	м — m	ч — ch
г — g	н — n	ш — sh
д — d	о — o	щ — shch
е — e	п — p	ъ — "
ё — io	р — r	ы — y
ж — zh	с — s	ь — '
з — z	т — t	э — e
и — i	у — u	ю — iu
й — i	ф — f	я — ia

A

а /a/ conj. and, but; eh?

абажур /abazhúr/ m. lampshade

абзац /abzáts/ m. paragraph

абонемент /abonemént/ m. subscription

абонент /abonént/ m. subscriber

аборт /abórt/ m. abortion; miscarriage

абрикос /abrikós/ m. apricot; apricot-tree

абсурд /absúrd/ m. nonsense, absurdity

авангард /avangárd/ m. vanguard

аванс /aváns/ m. advance payment

авантюрист /avantiuríst/ m. adventurer

авантюрный /avantiúrnyi/ adj. risky; shady

авария /aváriia/ f. crash, accident; breakdown

август /ávgust/ m. August

авиакомпания /aviakompániia/ f. airline

авиация /aviátsiia/ f. air force

автобиография /avtobiográfiia/ f. autobiography

автобус /avtóbus/ m. bus; coach

автогонки /avtogónki/ pl. motor race(s)

автомагистраль /avtomagistrál'/ f. motor-highway

автомат /avtomát/ m. automatic machine; slot machine; submachine gun

автомашина /avtomashína/ f. car, automobile

автономия /avtonómiia/ f. autonomy

автор /ávtor/ m. author

авторитет /avtoritét/ m. authority

авторитетный /avtoritétnyi/ adj. authoritative

авторский /ávtorskii/ adj. author's; copyright

авторское (право) /ávtorskoie právo/ adj.+ n. copyright

авторство /ávtorstvo/ n. authorship

агент /agént/ m. agent

агентство /agéntstvo/ n. agency

агрессивный /agressívnyi/ adj. aggressive

агрономия /agronómiia/ f. agronomy

ад /ad/ m. hell

адаптация /adaptátsiia/ f. adaptation

адвокат /advokát/ m. lawyer; barrister; advocate

администрация /administrátsiia/ f. administration

адмирал /admirál/ m. admiral

адрес /ádres/ m. address

адресат /adresát/ m. addressee

азарт /azárt/ m. excitement

азбука /ázbuka/ f. alphabet; the ABC

азиат /aziát/ m. Asian

академик /akadémik/ m. academician

акварель /akvarél'/ f. water-colour

аккредитив /akkreditív/ m. letter of credit

аккуратность /akkurátnost'/ f. neatness; punctuality; accuracy

аккуратный /akkurátnyi/ adj. tidy; punctual; exact

акр /akr/ m. acre

акт /akt/ m. act

актер /aktiór/ m. actor

актив /aktív/ m. assets; the activists

активизировать /aktivizírovat'/ v. intensify; activate

актуальный /aktuál'nyi/ adj. topical; urgent; pressing

акула /akúla/ f. shark

акушерка /akushérka/ f. midwife
акцент /aktsént/ m. accent
акционер /aktsionér/ m. shareholder
акционерный /aktsionérnyi/ adj. joint-stock
акция /áktsiia/ f. share; action
алименты /aliménty/ pl. alimony
алкоголик /alkogólik/ m. alcoholic
аллея /alléia/ f. avenue
алмаз /almáz/ m. diamond
алтарь /altár'/ m. altar
алфавит /alfavít/ m. alphabet, the ABC
алый /ályi/ adj. scarlet
альбом /al'bóm/ m. album
альпинизм /al'pinízm/ m. mountaineering
ампутация /amputátsiia/ f. amputation
анализ /análiz/ m. analysis
аналогичный /analogíchnyi/ adj. analogous
ананас /ananás/ m. pineapple
ангел /ángel/ m. angel
ангина /angína/ f. tonsillitis
английский /anglíiskii/ adj. English
англиканский /anglikánskii/ adj. Anglican
анекдот /anekdót/ m. anecdote
анкета /ankéta/ f. questionnaire
аннексия /annéksiia/ f. annexation
аннулировать /annulírovat'/ v. cancel, annul
анонимный /anonímnyi/ adj. anonymous
ансамбль /ansámbl'/ m.ensemble
антенна /anténna/ f. aerial; antenna

антиквар /antikvár/ m. antiquarian

антракт /antrákt/ m. interval

антрепренер /antrepreniór/ m. theatrical manager, impresario

аншлаг /anshlág/ m. full house; спектакль идет с аншлагом /spektákl' idiót s anshlágom/ the show is sold out

апатия /apátiia/ f. apathy

апеллировать /apellírovat'/ v. appeal

апельсин /apel'sín/ m. orange

аплодировать /aplodírovat'/ v. applaud

апогей /apogéi/ m. climax

аппарат /apparát/ m. apparatus; staff

аппетит /appetít/ m. appetite

апрель /aprél'/ m. April

аптека /aptéka/ f. drugstore; chemist's

арбуз /arbúz/ m. water-melon

арбитр /arbítr/ m. arbiter; referee

аргумент /argumént/ m. argument

арена /aréna/ f. arena; scene

аренда /arénda/ f. lease

арендная (плата) /aréndnaia pláta/ adj.+f. rent

арендатор /arendátor/ m. leaseholder; tenant

арест /arést/ m. arrest

армия /ármiia/ f. army

аромат /aromát/ m. aroma

артерия /artériia/ f. artery

артиллерия /artillériia/ f. artillery

артист /artíst/ m. actor

артрит /artrít/ m. arthritis
археолог /arkheólog/ m. archaeologist
археология /arkheológiia/ f. archaeology
архив /arkhív/ m. archives
архиепископ /arkhiepískop/ m. archbishop
архипелаг /arkhipelág/ m. archipelago
архитектор /arkhitéktor/ m. architect
архитектура /arkhitektúra/ f. architecture
аспирант /aspiránt/ m. post-graduate student
ассигнация /assignátsiia/ f. currency bill, note
ассигнование /assignovánie/ n. allocation
ассистент /assistént/ m. assistant
ассортимент /assortimént/ m. assortment
ассоциация /assotsiátsiia/ f. association
астма /ástma/ f. asthma
астролог /astrólog/ m. astrologer
ателье /atel'é/ n. studio; fashion house
атлас /átlas/ m. atlas
атлас /atlás/ m. satin
атлет /atlét/ n. athlete
атмосфера /atmosféra/ f. atmosphere
атомный /átomnyi/ adj. atomic
атомоход /atomokhód/ m. nuclear ship *or* ice-breaker
атташе /attashé/ m. attache
аттестат /attestát/ m. certificate; а. зрелости /a. zrélosti/
   school-leaving certificate
аттракцион /attraktsión/ m. side show
аудитория /auditóriia/ f. lecture room
аукцион /auktsión/ m. auction

афера /afióra/ f. swindle, fraud

афиша /afísha/ f. bill, poster

аэровокзал /aerovokzál/ m. air terminal; airport

аэродром /aerodróm/ m. airfield

аэрозоль /aerozól'/ m. aerosol

Б

баба /bába/ f. (old) woman; wife

бабочка /bábochka/ f. butterfly

бабье (лето) /báb'e léto/ adj. + n. Indian summer

бабушка /bábushka/ f. grandmother

багаж /bagázh/ m. baggage, luggage

багажная (квитанция) /bagázhnaia kvitántsiia/ adj. + f. luggage ticket

багажник /bagázhnik/ m. boot, luggage compartment

багажный (вагон) /bagázhnyi vagón/ adj. + m. luggage van

база /báza/ f. base, basis, foundation

базировать /bazírovat'/ v. base

бак /bak/ m. tank; seamen's mess

бакалейный /bakaléinyi/ adj. grocery

баланс /baláns/ m. balance

балет /balét/ m. ballet

балканский /balkánskii/ adj. Balkan

балкон /balkón/ m. balcony

баллотироваться /ballotírovat'sia/ v. be a candidate (for)

баловать /bálovat/ v. spoil; give a treat to

баловаться /bálovat'sia/ v. be naughty; indulge

банда /bánda/ f. gang; band

бандероль /banderól'/ f. (postal) wrapper

бандитизм /banditízm/ m. brigandage; gangsterism

банк /bank/ m. bank

банка /bánka/ f. jar, can, tin

банкет /bankét/ m. banquet

банкир /bankír/ m. banker

банкнота /banknóta/ m. bank-note, bill

банкрот /bankrót/ m. bankrupt

баня /bánia/ f. bath-house; public baths

барак /barák/ m. barrack, hut

баранина /baránina/ f. mutton

баранка /baránka/ f. ring-shaped roll

барашек /baráshek/ m. lamb

баррикада /barrikáda/ f. barricade

бархат /bárkhat/ m. velvet

барьер /bar'ér/ m. barrier

баснословный /basnoslóvnyi/ adj. fabulous, incredible

бассейн /basséin/ m. basin; pool

бастовать /bastovát'/ v. strike

батарейка /bataréika/ f. electric battery

батарея /bataréia/ f. battery; radiator

батист /batíst/ m. cambric

батон /batón/ m. long loaf

бацилла /batsílla/ f. bacillus

башня /báshnia/ f. tower

бдительность /bdítel'nost'/ f. vigilance

бег /beg/ m. run, race

беглость /béglost'/ f. fluency

беглый /béglyi/ adj. fluent, rapid; fugitive

беготня /begotniá/ f. running about

бегство /bégstvo/ n. flight, rout

бегун /begún/ m. runner

беда /bedá/ f. misfortune

беднеть /bednét'/ v. become poor

бедность /bédnost'/ f. poverty

бедный /bédnyi/ adj. poor

бедняк /bedniák/ m. poor man

бедро /bedró/ n. thigh, hip

бедственный /bédstvennyi/ adj. calamitous; disastrous

бедствие /bédstvie/ n. disaster

бежать /bezhát'/ v. run; escape, flee

беженец /bézhenets/ m. refugee

без /bez/ prep. without

безаварийный /bezavaríinyi/ adj. accident-free

безалкогольный /bezalkogól'nyi/ adj. non-alcoholic

безатомный /bezátomnyi/ adj. atom-free

безбедный /bezbédnyi/ adj. comfortable, well-to-do

безбилетный /bezbilétnyi/ adj. without a ticket

безбожие /bezbózhie/ n. atheism

безболезненный /bezboléznennyi/ adj. painless

безбоязненный /bezboiáznennyi/ adj. fearless

безвозмездный /bezvozmézdnyi/ adj. free, gratuitous

безволие /bezvólie/ n. lack of will

безвредный /bezvrédnyi/ adj. harmless

безвыходный /bezvýkhodnyi/ adj. hopeless

безграмотный /bezgrámotnyi/ adj. illiterate; ignorant

безграничный /bezgraníchnyi/ adj. boundless

бездействие /bezdéistvie/ n. inactivity, inertia

бездельник /bezdél'nik/ m. idler

безденежный /bezdénezhnyi/ adj. penniless

бездетный /bezdétnyi/ adj. childless

бездеятельный /bezdéiatel'nyi/ adj. inactive

бездомный /bezdómnyi/ adj. homeless; stray

безжалостный /bezzhálostnyi/ adj. merciless, ruthless

безжизненный /bezzhíznennyi/ adj. feeble, lifeless

беззаботный /bezzabótnyi/ adj. carefree

беззаконие /bezzakónie/ n. lawlessness

беззастенчивый /bezzasténchivyi/ adj. impudent, shameless

беззащитный /bezzashchítnyi/ adj. defenceless

безмятежный /bezmiatézhnyi/ adj. serene, tranquil

безнадежный /beznadiózhnyi/ adj. hopeless

безнаказанный /beznaкázannyi/ adj. unpunished

безнравственный /beznrávstvennyi/ adj. immoral

безобидный /bezobídnyi/ adj. harmless

безоблачный /bezóblachnyi/ adj. cloudless

безобразие /bezobrázie/ n. outrage

безобразный /bezobráznyi/ adj. ugly

безоговорочный /bezogovórochnyi/ adj. unconditional, unqualified

безопасность /bezopásnost'/ f. security

безопасный /bezopásnyi/ adj. safe

безоружный /bezorúzhnyi/ adj. unarmed

безостановочный /bezostanóvochnyi/ adj. non-stop

безответственный /bezotvétstvennyi/ adj. irresponsible

безотлагательный /bezotlagátel'nyi/ adj. pressing, urgent

безотчетный /bezotchótnyi/ adj. uncontrolled; unconscious

безошибочный /bezoshíbochnyi/ adj. unerring, correct

безработица /bezrabótitsa/ f. unemployment

безработный /bezrabótnyi/ m. unemployed

безрассудный /bezrassúdnyi/ adj. reckless, rash

безукоризненный /bezukoríznennyi/ adj. impeccable

безумие /bezúmie/ n. madness

безумный /bezúmnyi/ adj. mad

безупречный /bezupréchnyi/ adj. irreproachable, faultless

безусловный /bezuslóvnyi/ adj. absolute, indisputable, unconditional

безуспешный /bezuspéshnyi/ adj. unsuccessful

безысходный /bezyskhódnyi/ adj. hopeless, desperate

бекон /bekón/ m. bacon

белка /bélka/ f. squirrel

белок /belók/ m. white (of eye, egg)

белокровие /belokróvie/ n. leukaemia

белокурый /belokúryi/ adj. fair-haired

белый /bélyi/ adj. white; б. медведь /b. medvéd'/ polar bear

белье /bel'ió/ n. linen; washing; нижнее б. /nízhnee b./ underwear

бензин /benzín/ m. petrol

бензобак /benzobák/ m. petrol tank

берег /béreg/ m. bank; shore; coast

береговой /beregovói/ adj. waterside, coastal, riverside

бережливый /berezhlívyi/ adj. thrifty

бережный /bérezhnyi/ adj. careful

береза /berióza/ f. berch

беременеть /berémenet'/ v. be(come) pregnant

беречь /beréch'/ v. take care of, keep; spare

беречься /beréchsia/ v. beware (of)

беседа /beséda/ f. conversation, talk

беседовать /besédovat'/ v. talk, chat

бесконечность /beskonéchnost'/ f. infinity

бескорыстие /beskorýstie/ n. unselfishness

бескровный /beskróvnyi/ adj. bloodless, anaemic

бесперебойный /besperebóinyi/ adj. uninterrupted, constant

беспересадочный /besperesádochnyi/ adj. through, direct

бесперспективный /besperspektívnyi/ adj. without prospects; hopeless

беспечный /bespéchnyi/ adj. careless

бесплатный /besplátnyi/ adj. free

беспокоить /bespokóit'/ v. worry; trouble

бесполезный /bespoléznyi/ adj. useless

беспомощный /bespómoshchnyi/ adj. helpless

беспорядок /besporiádok/ m. disorder

беспорядочный /besporiádochnyi/ adj. irregular; unsystematic

беспересадочный (перелет) /besperesádochnyi pereliót/ adj. + m. non-stop flight

беспочвенный /bespóchvennyi/ adj. groundless

беспошлинный /bespóshlinnyi/ adj. duty-free

бесправие /besprávie/ n. lawlessness; lack of rights

беспрекословный /besprekoslóvnyi/ adj. absolute, unquestioning

беспрерывный /bespreryvnyi/ adj. continuous, ceaseless

беспрецедентный /bespretsedéntnyi/ adj. unprecedented

беспримерный /besprimérnyi/ adj. unparalleled

беспринципный /besprintsípnyi/ adj. unscrupulous

беспричинный /besprichínnyi/ adj. groundless, without motive

бессмертие /bessmértie/ n. immortality

бессмысленный /bessmýslennyi/ adj. senseless

бессовестный /bessóvestnyi/ adj. shameless; outrageous

бессодержательный /bessoderzhátel'nyi/ adj. empty; shallow

бессознательный /bessoznátel'nyi/ adj. unconscious; instinctive

бессонница /bessónitsa/ f. insomnia

бессрочный /bessróchnyi/ adj. permanent; termless

бессчетный /besschótnyi/ adj. innumerable, countless

бестактный /bestáktnyi/ adj. tactless

бестолковый /bestolkóvyi/ adj. muddle-headed, stupid; incoherent

бесцветный /bestsvétnyi/ adj. colourless, insipid

бесцельный /bestsél'nyi/ adj. aimless, pointless

бесценный /bestsénnyi/ adj. priceless

бесчеловечный /beschelovéchnyi/ adj. inhuman

бесчестный /beschéstnyi/ adj. dishonorable

бесшумный /besshúmnyi/ adj. noiseless

библиотека /bibliotéka/ f. library

билет /bilét/ m. ticket, pass, card; обратный б. /obrátnyi b./ return ticket

бинокль /binókl'/ m. binoculars

бинт /bint/ m. bandage

биография /biográfiia/ f. biography

биржа /bírzha/ f. stock exchange

биржевой маклер /birzhevói mákler/ adj. + m. stockbroker

бисквит /biskvít/ m. sponge-cake

бить /bit'/ v. hit, beat; strike; smash

биться /bít'sia/ v. fight; beat; struggle (with)

бифштекс /bifshtéks/ m. steak

благодарить /blagodarít'/ v. thank

благодаря /blagodariá/ conj. thanks to, owing to

благожелательный /blagozhelátel'nyi/ adj. well-disposed, favourable

благонамеренный /blagonamérennyi/ adj. loyal

благополучие /blagopolúchie/ n. well-being, prosperity

благоприятный /blagopriiátnyi/ adj. favourable

благоразумие /blagorazúmie/ n. prudence, discretion

благородный /blagoródnyi/ adj. noble

благословлять /blagoslovliát'/ v. bless

благотворительность /blagotvorítel'nost'/ f. charity

благоустроенный /blagoustróennyi/ adj. comfortable

бланк /blank/ m. form

блат /blat/ m. pull, protection

блеск /blesk/ m. brilliance

ближайший /blizháishii/ adj. nearest; next

близко /blízkó/ near, close

близнец /bliznéts/ m. twin

близорукий /blizorúkii/ adj. short-sighted

блин /blin/ m. pancake

блок /blok/ n. bloc; pulley

блокнот /bloknót/ m. writing pad

блондин /blondín/ m. fair-haired person

блузка /blúzka/ f. blouse

блюдечко /bliúdechko/ n. saucer

бог /bog/ m. god; боже, боже мой! /bózhe mói/ int. my goodness!; ей богу /éi bógu/ int. really and truly; сохрани бог /sokhraní bog/ God forbid

богатеть /bogatét'/ v. grow rich

богатство /bogátstvo/ n. wealth

богатый /bogátyi/ adj. rich

богослужение /bogosluzhénie/ n. divine service

бодрствовать /bódrstvovat'/ v. keep awake

бодрый /bódryi/ adj. cheerful; active

божество /bozhestvó/ n. divinity

бойкий /bóikii/ adj. shrewd, sharp; lively

бок /bok/ m. side

бокал /bokál/ m. glass, goblet

боковой /bokovói/ adj. side; lateral

более /bólee/ adj., adv. more; более или менее /bólee íli ménee/ more or less; более того /bólee togó/ moreover

болезненный /boléznennyi/ adj. ailing, unhealthy; painful

болезнь /bolézn'/ f. illness, disease

болельщик /bolél'shchik/ m. fan

болеть /bolét'/ v. be ill; ache, become sore

болеутоляющий /boleutoliáiushchii/ adj. sedative

боль /bol'/ f. pain

больница /bol'nítsa/ f. hospital

больше /ból'she/ adj. bigger; adv. more

большинство /bol'shinstvó/ n. majority

большой /bol'shói/ adj. big, large

борода /borodá/ f. beard

бороться /borót'sia/ v. struggle, fight, wrestle

борт /bort/ m. side (of ship); на борту /na bortú/ on board; за бортом /za bortóm/ overboard

бортпроводник /bortprovodník/ m. airline steward

борщ /borshch/ m. borshch

борьба /bor'bá/ f. struggle, fight; wrestling

босиком /bosikóm/ adv. barefoot

босоножка /bosonózhka/ f. sandal

бояться /boiát'sia/ v. fear, be afraid (of)

брак /brak/ m. marriage; spoilage, waste

браковать /brakovát'/ v. reject as defective

браконьер /brakon'ér/ m. poacher

браслет /braslét/ m. bracelet

брат /brat/ m. brother

брать /brat'/ v. take

брачный /bráchnyi/ adj. marriage

бредить /brédit'/ v. rave; be mad (on)

брезгливый /brezglívyi/ adj. fastidious

брелок /brelók/ m. pendant, charm

бригада /brigáda/ f. brigade, team, crew

бриллиант /brilliánt/ m. diamond

бритва /brítva/ f. razor; blade

брить /brit'/ v. shave

бровь /brov'/ f. brow, eyebrow

бронировать /broní rovat'/ v. reserve (seats)

бросать /brosát'/ v. throw

броситься /brósit'sia/ v. rush; dash

брошка, брошь /bróshka, brosh/ f. brooch

брошюра /broshiúra/ f. booklet, pamphlet

брызгать /brýzgat'/ v. splash, sprinkle

брюки /briúki/ pl. trousers

будильник /budíl'nik/ m. alarm-clock

будить /budít'/ v. wake

будто /búdto/ conj. as if, as though

будущий /búdushchii/ adj. future

буженина /buzhenína/ f. cold boiled pork

буйный /búinyi/ adj. wild, violent

буква /búkva/ f. letter

буквальный /bukvál'nyi/ adj. literal

букварь /bukvár'/ m. primer, ABC book

букет /bukét/ m. bouquet

букинист /bukiníst/ m. secondhand bookseller

булавка /bulávka/ f. pin; английская б. /anglíiskaia b./
  safety pin

булка /búlka/ f. roll

булочка /búlochka/ f. bun

булочная /búlochnaia/ f. baker's

булыжник /bulýzhnik/ m. cobble-stone

бульвар /bul'vár/ m. avenue, boulevard

бульон /bul'ón/ m. broth, clear soup

бум /bum/ m. sensation; boom

бумага /bumága/ f. paper

бумажник /bumázhnik/ m. wallet

бурный /búrnyi/ adj. stormy

буря /búria/ f. storm, tempest

бутерброд /buterbród/ m. open sandwich

бутылка /butýlka/ f. bottle

буфет /bufét/ m. sideboard; buffet, bar

буфетчик /bufétchik/ m. barman

буханка /bukhánka/ f. loaf

бухгалтер /bukhálter/ m. accountant

бухгалтерия /bukhaltériia/ f. book-keeping

бывать /byvát'/ v. be, happen; visit

бывший /bývshii/ adj. former, ex-

быстрота /bystróta/ f. speed

быстрый /býstryi/ adj. quick

быт /byt/ m. way of life

быть /byt'/ v. be

бюджет /biudzhét/ m. budget

бюллетень /bulletén'/ m. bulletin; избирательный б. /izbirátel'nyi b./ ballot-paper

бюро /biuró/ n. bureau, office

бюрократ /biurokrát/ m. bureaucrat

бюст /biust/ m. bust

бюстгальтер /biustgál'ter/ m. brassiere

В

в /v/ prep. into; within; on; at

вагон /vagón/ m. carriage, coach

вагон-ресторан /vagón-restorán/ m. restaurant-car

важность /vázhnost'/ f. importance

вакантный /vakántnyi/ adj. vacant

вакцина /vaktsína/ f. vaccine

валенок /válenok/ m. felt boot

валовой /valovói/ adj. gross

валюта /valiúta/ f. currency

валютный (курс) /valiútnyi kurs/ adj. + m. rate of exchange

ванна /vánna/ f. bath

ванная /vánnaia/ f. bathroom

варежка /várezhka/ f. mitten

варенки /variónki/ pl. sl. faded (stone-washed) jeans

вареный /variónyi/ adj. boiled

варенье /varén'e/ n. jam

вариант /variánt/ m. version

варить /varít'/ v. boil, cook

варьировать /var'írovat'/ v. vary

ватрушка /vatrúshka/ f. curd tart; cheesecake

вафля /váflia/ f. waffle

ваш /vash/ pron. your(s)

вбивать /vbivát'/ v. drive or hammer in

вблизи /vblizí/ adv. closely

введение /vvedénie/ n. introduction

вверх /vverkh/ adv. up, upward(s); в. дном /v. dnom/ upside down

вверху /vverkhú/ adv. above, overhead

ввиду /vvidú/ adv. in view (of)

вводить /vvodít'/ v. introduce; bring in

ввоз /vvoz/ m. import(s)

ввязываться /vviázyvat'sia/ v. get involved (in)

вглубь /vglub'/ adv. deep into

вдалеке /vdaleké/ adv. far off

вдаль /vdal'/ adv. into the distance

вдвое /vdvóe/ adv. double, twice; в.больше /v. bólshe/ twice as big/ as much; уменьшить в. /uménshit' v./ halve

вдвоем /vdvoióm/ adv. the two together

вдвойне /vdvoiné/ adv. twice, double; платить в. /platíť v./ pay double

вдова /vdová/ f. widow

вдовец /vdovéts/ m. widower

вдоволь /vdóvol'/ adv. in abundance, enough

вдогонку /vdogónku/ adv. in pursuit of; броситься в. /brósit'sia v./ rush after

вдоль /vdol'/ prep. along; в. и поперек /v. i poperiók/ far and wide

вдох /vdokh/ m. inhalation

вдохновлять /vdokhnovliát'/ v. inspire

вдруг /vdrug/ adv. suddenly

вдумчивый /vdúmchivyi/ adj. thoughtful

вдыхать /vdykhát'/ v. breathe in

вегетарианец /vegetariánets/ m. vegetarian

ведомость /védomost'/ f. list, register; платежная в. /platiózhnaia v./ pay-roll

ведомство /védomstvo/ n. department

ведро /vedró/ n. bucket

ведущий /vedúshchii/ adj. leading, basic

ведь /ved'/ conj. you see, you know; why, well

вежливый /vézhlivyi/ adj. polite

везде /vezdé/ adv. everywhere

везти /veztí/ v. carry, drive; have luck

век /vek/ m. age; century; lifetime; на моем веку /na moióm vekú/ in my lifetime

веко /véko/ n. eyelid

вековой /vekovói/ adj. age-old

вексель /véksel'/ m. bill of exchange

велеть /velét'/ v. order, command

великий /velíkii/ adj. great

великодержавный /velikoderzhávnyi/ adj. great-power

великодушный /velikodúshnyi/ adj. magnanimous

великолепный /velikolépnyi/ adj. magnificent

величественный /velíchestvennyi/ adj. majestic

величество /velíchestvo/ n. majesty; ваше в. /váshe v./
Your Majesty

величина /velichiná/ f. size

велосипед /velosipéd/ m. bicycle, cycle

велосипедист /velosipedíst/ m. cyclist

вельвет /vel'vét/ m. corduroy

вена /véna/ f. vein

венерический /venerícheskii/ adj. venereal

веник /vénik/ m. broom

венок /venók/ m. wreath, garland

вентилятор /ventiliátor/ m. ventilator, fan

венчание /venchánie/ n. wedding ceremony

вера /véra/ f. faith, belief

веранда /veránda/ f. veranda

верблюд /verbliúd/ m. camel

веревка /verióvka/ f. rope, string

верить /vérit'/ v. believe

верность /vérnost'/ f. faithfulness, loyality

вероисповедание /veroispovedánie/ n. religion; creed

вероломный /verolómnyi/ adj. perfidious, treacherous

вероятно /veroiátno/ adv. probably

вероятный /veroiátnyi/ adj. probable

версия /vérsiia/ f. version

вертеть /vertét'/ v. turn, twist

вертикальный /vertikál'nyi/ adj. vertical

вертолет /vertoliót/ m. helicopter

верующий /véruiushchii/ m. believer

верх /verkh/ m. top; summit

верховный /verkhóvnyi/ adj. supreme

вершина /vershína/ f. summit, peak

вес /vcs/ m. weight

веселиться /veselít'sia/ v. enjoy oneself, be merry

веселый /vesiólyi/ adj. gay, merry

весенний /vesénnii/ adj. spring

весить /vésit'/ v. weigh

веский /véskii/ adj. weighty

весна /vesná/ f. spring

вести /vestí/ v. lead, guide; в. себя /v. sebiá/ behave

вестибюль /vestibiúl'/ m. entrance hall

вестник /véstnik/ m. messenger; bulletin

весы /vesý/ pl. scales

весь /ves'/ pron. all, whole

ветвистый /vetvístyi/ adj. branchy

ветер /véter/ m. wind

ветеринар /veterinár/ m. veterinary surgeon

ветка /vétka/ f. branch, twig

ветреный /vétrenyi/ adj. windy; flippant

ветчина /vetchiná/ f. ham

веха /vékha/ f. landmark

вечер /vécher/ m. evening

вечеринка /vecherínka/ f. party

вечность /véchnost'/ f. eternity

вечный /véchnyi/ adj. eternal; perpetual

вешалка /véshalka/ f. peg. rack

вещественный /veshchéstvennyi/ adj. material

вещь /veshch/ f. thing

взад /vzad/ adv. back(wards); в. и вперед /v. i vperiód/ back and forth

взаимность /vzaímnost'/ f. reciprocity

взаимовыгодный /vzaimovýgodnyi/ adj. mutually advantageous

взаймы /vzaimý/ adv.: брать в. /brat' v./ borrow; давать в. /davát' v./ lend

взамен /vzamén/ adv. instead of

взбираться /vzbirát'sia/ v. climb up

взвешивать /vzvéshivat'/ v. weigh, weigh up

взволнованный /vzvolnóvannyi/ adj. excited

взгляд /vzgliad/ m. look, stare; на мой в. /na moi v./ in my opinion

вздор /vzdor/ m. nonsense

вздрагивать /vzdrágivat'/ v. shudder

вздутие /vzdútie/ n. swelling

вздыхать /vzdykhát'/ v. sigh; pine (for)

взламывать /vzlámyvat'/ v. break open

взлет /vzliot/ m. flight, take-off

взмахивать /vzmákhivat'/ v. flap, wave

взнос /vznos/ m. payment, dues

взрослый /vzróslyi/ m. adult

взрыв /vzryv/ m. explosion; outburst

взрывать /vzryvát'/ v. blow up

взыскание /vzyskánie/ n. penalty

взять /vziat'/ v. take

взятка /vziátka/ f. bribe

вид /vid/ m. sight, view; appearance, look; kind, sort; иметь в виду /imét' v vidú/ bear in mind; терять из виду /teriát' iz vídu/ lose sight of

видеокассета /videokasséta/ f. video casette

видеомагнитофон /videomagnitofón/ m. video recorder

видеть /vídet'/ v. see

видимость /vídimost'/ f. visibility; outward appearance

виза /víza/ f. visa

визит /vizít/ m. visit

викторина /viktorína/ f. quiz

вилка /vílka/ f. fork; electric plug

вина /viná/ f. fault, guilt

винегрет /vinegrét/ m. Russian salad

винить /vinít'/ v. blame (for)

вино /vinó/ n. wine

виноватый /vinovátyi/ adj. guilty (of)

виновник /vinóvnik/ m. culprit

виноторговец /vinotorgóvets/ m. wine merchant

винт /vint/ m. screw

винтовка /vintóvka/ f. rifle

висеть /visét'/ v. hang

виснуть /vísnut'/ v. hang

висок /visók/ m. temple

високосный /visokósnyi/ adj.: в. год /v. god/ leap-year

висячий /visiáchii/ adj. hanging; в. замок /v. zamók/ padlock; в. мост /v. most/ suspension bridge

витрина /vitrína/ f. shopwindow

вице-президент /vítse-presidént/ m. vice-president

вишня /víshnia/ f. cherry

вклад /vklad/ m. contribution (to); deposit (in bank)

вкладчик /vkládchik/ m. depositor

вкратце /vkrátse/ adv. briefly

вкрутую (яйцо в.) /iaitsó vkrutúiu/ n.+ adv. hard-boiled egg

вкус /vkus/ m. taste

влага /vlága/ f. moisture

владелец /vladélets/ m. owner, proprietor

владение /vladénie/ n. ownership, possession; property

владеть /vladét'/ v. own, possess

влажный /vlázhnyi/ adj. humid, damp

вламываться /vlámyvat'sia/ v. break into

властный /vlástnyi/ adj. imperious, commanding

власть /vlast'/ f. power, authority

влево /vlévo/ adv. to the left

влезать /vlezát'/ v. climb in, into, up

вливать /vlivát'/ v. pour in

влияние /vliiánie/ n. influence

влиятельный /vliiátel'nyi/ adj. influential

вложение /vlozhénie/ n. enclosure; investment

влюбленный /vliubliónnyi/ m. lover

влюбляться /vliubliát'sia/ v. fall in love (with)

вместе /vméste/ adv. together; в. с тем /v. s tem/ at the same time

вместимость /vmestímost'/ f. capacity

вместо /vmésto/ prep. instead of

вмешательство /vmeshátel'stvo/ n. interference, intervention

вмещать /vmeshchát'/ v. contain, accommodate

внаем /vnaióm/ adv.; отдать в. /otdát' v./ let, hire out; взять в. /vziát' v./ hire, rent

вначале /vnachále/ adv. at first

вне /vne/ prep. outside, out of

внедрять /vnedriát'/ v. introduce; inculcate

внезапный /vnezápnyi/ adj. sudden

внеочередной /vneocherednói/ adj. extraordinary

внешний /vnéshnii/ adj. outer, external; внешняя политика /vnéshniaia polítika/ foreign policy

вниз /vniz/ adv. down(wards)

внизу /vnizú/ adv. below, at the bottom

внимание /vnimánie/ n. attention

вновь /vnov'/ adv. again; newly

вносить /vnosít'/ v. carry or bring in; contribute

внук /vnuk/ m. grandson

внутренний /vnútrennii/ adj. inner, internal

внутренности /vnútrennosti/ pl. internal organs

внутри /vnutrí/ adv. inside, within

внутрь /vnutr'/. adv. into

внучка /vnúchka/ f. granddaughter

внушать /vnushát'/ v. inspire; в. ему уважение /v. emú uvazhénie/ fill him with respect

внушительный /vnushítel'nyi/ adj. impressive

вовлекать /vovlekát'/ v. involve

вовремя /vóvremia/ adv. in time

вовсе /vóvse/ adv. completely, quite; вовсе не /vóvse ne/ not at all

во-вторых /vo-vtorýkh/ adv. second(ly)

вода /vodá/ f. water

водитель /vodítel'/ m. driver

водить /vodít'/ v. lead, conduct; drive

водонепроницаемый /vodonepronitsáemyi/ adj. waterproof

водопад /vodopád/ m. waterfall

водопровод /vodoprovód/ m. water pipe

водопроводчик /vodoprovódchik/ m. plumber

водружать /vodruzhát'/ v. hoist, erect

воевать /voevát'/ v. wage war

военачальник /voenachál'nik/ m. military leader

военнослужащий /voennoslúzhashchii/ m. serviceman

военный /voénnyi/ adj. military, war

военное положение /voénnoe polozhénie/ adj. + n. martial law

вождь /vozhd'/ m. leader

возбуждать /vozbuzhdát'/ v. excite, arouse

возведение /vozvedénie/ n. raising, erection

возвещать /vozveshchát'/ n. announce, proclaim

возврат /vozvrát/ m. return, repayment

возглавлять /vozglavliát'/ v. head

возглас /vózglas/ m. exclamation

возгораемый /vozgoráemyi/ adj. inflammable

воздвигать /vozdvigát'/ v. erect

воздействовать /vozdéistvovat'/ v. have influence (on)

воздерживаться /vozdérzhivat'sia/ v. abstain, refrain (from)

воздух /vózdukh/ m. air

воздушный /vozdúshnyi/ adj. air; в. шар /v. shar/ balloon

воззвание /vozzvánie/ n. appeal, manifesto

возить /vozít'/ v. carry, drive, transport

возлагать /vozlagát'/ v. lay, place; в. надежду на /v. nadézhdu na/ place hopes on

возле /vózle/ adv. near

возлюбленный /vozliúblennyi/ adj. beloved

возмещать /vozmeshchát'/ v. compensate

возможно /vozmózhno/ adv. possibly

возмутительный /vozmutítel'nyi/ adj. disgraceful, scandalous

вознаграждать /voznagrazhdát'/ v. reward

возникать /voznikát'/ v. arise, crop up

возобновлять /vozobnovliát'/ v. renew, resume

возражать /vozrazhát'/ v. object (to)

возражение /vozrazhénie/ n. objection

возраст /vózrast/ m. age

возрождать /vozrozhdat'/ v. revive

воинский /vóinskii/ adj. military, martial; воинская повинность /vóinskaia povínnost'/ conscription

воинственный /voínstvennyi/ adj. martial, bellicose

война /voiná/ f. war

вокзал /vokzál/ m. railroad station

вокруг /vokrúg/ adv. (a)round

волевой /volevói/ adj. strong-willed

волей-неволей /vólei-nevólei/ adv. willy-nilly

волк /volk/ m. wolf

волна /volná/ f. wave

волнение /volnénie/ n. excitement

волноваться /volnovát'sia/ v. be excited

волокита /volokíta/ f. red tape

волос /vólos/ m. hair

волосатый /volosátyi/ adj. hairy

волшебный /volshébnyi/ adj. magic, fairy

вольный /vól'nyi/ adj. free, unrestricted

воля /vólia/ f. will; freedom

вон /von/ adv. away; over there; пошел вон /poshól von/ go away!

воображать /voobrazhát'/ v. imagine

воображение /voobrazhénie/ n. imagination

вообразимый /voobrazímyi/ adj. imaginable

вообще /voobshché/ adv. in general

воодушевлять /voodushevliát'/ v. inspire

вооружать /vooruzhát'/ v. arm

вооружение /vooruzhénie/ n. armament; arms

во-первых /vo-pérvykh/ adv. first(ly)

воплощать /voploshchát'/ v. embody

вопреки /voprekí/ prep. in spite of

вопрос /voprós/ m. question

вор /vor/ m. thief

воробей /vorobéi/ m. sparrow

воровать /vorovát'/ v. steal

ворона /voróna/ f. crow

ворота /voróta/ pl. gate(s)

воротник /vorotník/ m. collar

восемнадцать /vosemnádtsat'/ num. eighteen

восемь /vósem'/ num. eight

восемьдесят /vósem'desiat/ num. eighty

восемьсот /vosem'sót/ num. eight hundred

восклицать /vosklitsát'/ v. exclaim

восковой /voskovói/ adj. wax(en)

воскресенье /voskresén'e/ n. Sunday

воскрешать /voskreshát'/ v. revive, resuscitate

воспаление /vospalénie/ n. inflammation; в. легких /v. liógkikh/ pneumonia

воспитание /vospitánie/ n. upbringing, education

воспринимать /vosprinimát'/ v. take (up); conceive

воспроизводить /vosproizvodít'/ v. reproduce

воссоединять /vossoediniát'/ v. reunite

воссоздавать /vossozdavát'/ v. recreate

восстанавливать /vosstanávlivat'/ v. restore

восстание /vosstánie/ n. insurrection

восток /vostók/ m. east, orient

восторг /vostórg/ m. delight, rapture

востребование (до востребования) /do vostrébovaniia/ poste restante

восхвалять /voskhvaliát'/ v. praise, extol

восхитительный /voskhitíteľnyi/ adj. delightful

восход /voskhód/ m. sunrise

вот /vot/ part. here (is)

вотум /vótum/ m. vote; в.(не)доверия /v.(ne)dovériia/ vote of (no)confidence

впервые /vpervýe/ adv. for the first time

вперед /vperiód/ adv. forward, ahead; часы идут в. /chasý idút v./ the clock is fast; платить в. /platíť v./ pay in advance

впереди /vperedí/ adv. in front (of), before

впечатление /vpechatlénie/ n. impression

впитывать /vpítyvat'/ v. absorb

вплотную /vplotnúiu/ adv. close by

вплоть до /vplot' do/ adv. (right) up to

вполне /vpolné/ adv. quite, fully

впору /vpóru/ adv. just right

впоследствии /vposlédstvii/ adv. subsequently; afterwards

впотьмах /vpot'mákh/ adv. in the dark

вправе (быть в.) /byt' vpráve/ have the right

вправо /vprávo/ adv. to the right

впредь /vpred'/ adv. henceforth

впрочем /vpróchem/ conj. however

впрыскивание /vprýskivanie/ n. injection

впускать /vpuskát'/ v. let in, admit

впустую /vpustúiu/ adv. to no purpose

впутывать /vpútyvat'/ v. entangle

враг /vrag/ m. enemy

враждебный /vrazhdébnyi/ adj. hostile

вразрез /vrazréz/ adv.:идти в. /idtí v./ be contrary (to)

вразумительный /vrazumítel'nyi/ adj. intelligible

врасплох /vrasplókh/ adv. unawares

врассыпную /vrassypnúiu/ adv. in all directions

врать /vrat'/ m. lie

врач /vrach/ m. doctor

врачебный /vrachébnyi/ adj. medical

вращать /vrashchát'/ v. turn, rotate

вред /vred/ m. harm

вредить /vredít'/ v. harm, damage

вредный /vrédnyi/ adj. harmful

временный /vrémennyi/ adj. temporal

время /vrémia/ n. time; в то в. как /v to v. kak/ whilst; за
    последнее в. /za poslédnee v./ recently; временами
    /vremenámi/ (every) now and then; сколько времени?
    /skól'ko vrémeni/ What's the time?

врожденный /vrozhdiónnyi/ adj. innate

врозь /vroz'/ adv. separately, apart

вручать /vruchát'/ v. hand over, deliver

вручную /vruchnúiu/ adv. by hand

врываться /vryvát'sia/ v. burst in (to)

вряд ли /vriád li/ adv. hardly

всевозможный /vsevozmózhnyi/ adj. of all kinds of

всевышний /vsevýshnii/ m. the Most High

всегда /vsegdá/ adv. always

всего /vsegó/ m. all

вселенная /vselénnaia/ f. universe

вселяться /vseliát'sia/ v. move in (to)

всемерный /vsemérnyi/ adj. utmost

всемирный /vsemírnyi/ adj. world, universal

всемогущество /vsemogúshchestvo/ n. omnipotence

всенародный /vsenaródnyi/ adj. national, nationwide

всеобщий /vseóbshchii/ adj. general, universal

всеобъемлющий /vseob''émliushchii/ adj. all-embracing

всерьез /vser'ioz/ adv. in earnest, seriously

всесторонний /vsestorónnii/ adj. all-round

все-таки /vsió-takí/ conj. and part. nevertheless

всеуслышание (во в.) /vo vseuslýshanie/ n. for all to hear;
    in public

всецело /vsetsélo/ adv. entirely, wholly

вскользь /vskol'z'/ adv. casually, in passing

вскоре /vskóre/ adv. soon before long

вскрывать /vskryvát'/ v. open; reveal

вслед /vsled/ adv. (right) after; following

вследствие /vslédstvie/ adv. in consequence of

вслух /vslukh/ adv. aloud

всмятку (яйцо в.) /iaitsó vsmiátku/ n.+adv. soft-boiled egg

всплеск /vsplesk/ m. splash

всплывать /vsplyvát'/ v. rise to the surface; emerge

вспоминать /vspominát'/ v. remember, recall

вставать /vstavát'/ v. stand up; get up

вставной /vstavnói/ adj. double (windows); false (teeth)

встревоженный /vstrevózhennyi/ adj. alarmed

встречаться /vstrechát'sia/ v. meet; occur, happen

встреча /vstrécha/ f. meeting

вступать /vstupát'/ v. enter; join

вступительный /vstupítel'nyi/ adj. entrance, introductory

всхлипывать /vskhlípyvat'/ v. sob

всюду /vsiúdu/ adv. everywhere

всякий /vsiákii/ adj. any

всяческий /vsiácheskii/ adj. all kinds of; sundry

втайне /vtáine/ adv. in secret

втирать /vtirát'/ v. rub in

вторгаться /vtorgát'sia/ v. invade, penetrate

вторник /vtórnik/ m. Tuesday

второстепенный /vtorostepénnyi/ adj. secondary

в-третьих /v-trét'ikh/ adv. third(ly)

втридорога /vtrídoroga/ adv. at an exorbitant price; втрое
    /vtróe/ adv. three times; втроем /vtroióm/ adv. three
    together; втройне /vtroiné/ adv. three times as much

вуз /vuz/ abbr. m. higher educational institution

вход /vkhod/ m. entrance

входить /vkhodít'/ v. go in, enter

вчера /vcherá/ adv. yesterday

вчетверо /vchétvero/ adv. four times (as...)

въезд /v"ezd/ m. entrance

въсзжать /v"ezzhát'/ v. drive in

вы /vy/ pron. you

выбегать /vybegát'/ v. run out

выбирать /vybirát'/ v. choose; elect

выбор /výbor/ m. choice; selection; option; всеобщие выборы /vseóbshchie výbory/ general election

выбрасывать /vybrásyvat'/ v. throw out

выбывать /vybyvát'/ v. leave, quit

вывеска /výveska/ f. sign (board)

вывешивать /vyvéshivat'/ v. hang out, put up

вывинчивать /vyvínchivat'/ v. unscrew

вывих /vývikh/ m. dislocation

вывихнуть /vývikhnut'/ v. sprain

вывод /vývod/ m. withdrawal; conclusion

выводить /vyvodít'/ v. take out; remove; hatch, grow; conclude, infer

вывоз /vývoz/ m. export(s)

выглядеть /výgliadet'/ v. look, appear

выглядывать /vygliádyvat'/ v. look out, peep out

выгода /výgoda/ f. advantage; profit

выгонять /vygoniát'/ v. drive out

выгружать /vygruzhát'/ v. unload

выдавать /vydavát'/ v. hand out, distribute; betray; extradite выдавливать /vydávlivat'/ v. squeeze out

выдача /výdacha/ f. delivery, distribution, payment; extradition

выдвигать /vydvigát'/ v. put forward, propose, promote

выделять /vydeliát'/ v. pick out; detach; allot; emphasize; apportion; secrete

выдержанный /výderzhannyi/ adj. self-possessed; ripe, seasoned

выдерживать /vydérzhivat'/ v. sustain; pass (exams)

выдержка /výderzhka/ f. self-control; exposure (phot.)

выдох /výdokh/ m. exhalation

выдумка /výdumka/ f. invention

выдыхать /vydykhát'/ v. breathe out

выдыхаться /vydykhát'sia/ v. become stale; exhaust oneself

выезд /výezd/ m. departure; exit

выезжать /vyezzhát'/ v. leave, depart; drive *or* ride out

выживать /vyzhivát'/ v. survive

выжимать /vyzhimát'/ v. squeze out

выздоравливать /vyzdorávlivat'/ v. recover

вызов /výzov/ m. call; challenge

вызывать /vyzyvát'/ v. call, summon; rouse; evoke

выигрывать /vyígryvat'/ v. win

выигрыш /vyígrysh/ m. benefit, gain

выкапывать /vykápyvat'/ v. dig out

выкармливать /vykármlivat'/ v. bring up, rear

выкидыш /výkidysh/ m. miscarriage, abortion

выключатель /vykliuchátel'/ m. switch

выключать /vykliuchát'/ v. switch off

выкройка /výkroika/ f. pattern

выкуп /výkup/ m. ransom; redemption

вылезать /vylezát'/ v. climb out

вылет /výlet/ m. flight, take-off

вылечивать /vyléchivat'/ v. cure, heal

выливать /vylivát'/ v. pour out, empty

выменивать /vyménivat'/ v. exchange

вымирать /vymirát'/ v. die out, become extinct

вымогательство /vymogátel'stvo/ n. extortion, blackmail

вымокать /vymokát'/ v. wet through

вымысел /výmysel/ m. invention; fabrication

вынашивать /vynáshivat'/ v. bear (a child)

вынимать /vynimát'/ v. take out, produce

выносить /vynosít'/ v. carry out; endure

вынуждать /vynuzhdát'/ v. force, compel

вынужденный /výnuzhdennyi/ adj. forced

выпад /výpad/ m. lunge; thrust; attack

выпекать /vypekát'/ v. bake

выпивать /vypivát'/ v. drink (off)

выписка /výpiska/ f. writing out; extract

выплата /výplata/ f. payment

выполнять /vypolniát'/ v. carry out, implement

выпрашивать /vypráshivat'/ v. elicit by begging

выпуклый /výpuklyi/ adj. protuberant; bulging

выпуск /výpusk/ m. issue; output; discharge

выпускной (экзамен) /vypusknói ekzámen/ adj. + m. final
   exams

вырабатывать /vyrabátyvat'/ v. make, produce; develop

выравнивать /vyrávnivat'/ v. make even, level

выражать /vyrazhát'/ v. express

выразительный /vyrazítel'nyi/ adj. expressive

вырастать /vyrastát'/ v. grow (up)

вырезать /vyrezát'/ v. cut out; carve

вырезка /výrezka/ f. cutting-out; tender-loin

вырубать /vyrubát'/ v. cut down, fell

выручать /vyruchát'/ v. rescue, help out; gain

вырывать /vyryvát'/ v. pull *or* tear out; extort

выселять /vyseliát'/ v. evict, expel

высказывать /vyskázyvat'/ v. state, say

высказываться /vyskázyvat'sia/ v. speak out

выслеживать /vyslézhivat'/ v. track down, shadow

выслушивать /vyslúshivat'/ v. listen, hear out; sound
  (med.)

высмеивать /vysméivat'/ v. ridicule

высморкаться /výsmorkat'sia/ v. blow one's nose

высовывать /vysóvyvat'/ v. put out, push out

высовываться /vysóvyvat'sia/ v. lean out

высокий /vysókii/ adj. high, tall; lofty

высококачественный /vysokokáchestvennyi/ adj.
  high-quality

высококвалифицированный /vysokokvalifitsírovannyi/
  adj. highly skilled

высота /vysotá/ f. height; altitude

высохший /výsokhshii/ adj. dried up; withered

высочайший /vysocháishii/ adj. highest; imperial

выставка /výstavka/ f. exhibition

выстрел /výstrel/ m. shot

выступ /výstup/ m. prominence; projection

высушивать /vysúshivat'/ v. dry (up)

высчитывать /vyschítyvat'/ v. calculate

высший /výsshii/ adj. superior; highest

высылать /vysylát'/ v. sent out; banish

высыпать /vysypát'/ v. pour out

высыхать /vysykhát'/ v. dry up

вытаскивать /vytáskivat'/ v. take out, pull out

вытекать /vytekát'/ v. flow out; flow from; follow, result

вытеснять /vytesniát'/ v. force out; oust, expel

вытирать /vytirát'/ v. wipe, dry

вытряхивать /vytriákhivat'/ v. shake out

выть /vyt'/ v. howl

вытягивать /vytiágivat'/ v. draw out; stretch

выхаживать /vykházhivat'/ v. nurse; bring up

выход /výkhod/ m. going out; exit yield; publication

выходить /vykhodít'/ v. go or come out; withdraw; be published

вычеркивать /vychórkivat'/ v. cross out

вычисление /vychislénie/ n. calculation

вычитать /vychitát'/ v. subtract

вышвыривать /vyshvýrivat'/ v. fling out

выше /výshe/ adj. higher, beyond, above

вышивание /vyshivánie/ n. embroidery; needlework

выявлять /vyiavliát'/ v. expose, reveal

вьюга /v'iúga/ f. snowstorm, blizzard

вьющийся /v'iúshchiisia/ adj. curly (hair)

вязаный /viázanyi/ adj. knitted

вязать /viazát'/ v. bind; knit, crochet; be astringent

вязкий /viázkii/ adj. sticky; swampy

вялый /viályi/ adj. flabby, flaccid; sluggish, inert

вянуть /viánut'/ v. fade; droop

Г

г /g/ abbr., m. gram(me)

гавань /gávan'/ f. harbour

гадать /gadát'/ v. tell fortunes; guess

гадкий /gádkii/ adj. foul, nasty; bad

газ /gaz/ m. gas

газета /gazéta/ f. newspaper

газетный (киоск) /gazétnyi kiósk/ adj. + m. newsstand

газетчик /gazétchik/ m. newsman

газированная (вода) /gaziróvannaia vodá/ adj. + f. soda water

газон /gazón/ m. lawn

ГАИ /gai/ abbr., n. State Motor-vehicle Inspectorate

галантерея /galanteréia/ f. notions store; haberdashery

галантный /galántnyi/ adj. gallant, courtly

галстук /gálstuk/ m. (neck)tie

гараж /garázh/ m. garage

гарантировать /garantírovat'/ v. guarantee

гарантия /garántiia/ f. guarantee

гардероб /garderób/ m. cloakroom; wardrobe; clothes

гардина /gardína/ f. curtian

гарнир /garnír/ m. garnish; vegetables

гарнитур /garnitúr/ m. set, suite; спальный г. /spál'nyi g./ bedroom suite

гасить /gasít'/ v. extinguish

гаснуть /gásnut'/ v. go out, die away

гастролировать /gastrolírovat'/ v. tour, give performance(s) on a tour

гастроли /gastróli/ pl. starring (performance)

гастроном /gastronóm/ m. food store or shop

гвоздика /gvozdíka/ f. carnation

гвоздь /gvozd'/ m. nail

где /gde/ conj. where; где-либо, где-нибудь, где-то /gde-líbo, gde-nibúd', gde-to/ anywhere, somewhere

генерал /generál/ m. general; г.-майор /g.-maiór/ major-general

генеральный /generál'nyi/ adj. general; генеральная репетиция /generál'naia repetítsiia/ dress rehearsal

гениальный /geniál'nyi/ adj. of genius, brilliant

гений /génii/ m. genius

география /geográfiia/ f. geography

герб /gerb/ m. coat of arms

герметический /germetícheskii/ adj. hermetic

героиня /geroínia/ f. heroine

героический /geroícheskii/ adj. heroic

герой /gerói/ m. hero

гибель /gíbel'/ f. destruction

гибкий /gíbkii/ adj. flexible, supple

гиблый /gíblyi/ adj. wretched, ruinous

гибнуть /gíbnut'/ v. perish

гигантский /gigántskii/ adj. gigantic

гигиенический /gigienícheskii/ adj. hygienic, sanitary

гид /gid/ m. guide

гимн /gimn/ m. hymn; anthem; государственный г. /gosudárstvennyi g./ national anthem

гитара /gitára/ f. guitar

глава /glavá/ f. head, chief; chapter

главный /glávnyi/ adj. chief, main; главным образом /glávnym óbrazom/ mainly

гладить /gládit'/ v. iron

глаз /glaz/ m. eye; на глазок /na glazók/ approximately; с глазу на глаз /s glázu na glaz/ tete-a-tete

глазунья /glazún'ia/ f. fried eggs

глиняная (посуда) /glínianaia posúda/ adj. + f. earthenware

глиссер /glísser/ m. speed-boat

глотать /glotát'/ v. swallow

глоток /glotók/ m. gulp

глубокий /glubókii/ adj. deep, profound

глупость /glúpost'/ f. stupidity

глупый /glúpyi/ adj. stupid

глухой /glukhói/ adj. deaf

глухонемой /glukhonemói/ adj. deaf-mute

глухота /glukhotá/ f. deafness

глушить /glushít'/ v. muffle; jam; suppress

глядеть /gliadét'/ v. look, glance (at)

гнев /gnev/ m. anger

гневный /gnévnyi/ adj. angry

гнездо /gnezdó/ n. nest

гнет /gniót/ m. oppression; press(ure)

гнилой /gnilói/ adj. rotten

говорить /govorít'/ v. speak *or* talk; говорят /govoriát/ they say; г. по-русски /g. po-rússki/ speak Russian; иначе говоря /ináche govoriá/ in other words

говядина /goviádina/ f. beef

год /god/ m. year; в этом (прошлом) году /v étom (próshlom) godú/ this (last) year; круглый г. /krúglyi g./ all the year round; из года в год /iz góda v god/ year in year out

годичный /godíchnyi/ adj. annual

годный /gódnyi/ adj. fit, suitable

годовалый /godovályi/ adj. one-year-old

годовой /godovói/ adj. annual

годовщина /godovshchína/ f. anniversary

гол /gol/ m. goal; забивать г. /zabivát' g./ score a goal

голова /golová/ f. head

головка /golóvka/ f. head (pin, nail, etc.)

головной /golovnói/ adj. head; головная боль /golovnáia bol'/ headache

головокружение /golovokruzhénie/ n. giddiness, dizziness

головоломка /golovolómka/ f. puzzle

голод /gólod/ m. hunger; famine

голодать /golodát'/ v. starve

голодный /golódnyi/ adj. hungry

голодовка /golodóvka/ f. hunger-strike

голос /gólos/ m. voice; vote; право голоса /právo gólosa/ suffrage

голосовать /golosovát'/ v. vote

голый /gólyi/ adj. naked; bare

гонорар /gonorár/ m. fee

гора /gorá/ f. mountain, hill; идти в/на гору /idtí v/na góru/ go uphill; под гору /pod góru/ downhill

гораздо /gorázdo/ adv. much, far

гордиться /gordít'sia/ v. be proud (of)

гордость /górdost'/ f. pride

горе /góre/ n. sorrow, grief

горевать /gorevát'/ v. grieve

гореть /gorét'/ v. glow, gleam

горечь /górech/ f. bitter taste; bitterness

горизонтальный /gorizontál'nyi/ adj. horizontal

горло /górlo/ n. throat

горничная /górnichnaia/ f. housemaid

горный /górnyi/ adj. mountainous; mining

город /górod/ m. town, city

горожанин /gorozhánin/ m. townsman; pl. townspeople

горсть /gorst'/ f. handful

гортань /gortán'/ f. larynx

горчица /gorchítsa/ f. mustard

горшок /gorshók/ m. pot

горький /gór'kii/ adj. bitter

горючее /goriúchee/ n. fuel

горячий /goriáchii/ adj. hot; cordial, fervent

госпиталь /góspital'/ m. hospital

господин /gospodín/ m. gentleman; Mr.

господство /gospódstvo/ n. supremacy; rule

господь /gospód'/ m. Lord, God

госпожа /gospozhá/ f. lady, Mrs, Miss

гостеприимство /gosteprиímstvo/ n. hospitality

гостиная /gostínaia/ f. drawing-room

гостиница /gostínitsa/ f. hotel

гостить /gostít'/ v. be on a visit, stay with

государственный /gosudárstvennyi/ adj. state

государство /gosudárstvo/ n. state

готовить /gotóvit'/ v. prepare (for); cook

готовый /gotóvyi/ adj. ready

грабеж /grabiózh/ m. robbery

грабитель /grabítel'/ m. robber

град /grad/ m. hail

градус /grádus/ m. degree

градусник /grádusnik/ m. thermometer

гражданин /grazhdanín/ m. citizen

гражданство /grazhdánstvo/ m. citizenship

грамзапись /gramzápis'/ f. recording

грамм /gramm/ m. gram(me)

грамотность /grámotnost'/ f. literacy

грампластинка /gramplastínka/ f. record

граница /granítsa/ f. boundary, frontier; ехать за границу /ékhat' za granítsu/ go abroad

графин /grafín/ m. decanter

грациозный /gratsióznyi/ adj. graceful

гребец /grebéts/ m. oarsman

грелка /grélka/ f. hot-water bottle

гренки /grénki/ pl. toast(s)

грести /grestí/ v. row; scull

греть /gret'/ v. warm, heat

гриб /grib/ m. mushroom

грим /grim/ m. make-up

грипп /gripp/ m. influenza

гроза /grozá/ f. (thunder)storm

гроздь /grozd'/ f. bunch

грозить /grozít'/ v. threaten, menace

гром /grom/ m. thunder

громкий /grómkii/ adj. loud

грубый /grúbyi/ adj. coarse; rude

грудинка /grudínka/ f. bacon

грудь /grud'/ f. breast

груз /gruz/ m. load, cargo

грузить /gruzít'/ v. load

грузный /grúznyi/ adj. massive

грузовик /gruzovík/ m. truck

группа /grúppa/ f. group

грустный /grústnyi/ adj. sad

грусть /grust'/ f. sadness, melancholy

груша /grúsha/ f. pear

грызть /gryzt'/ v. gnaw; crack (nuts)

грязный /griáznyi/ adj. dirty, sordid

губа /gubá/ f. lip; bay

губка /gúbka/ f. sponge

гудеть /gudét'/ v. buzz

гулять /guliát'/ v. go for a walk, stroll

ГУМ /gum/ abbr., m. State department store

гуманный /gemánnyi/ adj. humane

густой /gustói/ adj. thick, dense; deep, rich (colour, sound)

гусь /gus'/ m. goose

Д

да /da/ part. yes; conj. and; but; да и /da i/ and besides

давать /davát'/ v. give; grant, let; давайте /daváite/ let us

давить /davít'/ v. press; crush, run over

давка /dávka/ f. throng, jam

давление /davlénie/ n. pressure

давний /dávnii/ adj. old, ancient

давно /davnó/ adv. long ago

даже /dázhe/ adv. even

далее /dálee/ adv. further, later; и так д. /i tak d./ and so on

далекий /daliókii/ adj. distant

далеко /dalekó/ adv. far (off, away); д. за полночь /d. zá polnoch/ long after midnight; д. не /d. ne/ far from, by no means

дальневосточный /dal'nevostóchnyi/ adj. Far Eastern

дальнейший /dal'néishii/ adj. further

дальний /dál'nii/ adj. distant, remote

дальнозоркий /dal'nozórkii/ adj. long-sighted

данный /dánnyi/ adj. given

данные /dánnye/ pl. data, facts

дантист /dantíst/ m. dentist

дань /dan'/ f. tribute, contribution

дар /dar/ m. gift

дарить /darít'/ v. present

даром /dárom/ adv. gratis, free

дата /dáta/ f. date

датировать /datírovat'/ v. date

дача /dácha/ f. dacha, summer residence; на даче /na dáche/ out of town, in the country

два /dva/ num. two

двадцатилетний /dvadtsatilétnii/ adj. twenty-year-old

двадцать /dvádtsat'/ num. twenty

дважды /dvázhdy/ adv. twice

двенадцать /dvenádtsat'/ num. twelve

дверь /dver'/ f. door

двести /dvésti/ num. two hundred

двигатель /dvígatel'/ m. motor, engine

двигать /dvígat'/ v. push, drive; further; motivate

движение /dvizhénie/ n. movement; traffic

движимость /dvízhimost'/ f. movable property

двое /dvóe/ num. two

двойной /dvoinói/ adj. double

двойственный /dvóistvennyi/ adj. dual; double-faced

двор /dvor/ m. court; yard; farm(stead)

дворец /dvoréts/ m. palace

дворник /dvórnik/ m. street cleaner; windshield (windscreen) wiper

двоюродный (брат), двоюродная (сестра) /dvoiúrodnyi brat, dvoiúrodnaia sestrá/ adj. + m., f. cousin

двоякий /dvoiákii/ adj. double, of two kinds

двубортный /dvubórtnyi/ adj. doublebreasted

двукратный /dvukrátnyi/ adj. double, done twice

двусмысленный /dvusmýslennyi/ adj. ambiguous

двусторонний /dvustorónnii/ adj. two-way; bilateral

двухгодовалый /dvukhgodovályi/ adj. two-year-old

двухдневный /dvukhdnévnyi/ adj. of two days

двухлетний /dvukhlétnii/ adj. biennial; two-year-old

двухмесячный /dvukhmésiachnyi/ adj. two months', two-month-old

двухнедельный /dvukhnedél'nyi/ adj. two-week-old, fortnightly

двухэтажный /dvukhetázhnyi/ adj. two-storeyed

двуязычный /dvuiazýchnyi/ adj. bilingual

дебаты /debáty/ pl. debate

дебри /débri/ pl. dense forest; maze, labyrinth

девальвация /deval'vátsia/ f. devaluation

деваться /devát'sia/ v. get to, disappear to

девочка /dévochka/ f. (little) girl

девушка /dévushka/ f. girl; miss

девяносто /devianósto/ num. ninety

девятнадцать /deviatnádtsat'/ num. nineteen

девять /déviat'/ num. nine

девятьсот /deviat'sót/ num. nine hundred

дегустация /degustátsiia/ f. tasting

дед, дедушка /ded, dédushka/ m. grandfather; old man

дезориентировать /dezorientírovat'/ v. confuse, mislead

действенный /déistvennyi/ adj. effective, active

действие /déistvie/ n. action; act; operation

действительный /deistvítel'nyi/ adj. actual, real, valid

действительность /deistvítel'nost'/ f. reality

действовать /déistvovat'/ v. act, operate, function; have effect (on)

декабрь /dekábr'/ m. December

деквалификация /dekvalifikátsiia/ f. loss of professional skill

декламировать /deklamírivat'/ v. recite

декорация /dekorátsiia/ f. scenery

декретный (отпуск) /dekrétnyi ótpusk/ adj. + m. maternity leave

делать /délat'/ v. make; нечего делать /néchego délat'/ it can't be helped

делаться /délat'sia/ v. become, grow, turn; happen; что с
  ним сделалось? /chto s nim sdélalos'?/ what has become
  of him?

делец /deléts/ m. (sharp) businessman

деликатес /delikatés/ m. dainty

деликатный /delikátnyi/ adj. delicate, tactful

делить /delít'/ v. divide, share

делиться /delít'sia/ v. exchange; confide; be divisible

дело /délo/ n. matter, business, affair; deed; говорить д.
  /govorít' d./ talk sense; на самом деле /na sámom déle/
  in reality, in fact

деловой /delovói/ adj. business-like

делопроизводитель /deloproizvodítel'/ m. secretary

дельный /dél'nyi/ adj. competent; sensible

денежный /dénezhnyi/ adj. money, pecuniary

день /den'/ m. day; на днях /na dniákh/ the other day; три
  часа дня /tri chasá dniá/ 3 p.m.

деньги /dén'gi/ pl. money

депозит /depozít/ m. deposit

депрессия /depréssiia/ f. depression

дергать /diórgat'/ v. pull, tug

деревенский /derevénskii/ adj. rural

деревня /derévnia/ f. village; country(side)

дерево /dérevo/ n. tree; красное д. /krásnoe d./
  mahogany; черное д. /chórnoe d./ ebony

деревянный /dereviánnyi/ adj. wooden

держава /derzháva/ f. power, state

держать /derzhát'/ v. hold, keep; д. себя /d. sebiá/
  behave

держаться /derzhát'sia/ v. hold (onto); hold out, stand; д. в стороне /d. v storoné/ hold aloof

дерзкий /dérzkii/ adj. impudent; bold, daring

дерзость /dérzost'/ f. impudence, cheek

десерт /desért/ m. dessert

десна /desná/ f. gum

десятилетие /desiatilétie/ n. decade; tenth anniversary

десять /désiat/ num. ten

деталь /detál'/ f. detail; component

детальный /detál'nyi/ adj. detailed, minute

детектив /detektív/ m. detective; detective story

детеныш /detiónysh/ m. young one, cub

дети /déti/ pl. children

детский (сад) /détskii sad/ adj. + m. kindergarten

детство /détstvo/ n. childhood

дефект /defékt/ m. defect

дефектный /deféktnyi/ adj. faulty

дефицит /defitsít/ m. shortage

дефицитный /defitsítnyi/ adj in short supply, scarce

дешевизна /deshevízna/ f. cheapness

дешевый /deshóvyi/ adj. cheap

деятель (политический д.) /politícheskii déiatel'/ adj. + m. politican; государственный д. /gosudárstvennyi d./ statesman; общественный д. /obshchéstvennyi d./ public figure

деятельность /déiatel'nost'/ f. activity

джемпер /dzhémper/ m. jumper, pullover

диагноз /diágnoz/ m. diagnosis

диапазон /diapazón/ m. range, compass

диван /diván/ m. settee; divan; sofa

диета /diéta/ f. diet

дизентерия /dizenteríia/ f. dysentery

дикий /díkii/ adj. wild; shy

диктатор /diktátor/ m. dictator

диктовать /diktovát'/ v. dictate

диктор /díktor/ m. announcer

дилетант /diletánt/ m. amateur, dilettante

динамика /dinámika/ f. dynamics

диплом /diplóm/ m. diploma

дипломат /diplomát/ m. diplomat; sl. attache case

директива /direktíva/ f. instruction, directive

директор /diréktor/ m. director, manager

дирекция /diréktsiia/ f. management; board of directors

дирижер /dirizhór/ m. conductor

дисквалифицировать /diskvalifitsírovat'/ v. disqualify

дискредитировать /diskreditírovat'/ v. discredit

дискриминация /diskriminátsiia/ f. discrimination

дискутировать /diskutírovat'/ v. discuss, debate

диспетчер /dispétcher/ m. controller

диспут /dísput/ m. public debate

диссертация /dissertátsiia/ f. thesis, dissertation

дисциплина /distsiplína/ f. discipline

дитя /ditiá/ n. child

длина /dliná/ f. length

длинный /dlinnyi/ adj. long

длиться /dlít'sia/ v. last

для /dliá/ prep. for; для того чтобы /dlia togó chtóby/ in order to

дневник /dnevník/ m. diary

дневной /dnevnói/ adj. daily

дно /dno/ n. bottom; ground

до /do/ prep. up to, until, before; мне не до шуток /mne ne do shútok/ I'm not in the mood for jokes

добавка /dobávka/ f. addition, supplement

добавлять /dobavliát'/ v. add

добиваться /dobivát'sia/ v. achieve, obtain; д. своего /d. svoegó/ gain one's end

добираться /dobirát'sia/ v. get to, reach

добро /dobró/ n. good; д. пожаловать! /d. pozhálovat'!/ welcome (to)!

добровольный /dobrovól'nyi/ adj. voluntary

добродетель /dobrodétel'/ f. virtue

добродушие /dobrodúshie/ n. good-nature

доброжелательный /dobrozhelátel'nyi/ adj. benevolent

доброкачественный /dobrokáchestvennyi/ adj. of high quality; benign

добросовестный /dobrosóvestnyi/ adj. conscientious

добрососедский /dobrososédskii/ adj. neighbourly, friendly

доброта /dobrotá/ f. goodness, kindness

добротный /dobrótnyi/ adj. of high quality

добрый /dóbryi/ adj. good, kind

добывать /dobyvát'/ v. get, obtain

добыча /dobýcha/ f. output; booty, loot; extraction, mining

доверенность /dovérennost'/ f. warrant, power of attorney

доверие /dovérie/ n. confidence, trust

доверить /dovérit'/ v. entrust (to)

доверху /dóverkhu/ adv. to the top

доверчивый /dovérchivyi/ adj. trusting, credulous

доверять /doveriát'/ v. trust, confide (in)

довод /dóvod/ m. reason, argument

доводить /dovodít'/ v. lead, bring (to)

довольно /dovól'no/ adv. enough; rather

довольный /dovól'nyi/ adj. pleased, content (with)

догадливый /dogádlivyi/ adj. quick-witted

догадываться /dogádyvat'sia/ v. guess

договариваться /dogovárivat'sia/ v. come to an agreement

договор /dogovór/ m. agreement, contract, treaty

договорный /dogovórnyi/ adj. contractual, agreed

догонять /dogoniát'/ v. catch up

дождевик /dozhdevík/ m. raincoat; puffball

дождливый /dozhdlívyi/ adj. rainy

дождь /dozhd'/ m. rain

дожидаться /dozhidát'sia/ v. wait for

доза /dóza/ f. dose

дозвониться /dozvonít'sia/ v. ring till one gets an answer; ring through

дозировка /doziróvka/ f. dosage

доисторический /doistorícheskii/ adj. prehistoric

доить /doít'/ v. milk

доказательный /dokazátel'nyi/ adj. conclusive

доказательство /dokazátel'stvo/ n. proof, evidence

доказывать /dokázyvat'/ v. prove

докапываться /dokápyvat'sia/ v. find out

доклад /doklád/ m. report

докладчик /dokládchik/ m. speaker

докладывать /dokládyvat'/ v. make a report

доктор /dóktor/ m. doctor; physician

документ /dokumént/ m. document

долг /dolg/ m. debt; брать в д. /brat' v d./ borrow; давать в д. /davát' v d./ lend

долгий /dólgii/ adj. long

долго /dólgo/ adv. for a long time

долговременный /dolgovrémennyi/ adj. lasting, permanent

должник /dolzhník/ m. debtor

должность /dólzhnost'/ post, position

долина /dolína/ f. valley

дольше /dól'she/ adv. longer

доля /dólia/ f. portion, share; fate

дом /dom/ m. house; building

дома /dóma/ adv. at home

домашний /domáshnii/ adj. domestic

домовладелец /domovladélets/ m. house-owner; landlord

домогательство /domogátel'stvo/ n. solicitation; importunity

домой /domói/ adv. home, homewards

донизу /dónizu/ adv. to the bottom; сверху д. /svérkhu d./ from top to bottom

доносить /donosít'/ v. report, inform (against)

доносчик /donóschik/ m. informer

доплата /dopláta/ f. extra payment; excess fare

доплачивать /dopláchivat'/ v. pay the remainder; pay in addition

дополнение /dopolnénie/ n. addition, supplement

дополнительный /dopolnítel'nyi/ adj. additional

допрашивать /dopráshivat'/ v. question, interrogate

допрос /doprós/ m. interrogation

допускать /dopuskát'/ v. admit

допустимый /dopustímyi/ adj. permissible, possible

дорога /doróga/ f. road, way; железная д. /zheléznaia d./ railway, railroad; туда ему и д. /tudá emú i d/ in serves him right!

дороговизна /dorogovízna/ f. high prices

дорогой /dorogói/ adj. dear; expensive

дорожать /dorozhát'/ v. rise in prise

дорожить /dorozhít'/ v. value

дорожка /dorózhka/ f. path; track; strip (of carpet)

досада /dosáda/ f. vexation, disappointment

доска /doská/ f. board; slab

дословный /doslóvnyi/ adj. word-for-word, literal

досрочный /dosróchnyi/ adj. ahead of schedule

доставать /dostavát'/ v. get, obtain; suffice; reach; touch

доставка /dostávka/ f. delivery

достаток /dostátok/ m. prosperity

достаточный /dostátochnyi/ adj. sufficient, enough

достигать /dostigát'/ v. reach, achive

достижение /dostizhénie/ n. achivement

достоверный /dostovérnyi/ adj. authentic

достоинство /dostóinstvo/ n. dignity; merit

достойный /dostóinyi/ adj. worth (of)

достопримечательность /dostoprimechátel'nost'/ f. sight; осматривать (достопримечательности) /osmátrivat' dostoprimechátel'nosti/ go sightseeing достояние /dostoiánie/ n. property

доступный /dostúpnyi/ adj. accessible

досуг /dosúg/ m. leisure; на досуге /na dosúge/ in one's spare time

досягаемый /dosiagáemyi/ adj. attainable

дотация /dotátsia/ f. State grant, subsidy

дотрагиваться /dotrágivat'sia/ v. touch

доход /dokhód/ m. income

доходный /dokhódnyi/ adj. profitable

доходчивый /dokhódchivyi/ adj. intelligible, easy to understand

дочка, дочь /dóchka, doch/ f. daughter

дошкольник /doshkól'nik/ m. child under school age

дошкольный /doshkól'nyi/ adj. preschool

драгоценность /dragotsénnost'/ f. jewel

драгоценный /dragotsénnyi/ adj. precious

дразнить /draznít'/ v. tease

драка /dráka/ f. fight

драма /dráma/ f. drama

драматург /dramatúrg/ m. playwright

драться /drát'sia/ v. fight

драчливый /drachlívyi/ adj. pugnacious

древесина /drevesína/ f. wood, wood-pulp

древнерусский /drevnerússkii/ adj. Old Russian

древний /drévnii/ adj. ancient

дремать /dremát'/ v. doze

дрессировать /dressirovát'/ v. train (animals)

дрова /drová/ pl. firewood

дрожать /drozhát'/ v. tremble

дрожжи /drózhzhi/ pl. yeast, leaven

друг /drug/ m. friend; друг друга /drug drúga/ each other

другой /drugói/ adj. other, different; и тот и д. /i tot i d./ both; ни тот ни д. /ni tot ni d./ neither

дружба /drúzhba/ f. friendship

дружелюбный /druzheliúbnyi/ adj. amicable

дружеский /drúzheskii/ adj. friendly

дряхлый /driákhlyi/ adj. decrepit

дуб /dub/ m. oak

дубинка /dubínka/ f. truncheon, club

дуло /dúlo/ n. muzzle

дурак /durák/ m. fool, ass

дуть /dut'/ v. blow

дух /dukh/ m. spirit; breath; mind; spectre, ghost; захватывает дух /zakhvátyvaet dukh/ it takes one's breath away; присутствие духа /prisútstvie dúkha/ presence of mind; о нем ни слуху ни духу /o nióm ni slúkhu ni dúkhu/ nothing has been heard of him

духи /dukhí/ pl. perfume

духовенство /dukhovénstvo/ n. clergy

духовка /dukhóvka/ f. oven

душ /dush/ m. shower (-bath)

душа /dushá/ f. soul

душевнобольной /dushevnobol'nói/ adj. insane

душевный /dushévnyi/ adj. mental, psychical; sincere

душистый /dushístyi/ adj. fragrant

душить /dushít'/ v. smother, stifle, strangle; scent, perfume

душный /dúshnyi/ adj. stuffy

дым /dym/ m. smoke

дымить /dymít'/ v. smoke

дыня /dýnia/ f. melon

дыра /dyrá/ f. hole

дырявый /dyriávyi/ adj. full of holes

дыхание /dykhánie/ n. breathing; breath

дыхательный /dykhátel'nyi/ adj. respiratory

дышать /dyshát'/ v. breathe

дьявол /d'iávol/ m. devil

дюйм /diúim/ m. inch

дядя /diádia/ m. uncle

Е

Евангелие /evángelie/ n. the Gospels

еда /edá/ f. food, meal

едва /edvá/ adv. hardly, just, scarcely; е. не /e. ne/ nearly, all but

единица /edinítsa/ f. one; unit; individual

единичный /ediníchnyi/ adj. single, isolated

единодушие /edinodúshie/ n. unanimity

единомыслие /edinomýslie/ n. agreement of opinion

единообразие /edinoobrázie/ n. uniformity

единственный /edínstvennyi/ adj. only, sole

единство /edínstvo/ n. unity

единый /edínyi/ adj. united, common; single

ежегодник /ezhegódnik/ m. yearbook

ежегодный /ezhegódnyi/ adj. annual

ежедневный /ezhednévnyi/ adj. daily

ежемесячник /ezhemésiachnik/ m. monthly (magazine)

еженедельник /ezhenedél'nik/ m. weekly (newspaper, magazine)

ежечасный /ezhechásnyi/ adj. hourly

ездить /ézdit'/ v. ride, drive, go

ей-богу /ei bógu/ int. really and truly

елка /iólka/ f. fir(-tree); рождественская е. /rozhdéstvenskaia io./ Christmas-tree

ель /el'/ f. fir-tree

епископ /epískop/ m. bishop

ерунда /erundá/ f. nonsense

если /ésli/ conj. if; e. не /e. ne/ unless

естественный /estéstvennyi/ adj. natural

есть /est'/ v. eat; there is, there are; у меня е. /u meniá e./ I have

ехать /ékhat'/ v. go, drive, ride

еще /eshchió/ adv. still, yet; e. раз /e. raz/ once more, again

Ж

ж /zh/ - же

жадный /zhádnyi/ adj. greedy (for)

жажда /zházhda/ f. thirst

жакет /zhakét/ m. (ladies') jacket

жалеть /zhalét'/ v. feel sorry (for); regret

жалить /zhálit'/ v. sting

жалкий /zhálkii/ adj. pitiful, pathetic, wretched

жалоба /zháloba/ f. complaint

жалобный /zhálobnyi/ adj. plaintive; жалобная книга /zhálobnaia kníga/ complaints book

жаловаться /zhálovat'sia/ v. complain (of, about)

жалость /zhálost'/ f. pity

жаль /zhal'/ as pred. (it is a) pity; ему жаль сестру /emú zhal' sestrú/ he is sorry for his sister

жара /zhará/ f. heat

жареный /zhárenyi/ adj. fried, grilled, roasted

жарить /zhárit'/ v. fry, grill

жаркий /zhárkii/ adj. hot

жаркое /zharkóe/ n. roast (meat)

жать /zhat'/ v. press, squeeze, be too tight; reap

жвачка /zhváchka/ f. chewing-gum

ждать /zhdat'/ v. wait (for)

же /zhe/ conj. as for, after all

же /zhe/ emphatic particle: когда же они приедут? /kogdá zhe oní priédut?/ whenever will they come?

же /zhe/ particle expressing identity: тот же /tot zhe/ the same; там же /tam zhe/ in the same place

жевать /zhevát'/ v. chew

желание /zhelánie/ n. wish, desire

железо /zhelézo/ n. iron

железобетон /zhelezobetón/ m. reinforced concrete

желток /zheltók/ m. yolk

желтый /zhéltyi/ adj. yellow

желудок /zhelúdok/ m. stomach

желудочный /zhelúdochnyi/ adj. stomach, gastric

желчный /zhélchnyi/ adj. bilious; bitter; ж. пузырь /zh. puzýr'/ gall-bladder

жемчуг /zhémchug/ m. pearl(s)

жена /zhená/ f. wife

женатый /zhenátyi/ adj. married

жениться /zheníťsia/ v. marry, get married

жених /zheníkh/ m. fiancé

женский /zhénskii/ adj. female, feminine

женственный /zhénstvennyi/ adj. womanly

женщина /zhénshchina/ f. woman

жеребец /zherebéts/ m. stallion

жертва /zhértva/ f. victim

жертвовать /zhértvovat'/ v. sacrifice

жест /zhest/ m. gesture

жестокий /zhestókii/ adj. hard, rigid

жестокость /zhestókost'/ f. cruelty

жетон /zhetón/ v. counter

жечь /zhech/ v. burn

живой /zhivói/ adj. living, alive

живописный /zhivopísnyi/ adj. picturesque

живость /zhívost'/ f. liveliness

живот /zhivót/ m. abdomen, belly

животное /zhivótnoe/ n. animal

живучий /zhivúchii/ adj. hardy, tough; enduring

жидкий /zhídkii/ adj. liquid; thin

жидкость /zhídkost'/ f. liquid; fluid

жизненный /zhíznennyi/ adj. vital, living; ж. уровень /zh. úroven'/ standard of living

жизнеспособный /zhiznesposóbnyi/ adj. viable

жизнь /zhizn'/ f. life

жилет /zhilét/ m. waistcoat

жилец /zhiléts/ m. tenant, lodger

жилище /zhilíshche/ n. dwelling

жилищные (условия) /zhilíshchnye uslóviia/ adj. + pl.
  housing conditions

жилой /zhilói/ adj. dwelling; ж. дом /zh. dom/ dwelling
  house

жир /zhir/ m. fat, grease

жирный /zhírnyi/ adj. fat; rich; greasy

житейский /zhitéiskii/ adj. everyday; worldly

житель /zhítel'/ m. inhabitant, resident

жительство /zhítel'stvo/ n. residence

жить /zhit'/ v. live

жук /zhuk/ m. beetle

жулик /zhúlik/ m. swindler

жульничать /zhúlnichat'/ v. cheat

журнал /zhurnál/ m. periodical, magazine, journal

жуткий /zhútkii/ adj. terrible

жюри /zhurí/ n. jury

З

за /za/ prep. behind, beyond; at; for; after; because of; за
  городом /za górodom/ out of town; за столом /za stolóm/
  at the table; за работой /za rabótoi/ at work; ехать за
  город /ékhat' zá gorod/ go out of town; ему за 50 лет /emú
  za 50 let/ he is over 50; далеко за полночь /dalekó za
  pólnoch/ long after midnight; за 100 км от /za 100 km ot/
  100 km from...; за последние пять лет /za poslédnie piat'
  let/ for the past five years; за два дня до этого /za dva dniá
  do étovo/ two days before that; покупать за 10 руб.
  /pokupát' za 10 rubléi/ buy for 10 rubles; я расписался
  за него /ia raspisálsia za nevó/ I have signed for him; за и

против /za i prótiv/ pros and cons; взять за руку /vziát' zá ruku/ take by the hand

забавлять /zabavliát'/ v. amuse, entertain

забастовка /zabastóvka/ f. strike

забег /zabég/ m. heat, race

забегать /zabegát'/ v. drop in (to see); з. вперед /z. vperiód/ run ahead; anticipate

забеременеть /zaberémenet'/ v. become pregnant

забирать /zabirát'/ v. take away

заблаговременный /zablagovrémennyi/ adj. timely

заблудиться /zabludít'sia/ v. get lost

заблуждаться /zabluzhdát'sia/ v. be mistaken

заболевать /zabolevát'/ v. begin to ache; fall ill

забор /zabór/ m. fence

забота /zabóta/ f. care

заботиться /zabótit'sia/ v. take care of

заботливый /zabótlivyi/ adj. considerate, solicitous

забывать /zabyvát'/ v. forget

забывчивый /zabývchivyi/ adj. forgetful

заваливать /zaválivat'/ v. heap up, block up; overload

заваривать (чай) /zavárivat' chái/ v. + m. brew tea

заведение /zavedénie/ n. establishment

заведовать /zavédovat'/ v. manage

заведующий /zavéduiushchii/ m. manager, head

завертывать /zaviórtyvat'/ v. wrap in; turn off

завершать /zavershát'/ v. complete, conclude

заверять /zaveriát'/ v. assure; certify

завет /zavét/ m. behest; Ветхий, Новый з. /vétkhii, nóvyi z./ the Old, the New Testament завещание /zaveshchánie/ n. testament, will

завещать /zaveshchát'/ v. bequeath

завидовать /zavídovat'/ v. envy

завинчивать /zavínchivat'/ v. screw up

зависеть /zavíset'/ v. depend (on)

зависимый /zavísimyi/ adj. dependent

завистливый /zavístlivyi/ adj. envious

завитой /zavitói/ adj. curled; waved

завладеть /zavladét'/ v. take possession of; seize

завод /zavód/ m. factory, works; stud (-farm); winding up

заводить /zavodít'/ v. bring, lead; acquire; establish; wind up

заводной /zavodnói/ adj. clockwork

завоеватель /zavoevátel'/ m. conqueror

завоёвывать /zavoióvyvat'/ v. conquer, win

завозить /zavozít'/ v. convey, deliver

завтра /závtra/ adv. tomorrow

завтрак /závtrak/ m. breakfast

завязывать /zaviázyvat'/ v. tie up

загадка /zagádka/ f. enigma, riddle

загадочный /zagádochnyi/ adj. mysterious

загадывать /zagádyvat'/ v. make plans, look ahead

загар /zagár/ m. (sun-)tan

загибать /zagibát'/ v. bend

заглавие /zaglávie/ n. title, heading

заглушать /zaglushát'/ v. muffle, jam (broadcast); soothe (pain)

заглядывать /zagliádyvat'/ v. peep in; call on

загнивать /zagnivát'/ v. rot

заговор /zágovor/ m. plot; exorcism

заговорщик /zagovórshchik/ m. conspirator

заголовок /zagolóvok/ m. heading, title; headline

загораживать /zagorázhivat'/ v. enclose; obstruct

загораться /zagorát'sia/ v. catch fire

загорелый /zagorélyi/ adj. sunburnt

загородный /zágorodnyi/ adj. country, out-of-town

заграница /zagranítsa/ f. foreign countries; поехать за границу /poékhat' za granítsu/ go abroad

заграничный /zagraníchnyi/ adj. foreign

загружать /zagruzhát'/ v. load; feed (machine); keep fully occupied

загрязнять /zagriazniát'/ v. pollute

загс /zags/ abbr. m. registry office

зад /zad/ m. back; buttocks; задом /zádom/ with one's back (to)

задавать /zadavát'/ v. give, set

задаваться (целью) /zadavát'sia tsél'iu/ v. + f. set oneself (to)

задание /zadánie/ n. task

задаток /zadátok/ m. advance, deposit; природные задатки /priródnye zadátki/ instincts, inclinations

задача /zadácha/ f. problem, task

задевать /zadevát'/ v. touch; offend, wound

задергивать /zadiórgivat'/ v. pull, shut

задерживать /zadérzhivat'/ v. hold back; arrest

задерживаться /zadérzhivat'sia/ v. stay too long

задержка /zadérzhka/ f. delay

задний /zádnii/ adj. back, rear; з. план /z. plan/ background задолго /zadólgo/ adv. long before

задолженность /zadólzhennost'/ f. debts

задумчивый /zadúmchivyi/ adj. thoughtful

задумывать /zadúmyvat'/ v. plan, intend

задумываться /zadúmyvat'sia/ v. become lost in thought

задушевный /zadushévnyi/ adj. sincere; intimate

задыхаться /zadykhát'sia/ v. choke, suffocate

заезжать /zaezzhát'/ v. call (at)

заем /zaióm/ m. loan

заживать /zazhivát'/ v. heal

заживо /zázhivo/ adv. alive

зажигалка /zazhigálka/ f. lighter

зажигать /zazhigát'/ v. set fire to; light

зажигаться /zazhigát'sia/ v. catch fire; inflame

зажиточный /zazhítochnyi/ adj. prosperous

зазнаваться /zaznavát'sia/ v. give oneself airs

зазубривать /zazúbrivat'/ v. learn by rote

заика /zaíka/ m. and f. stammerer

заикаться /zaikát'sia/ v. stammer, clutter

заимствовать /zaímstvovat'/ v. borrow

заинтересовывать /zainteresóvyvat'/ v. interest

заискивать /zaískivat'/ v. ingratiate oneself (with)

заказ /zakáz/ m. order

заказное письмо /zakaznóe pis'mó/ adj. + n. registered
   letter

заказчик /zakázchik/ m. client, customer

заказывать /zakázyvat'/ v. order

заканчивать /zakánchivat'/ v. finish

закапывать /zakápyvat'/ v. bury; fill up

закат /zakát/ m. sunset

закатывать /zakátyvat'/ v. roll up, wrap in

заклад /zaklád/ m. pawning; биться об з. /bít'sia ob z./ bet

закладная /zakladnáia/ f. mortgage

закладывать /zakládyvat'/ v. put (behind); block up; lay (the foundation of); pawn

заключать /zakliuchát'/ v. conclude; infer; close; finish; contract; contain; imprison

заключаться /zakliuchát'sia/ v. consist (in)

заключение /zakliuchénie/ n. conclusion; imprisonment

заключенный /zakliuchónnyi/ m. prisoner

заключительный /zakliuchítel'nyi/ adj. final

заколачивать /zakoláchivat'/ v. drive in; nail up

заколка /zakólka/ f. hairpin

закон /zakón/ m. law

законность /zakónnost'/ f. legality

законный /zakónnyi/ adj. legal, legitimate

законодательный /zakonodátel'nyi/ adj. legislative

законодательство /zakonodátel'stvo/ n. legislation

закономерность /zakonomérnost'/ f. regularity, conformity with a law

закономерный /zakonomérnyi/ adj. regular, natural

законопроект /zakonoproékt/ m. bill

закреплять /zakrepliát'/ v. fasten, fix; consolidate; allot

закрывать(ся) /zakryvát'(sia)/ v. close, shut

закрытие /zakrýtie/ n. closing

закрытый /zakrýtyi/ adj. shut, closed; private

закупать /zakupát'/ v. buy up (wholesale)

закупка /zakúpka/ f. purchase

закупоривать /zakupórivat'/ v. cork

закуривать /zakúrivat'/ v. light up (cigarette, etc.)

закуска /zakúska/ f. hors-d'oeuvre; snack

закусочная /zakúsochnaia/ f. snack bar

закусывать /zakúsyvat'/ v. have a snack

закутывать /zakútyvat'/ v. wrap up, muffle

зал /zal/ m. hall; (reception) room

залезать /zalezát'/ v. climb (up, onto), creep (into)

залечивать /zaléchivat'/ v. cure, heal

залив /zalív/ m. bay, gulf

заливать /zalivát'/ v. flood; quench; extinguish

залог /zalóg/ m. deposit; security

заложник /zalózhnik/ m. hostage

залп /zalp/ m. volley, salvo; выпить залпом /výpit' zálpom/ drink at one draught

замалчивать /zamálchivat'/ v. hush up

заманивать /zamánivat'/ v. entice

заманчивый /zamánchivyi/ adj. tempting

замахиваться /zamákhivat'sia/ v. lift one's arm threateningly

замедлять /zamedliát'/ v. slow down

замена /zaména/ f. substitution

заменять /zameniát'/ v. substitute, replace

замерзание /zamerzánie/ n. freezing; точка замерзания /tóchka zamerzániia/ freezing point

замертво /zámertvo/ adv. as good as dead

заместитель /zamestítel'/ m. deputy, assistant, vice-...

заметка /zamétka/ f. note, notice

заметный /zamétnyi/ adj. appreciable; noticeable; visible

замечание /zamechánie/ n. remark

замечательный /zamechátel'nyi/ adj. remarkable

замечать /zamechát'/ v. notice, observe, remark

замешательство /zameshátel'stvo/ n. embarrassment

замешивать /zaméshivat'/ v. involve; implicate; mix; з. тесто /z. tésto/ knead dough

замещать /zameshchát'/ v. replace

замещение /zameshchénie/ n. substitution

замкнутость /zámknutost'/ f. reserve

замкнутый /zámknutyi/ adj. excessive; reserved

замок /zámok/ m. castle

замок /zamók/ m. lock

замолкать /zamolkát'/ v. fall silent

замораживать /zamorázhivat'/ v. freeze

замуж (выдавать з.) /vydavát' zámuzh/ v. + adv. give in marriage (to); выходить з. /vykhodít' z./ get married (to)

замужем /zámuzhem/ adv. married (to)

замша /zámsha/ f. suede

замыкание (короткое з.) /korótkoe zamykánie/ adj. + n. short circuit

замыкать /zamykát'/ v. lock, close

замысел /zámysel/ m. project, plan

замышлять /zamyshliát'/ v. plan; contemplate

замять (разговор) /zamiát' razgovór/ v. + m. change the subject

занавес /zánaves/ m. curtain

занавеска /zanavéska/ f. curtain

занимательный /zanimátel'nyi/ adj. entertaining

занимать /zanimát'/ v. occupy; engage; interest

заниматься /zanimát'sia/ v. be occupied (with); be engaged (in); study

заново /zánovo/ adv. anew

заноза /zanóza/ f. splinter

заносчивый /zanóschivyi/ adj. arrogant

занятие /zaniátie/ n. occupation

занятный /zaniátnyi/ adj. entertaining, amusing

занятой /zaniatói/ adj. occupied, busy

заочный (курс) /zaóchnyi kurs/ adj. + m. correspondence course

запад /západ/ m. west

западный /západnyi/ adj. western

западня /zapadniá/ f. trap

запаздывать /zapázdyvat'/ v. be late

запаковывать /zapakóvyvat'/ v. pack, wrap up

запас /zapás/ m. stock, supply

запасать /zapasát'/ v. store

запасаться /zapasát'sia/ v. provide oneself (with)

запасливый /zapáslivyi/ adj. thrifty

запасной /zapasnói/ adj. spare, reserve

запах /západh/ m. smell

запеканка /zapekánka/ f. baked pudding

запекать /zapekát'/ v. bake

запечатывать /zapechátyvat'/ v. seal up

запивать /zapivát'/ v. wash down

запить /zapít'/ v. take to drinking

запинаться /zapinát'sai/ v. stammer, falter

запирать /zapirát'/ v. lock

записка /zapíska/ f. note

записывать /zapísyvat'/ v. note; enter; record

записываться /zapísyvat'sia/ v. register, enroll

запись /zápis'/ f. writing down, entry; record, recording

заплакать /zaplákat'/ v. start crying

заплата /zapláta/ f. patch

заплесневелый /zaplesnevélyi/ adj. mouldy

заплетать /zapletát'/ v. braid, plait

заповедник /zapovédnik/ m. preserve; reserve

заповедь /zápoved'/ f. commandment

заподозрить /zapodózrit'/ v. suspect (of)

запоздалый /zapozdályi/ adj. belated

заполнять /zapolniát'/ v. fill in, fill up

запоминать /zapominát'/ v. memorize

запонка /záponka/ f. cuff-link

запор /zapór/ m. lock, bolt; constipation

заправка /zaprávka/ f. seasoning; refuelling

заправлять /zapravliát'/ v. season; trim; refuel

заправочная (станция) /zaprávochnaia stántsiia/ adj. + f.
  filling (gas) station

запрет /zaprét/ m. interdiction

запретный /zaprétnyi/ adj. forbidden

запрещать /zapreshchát'/ v. forbid

запрещение /zapreshchénie/ n. prohibition

запугивать /zapúgivat'/ v. intimidate

запуск /zápusk/ m. launching

запускать /zapuskát'/ v. start, launch; neglect

запутывать /zapútyvat'/ v. dangle, confuse

запутываться /zapútyvat'sia/ v. become entangled

запутанный /zapútannyi/ adj. intricate

запущенный /zapúshchennyi/ adj. neglected

запястье /zapiást'e/ n. wrist

зарабатывать /zarabátyvat'/ v. earn

заработная (плата) /zárabotnaia pláta/ adj. + f. wage, pay

заработок /zárabotok/ m. earnings

заражение /zarazhénie/ n. infection

заразный /zaráznyi/ adj. infectious, contagious

заранее /zaránee/ adv. beforehand

зарекомендовать (себя) /zarekomendovát' sebiá/ v. +
  pron. show oneself (to be)

зарплата /zarpláta/ f. pay, wages

зарубежный /zarubézhnyi/ adj. foreign

заручаться /zaruchát'sia/ v. secure; з. поддержкой /z.
  poddérzhkoi/ enlist support

зарывать /zaryvát'/ v. bury

заря /zariá/ f. dawn, daybreak; sunset

заряд /zariád/ m. charge

заряжать /zariazhát'/ v. load; charge

засада /zasáda/ f. ambush

заседание /zasedánie/ n. session

заселять /zaseliát'/ v. populate; settle

заслуга /zaslúga/ f. merit

заслуженный /zaslúzhennyi/ adj. honoured

заслуживать /zaslúzhivat'/ v. deserve

засорять /zasoriát'/ v. litter

заставлять /zastavliát'/ v. make, compel; block up

застегиваться /zastiógivat'sia/ v. button oneself up

застежка /zastiózhka/ f. clasp; з.-молния /z.-mólnia/ zip
  fastener

застенчивый /zasténchivyi/ adj. shy
застой /zastói/ m. stagnation
застраивать /zastráivat'/ v. build (over, on, up)
застраховывать /zastrachóvyvat'/ v. insure
застревать /zastrevát'/ v. get stuck
застрелить /zastrelít'/ v. shoot (dead)
застрелиться /zastrelít'sia/ v. shoot oneself
заступаться /zastupát'sia/ v. intercede (for); stand up for
засуха /zásukha/ f. drought
засыпать /zasýpat'/ v. fill up
засыпать /zasypát'/ v. fall asleep
затем /zatém/ adv. then
затихать /zatikhát'/ v. calm down
затишье /zatísh'e/ n. lull
затмение /zatménie/ n. eclipse
зато /zató/ conj. but on the other hand
затоваривание /zatovárivanie/ n. glut (of goods)
затор /zatór/ m. (traffic) jam
затрагивать /zatrágivat'/ v. affect
затрата /zatráta/ f. expenditure
затрачивать /zatráchivat'/ v. spend
затребовать /zatrébovat'/ v. require; ask for
затруднение /zatrudnénie/ n. difficulty
затруднять /zatrudniát'/ v. hamper
затылок /zatýlok/ m. back of the head
затягивать /zatiágivat'/ v. tighten; drag down
затяжка /zatiázhka/ f. delay; inhaling (in smoking)
затяжной /zatiazhnói/ adj. protracted
заурядный /zauriádnyi/ adj. ordinary, mediocre

захватить /zakhvatít'/ v. seize, capture

защита /zashchíta/ f. defence

защитник /zashchítnik/ m. defender

защитный /zashchítnyi/ adj. protective

защищать /zashchishchát'/ v. protect

заявка /zaiávka/ f. claim

заявление /zaiavlénie/ n. application

заявлять /zaiavliát'/ v. declare

звание /zvánie/ n. rank

звать /zvat'/ v. call; name; как вас зовут? /kak vas zovút?/ what is your name?

звезда /zvezdá/ f. star

звено /zvenó/ n. link; team

зверский /zvérskii/ adj. brutal

зверствовать /zvérstvovat'/ v. commit atrocities

зверь /zver'/ m. wild beast

звонить /zvonít'/ v. ring; з. в колокол /z. v kólokol/ toll a bell; з. по телефону /z. po telefónu/ give (smb.) a ring

звонок /zvonók/ m. bell

звук /zvuk/ m. sound

звукозапись /zvukozápis'/ f. recording

звуконепроницаемый /zvukonepronitsáemyi/   adj. sound-proof

звучать /zvuchát'/ v. sound

здание /zdánie/ n. building

здесь /zdes'/ adv. here

здороваться /zdoróvat'sia/ v. greet

здорово! /zdórovo!/ int. well done; adv. splendidly

здоровый /zdoróvyi/ adj. healthy

здоровье /zdoróv'e/ n. health

здравоохранение /zdravookhranénie/ n. public health

здравствовать /zdrávstvovat'/ v. be well; да здравствует! /da zdrávstvuet/ long live!

здравствуйте /zdrávstvuite/ how do you do

здравый /zdrávyi/ adj. sensible; з. смысл /z. smysl/ common sense

зевака /zeváka/ m. and f. idler

зевать /zevát'/ v. yawn

зеленщик /zelénshchik/ m. greengrocer

зеленый /zeliónyi/ adj. green

зелень /zélen'/ f. greenery

земельный /zemél'nyi/ adj. land

землевладелец /zemlevladélets/ m. landowner

земледелец /zemledélets/ m. farmer

земледелие /zemledélie/ n. agriculture

землетрясение /zemletriasénie/ n. earthquake

земля /zemliá/ m. earth; land

земляк /zemliák/ m. fellow-countryman

земляника /zemlianíka/ f. strawberry

земной /zemnói/ adj. earthly; з. шар /z. shar/ globe

зеркало /zérkalo/ n. mirror

зернистый /zernístyi/ adj. grainy; unpressed (caviar)

зерно /zernó/ n. grain

зима /zimá/ f. winter

злак /zlak/ m. cereal

злить /zlit'/ v. irritate

злиться /zlít'sia/ v. be angry, annoyed

зло /zlo/ n. evil

злободневный /zlobodnévnyi/ adj. topical

зловещий /zlovéshchii/ adj. ominous

злой /zloi/ adj. vicious; cruel; malicious

злокачественный /zlokáchestvennyi/ adj. malignant

злопамятный /zlopámiatnyi/ adj. unforgiving

злополучный /zlopolúchnyi/ adj. ill-fated

злорадный /zlorádnyi/ adj. gloating

злословие /zloslóvie/ n. scandal

злоупотреблять /zloupotrebliát'/ v. abuse

змей /zmei/ m. serpent; kite

змея /zmeiá/ f. snake

знак /znak/ m. sing, symbol, mark

знакомить /znakómit'/ v. introduce; acquaint

знакомиться /znakómit'sia/ v. make acquaintance (of)

знакомство /znakómstvo/ n. acquaintance

знакомый /znakómyi/ adj. familiar; m. acquaintance

знаменательный /znamenátel'nyi/ adj. significant

знаменитость /znamenítost'/ f. celebrity

знаменитый /znamenítyi/ adj. famous

знание /znánie/ n. knowledge

знаток /znatók/ m. expert, connoisseur

знать /znat'/ v. know

значение /znachénie/ n. significance; meaning

значительный /znachítel'nyi/ adj. important

значить /znáchit'/ v. mean

значок /znachók/ m. badge

знойный /znóinyi/ adj. sultry

золото /zóloto/ n. gold

зона /zóna/ f. zone

зонт /zont/ umbrella

зоопарк /zoopárk/ m. zoo

зрачок /zrachók/ m. pupil (of the eye)

зрелище /zrélishche/ n. spectacle; sight

зрелость /zrélost'/ f. maturity

зрелый /zrélyi/ adj. ripe

зрение /zrénie/ n. sight; с точки зрения /s tóchki zréniia/
  from the point of view

зреть /zret'/ v. ripen; mature

зритель /zrítel'/ m. spectator

зрительный /zrítel'nyi/ adj. visual; з. зал /z. zal/
  auditorium

зря /zria/ adv. to no purpose, in vain

зуб /zub/ m. tooth

зубной /zubnói/ adj. dental

зубоврачебный /zubovrachébnyi/ adj. dental; dentist's

зубочистка /zubochístka/ f. toothpick

зябкий /ziábkii/ adj. chilly

зябнуть /ziábnut'/ v. be chilled

зять /ziat'/ m. son-in-law (daughter's husband);
  brother-in-law (sister's husband)

И

и /i/ conj. and

ибо /íbo/ conj. for

игла /iglá/ f. needle

игнорировать /ignorírovat'/ v. ignore

игорный /igórnyi/ adj. gambling

игра /igrá/ f. game, play; performance

играть /igrát'/ play; act

игрок /igrók/ m. player, gambler

игрушка /igrúshka/ f. toy

идейный /idéinyi/ adj. ileological

идентичный /identíchnyi/ adj. identical

идея /idéia/ f. concept

идти /idtí/ v. go, be going

иждивенец /izhdivénets/ m. dependant

из /iz/ prep. out of, from

изба /izbá/ hut, peasant house

избавлять /izbavliát'/ v. save

избаловать /izbálovat'/ v. spoil (children)

избегать /izbegát'/ v. avoid, evade

избиратель /izbirátel'/ m. elector, voter

избирательный /izbirátel'nyi/ adj. electoral; и. округ /i. ókrug/, и. участок /i. uchástok/ electoral district, constituency

избирать /izbirát'/ v. choose, elect

избыток /izbýtok/ m. surplus; abundance

известие /izvéstie/ n. news

известный /izvéstnyi/ adj. known; popular

извещать /izveshchát'/ v. inform

извещение /izveshchénie/ n. notification

извинение /izvinénie/ n. apology

извинять /izviniát'/ v. excuse; извините! /izviníte/ excuse me! I'm sorry

извиняться /isviniát'sia/ v. apologize

извне /izvné/ adv. from without

извращать /izvrashchát'/ v. distort

изгнание /izgnánie/ n. exile

изгонять /izgoniát'/ v. banish

изгородь /ízgorod'/ f. fence; живая и. /zhiváia i./ hedge

изготавливать /izgotávlivat'/ v. manufacture

издавать /izdavát'/ v. publish

издание /izdánie/ n. edition

издатель /izdátel'/ m. publisher

издательство /izdátel'stvo/ n. publishing house

издеваться /izdevát'sia/ v. scoff (at), mock

изделие /izdélie/ n. make; article

издержки /izdérzhki/ pl. outlay

из-за /iz-za/ prep. from behind; because of

излагать /izlagát'/ v. set forth; state

излечение /izlechénie/ n. recovery

излечивать /izléchivat'/ v. cure

излечимый /izlechímyi/ adj. curable

излишек /izlíshek/ m. surplus

излишество /izlíshestvo/ n. excess

изложение /izlozhénie/ n. exposition; rendering

излюбленный /izliúblennyi/ adj. pet, favourite

измена /izména/ f. treason

изменение /izmenénie/ n. change

изменник /izménnik/ m. traitor

изменять /izmeniát'/ v. change, alter; be unfaithful to, betray

измерение /izmerénie/ n. measuring

измерять /izmeriát'/ v. measure

измученный /izmúchennyi/ adj. exhausted

изнасилование /iznasílovanie/ n. rape

изнемогать /iznemogát'/ v. be(come) exhausted
изнурительный /iznurítel'nyi/ adj. exhausting
изнутри /iznutrí/ adv. from within
изобилие /izobílie/ n. abundance
изобличать /izoblichát'/ v. expose
изображать /izobrazhát'/ v. depict, portray
изобретать /izobretát'/ v. invent
изобретение /izobreténie/ v. invention
из-под /iz-pod/ prep. from under
изразцовый /izraztsóvyi/ adj. tiled
изредка /ízredka/ adv. now and then
изувечить /izuvéchit'/ v. maim, mutilate
изумительный /izumítel'nyi/ adj. amazing
изумлять /izumliát'/ v. amaze
изумруд /izumrúd/ m. emerald
изучать /izuchát'/ v. study
изюм /iziúm/ m. raisins
изящество /iziáshchestvo/ n. grace; elegance
икать /ikát'/ v. hiccup
икона /ikóna/ f. icon
икра /ikrá/ f. caviar
или /íli/ conj. or
иллюзия /illiúziia/ f. illusion
иллюстрация /illustrátsiia/ f. illustration
имение /iménie/ n. estate
именины /imeníny/ pl. name-day
именно /ímenno/ adv. namely; precisely
именовать /imenovát'/ v. name

иметь /imét'/ v. have; и. дело /i. délo/ have dealings (with); и. место /i. mésto/ take place

иммигрант /immigránt/ m. immigrant

иммунитет /immunitét/ m. immunity

империя /impériia/ f. empire

импорт /ímport/ m. import

имущество /imúshchestvo/ n. property

имя /ímia/ n. name

иначе /ináche/ adv. differently, otherwise; так или и. /tak íli i./ in any case

инвалид /invalíd/ m. invalid

инвалидность /invalídnost'/ f. disablement

инвентарь /inventár'/ m. inventory; stock

индейка /indéika/ f. turkey

индивидуальный /individuál'nyi/ adj. individual

индустриализация /industrializátsiia/ f. industrialization

индустрия /industríia/ f. industry

инженер /inzhenér/ m. engineer

инжир /inzhír/ m. fig

инициал /initsiál/ m. initial

инициатива /initsiatíva/ f. initiative

иногда /inogdá/ adv. sometimes

иной /inói/ adj. different, other

иностранец /inostránets/ m. foreigner

иностранный /inostránnyi/ adj. foreign

инстинкт /instínkt/ m. instinct

институт /institút/ m. intsitute

инсулин /insulín/ m. insulin

интеллектуальный /intellektuál'nyi/ adj. intellectual

интеллигент /intelligént/ m. intellectual
интервью /interv'iú/ n. interview
интерес /interés/ m. interest
интересный /interésnyi/ adj. interesting
интерьер /inter'ér/ m. interior
интимный /intímnyi/ adj. intimate
интрига /intríga/ f. intrigue
интуиция /intuítsiia/ f. intuition
инфекция /inféktsiia/ f. infection
инфляция /infliátsiia/ f. inflation
инцидент /intsidént/ m. incident
инъекция /in''éktsiia/ f. injection
ирония /iróniia/ f. irony
иррациональный /irratsionál'nyi/ adj. irrational
ирригация /irrigátsiia/ f. irrigation
иск /isk/ m. suit
искажать /iskazhát'/ v. distort
искать /iskát'/ v. seek, look for
исключать /iskliuchát'/ v. exclude; expel
исключительный /isluchítel'nyi/ adj. exclusive
ископаемое /iskopáemoe/ n. fossil; mineral
искренний /ískrennii/ adj. sincere
искусный /iskúsnyi/ adj. skilled
искусственный /iskússtvennyi/ adj. artificial
искусство /iskússtvo/ n. art
искушать /iskushát'/ v. tempt; seduce
ислам /islám/ m. Islam
испачкать /ispáchkat'/ v. dirty
исповедь /íspoved'/ f. confession

исполнение /ispolnénie/ n. fulfilment

исполнительный /ispolnítel'nyi/ adj. executive; efficient

исполнять /ispolniát'/ v. fulfil

использование /ispól'zovanie/ n. use

испорченный /ispórchennyi/ adj. rotten

исправлять /ispravliát'/ v. correct

испуг /ispúg/ m. fright

испытание /ispytánie/ n. trial

испытанный /ispýtannyi/ adj. proved

испытывать /ispýtyvat'/ v. try, test; feel, experience

исследовать /isslédovat'/ v. explore

истец /istéts/ m. plaintiff

истина /ístina/ f. truth

истинный /ístinnyi/ adj. true

истолкование /istolkovánie/ n. interpretation

история /istóriia/ f. history

источник /istóchnik/ m. source; spring

истощать /istoshchát'/ v. exhaust, wear out

истреблять /istrebliát'/ v. destroy; exterminate

исходить /iskhodít'/ v. proceed; walk all over

исходный /iskhódnyi/ adj. initial

исчезать /ischezát'/ v. disappear

исчерпывать /ischérpyvat'/ v. exhaust; complete

исчислять /ischisliát'/ v. estimate

итак /iták/ conj. and so

итог /itóg/ m. total; result

иудейство /iudéistvo/ n. Judaism

июль /iiúl'/ m. July

июнь /iiún'/ m. June

Й

йод /iod/ m. iodine

йог /iog/ m. yogi

йодистый (калий) /iódistyi kálii/ adj. + m. potassium
  iodide

йота /ióta/ f. iota; ни на йоту /ni na iótu/ not a whit

К

к /k/ prep. to; for; by

кабина /kabína/ f. booth, cabin

кабинет /kabinét/ m. study; cabinet (of ministers)

каблук /kablúk/ m. heel

кадр /kadr/ m. still; personnel

кадык /kadýk/ m. Adam's apple

каемка /kaiómka/ f. edging

каждый /kázhdyi/ adj. every, each

кажущийся /kázhushchiisia/ adj. apparent

казаться /kazát'sia/ v. seem

казино /kazinó/ n. casino

казна /kazná/ f. treasury

казнь /kazn'/ f. execution

кайма /kaimá/ f. edging

как /kak/ adv. how; conj. as

какао /kakáo/ n. cocoa, cacao

как-либо /kak-líbo/ adv. anyhow

как-нибудь /kak-nibúd'/ adv. anyhow, somehow

как-никак /kak-nikák/ adv. after all

какой /kakói/ pron. what

как-то /kak-to/ adv. somehow; one day

калека /kaléka/ m. and f. cripple

календарь /kalendár'/ m. calendar

калитка /kalítka/ f. wicket-gate

калькулировать /kal'kulírovat'/ v. calculate

кальсоны /kal'sóny/ pl. drawers

камбала /kámbala/ f. flounder

каменный /kámennyi/ adj. stone

камень /kámen'/ m. stone

камера /kámera/ f. cell; camera; к. хранения /k. khranéniia/ cloak-room

камерный /kámernyi/ adj. chamber

камин /kamín/ m. fire-place

кампания /kampániia/ f. campaign

канава /kanáva/ f. ditch

канал /kanál/ m. canal; channel

канализация /kanalizátsiia/ f. sewerage

кандидат /kandidát/ m. candidate

каникулы /kaníkuly/ pl. vacation, holidays

канун /kanún/ m. eve

канцелярия /kantseliáriia/ f. office

капать /kapát'/ v. drip

капельница /kápelnitsa/ f. dropper (med.)

капитал /kapitál/ m. capital

капитализм /kapitalízm/ m. capitalism

капиталовложение /kapitalovlozhénie/ n. investment

капитан /kapitán/ m. captain

капля /káplia/ f. drop, drip

капот /kapót/ m. bonnet, hood

каприз /kapríz/ m. whim

капризничать /kapríznichat'/ v. be capricious

капуста /kapústa/ f. cabbage; брюссельская к. /brussél'skaia k./ Brussels sprouts; кислая к. /kíslaia k./ sauerkraut

капюшон /kapiushón/ m. hood

карамель /karamél'/ f. caramel

карандаш /karandásh/ m. pencil

карась /karás'/ m. crucian carp

карман /karmán/ m. pocket

карп /karp/ m. carp

карта /kárta/ m. map; card

картина /kartína/ f. picture; scene

картон /kartón/ m. cardboard

картотека /kartotéka/ f. card index

картофель /kartófel'/ m. potatoes

карточка /kártochka/ f. card, photograph

карточная система /kártochnaia sistéma/ adj. + f. rationing system

картошка /kartóshka/ f. potato

карусель /karusél'/ f. merry-go-round

карьера /kar'éra/ f. career

касаться /kasát'sia/ v. touch; concern

касса /kássa/ f. box-office

кассета /kasséta/ f. cassette

кассир /kassír/ m. cashier

кассировать /kassírovat'/ v. annul; reverse (legal)

кастрюля /kastriúlia/ f. saucepan

каталог /katalóg/ m. catalogue

катар /katár/ m. catarrh
катаракта /katarákta/ f. cataract
катастрофа /katastrófa/ f. catastrophe
катать /katát'/ v. drive; roll
кататься /katát'sia/ v. go for a ride
катафалк /katafálk/ m. catafalque
категория /kategória/ f. category
катер /káter/ m. patrol boat
катить /katít'/ v. roll
каток /katók/ m. skating-rink
католик /katólik/ m. Roman Catholic
катушка /katúshka/ f. bobbin, reel
кафе /kafé/ n. cafe
кафедра /káfedra/ f. chair; rostrum; department
кафель /káfel'/ m. glazed tile
кафетерий /kafetérii/ m. cafeteria
качалка /kachálka/ f. rocking-chair
качать /kachát'/ v. swing
качество /káchestvo/ n. quality
каша /kásha/ f. porridge
кашлять /káshlait'/ v. cough
каюта /kaiúta/ f. cabin
каяться /káiat'sia/ v. repent; confess
квалификация /kvalifikátsiia/ f. qualification
квартал /kvartál/ m. block; district
квартира /kvartíra/ f. flat, apartment
квартирант /kvartiránt/ m. tenant
квартирная плата /kvartírnaia pláta/ adj. + f. rent
кверху /kvérkhu/ adv. up(wards)

квитанция /kvitántsiia/ f. receipt ticket

кегельбан /kegel'bán/ m. bowling-alley

кедр /kedr/ m. cedar

кеды /kédy/ pl. light sports boots

кекс /keks/ m. cake

кепка /képka/ f. cap

керамика /kerámika/ f. ceramics

кесарево сечение /késarevo sechénie/ adj. + n. Caesarean operation

кета /ketá/ f. Siberian salmon

кетовая икра /ketóvaia ikrá/ f. red caviar

кефир /kefír/ m. yoghurt

кидать /kidát'/ v. throw

кило /kiló/ n. kilogram

кино /kinó/ n. cinema

киножурнал /kinozhurnál/ m. newsreel

кинозвезда /kinozvezdá/ f. film star

киносъемка /kinos''iómka/ f. filming

киоск /kiósk/ m. stall

кипеть /kipét'/ v. boil

кипучий /kipúchii/ adj. seething

кипяток /kipiatók/ m. boiling water

кипяченый /kipiachiónyi/ adj. boiled

кириллица /kiríllitsa/ f. Cyrillic alphabet

кирпич /kirpích/ m. brick

кисель /kisél'/ m. jelly

кислый /kíslyi/ adj. sour

киста /kistá/ f. cyst

кисть /kist'/ f. brush; cluster; hand

кишечник /kishéchnik/ m. bowels

кишечный /kishéchnyi/ adj. testinal

кишка /kishká/ f. gut

клавиатура /klaviatúra/ f. keyboard

клад /klad/ m. treasure

кладбище /kládbishche/ n. cemetery

кладовая /kladováia/ f. store-room

кланяться /klániat'sia/ v. bow

клапан /klápan/ m. valve

класс /klass/ m. class

класть /klast'/ v. put; lay

клевета /klevetá/ f. slander

клеенка /kleiónka/ f. oilcloth

клеить /kléit'/ v. glue, gum, paste

клейкий /kléikii/ adj. sticky

клетка /klétka/ f. cage; check (on fabric)

клещи /kléshchi/ pl. tongs; pincers

клиент /kliént/ m. client

клиентура /klientúra/ f. clientele

клизма /klízma/ f. enema

климат /klímat/ m. climate

клиника /klínika/ f. clinic

клоп /klop/ m. bug

клоун /klóun/ m. clown

клуб /klub/ m. club (house)

клубника /klubníka/ f. strawberries

клубок /klubók/ m. ball

клумба /klúmba/ f. flower-bed

клюква /kliúkva/ f. cranberries

ключ /kliuch/ m. key; spring

ключица /kliuchítsa/ f. collar-bone

клясться /kliást'sia/ v. swear, vow

клятва /kliátva/ f. oath

книга /kníga/ f. book

книзу /knízu/ adv. downwards

кнопка /knópka/ f. press-button

кнопочное управление /knópochnoe upravlénie/ adj. + n.
   pushbutton control

ковбойка /kovbóika/ f. checked shirt

ковер /koviór/ m. carpet

когда /kogdá/ pron. when

коготь /kógot'/ m. claw

код /kod/ m. code

коечный больной /kóechnyi bol'nói/ adj. + m. in-patient

кожа /kózha/ f. skin

кожаный /kózhanyi/ adj. leather

кожура /kozhurá/ f. peel

койка /kóika/ f. berth; bed

коклюш /kókliush/ m. whooping cough

коктейль /koktéil'/ m. cocktail

колбаса /kolbasá/ f. sausage

колготки /kolgótki/ pl. tights

колебаться /kolebát'sia/ v. hesitate

колено /koléno/ n. knee

колесо /kolesó/ n. wheel

колики /kóliki/ pl. colic

количество /kolíchestvo/ n. number, quantity

коллега /kolléga/ m. colleague

коллегия /kollégiia/ f. board

колледж /kólledzh/ m. college

коллектив /kollektív/ m. collective (body)

колонка /kolónka/ f. column; petrol pump

колонна /kolónna/ f. column

колхоз /kolkhóz/ m. kolkhoz, collective farm

колыбель /kolybél'/ f. cradle

колье /kol'é/ n. necklace

кольцо /kol'tsó/ n. ring

команда /kománda/ f. order; team

командир /komandír/ m. commander

командировка /komandiróvka/ f. business trip

командировочные /komandiróvochnye/ pl. travelling expenses

комар /komár/ m. mosquito

комбайн /kombáin/ m. combine

комбинация /kombinátsiia/ f. combination; slip

комбинезон /kombinezón/ m. overalls

комбинировать /kombinírovat'/ v. combine

комедия /komédiia/ f. comedy

комик /kómik/ m. comic (actor)

комиссионер /komissionér/ m. agent, broker

комиссионный /komissiónnyi/ adj. commission; к. магазин /k. magazín/ second-hand shop

комиссия /komíssiia/ f. comission

комитет /komitét/ m. committee

коммерсант /kommersánt/ m. businessman

коммерческий /kommércheskii/ adj. commercial

коммуна /kommúna/ f. commune

коммуникация /kommunikátsiia/ f. communication
коммутатор /kommutátor/ m. switchboard
коммюнике /kommiuniké/ n. communique
комната /kómnata/ f. room
комод /komód/ m. chest of drawers, locker
компания /kompániia/ f. company
компаньон /kimpan'ón/ m. partner
компенсация /kompensátsiia/ f. compensation
компенсировать /kompensírovat'/ v. compensate
компетентный /kompeténtnyi/ adj. competent; authorized
комплект /komplékt/ m. set
комплектовать /komplektovát'/ v. staff
комплекция /kompléktsiia/ f. build
комплимент /komplimént/ m. compliment
композитор /kompozítor/ m. composer
компрометировать /komprometírovat'/ v. compromise
компромисс /kompromíss/ m. compromise
компьютер /komp'iúter/ m. computer
комфортабельный /komfortábel'nyi/ adj. comfortable
конвейер /konvéier/ m. production line, belt
конвенция /konvéntsiia/ f. convention
конвергенция /konvergéntsiia/ f. convergence
конверсия /konvérsiia/ f. conversion
конверт /konvért/ m. envelope
кондитерская /kondíterskaia/ f. confectioner's shop
кондиционирование /konditsionírovanie/ n. conditioning;
  к. воздуха /k. vózdukha/ air-conditioning
кондуктор /kondúktor/ m. conductor
конец /konéts/ m. end

конечно /konéchno/ part. of course; sure
конечный /konéchnyi/ adj. final; ultimate
конкретный /konkrétnyi/ adj. specific, concrete
конкурент /konkurént/ m. competitor
конкуренция /konkuréntsiia/ f. competition
конкурировать /konkurírovat'/ v. compete
конкурс /kónkurs/ m. competition
консерватор /konservátor/ m. conservative
консерватория /konservatóriia/ f. conservatoire
консервировать /konservírovat'/ v. can, bottle
консервный нож /konsérvnyi nozh/ adj. + m. tinopener
консервы /konsérvy/ pl. canned food
констатировать /konstatírovat'/ v. ascertain; note
конституция /konstitútsiia/ f. constitution
конструкция /konstrúktsiia/ f. construction, design
консул /kónsul/ m. consul
консульство /kónsul'stvo/ n. consulate
консультировать /konsul'tírovat'/ v. advise; consult
контакт /kontákt/ m. contact
контейнер /kontéiner/ m. container
контекст /kontékst/ m. context
континент /kontinént/ m. continent
контора /kontóra/ f. office
контрабанда /kontrabánda/ f. contraband
контрабандист /kontrabandíst/ m. smuggler
контрабас /kontrabás/ m. doublebass
контракт /kontrákt/ m. contract
контролер /kontroliór/ m. inspector
контролировать /kontrolírovat'/ v. check

контроль /kontról'/ m. control

контрразведка /kontrrazvédka/ f. counter-expionage; security service

конфедерация /konfederátsiia/ f. confederation

конференция /konferéntsiia/ f. conference

конфета /konféta/ f. sweet, candy

конфиденциальный /konfidentsiál'nyi/ adj. confidential

конфискация /konfiskátsiia/ f. confiscation

конфликт /konflíkt/ m. conflict

концентрация /kontsentrátsiia/ f. concentration

концепция /kontséptsiia/ f. conception

концерн /kontsérn/ m. concern; enterprise

концерт /kontsért/ m. concert

концессия /kontséssiia/ f. concession

кончать /konchát'/ v. finish

конь /kon'/ m. horse, steed

коньки /kon'kí/ pl. skates; роликовые к. /rólikovye k./ roller- skates

коньяк /kon'iák/ m. cognac

копать /kopát'/ v. dig

копейка /kopéika/ f. kopeck

копировать /kopírovat'/ v. copy; imitate

копить /kopít'/ v. accumulate

копия /kópiia/ f. copy

копченый /kopchiónyi/ adj. smoked

корабль /korábl'/ m. ship

корень /kóren'/ m. root

корзина /korzína/ f. basket

коридор /koridór/ m. corridor

корица /korítsa/ f. cinnamon

коричневый /koríchnevyi/ adj. brown

корка /kórka/ f. crust

кормилец /kormílets/ m. bread-winner

кормить /kormít'/ v. feed

коробка /koróbka/ f. box

корова /koróva/ f. cow

королева /koroléva/ f. queen

королевский /korolévskii/ adj. royal

королевство /korolévstvo/ n. kingdom

король /koról'/ m. king

корона /koróna/ f. crown

коронка /korónka/ f. crown (on tooth)

короткий /korótkii/ adj. short

коротковолновый /korotkovolnóvyi/ adj. short-wave

корпорация /korporátsiia/ f. corporation

корпус /kórpus/ m. building; corps

корректировать /korrektírovat'/ v. correct

корреспондент /korrespondént/ m. correspondent

корреспонденция /korrespondéntsiia/ f. correspondence; report

коррупция /korrúpsiia/ f. corruption

корт /kort/ m. (tennis) court

корыстолюбие /korystoliúbie/ n. mercenary spirit

коса /kosá/ f. plait; scythe

косвенный /kósvennyi/ adj. indirect

косилка /kosílka/ f. mowing-machine

косичка /kosíchka/ f. pigtail

косметика /kosmétika/ f. cosmetics

космический /kosmícheskii/ adj. space

космодром /kosmodróm/ m. spacedrom

космонавт /kosmonávt/ m. spaceman

космополит /kosmopolít/ m. cosmopolitan

космос /kósmos/ m. space

косный /kósnyi/ adj. stagnant, inert

косой /kosói/ adj. slanting

костер /kostiór/ m. bonfire

костлявый /kostliávyi/ adj. bony

костыль /kostýl'/ m. crutch

кость /kost'/ f. bone

костюм /kostiúm/ m. suit

косынка /kosýnka/ f. scarf

кот /kot/ m. tom-cat

котел /kotiól/ m. boiler

котенок /kotiónok/ m. kitten

котлета /kotléta/ f. cutlet, chop

который /kotóryi/ pron. which, who

коттедж /kottédzh/ m. cottage

кофе /kófe/ m. coffee

кофеин /kofeín/ m. caffeine

кофейник /koféinik/ m. coffee-pot

кофта /kófta/ f. cardigan

кофточка /kóftochka/ f. blouse

кочан /kochán/ m. head (e.g. of cabbage)

кошелек /kosheliók/ m. purse

кошка /kóshka/ f. cat

кошмар /koshmár/ m. nightmare

кощунство /koshchúnstvo/ n. blasphemy

коэффициент /koeffitsiént/ m. coefficient

краб /krab/ m. crab

краденый /krádenyi/ adj. stolen

кража /krázha/ f. theft; к. со взломом /k. so vzlómom/ burglary

край /krai/ m. edge; brink; land; territory

крайний /kráinii/ adj. extreme; по крайней мере /po kráinei mére/ at least

кран /kran/ m. crane

красавец /krasávets/ m. handsome man

красавица /krasávitsa/ f. beauty

красить /krásit'/ v. paint, dye

краска /kráska/ f. colour, paint, dye

краснеть /krasnét'/ v. go red

красноречие /krasnoréchie/ n. eloquence

красный /krásnyi/ adj. red; красное дерево /krásnoe dérevo/ mahogany

красота /krasotá/ f. beauty

красочный /krásochnyi/ adj. colourful

красть /krast'/ v. steal

краткий /krátkii/ adj. brief

кратковременный /kratkovrémennyi/ adj. short; short-lived

краткосрочный /kratkosróchnyi/ adj. short-term, short-dated

крах /krakh/ m. crash

крахмал /krakhmál/ m. starch

креветка /krevétka/ f. shrimp

кредит /kredít/ m. credit

крем /krem/ m. cream

крематорий /krematórii/ m. crematorium

кремль /kreml'/ m. Kremlin

крепкий /krépkii/ adj. firm

кресло /kréslo/ n. armchair

крест /krest/ m. cross

крестить /krcstít'/ v. christen

крестьянин /krest'iánin/ m. peasant

кривой /krivói/ adj. crooked

кризис /krízis/ m. crisis

крик /krik/ m. cry, shout

криминальный /kriminál'nyi/ adj. criminal

критерий /kritérii/ m. criterion

критик /krítik/ m. critic

кричать /krichát'/ v. shout

кровавый /krovávyi/ adj. bloody

кровать /krovát'/ f. bed

кровля /króvlia/ f. roof

кровный /króvnyi/ adj. blood

кровоизлияние /krovoizliiánie/ n. haemorrhage

кровообращение /krovoobrashchénie/ n. circulation

кровоостанавливающий /krovoostanávlivaiushchii/ adj. styptic

кровоподтек /krovopodtiók/ m. internal bruise

кровотечение /krovotechénie/ n. blooding; haemorrhage

кровь /krov'/ f. blood

кроить /kroít'/ v. cut out

кролик /królik/ m. rabbit

кроме /króme/ prep. except; besides, apart from

кроткий /krótkii/ adj. gentle

крошка /króshka/ f. crumb

круг /krug/ m. circle

круглосуточный /kruglosútochnyi/ adj. round-the-clock

круглый /krúglyi/ adj. round

кругом /krugóm/ adv. round, about

кружево /krúzhevo/ n. lace

кружить /rkuzhít'/ spin, whirl

кружка /krúzhka/ f. mug

кружок /kruzhók/ m. small circle; group

крупа /krupá/ f. groats; cereals

крупный /krúpnyi/ adj. large

крутить /krutít'/ v. twist; twirl

крутой /krutói/ adj. steep

крушение /krushénie/ n. downfall

крыло /kryló/ n. wing

крыльцо /kryl'tsó/ n. porch

крыса /krýsa/ f. rat

крысиный яд /krysínyi iád/ adj. + m. rat poison

крыть /kryt'/ v. cover; roof

крыша /krýsha/ f. roof

крышка /krýshka/ f. lid

крюк /kriúk/ m. hook

крючок /kriuchók/ m. hook; catch

кстати /kstáti/ adv. by the way

кто /kto/ pron. who

кувшин /kuvshín/ m. pitcher

куда /kudá/ adv. where

кудри /kúdri/ pl. curls

кузен /kuzén/ m. cousin

кузина /kuzína/ f. cousin

кузов /kúzov/ m. body (of car)

кукла /kúkla/ f. doll

кукольный /kúkol'nyi/ adj. puppet

кукуруза /kukurúza/ f. corn

кулак /kulák/ m. fist

кулебяка /kulebiáka/ f. pie

кулинарный /kulinárnyi/ adj. culinary

культура /kultúra/ f. culture

купальный /kupál'nyi/ adj. bathing

купаться /kupát'sia/ v. bath(e)

купе /kupé/ n. compartment

купец /kupéts/ m. merchant

купюра /kupiúra/ f. note

курить /kurít'/ v. smoke

курица /kúritsa/ f. hen, chicken

курорт /kurórt/ m. health resort

курс /kurs/ m. course; rate of exchange

курсы /kúrsy/ pl. school; college

куртка /kúrtka/ f. jacket

курьер /kur'ér/ m. messenger

кусать /kusát'/ v. bite

кусок /kusók/ m. piece; morsel

куст /kust/ m. bush

кухня /kúkhnia/ f. kitchen

кушанье /kúshan'e/ n. dish

кушать /kúshat'/ v. eat

кушетка /kushétka/ f. couch

кювет /kiuvét/ m. ditch

Л

лагерь /láger'/ m. camp

ладно /ládno/ adv., part. all right, O.K.

ладонь /ladón'/ f. palm

лайнер /láiner/ m. liner

лак /lak/ m. lacquer

лакей /lakéi/ m. lackey

лаковый /lákovyi/ adj. varnished

лакомиться /lákomit'sia/ v. treat oneself (to)

лаконичный /lakoníchnyi/ adj. concise, laconic

лампа /lámpa/ f. lamp; valve

лапа /lápa/ f. paw

лапша /lapshá/ f. noodles

ларек /lariók/ m. stall

ласка /láska/ f. caress

ласковый /láskovyi/ adj. affectionate; tender; gentie

лацкан /látskan/ m. lapel

лаять /láiat'/ v. bark

лгать /lgat'/ v. tell lies

лебедь /lébed'/ m. swan

лев /lev/ m. lion

левый /lévyi/ adj. left

легкий /liógkii/ adj. easy; light

легкоатлет /liogkoatlét/ m. athlete

легковой автомобиль /legkovói avtomobíl'/ adj. + m. car

легкое /liógkoe/ n. lung

легкомысленный /legkomýslennyi/ adj. thoughtless; frivolous

лед /liod/ m. ice

леденец /ledenéts/ m. lollipop; rock

лезвие /lézvie/ n. blade

лезть /lezt'/ v. climb; push forward

лекарство /lekárstvo/ n. medicine

лен /lion/ m. flax

ленивый /lenívyi/ adj. lazy

лениться /lenít'sia/ v. be lazy

лента /lénta/ f. ribbon

лень /len'/ f. idleness

лепить /lepít'/ v. model

лес /les/ m. forest

лестница /léstnitsa/ f. staircase; ladder

лесть /lest'/ f. flattery

летать /letát'/ v. fly

лето /léto/ n. summer

летчик /liótchik/ m. pilot

лечебница /lechébnitsa/ f. hospital

лечебный /lechébnyi/ adj. medical

лечить /lechít'/ v. treat (for)

лжесвидетельство /lzhesvidétel'stvo/ n. false evidence

лжец /lzhets/ m. liar

лживый /lzhívyi/ adj. false; untruthful

ли /li/ part. whether

либерал /liberál/ m. liberal

либо /líbo/ part. or; либо ... либо... /líbo... líbo.../ conj. either... or...

ливень /líven'/ m. downpour

ливер /líver/ m. liver

лидер /líder/ m. leader

лизать /lizát'/ v. lick

ликвидация /likvidátsiia/ f. liquidation

ликер /likiór/ m. liqueur

ликовать /likovát'/ v. rejoice

лиловый /lilóvyi/ adj. lilac

лимон /limón/ m. lemon

лимонад /limonád/ m. lemonade

линейка /linéika/ f. ruler

линия /líniia/ f. line

линять /liniát'/ v. moult; fade

липа /lípa/ f. lime

лиса /lisá/ f. fox

лист /list/ m. sheet; leaf

листовка /listóvka/ f. leaflet

листопад /listopád/ m. fall

литератор /literátor/ m. man of letters

литература /literatúra/ f. literature

литр /litr/ m. litre

лить /lit'/ v. pour

лиф /lif/ m. bodice

лифт /lift/ m. elevator; lift

лифчик /lífchik/ m. brassiere

лихорадка /likhorádka/ f. fever

лицевой /litsevói/ adj. front; л. счет /l. schiot/ personal account

лицемерие /litsemérie/ n. hypocrisy

лицо /litsó/ n. face; person
личность /líchnost'/ f. personality
личный /líchnyi/ adj. private
лишать /lishát'/ v. deprive of
лишний /líshnii/ adj. superfluous; unnecessary
лишь /lish/ part. only; conj. as soon as
лоб /lob/ m. forehead
ловить /lovít'/ v. catch
ловкий /lóvkii/ adj. adroit; smart
ловушка /lovúshka/ f. trap
логика /lógika/ f. logic
лодка /lódka/ f. boat
лодыжка /lodýzhka/ f. ankle
ложиться /lozhít'sia/ v. lie down
ложка /lózhka/ f. spoon
ложный /lózhnyi/ adj. false
ложь /lozh/ f. lie
локаут /lokáut/ m. lock-out
локоть /lókot'/ m. elbow
ломаный /lómanyi/ adj. broken
ломать /lomát'/ v. break
ломбард /lombárd/ m. pawnshop
ломкий /lómkii/ adj. fragile
ломота /lomotá/ f. rheumatic pain
ломоть /lomót'/ m. chunk
ломтик /lómtik/ m. slice
лопата /lopáta/ f. shovel; spade
лопатка /lopátka/ f. shoulder-blade
лопаться /lópat'sia/ v. burst; collapse

лосось /losós'/ m. salmon
лотерея /loteréia/ f. lottery
лохматый /lokhmátyi/ adj. shaggy
лохмотья /lokhmót'ia/ pl. rags
лошадь /lóshad'/ f. horse
лояльный /loiál'nyi/ adj. loyal
луг /lug/ m. meadow
лужа /lúzha/ f. puddle
лужайка /luzháika/ f. lawn
лук /luk/ m. onions; bow
луковица /lúkovitsa/ f. onion; bulb
луна /luná/ f. moon
луч /luch/ m. ray
лучше /lúchshe/ adj., adv. better
лучший /lúchshii/ adj. best
лыжи /lýzhi/ pl. ski
лысеть /lysét'/ v. go bald
льгота /l'góta/ f. privilege
льняной /l'nianói/ adj. flax, linen
льстить /l'stít'/ v. flatter
любезничать /liubéznichat'/ v. pay complements
любезность /liubéznost'/ f. courtesy
любимец /liubímets/ m. favourite
любительский /liubítel'skii/ adj. amateur
любить /liubít'/ v. love; like
любоваться /liubovát'sia/ v. admire
любовник /liubóvnik/ n. lover
любовница /liubóvnitsa/ f. mistress
любовь /liubóv'/ f. love

любознательный /liuboznátel'nyi/ adj. curious
любой /liubói/ adj. any
любопытный /liubopýtnyi/ adj. curious; interesting
люди /liúdi/ pl. people
людный /liúdnyi/ adj. crowded
люкс /liuks/ m. de-luxe
лютеранин /liuteránin/ m. Lutheran
лягушка /liagúshka/ f. frog
ляжка /liázhka/ f. thigh

M

магазин /magazín/ m. shop
магистраль /magistrál'/ f. highway
магнат /magnát/ m. magnate
магнитофон /magnitofón/ m. tape-recorder
мазать /mázat'/ v. paint; smear; oil
мазь /maz'/ f. ointment
май /mai/ m. May
майка /máika/ f. sports-shirt
макароны /makaróny/ pl. macaroni
маклер /mákler/ m. broker
максимум /máksimum/ m. maximum
макулатура /makulatúra/ f. waste paper
макушка /makúshka/ f. top
малейший /maléishii/ adj. smallest
маленький /málen'kii/ adj. little; small
малина /malína/ f. raspberry
мало /málo/ adv. little, few; not much; not many
маловероятный /maloveroiátnyi/ adj. improbable

малознакомый /maloznakómyi/ adj. unfamiliar

малоизвестный /maloizvéstnyi/ adj. little-known

малоимущий /maloimúshchii/ m. needy, poor

малокровие /malokróvie/ n. anaemia

малолетний /malolétnii/ adj. young; m. juvenile

малоподвижный /malopodvízhnyi/ adj. slow, inactive

малопродуктивный /maloproduktívnyi/ adj. unproductive

малосемейный /maloseméinyi/ adj. with a small family

малоубедительный /maloubedítel'nyi/ adj. not very convincing

мальчик /mál'chik/ m. boy

малютка /maliútka/ m., f. baby

мама /máma/ f. mummy

мандарин /mandarín/ m. tangerine

манекен /manekén/ m. tailor's dummy

манекенщик /manekénshchik/ m. model

манекенщица /manekénshchitsa/ f. model

манера /manéra/ f. manner

манжета /manzhéta/ f. cuff

маникюр /manikiúr/ m. manicure

манипулировать /manipulírovat'/ v. manipulate

манная каша /mánnaia kásha/ adj. + f. (boiled) semolina

маргарин /margarín/ m. margarine

маргаритка /margarítka/ f. daisy

мариновать /marinovát'/ v. pickle

марка /márka/ f. stamp; mark; brand; make

мармелад /marmelád/ m. fruit sweets

март /mart/ m. March

маршрут /marshrút/ m. route

маскировать /maskirovát'/ v. mask; disguise; camouflage

масленка /masliónka/ f. butter-dish

маслина /maslína/ f. olive

масло /máslo/ n. butter; oil

массаж /massázh/ m. massage

массовый /mássovyi/ adj. mass

мастер /máster/ m. master; expert

мастерить /masterít'/ v. make

мастерская /masterskáia/ f. workshop

мастерство /masterstvó/ n. skill

масштаб /masshtáb/ m. scale

материал /materiál/ m. material

материк /materík/ m. continent

материнство /materínstvo/ n. maternity

материя /matériia/ f. fabric

матрас /matrás/ m. mattress

матрос /matrós/ m. sailor; seaman

матч /match/ m. match

мать /mat'/ f. mother

махать /makhát'/ v. wave

махинация /makhinátsiia/ f. trick, machination

мачеха /máchekha/ f. step-mother

машина /mashína/ f. machine; car

машинист /mashiníst/ m. engine-driver

машинистка /mashinístka/ f. typist

машинка /mashínka/ f. typewriter

мгновение /mgnovénie/ n. moment

мебель /mébel'/ f. furniture

мед /miod/ m. honey

медаль /medál'/ f. medal

медведь /medvéd'/ m. bear

медик /médik/ m. doctor

медикамент /medikamént/ m. medicine, drug

медицина /meditsína/ f. medicine

медленный /médlennyi/ adj. slow

медлить /médlit'/ v. linger; delay

медный /médnyi/ adj. brass

медосмотр /medosmótr/ m. medical examination

медпомощь /medpómoshch/ f. medical service

медпункт /medpúnkt/ m. surgery

медсестра /medsestrá/ f. nurse

медуза /medúza/ f. jellyfish

медь /med'/ f. copper

между /mézhdu/ prep. between, amongst

междугородный /mezhdugoródnyi/ adj. inter-city

международный /mezhdunaródnyi/ adj. international

межконтинентальный /mezhkontinentál'nyi/ adj. intercontinental

мел /mel/ m. chalk

мелкий /mélkii/ adj. fine; small; petty; shallow

мелодия /melódiia/ f. melody, tune

мелочь /méloch/ f. trifle; small change (money)

мелькать /mel'kát'/ v. flash

мельчайший /mel'cháishii/ adj. smallest

мемуары /memuáry/ pl. memoirs

менее /ménee/ adv. less

меньше /mén'she/ adv. smaller, less, fewer

меньшинство /men'shinstvó/ n. minority

меню /meniú/ n. menu
менять /meniát'/ v. change
мера /méra/ f. measure
мерзнуть /miórznut'/ v. freeze
мерить /mérit'/ v. measure; try on
мерка /mérka/ f. measure
мертвый /miórtvyi/ adj. dead
мести /mestí/ v. sweep
местность /méstnost'/ f. locality
место /mésto/ m. place; site; seat
местожительство /mestozhítel'stvo/ n. residence
месяц /mésiats/ m. month; moon
металл /metáll/ m. metal
метла /metlá/ f. broom
метод /métod/ m. method
метр /metr/ m. metre
метро /metró/ n. metro, underground
мех /mekh/ m. fur
механизм /mekhanízm/ m. mechanism
механик /mekhánik/ m. mechanical engineer
мечтать /mechtát'/ v. dream
мешать /meshát'/ v. mix; hinder
мешок /meshók/ m. sack
мещанский /meshchánskii/ adj. vulgar
миг /mig/ m. moment
мигать /migát'/ v. blink, wink
миграция /migrátsiia/ f. migration
мизинец /mizínets/ m. little finger/toe
микроскоп /mikroskóp/ m. microscope

микрофон /mikrofón/ m. microphone

микстура /mikstúra/ f. mixture

миллиметр /millimétr/ m. millimetre

миллион /millión/ m. million

миллионер /millionér/ m. millionaire

милосердие /milosérdie/ n. charity

милостыня /mílostynia/ f. alms

милость /mílost'/ f. favour

милый /mílyi/ adj. dear; sweet; m. darling

миля /mília/ f. mile

мимо /mímo/ adv. past; by

минерал /minerál/ m. mineral

миниатюра /miniatiúra/ f. miniature

минимум /mínimum/ m. minimum

министерство /ministérstvo/ n. ministry

министр /minístr/ m. minister

минувший /minúvshii/ adj. past

минус /mínus/ m. minus

минута /minúta/ f. minute

мир /mir/ m. world; peace

мирить /mirít'/ v. reconcile

мирный /mírnyi/ adj. peaceful

мировой /mirovói/ adj. world

мироздание /mirozdánie/ n. universe

миролюбивый /miroliúbivyi/ adj. peace-loving

миска /míska/ f. bowl

миссионер /missionér/ m. missionary

миссия /míssiia/ f. mission

мистика /místika/ f. mysticism

митинг /míting/ m. meeting

митрополит /mitropolít/ m. Metropolitan

мишень /mishén'/ f. target

младенец /mladénets/ m. infant

младший /mládshii/ adj. junior

млекопитающее /mlekopitáiushchee/ n. mammal

мнение /mnénie/ n. opinion

мнимый /mnímyi/ adj. imaginary; illusory

мнительный /mnítel'nyi/ adj. health-conscious; suspicious

многие /mnógie/ adj. many

много /mnógo/ adv. much; many, a lot

многодетная семья /mnogodétnaia sem'iiá/ adj. + f. large
   family

многолетний /mnogolétnii/ adj. many years' standing

многолюдный /mnogoliúdnyi/ adj. crowded

многообразный /mnogoobráznyi/ adj. varied

многоуважаемый /mnogouvazháemyi/ adj. respected;
   dear (in letter)

многочисленный /mnogochíslennyi/ adj. numerous

многоэтажный /mnogoetázhnyi/ adj. many-storeyed

множество /mnózhestvo/ n. great number

могила /mogíla/ f. grave

могущество /mogúshchestvo/ n. power

мода /móda/ f. fashion

модель /modél'/ f. pattern, model

модный /módnyi/ adj. fashionable

может быть /mózhet byt'/ paren. perhaps

можно /mózhno/ pred. it is possible; можно (мне)..?
   /mózhno mne/ may I...?

мозг /mozg/ m. brain

мой /moi/ pron. my

мойка /móika/ f. washing; sink

мокрый /mókryi/ adj. moist, wet

молитва /molítva/ f. prayer

молния /mólniia/ f. lightning

молодежь /molodiózh'/ f. young people

молодец /molodéts/ m. fine fellow; молодец! paren. well done!

молодожены /molodozhióny/ pl. newly-weds

молодой /molodói/ adj. young

молодость /mólodost'/ f. youth

молоко /molóko/ n. milk

молоток /molotók/ m. hammer

молочная /molóchnaia/ f. dairy

молчание /molchánie/ n. silence

молчать /molchát'/ v. be silent

моль /mol'/ f. moth

момент /momént/ m. moment

моментальный /momentál'nyi/ adj. instant

монарх /monárkh/ m. monarch

монастырь /monastýr'/ m. monastery; convent

монах /monákh/ m. monk

монахиня /monákhinia/ f. nun

монета /monéta/ f. coin

монополия /monopóliia/ f. monopoly

мораль /morál'/ f. moral

мораторий /moratórii/ m. moratorium

морг /morg/ m. morgue

моргать /morgát'/ v. blink

море /móre/ n. sea

мореходный /morekhódnyi/ adj. nautical

морковь /morkóv'/ f. carrots

мороженое /morózhenoe/ n. ice-cream

мороз /moróz/ m. frost

морозоустойчивый /morozoustóichivyi/ adj. frost-resistant

моросить /morosít'/ v. drizzle

морской /morskói/ adj. sea, maritime; морская звезда /morskáia zvezdá/ starfish; м. болезнь /m. bolézn'/ sea-sickness

морфий /mórfii/ m. morphine

морщина /morshchína/ f. wrinkle

морщиться /mórshchit'sia/ v. wrinkle

моряк /moriák/ m. sailor

мост /most/ m. bridge

мостовая /mostováia/ f. pavement; roadway

мотель /motél'/ m. motel

мотив /motív/ m. motive

моток /motók/ m. ball

мотор /motór/ m. motor, engine

мотылек /motyliók/ m. moth; butterfly

мочевой пузырь /mochevói puzýr'/ adj. + m. bladder

мочить /mochít'/ v. soak, wet

мочиться /mochít'sia/ v. urinate

мочка /móchka/ f. lobe of ear

мочь /moch/ v. be able

мошенник /moshénnik/ m. rogue, swindle

мошенничать /moshénnichat'/ v. cheat

мощность /móshchnost'/ f. capacity

мощь /moshch/ f. power

мрак /mrak/ m. gloom

мрачный /mráchnyi/ adj. gloomy

мстить /mstit'/ v. avenge; have revenge on

мудрость /múdrost'/ f. wisdom

мудрый /múdryi/ adj. wise

муж /muzh/ m. husband

мужество /múzhestvo/ n. courage

мужской /muzhskói/ adj. masculine; male, men's

мужчина /muzhchína/ n. man

музей /muzéi/ m. museum

музыка /múzyka/ f. music

музыкант /muzykánt/ m. musician

мука /muká/ f. flour

мультипликационный (фильм) /mul'tiplikatsiónnyi
  fil'm/ adj. + m. cartoon film

мундир /mundír/ m. uniform

муниципальный /munitsipál'nyi/ adj. municipal

муравей /muravéi/ m. ant

муравейник /muravéinik/ m. ant-hill

мускул /múskul/ m. muscle

мусульманин /musul'mánin/ m. Moslem

мутный /mútnyi/ adj. muddy

муха /múkha/ f. fly

мучение /muchénie/ n. torment

мучительный /muchítel'nyi/ adj. agonizing

мучить /múchit'/ v. torture

мы /my/ pron. we

мыло /mýlo/ n. soap

мыльница /mýl'nitsa/ f. soap-dish

мыльный /mýl'nyi'/ adj. soap(y); мыльная пена /mýl'naia péna/ foam

мыс /mys/ m. cape

мыслить /mýslit'/ v. think

мысль /mysl'/ f. idea; thought

мыть /myt'/ v. wash

мышца /mýshtsa/ f. muscle

мышь /mysh/ f. mouse

мышьяк /mush'iák/ m. arsenic

мягкий /miágkii/ adj. soft; gentle; mild

мясник /miasník/ m. butcher

мясо /miáso/ n. meat; flesh

мятый /miátyi/ adj. crumpled; rumpled

мяч /miach/ n. ball

Н

на /na/ prep. on, in, for (period of time); to; by; at; during

на /na/ part. here; на, возьми! /na voz'mí/ here, take this!

набережная /náberezhnaia/ f. embankment

набивать /nabivát'/ v. stuff

набирать /nabirát'/ v. gather; make up

наблюдатель /nabliudátel'/ m. observer

наблюдать /nabliudát'/ v. watch; observe; keep an eye on

набок /nábok/ adv. awry

набор /nabór/ m. recruitment; enrolment

навек /navék/ adv. for ever

наверно(е) /navérno(e)/ adv. probably

наверняка /naverniaká/ adv. for certain

наверстывать /naviórstyvat'/ v. make up (for)

наверх /navérkh/ adv. upstairs; up

навещать /naveshchát'/ v. visit

навзничь /návznich/ adv. backwards; on one's back

наводнение /navodnénie/ n. flood

наволочка /návolochka/ f. pillowcase

навряд (ли) /navriád (li)/ adv. hardly

навсегда /navsegdá/ adv. for ever

навстречу /navstréchu/ adv. in: идти н. /idtí n./ meet smb. half-way

навык /návyk/ m. habit

навязывать /naviázyvat'/ v. tie (on); impose; thrust (on)

нагибаться /nagibát'sia/ v. stoop

наглухо /náglukho/ adv. tight(ly)

наглый /náglyi/ adj. impudent

наглядный /nagliádnyi/ adj. graphic

нагноение /nagnoénie/ n. suppuration

нагой /nagói/ adj. naked

награда /nagráda/ f. reward; decoration; prize

награждать /nagrazhdát'/ v. award

нагревать /nagrevát'/ v. heat

нагрудник /nagrúdnik/ m. (child's) bib

нагружать /nagruzhát'/ v. load

над /nad/ prep. over, above

надавливать /nadávlivat'/ v. press

надбавка /nadbávka/ f. increment

надвигаться /nadvigát'sia/ v. approach; be imminent

надводный /nadvódnyi/ adj. surface

надвое /nádvoe/ adv. in two

надевать /nadevát'/ v. put on

надежда /nadézhda/ f. hope

надежный /nadiózhnyi/ adj. reliable

надеяться /nadéiat'sia/ v. hope

надзиратель /nadzirátel'/ m. supervisor

надо /nádo/ pred. it is necessary

надоедать /nadoedát'/ v. pester; bother

надоедливый /nadoédlivyi/ adj. tiresome

надолго /nadólgo/ adv. for long

надпись /nádpis'/ f. inscription

надувать /naduvát'/ v. inflate; swindle, cheat

наедине /naediné/ adv. in private

наездник /naézdnik/ m. rider

наем /naióm/ m. hiring; renting

наемник /naiómnik/ m. mercenary

наемный /naiómnyi/ adj. hired

наживать /nazhivát'/ v. acquire

наживаться /nazhivát'sia/ v. make a fortune

нажим /nazhím/ m. pressure

нажимать /nazhimát'/ v. press

назад /nazád/ adv. backwards; back

название /nazvánie/ n. name

наземный /nazémnyi/ adj. ground

назло /nazló/ adv. out of spite

назначать /naznachát'/ v. appoint

назначение /naznachénie/ n. appointment

назревать /nazrevát'/ v. mature

называть /nazyvát'/ v. name

называться /nazyvát'sia/ v. be called

наиболее /naibólee/ adv. most

наибольший /naiból'shii/ adj. greatest, largest

наивный /naívnyi/ adj. naive

наивысший /naivýsshii/ adj. highest

наизнанку /naiznánku/ adv. inside out

наизусть /naizúst'/ adv. by heart

наилучший /nailúchshii/ adj. best

наименее /naiménee/ adv. least of all

наименование /naimenovánie/ n. name

наименьший /naimén'shii/ adj. least

наискось /náiskos'/ adv. obliquely

наихудший /naikhúdshii/ adj. worst

наказание /nakazánie/ n. punishment

наказывать /nakázyvat'/ v. punish

накануне /nakanúne/ adv. the day before; prep. on the eve

накапливать /nakáplivat'/ v. accumulate

накачивать /nakáchivat'/ v. pump

накидка /nakídka/ f. cushion-cover; cape

накипь /nákip'/ f. scum

накладная /nakladnáia/ f. invoice

наклеивать /nakléivat'/ v. stick on

наклейка /nakléika/ f. label

наклонный /naklónnyi/ adj. sloping

наклонять /nakloniát'/ v. incline; tilt

наклоняться /nakloniát'sia/ v. bend

наконец /nakonéts/ adv. at last; finally

наконечник /nakonéchnik/ m. tip

накоплять /nakopliát'/ v. accumulate

накрепко /nákrepko/ adv. fast

накрест /nákrest/ adv. crosswise

накрывать /nakryvát'/ v. cover; н. на стол /n. na stol/ lay the table

налаживать /nalázhivat'/ v. adjust; organize

налево /nalévo/ adv. to the left

налегке /nalegké/ adv. light

налетчик /naliótchik/ m. robber

наливать /nalivát'/ v. pour out; fill

наличие /nalíchie/ n. availability

наличность /nalíchnost'/ f. cash

налог /nalóg/ m. tax

налогоплательщик /nalogoplatél'shchik/ m. taxpayer

наложенным платежом /nalózhennym platezhóm/ adj. + m. cash on delivery

намазывать /namázyvat'/ v. spread

намек /namiók/ m. hint

намекать /namekát'/ v. hint (at)

намереваться /namerevát'sia/ v. intend

намечать /namechát'/ v. plan; outline

намного /namnógo/ adv. by far

намордник /namórdnik/ m. muzzle

нанизывать /nanízyvat'/ v. string

нанимать /nanimát'/ v. hire; rent

наоборот /naoborót/ adv. the other way round; paren. on the contrary

наотмашь /naótmash/ in: ударить н. /udárit' n./ deal smb.
a smashing blow

наотрез /naotréz/ adv. pointblank

нападать /napadát'/ v. attack; assault

нападение /napadénie/ n. attack

наперекор /naperekór/ adv. counter to

наперерез /napereréz/ adv. cutting across

наперсток /napiórstok/ m. thimble

напиток /napítok/ m. drink

наподобие /napodóbie/ adv. like; resembling

напоказ /napokáz/ adv. on show, for show

наполовину /napolovínu/ adv. half

напоминать /napominát'/ v. remind

напор /napór/ m. pressure

напоследок /naposlédok/ adv. by way of farewell

направление /napravlénie/ n. direction

направо /naprávo/ adv. to the right

напрасный /naprásnyi/ adj. vain

например /naprimér/ paren. for example

напрокат /naprokát/ adv. for hire

напротив /naprótiv/ adv. on the contrary; opposite

напряженный /napriazhónnyi/ adj. tense; strained

напрямик /napriamík/ adv. straight

напуганный /napúgannyi/ adj. scared

наравне /naravné/ adv. on equal terms

наркоз /narkóz/ m. narcosis

наркоман /narkomán/ m. drug addict

наркотик /narkótik/ m. dope

народ /naród/ m. people; nation

нарочно /naróchno/ adv. on purpose

наружный /narúzhnyi/ adj. external

наручники /narúchniki/ pl. handcuffs

нарушать /narushát'/ v. break, infringe

наряд /nariád/ m. dress

нарядный /nariádnyi/ adj. smart

насекомое /nasekómoe/ n. insect

население /naselénie/ n. population

населять /naseliát'/ v. settle

насилие /nasílie/ n. violence

насиловать /nasílovat'/ v. rape

насладиться /nasladít'sia/ v. enjoy

наследие /naslédie/ n. legacy

наследник /naslédnik/ m. heir

наследовать /naslédovat'/ v. inherit

наследственный /naslédstvennyi/ adj. hereditary

насмехаться /nasmekhát'sia/ v. mock

насморк /násmork/ m. cold

насос /nasós/ m. pump

настаивать /nastáivat'/ v. insist (on)

настойчивый /nastóichivyi/ adj. persistent

настолько /nastól'ko/ adv. so much

настоящий /nastoiáshchii/ adj. real, genuine

настраивать /nastráivat'/ v. tune; adjust

настроение /nastroénie/ n. mood

наступление /nastuplénie/ n. offensive

насущный /nasúshchnyi/ adj. vital

натирать /natirát'/ v. rub

натощак /natoshchák/ adv. on an empty stomach

натрий /nátrii/ m. sodium

натуральный /naturál'nyi/ adj. natural

наугад /naugád/ adv. at random

наука /naúka/ f. science

научный /naúchnyi/ adj. scientific

наушник /naúshnik/ m. ear-phone

нахал /nakhál/ m. impudent person

нахмуривать /nakhmúrivat'/ v. frown

находить /nakhodít'/ v. find

находиться /nakhodít'sia/ v. be situated

находчивый /nakhódchivyi/ adj. quick; resourceful

нацеливать /natsélivat'/ v. aim

национальность /natsionál'nost'/ f. nationality

нация /nátsiia/ f. nation, people

начало /nachálo/ n. beginning

начальник /nachál'nik/ m. chief

начальный /nachál'nyi/ adj. elementary

начинать /nachinát'/ v. begin

начинка /nachínka/ f. stuffing

начистоту /nachistotú/ adv. frankly

начитанный /nachítannyi/ adj. well-read

наш /nash/ pron. our

нашатырь /nashatýr'/ m. sal-ammoniac

не /ne/ part. not

небо /nébo/ n. sky; heaven

небо /nióbo/ n. palate

небольшой /nebol'shói/ adj. small, little

небоскреб /neboskriób/ m. skyscraper

небрежный /nebrézhnyi/ adj. careless

невдалеке /nevdaleké/ adv. not far off

невежливый /nevézhlivyi/ adj. rude, impolite

невероятный /neveroiátnyi/ adj. incredible

невеста /nevésta/ f. bride; fiancée

невестка /nevéstka/ f. daughter-in-law (son's wife), sister-in-law (brother's wife)

невидимый /nevídimyi/ adj. invisible

невинность /nevínnost'/ f. innocence

невозможный /nevozmózhnyi/ adj. impossible

невольно /nevól'no/ adv. unintentionally; involuntarily

невооруженный /nevooruzhónnyi/ adj. unarmed; naked (eye)

невроз /nevróz/ m. neurosis

невыгодный /nevýgodnyi/ adj. unprofitable; unfavorable

невыносимый /nevynosímyi/ adj. unbearable

негр /negr/ m. Negro, Black

неграмотный /negrámotnyi/ adj. illiterate

недавний /nedávnii/ adj. recent

недавно /nedávno/ adv. lately

недаром /nedárom/ adv. not for nothing

недвижимость /nedvízhimost'/ f. real estate

неделя /nedélia/ f. week

недоверие /nedovérie/ n. distrust

недовольство /nedovól'stvo/ n. displeasure

недоедание /nedoedánie/ n. malnutrition

недооценивать /nedootsénivat'/ v. underestimate

недопустимый /nedopustímyi/ adj. inadmissible

недоразумение /nedorazuménie/ n. misunderstanding

недорогой /nedorogói/ adj. inexpensive

недоставать /nedostavát'/ v. lack

недостаток /nedostátok/ m. lack; defect; fault

недоступный /nedostúpnyi/ adj. inaccessible; incomprehensible

нежный /nézhnyi/ adj. gentle

независимость /nezavísimost'/ f. independence

незаконнорожденный /nezakonnorózhdionnyi/ adj. illegitimate

незаменимый /nezamenímyi/ adj. irreplaceable

незнакомец /neznakómets/ m. stranger

незнакомый /neznakómyi/ adj. unknown

незрелый /nezrélyi/ adj. unripe; immature

неизбежный /neizbézhnyi/ adj. inevitable

неизменный /neizménnyi/ adj. invariable; constant

неимущий /neimúshchii/ adj. indigent

неисполнимый /neispolnímyi/ adj. impracticable

неисправный /neisprávnyi/ adj. defective

неисчислимый /neischislímyi/ adj. innumerable

нейлон /neilón/ m. nylon

нейтралитет /neitralitét/ m. neutrality

некоторый /nékotoryi/ pron. certain; some

некрасивый /nekrasívyi/ adj. ugly; unattractive; unseemly

некролог /nekrológ/ m. obituary

некуда /nékuda/ pron. nowhere

нелегкий /neliógkii/ adj. difficult; not easy

неловкий /nelóvkii/ adj. awkward

нельзя /nel'ziá/ pred. (it is) impossible

немедленный /nemédlennyi/ adj. immediate

немец /némets/ m. German

немецкий /nemétskii/ adj. German

немногие /nemnógie/ pl. few

немного /nemnógo/ adv. a little

немой /nemói/ adj. dumb

ненавидеть /nenavídet'/ v. hate

необоснованный /neobosnóvannyi/ adj. groundless

необходимость /neobkhodímost'/ f. necessity

необыкновенный /neobyknovénnyi/ adj. extraordinary; uncommon

неограниченный /neograníchennyi/ adj. unlimited

неожиданный /neozhídannyi/ adj. unexpected

неопределенный /neopredeliónnyi/ adj. indefinite; vague

неосторожный /neostorózhnyi/ adj. careless

неотложный /neotlózhnyi/ adj. urgent

неотразимый /neotrazímyi/ adj. irresistible

неплатежеспособный /neplatiozhesposóbnyi/ adj. insolvent

непобедимый /nepobedímyi/ adj. invincible

непогода /nepogóda/ f. bad weather

неподвижный /nepodvízhnyi/ adj. motionless

неполадка /nepoládka/ f. defect

непослушание /neposlushánie/ n. disobedience

неправда /neprávda/ f. untruth

неправильный /neprávil'nyi/ adj. incorrect

непременно /nepreménno/ adv. certainly

непрерывный /neprerývnyi/ adj. continuous

неприличный /neprilíchnyi/ adj. improper

непринужденный /neprinuzhdiónnyi/ adj. relaxed, easy

непроизводительный /neproizvodítel'nyi/ adj. unproductive

непромокаемый /nepromokáemyi/ adj. waterproof

неравный /nerávnyi/ adj. unequal

нерв /nerv/ m. nerve

нервничать /nérvnichat'/ v. be nervous

нерешительный /nereshítel'nyi/ adj. irresolute

нержавеющий /nerzhavéiushchii/ adj. stainless (steel)

неряшливый /neriáshlivyi/ adj. slovenly

несварение /nesvarénie/ n. indigestion

несгораемый /nesgoráemyi/ adj. fireproof

несколько /néskol'ko/ pron. several, some

несмотря (на) /nesmotriá na/ adv. + prep. in spite of

несовершеннолетний /nesovershennolétnii/ adj. under age; m. minor

несомненно /nesomnénno/ adv. undoubtedly

несправедливый /nespravedlívyi/ adj. unjust

нести /nestí/ v. carry; bear

несчастный /neschástnyi/ adj. unhappy; н. случай /n. slúchai/ accident

несчастье /neschást'e/ n. misfortune

нет /net/ part. no; not

нетерпение /neterpénie/ n. impatience

нетрудоспособный /netrudosposóbnyi/ adj. disabled

нетто /nétto/ adj. net

неуверенный /neuvérennyi/ adj. uncertain

неудача /neudácha/ f. failure

неудачный /neudáchnyi/ adj. unsuccessful

неудобный /neudóbnyi/ adj. inconvenient

неужели /neuzhéli/ part. really?

неуклюжий /neukliúzhii/ adj. clumsy

неустойка /neustóika/ f. forfeit

неустойчивый /neustóichivyi/ adj. unstable

нефть /neft'/ f. oil, petroleum

нехватка /nekhvátka/ f. shortage

неходовой /nekhodovói/ adj. unmarketable

нехотя /nékhotia/ adv. unwillingly

нечестный /nechéstnyi/ adj. dishonest

нечетный /nechótnyi/ adj. odd

ни /ni/ conj. not a; nor; ни... ни... /ni... ni.../ neither... nor

нигде /nigdé/ adv. nowhere

нижний /nízhnii/ adj. lower; нижнее белье /nízhnee bel'ió/ underclothes, underwear

низ /niz/ m. bottom

низкий /nízkii/ adj. low; mean

никакой /nikakói/ pron. no

никогда /nikogdá/ adv. never

никотин /nikotín/ m. nicotine

никто /niktó/ pron. nobody, no one

никуда /nikudá/ adv. nowhere

никчемный /nikchómnyi/ adj. good-for-nothing

нитка /nítka/ f. thread

ничего /nichevó/ pron. nothing; adv. so-so; passably

ничей /nichéi/ pron. nobody's

ничто /nichtó/ pron. nothing

ничуть /nichút'/ adv. not a bit

ничья /nich'iá/ f. draw, draw game

нищета /nishchetá/ f. poverty

нищий /níshchii/ m. beggar

но /no/ conj. but, and

новичок /novichók/ m. novice

новобранец /novobránets/ m. recruit

новорожденный /novorozhdiónnyi/ adj. new-born

новоселье /novosél'ie/ n. housewarming

новость /nóvost'/ f. news

новый /nóvyi/ adj. new

нога /nogá/ f. foot, leg

ноготь /nógot'/ m. nail

нож /nozh/ m. knife

ножницы /nózhnitsy/ pl. scissors

ноздря /nozdriá/ f. nostril

ноль /nol'/ m. nought; zero; nil

номер /nómer/ m. number; size; (hotel) room

нора /norá/ f. burrow; hole

норвежский /norvézhskii/ adj. Norwegian

норка /nórka/ f. mink

норма /nórma/ f. standard

нормальный /normál'nyi/ adj. normal

нос /nos/ m. nose

носилки /nosílki/ pl. stretcher

носильщик /nosíl'shchik/ m. porter

носить /nosít'/ v. carry; wear

носовой /nosovói/ adj. nasal; н. платок /n. platók/ handkerchief

носок /nosók/ m. toe (of boot or stocking); sock

нота /nóta/ f. note

ночевать /nochevát'/ v. spend the night

ночь /noch/ f. night
ноябрь /noiábr'/ m. November
нравиться /nrávit'sia/ v. please
ну /nu/ int. well now!
нужда /nuzhdá/ f. want, straits; need
нужный /núzhnyi/ adj. necessary
нырять /nyriát'/ v. dive
ныть /nyt'/ v. ache; whine
нюхать /niúkhat'/ v. sniff
нянчить /niánchit'/ v. nurse

O

о /o/ prep. about; with; on; against
оба /óba/ num. m., n. both
обаяние /obaiánie/ n. charm
обвешивать /obvéshivat'/ v. cheat (in weighing goods)
обвинитель /obvinítel'/ m. prosecutor
обвинять /obviniát'/ v. accuse (of)
обгонять /obgoniát'/ v. outstrip
обдумывать /obdúmyvat'/ v. consider
обе /óbe/ num. f. both
обед /obéd/ m. dinner; lunch
обедать /obédat'/ v. have dinner
обезболивать /obezbólivat'/ v. anesthetize
обезоруживать /obezorúzhivat'/ v. disarm
обезуметь /obezúmet'/ v. go mad
обезьяна /obez'iána/ f. monkey
оберегать /oberegát'/ v. guard

обертывать /obió́rtyvat'/ v. wrap up

обеспечивать /obespéchivat'/ v. provide for

обесценивать /obestsénivat'/ v. devalue

обещать /obeshchát'/ v. promise

обжаловать /obzhálovat'/ v. appeal against

обжигать /obzhigát'/ v. burn

обжора /obzhóra/ m., f. glutton

обзор /obzór/ m. review

обида /obída/ f. offence

обижать /obizhát'/ v. offend

обилие /obílie/ n. abundance

обитаемый /obitáemyi/ adj. inhabited

обкрадывать /obkrádyvat'/ v. rob

облагать (налогом) /oblagát' nalógom/ v. + m. tax

обладать /obladát'/ v. possess

облако /óblako/ n. cloud

область /óblast'/ f. region; province; sphere

облегчать /oblegchát'/ v. facilitate; ease

обливать /oblivát'/ v. pour (over); spill (over)

облигация /obligátsiia/ f. bond

облик /óblik/ m. appearance

обложка /oblózhka/ f. cover

облокачиваться /oblokáchivat'sia/ v. lean

обломок /oblómok/ m. fragment

облысеть /oblysét'/ v. grow bold

обман /obmán/ m. deception

обманывать /obmányvat'/ v. deceive

обматывать /obmátyvat'/ v. wind

обмен /obmén/ m. exchange

обмолвка /obmólvka/ f. slip of the tongue

обморок /óbmorok/ m. faint

обнажать /obnazhát'/ v. bare; lay bare

обнаруживать /obnarúzhivat'/ v. reveal; display

обнимать /obnimát'/ v. embrace

обновление /obnovlénie/ n. renewal, renovation

обобщать /obobshchát'/ v. summarize

обогащать /obogashchát'/ v. enrich

обогреватель /obogrevátel'/ m. heater

ободрять /obodriát'/ v. encourage

обожать /obozhát'/ v. adore

обознаться /oboznát'sia/ v. take someone for someone else

обозначать /oboznachát'/ v. designate

обои /obói/ pl. wallpaper

обойщик /oboishchik/ m. upholsterer

оболочка /obolóchka/ f. cover; shell; радужная о. /ráduzhnaia o./ iris

обольщать /obol'shchát'/ v. seduce

обонять /oboniát'/ v. smell

оборачиваться /oboráchivat'sia/ v. turn (round)

оборона /oboróna/ f. defence

оборотный /oborótnyi/ adj. reverse; working (capital)

оборудование /oborúdovanie/ n. equipment

обоснование /obosnovánie/ n. basis, ground

обострять /obostriát'/ v. sharpen; aggravate

обочина /obóchina/ f. edge; side

обоюдный /oboiúdnyi/ adj. mutual

обрабатывать /obrabátyvat'/ v. process; till

образ /óbraz/ m. image; mode, manner; icon

образец /obrazéts/ m. model, pattern

образование /obrazovánie/ n. education

обратно /obrátno/ adv. back(wards)

обратный /obrátnyi/ adj. return; reverse

обращение /obrashchénie/ n. address; appeal; treatment

обрезать /obrezát'/ v. cut off; clip, trim

обручальное (кольцо) /obruchál'noe kol'tsó/ adj. + n. engagement ring

обрыв /obrýv/ m. precipice

обрывать /obryvát'/ v. tear off; cut short

обряд /obriád/ m. rite

обсерватория /observatóriia/ f. observatory

обследование /obslédovanie/ n. enquiry, inspection; investigation

обслуживание /obslúzhivanie/ n. service

обстановка /obstanóvka/ f. conditions, situation; furniture

обстоятельство /obstoiátel'stvo/ n. circumstance

обстрел /óbstrel/ m. firing

обсчитывать /obschítyvat'/ v. cheat, overcharge

обуваться /obuvát'sia/ v. put on one's shoes/boots

обувь /óbuv'/ f. footwear

обуза /obúza/ f. burden

обучать /obuchát'/ v. teach, train

обучаться /obuchát'sia/ v. learn

обучение /obuchénie/ n. instruction; teaching

обширный /obshírnyi/ adj. vast

обшлаг /obshlág/ m. cuff

общаться /obshchát'sia/ v. associate (with)

общежитие /obshchezhítie/ n. hostel

общенародный /obshchenaródnyi/ adj. public, national

общение /obshchénie/ n. intercourse; relations

общепринятый /obshchepríniatyi/ adj. generally accepted

общественный /obshchéstvennyi/ adj. public, social; общественное мнение /obshchéstvennoe mnénie/ public opinion

общество /óbshchestvo/ n. society; company

общий /óbshchii/ adj. general, common; в общем /v óbshchem/ in general

община /obshchína/ f. commune, community

общительный /obshchítel'nyi/ adj. sociable

объединение /ob''edinénie/ f. unification; union

объект /ob''ékt/ m. object

объектив /ob''ektív/ m. lens

объем /ob''ióm/ m. volume

объявление /ob''iavlénie/ n. announcement; notice

объявлять /ob''iavliát'/ v. declare, announce

объяснять /ob''iasniát'/ v. explain

объятие /ob''iátie/ n. embrace

обыкновенный /obyknovénnyi/ adj. ordinary

обыск /óbysk/ m. search

обычай /obýchai/ m. custom

обычный /obýchnyi/ adj. usual

обязанность /obiázannost'/ f. duty, obligation

овдоветь /ovdovét'/ v. become a widow(er)

овес /oviós/ m. oats

овладевать /ovladevát'/ v. seize, take; master

овощи /óvoshchi/ pl. vegetables

овраг /ovrág/ m. ravine

овсянка /ovsiánka/ f. oatmeal porridge

овца /ovtsá/ f. sheep

овчарка /ovchárka/ f. Alsatian

огибать /ogibát'/ v. bend round; skirt

оглавление /oglavlénie/ n. contents

оглядываться /ogliádyvat'sia/ v. glance back

огнеопасный /ogneopásnyi/ adj. inflammable

огнетушитель /ognetushítel'/ m. fire-extinguisher

оговорка /ogovórka/ f. reservation; slip of the tongue

огонь /ogón'/ m. fire; light

огород /ogoród/ m. kitchen-garden

огорчать /ogorchát'/ v. grieve, pain

ограбление /ograblénie/ n. robbery

ограда /ográda/ f. fence

ограничение /ogranichénie/ n. restriction

ограниченный /ograníchennyi/ adj. narrow-minded;
  limited

огромный /ogrómnyi/ adj. huge

огурец /oguréts/ m. cucumber

одалживать /odálzhivat'/ v. lend; borrow (from)

одеваться /odevát'sia/ v. dress (oneself)

одежда /odézhda/ f. clothes

одеколон /odekolón/ m. eau-de-Cologne

одеяло /odeiálo/ n. blanket

один /odín/ num. and pron. one; only; certain

одинаковый /odinákovyi/ adj. identical, the same

одиннадцать /odínnadtsat'/ num. eleven

одинокий /odinókii/ adj. lonely

однажды /odnázhdy/ adv. once

однако /odnáko/ adv. however

одновременный /odnovreménnyi/ adj. simultaneous

однообразный /odnoobráznyi/ adj. monotonous

однородный /odnoródnyi/ adj. homogeneous

однофамилец /odnofamílets/ m. namesake

одноэтажный /odnoetázhnyi/ adj. one-storeyed

одобрение /odobrénie/ n. approval

одышка /odýshka/ f. short breath

ожерелье /ozherél'e/ n. necklace

ожесточенный /ozhestochónnyi/ adj. embittered; violent

оживать /ozhivát'/ v. come to life, revive

ожидать /ozhidát'/ v. wait for, expect

ожирение /ozhirénie/ n. obesity

ожог /ozhóg/ m. burn

озеро /ózero/ n. lake

озимый /ozímyi/ adj. winter (crops)

означать /oznachát'/ v. mean

озноб /oznób/ m. shivering; chill

озон /ozón/ m. ozone

оказывать (помощь) /okázyvat' pómoshch/ v. + f. render
  assistance; о. влияние /o. vliiánie/ exert influence (upon)

океан /okeán/ m. ocean

оккупация /okkupátsiia/ f. occupation

оклад /oklád/ m. salary

окно /oknó/ n. window

оковы /okóvy/ pl. fetters

около /ókolo/ prep. around; by, near; about

окончательный /okonchátel'nyi/ adj. final

окорок /ókorok/ m. ham

окраина /okráina/ f. outskirts

окрестность /okréstnost'/ f. environs

окружать /okruzhát'/ v. encircle, surround

октябрь /oktiábr/ m. October

окулист /okulíst/ m. oculist

окунь /ókun'/ m. perch (fish)

окупать /okupát'/ v. repay

окурок /okúrok/ m. cigarette end

оладья /olád'ia/ f. pancake

олень /olén'/ m. deer

омар /omár/ m. lobster

омерзительный /omerzítel'nyi/ adj. loathsome, sickening

омлет /omlét/ m. omelette

он, она, оно, они /on, oná, onó, oní/ pron. he, she, it, they

онкология /onkológiia/ f. oncology

ООН /oon/ abbr. U.N.O.

опаздывать /opázdyvat'/ v. be late

опасаться /opasát'sia/ v. fear

опасный /opásnyi/ adj. dangerous

опека /opéka/ f. trusteeship

опекун /opekún/ m. guardian

опера /ópera/ f. opera

оператор /operátor/ m. cameraman

операция /operátsiia/ f. operation

опережать /operezhát'/ v. outstrip; forestall

опечатка /opechátka/ f. misprint

описание /opisánie/ n. description

опись /ópis'/ f. inventory; list; о. имущества /o. imúshchestva/ distraint

оплата /opláta/ f. payment

оплачивать /opláchivat'/ v. pay

опоздание /opozdánie/ n. delay

опора /opóra/ f. support

оппозиция /oppozítsiia/ f. opposition

оправа /opráva/ f. setting; rim, frame

оправдывать /oprávdyvat'/ v. justify; acquit

определение /opredelénie/ n. definition

определенный /opredeliónnyi/ adj. definite; fixed

опровергать /oprovergát'/ v. refute

опрокидывать /oprokídyvat'/ v. overturn

опрятный /opriátnyi/ adj. tidy

оптика /óptika/ f. optics

оптимизм /optimízm/ m. optimism

оптовый /optóvyi/ adj. wholesale

опускать /opuskát'/ v. lower; post (letter); omit

опускаться /opuskát'sia/ v. sink; fall

опухоль /ópukhol'/ f. swelling, tumor

опыт /ópyt/ m. experiment, test; experience

опьянение /op'ianénie/ n. intoxication

опять /opiát'/ adv. again

оранжевый /oránzhevyi/ adj. orange

орать /orát'/ v. yell

орбита /orbíta/ f. orbit

орган /órgan/ m. organ; agency

организация /organizátsiia/ f. organization

организм /organízm/ m. organism

организовывать /organizóvyvat'/ v. organize

орден /órden/ m. order; decoration

ордер /órder/ m. order; warrant

орел /oriól/ m. eagle

орех /orékh/ m. nut

оригинал /originál/ m. original

ориентация /orientátsiia/ f. orientation

оркестр /orkéstr/ m. orchestra, band

орнамент /ornáment/ m. ornament

орудие /orúdie/ n. instrument, tool; gun

оружие /orúzhie/ n. weapons, arm(s)

орфография /orfográfiia/ f. spelling

оса /osá/ f. wasp

осада /osáda/ f. siege

осадок /osádok/ m. sediment; aftertaste; pl. precipitation

осанка /osánka/ f. bearing, carriage

освобождать /osvobozhdát'/ v. free, liberate

осел /osiól/ m. donkey; ass

осень /ósen'/ f. autumn

осетр /osiótr/ m. sturgeon

осина /osína/ f. asp(en)

осколок /oskólok/ m. splinter

оскорбление /oskorblénie/ n. insult

осложнение /oslozhnénie/ n. complication

осматривать /osmátrivat'/ v. examine

осмеливаться /osmélivat'sia/ v. dare

основа /osnóva/ f. base

основной /osnovnói/ adj. fundamental; principal

особенно /osóbenno/ adv. especially

особенный /osóbennyi/ adj. (e)special, particular

осознавать /osoznavát'/ v. realize

оспа /óspa/ f. smallpox; ветряная о. /vetrianáia o./ chicken-pox

оставаться /ostavát'sia/ v. remain, stay

оставлять /ostavliát'/ v. leave, abandon

останавливать /ostanávlivat'/ v. stop

остановка /ostanóvka/ f. stop

остаток /ostátok/ m. remainder

остерегаться /osteregát'sia/ v. beware (of)

осторожный /ostorózhnyi/ adj. cautious

остров /óstrov/ m. island

остроумие /ostroúmie/ n. wit

острый /óstryi/ adj. sharp

остывать /ostyvát'/ v. cool down

осуждать /osuzhdát'/ v. condemn

осуществлять /osushchestvliát'/ v. carry out

осуществляться /osushchestvliát'sia/ v. come true

ось /os'/ f. axis

осьминог /os'minóg/ m. octopus

осязаемый /osiazáemyi/ adj. tangible

от /ot/ prep. from

отбелить /otbelít'/ v. bleach

отбивная (котлета) /otbivnáia kotléta/ adj. + f. chop

отбрасывать /otbrásyvat'/ v. throw off, cast away

отвага /otvága/ f. courage

отвергать /otvergát'/ v. reject

отверстие /otvérstie/ n. opening

отвертка /otvió rtka/ f. screwdriver

ответ /otvét/ m. answer

ответственность /otvétstvennost'/ f. responsibility

ответчик /otvétchik/ m. defendant
отвечать /otvechát'/ v. answer
отвлекать /otvlekát'/ v. distract
отворачиваться /otvoráchivat'sia/ v. turn away
отворять /otvoriát'/ v. open
отвратительный /otvratítel'nyi/ adj. disgusting
отдавать /otdavát'/ v. give back, return
отдаленный /otdaliónnyi/ adj. remote
отдел /otdél/ m. department
отдельный /otdél'nyi/ adj. separate
отдирать /otdirát'/ v. rip off
отдых /otdýkh/ m. rest; relaxation
отель /otél'/ m. hotel
отец /otéts/ m. father
отзвук /ótzvuk/ m. echo
отказ /otkáz/ m. refusal
откладывать /otkládyvat'/ v. put aside
откликаться /otklikát'sia/ v. respond (to)
откровенный /otkrovénnyi/ adj. frank
открывать /otkryvát'/ v. open
открытие /otkrýtie/ n. discovery
открытка /otrýtka/ f. postcard
открытый /otrýtyi/ adj. open; frank
откуда /otkúda/ adv. where from; whence
откусывать /otkúsyvat'/ v. bite off
отличать /otlichát'/ v. distinguish
отличаться /otlichát'sia/ v. differ
отличный /otlíchnyi/ adj. excellent; different (from)
отменять /otmeniát'/ v. abolish, annul

отметка /otmétka/ f. note; mark

отнимать /otnimát'/ v. take away

относительно /otnosítel'no/ adv. relatively; prep. concerning

относиться /otnosít'sia/ v. concern; treat

отношение /otnoshénie/ n. attitude

отовсюду /otovsiúdu/ adv. from every quarter

отопление /otoplénie/ n. heating

отпечаток /otpechátok/ m. imprint

отплывать /otplyvát'/ v. sail

отпор /otpór/ m. rebuff

отправитель /otpravítel'/ m. sender

отправка /otprávka/ f. dispatch

отправляться /otpravliát'sia/ v. set off

отпуск /ótpusk/ m. leave; holiday

отпускать /otpuskát'/ v. let go

отрава /otráva/ f. poison

отражать /otrazhát'/ reflect; repulse

отрасль /ótrasl'/ f. branch, sphere

отрезать /otrézat'/ v. cut off

отрезок /otrézok/ m. piece; section

отрицательный /otritsátel'nyi/ adj. negative

отрицать /otritsát'/ v. deny

отроческий /ótrocheskii/ adj. adolescent

отруби /ótrubi/ pl. bran

отрывать /otryvát'/ v. tear off

отрывок /otrývok/ m. excerpt

отряд /otriád/ m. detachment

отряхивать /otriákhivat'/ v. shake down

отсекать /otsekát'/ v. cut off

отсрочивать /otsróchivat'/ v. postpone

отставать /otstavát'/ v. lag behind, be slow (of a clock or watch)

отставка /otstávka/ f. resignation

отсталость /otstálost'/ f. backwardness

отстранять /otstraniát'/ v. push aside

отступление /otstuplénie/ n. retreat

отсутствие /otsútstvie/ n. absence

отсутствовать /otsútstvovat'/ v. be absent

отсылать /otsylát'/ v. send back; refer(to)

отсюда /otsiúda/ adv. from here; hence

отталкивать /ottálkivat'/ v. push away

оттенок /otténok/ m. shade

оттепель /óttepel'/ f. thaw

оттуда /ottúda/ adv. from there

отход /otkhód/ m. withdrawal

отходы /otkhódy/ pl. waste

отцовский /ottsóvskii/ adj. paternal

отчаяние /otcháianie/ n. despair

отчаянный /otcháiannyi/ adj. desperate

отчего /otchevó/ adv. why

отчество /ótchestvo/ n. patronymic

отчет /otchót/ m. account

отчетливый /otchótlivyi/ adj. distinct

отчизна /otchízna/ f. native country

отчим /ótchim/ m. step-father

отчислять /otchisliát'/ v. deduct

отъезд /ot''ézd/ m. departure

отыскивать /otýskivat'/ v. find

офицер /ofitsér/ m. officer

официальный /ofitsiál'nyi/ adj. official

официант /ofitsiánt/ m. waiter

официантка /ofitsiántka/ f. waitress

оформление /oformlénie/ n. official registration

охлаждать /okhlazhdát'/ v. cool

охота /okhóta/ f. hunt(ing)

охотно /okhótno/ adv. willingly

охрана /okhrána/ f. guard; protection

оценивать /otsénivat'/ v. estimate

оценка /otsénka/ f. estimate

очаг /ochág/ m. hearth

очаровательный /ocharovátel'nyi/ adj. charming

очевидец /ochevídets/ m. eye-witness

очевидный /ochevídnyi/ adj. obvious

очень /óchen'/ adv. very; very much

очередной /ocherednói/ adj. next in turn; periodical;
  regular

очередь /óchered'/ f. turn; queue, line

очерк /ócherk/ m. essay

очищать /ochishchát'/ v. clean

очки /ochkí/ pl. spectacles

очко /ochkó/ n. pip; point

очутиться /ochutít'sia/ v. find oneself

ошейник /oshéinik/ m. collar

ошибаться /oshibát'sia/ v. make a mistake

ошибка /oshíbka/ f. mistake, error

ощипывать /oshchípyvat'/ v. pluck

ощущать /oshchushchát'/ v. feel, sense

П

павильон /pavil'ón/ m. pavilion

павлин /pavlín/ m. peacock

падать /pádat'/ v. fall

падеж /padézh/ m. (gram.) case

падчерица /pádcheritsa/ f. step-daughter

паек /paiók/ m. ration

пай /pai/ m. share

пайщик /páishchik/ m. shareholder

пакет /pakét/ m. parcel, package

паковать /pakovát'/ v. pack

палата /paláta/ f. chamber; house

палатка /palátka/ f. tent

палец /pálets/ m. finger; toe

палка /pálka/ f. stick

палтус /páltus/ m. halibut

палуба /páluba/ f. deck

пальма /pál'ma/ f. palm (tree)

пальто /pal'tó/ n. (over)coat

памятник /pámiatnik/ m. monument

память /pámiat'/ f. memory

паника /pánika/ f. panic

панихида /panikhída/ f. office for the dead

пантера /pantéra/ f. panther

папа /pápa/ m. dad, daddy; pope

папироса /papirósa/ f. cigarette

папка /pápka/ f. file; document case

пар /par/ m. steam
пара /pára/ f. pair
парад /parád/ m. parade
паразит /parazít/ m. parasite
парализовать /paralizovát'/ v. paralyze
парень /páren'/ m. guy; fellow
парикмахер /parikmákher/ m. hairdresser
парк /park/ m. park
паркет /parkét/ m. parquet
парламент /parláment/ m. parliament
парник /parník/ m. hotbed
парной /parnói/ adj. fresh
пароход /parokhód/ m. steamer
парта /párta/ f. (school) desk
партер /partér/ m. the stalls; pit
партия /pártiia/ f. party; game
партнер /partniór/ m. partner
парус /párus/ m. sail
пасмурный /pásmurnyi/ adj. gloomy
паспорт /pásport/ m. passport
пассажир /passazhír/ m. passenger
пассив /passív/ m. liabilities
пассивный /passívnyi/ adj. passive
паста /pásta/ f. paste
пастух /pastúkh/ m. shepherd
пасха /páskha/ f. Easter
патент /patént/ m. patent
патриот /patriót/ m. patriot
патрон /patrón/ m. patron; cartridge

патруль /patri'/ m. patrol
пауза /páuza/ f. pause
паук /pak/ m. spider
пах /pakh/ m. groin
пахать /pakhát'/ v. plough
пахнуть /pákhnut'/ v. smell
пациент /patsiént/ m. patient
пачка /páchka/ f. bundle
пачкать /páchkat'/ v. dirty
паштет /pashtét/ m. pâté, paste
паять /paiát'/ v. solder
певец /pevéts/ m. singer
педагог /pedagóg/ m. teacher
педаль /pedál'/ f. pedal
пейзаж /peizázh/ m. landscape
пекарня /pekárnia/ f. bakery
пеленка /peliónka/ f. nappie
пена /péna/ f. foam
пенал /penál/ m. pencil-case
пенициллин /penitsilin/ m. penicillin
пенсия /pénsiia/ f. pension
пень /pen'/ m. stump
пеня /pénia/ f. fine
пепел /pépel/ m. ashes
первобытный /pervobýtnyi/ adj. primitive; prehistoric
первосортный /pervosórtnyi/ adj. first class
первый /pérvyi/ adj. first
перебегать /perebegát'/ v. desert; run across
перебивать /perebivát'/ v. interrupt

перевод /perevód/ m. transfer; translation

переводчик /perevódchik/ m. translator, interpreter

перевозить /perevozít'/ v. transport

переворот /perevorót/ m. coup

перевязка /pereviázka/ f. bandaging

переговоры /peregovóry/ pl. negotiations

перегревать /peregrevát'/ v. overheat

перегружать /peregruzhát'/ v. overload

перед /péred/ conj. before; in front of

перед /periód/ m. front

передавать /peredavát'/ v. pass; transmit; convey; hand over

передача /peredácha/ f. transfer; broadcast

переделывать /peredélyvat'/ v. remake

передний /perédnii/ adj. front

передник /perédnik/ m. apron

передовица /peredovítsa/ f. editorial

передумывать /peredúmyvat'/ v. change one's mind

переживание /perezhivánie/ n. experience

пережиток /perezhítok/ m. survival

переизбирать /pereizbirát'/ v. re-elect

переиздавать /pereizdavát'/ v. reprint

перекись /pérekis'/ f. peroxide

переключать /perekliuchát'/ v. switch (over)

перекресток /perekrióstok/ m. crossroads

перелезать /perelezát'/ v. climb over

перелетная птица /pereliótnaia pútsa/ adj. + f. bird of passage

перелом /perelóm/ m. break; turning-point

перематывать /peremátyvat'/ v. (re)wind

перемена /pereména/ f. interval; break; change

перемешивать /pereméshivat'/ v. mix; shuffle

перемирие /peremírie/ n. truce

перенаселенный /perenaseliónnyi/ adj. overpopulated

перенасыщенный /perenasýshchennyi/ adj. oversaturated

переносить /perenosít'/ v. carry across; put off; endure

переносица /perenósitsa/ f. bridge of the nose

переносный /perenósnyi/ adj. portable; figurative

переоборудовать /pereoborúdovat'/ v. re-equip

переобуваться /pereobuvát'sia/ v. change one's footwear

переодевать /pereodevát'/ v. change (someone's clothes)

перепел /pérepel/ m. quail

перепечатывать /perepechátyvat'/ v. reprint; type

переписка /perepíska/ f. correspondence

переписывать /perepísyvat'/ v. copy

переплачивать /perepláchivat'/ v. overpay

переплет /perepliót/ m. binding; cover

переплывать /pereplyvát'/ v. swim across

переполнять /perepolniát'/ v. fill (smth.) to overflowing; overwhelm

перепонка /perepónka/ f. membrane

переправа /perepráva/ f. crossing

перепродавать /pereprodavát'/ v. resell

перепроизводство /pereproizvódstvo/ n. overproduction

перепрыгивать /pereprýgivat'/ v. jump over

перерасход /pereraskhód/ m. overexpenditure

перерыв /pererýv/ m. interval

пересадка /peresádka/ f. transplantation; change

пересекать /peresekát'/ v. cross

переселять /pereseliát'/ v. move

пересечение /peresechénie/ n. intersection

переставать /perestavát'/ v. stop

перестраивать /perestráivat'/ v. rebuild

перестрелка /perestrélka/ f. exchange of fire

перестройка /perestróika/ f. perestroika; reorganization

пересчитывать /pereschítyvat'/ v. count again; recalculate

переулок /pereúlok/ m. by-street; lane

переутомлять(ся) /pereutomliát'sia/ v. overstrain

перехитрить /perekhitrít'/ v. outwit; be too smart

переход /perekhód/ m. passage

переходить /perekhodít'/ v. cross

переходный /perekhódnyi/ adj. transition(al)

перец /pérets/ m. pepper

перечень /pérechen'/ m. list

перечеркивать /perechiórkivat'/ v. cross out

перечислять /perechisliát'/ v. enumerate; transfer (fin.)

перешеек /pereshéek/ m. isthmus

перила /períla/ pl. (hand) rail

период /períod/ m. period

периодика /periódika/ f. periodicals

периферия /periferíia/ f. periphery

перламутр /perlamútr/ m. mother-of-pearl

перловая крупа /perlóvaia krupá/ adj. + f. pearl-barley

перо /peró/ n. feather; pen

перочинный нож /perochínnyi nozh/ adj. + m. penknife

перпендикуляр /perpendikuliár/ m. perpendicular

перрон /perrón/ m. platform

персик /pérsik/ m. peach

персонал /personál/ m. staff

перспектива /perspektíva/ f. prospects

перхоть /pérkhot'/ f. dandruff

перчатка /perchátka/ f. glove

песня /pésnia/ f. song

песок /pesók/ m. sand; сахарный п. /sákharnyi p./
  granulated sugar

петиция /petítsiia/ f. petition

петля /petliá/ f. loop

петрушка /petrúshka/ f. parsley

петух /petúkh/ m. cock, rooster

петь /pet'/ v. sing

пехота /pekhóta/ f. infantry

печаль /pechál'/ f. sorrow; grief

печатать /pechátat'/ v. print; type

печать /pechát'/ f. seal; the press

печеный /pechónyi/ adj. baked

печень /péchen'/ f. liver

печенье /pechén'e/ n. biscuit; cookies

печь /pech/ f. stove; v. bake

пешеход /peshekhód/ m. pedestrian

пешка /péshka/ f. pawn (chess)

пешком /peshkóm/ adv. on foot

пещера /peshchéra/ f. cave

пианино /pianíno/ n. piano

пивная /pivnáia/ f. pub; tavern

пиво /pívo/ n. beer
пиджак /pidzhák/ m. jacket, coat
пижама /pizháma/ f. pyjamas
пик /pik/ m. peak; час п. /chas p./ rush hour
пила /pilá/ f. saw
пилот /pilót/ m. pilot
пилюля /piliúlia/ f. pill
пион /pión/ m. peony
пипетка /pipétka/ f. dropper
пир /pir/ m. feast
пирамида /piramída/ f. pyramid
пират /pirát/ m. pirate
пирог /piróg/ m. pie
пирожное /pirózhnoe/ n. pastry
писатель /pisátel'/ m. writer, author
писать /pisát'/ v. write
пистолет /pistolét/ m. pistol
письменный /pís'mennyi/ adj. written
письмо /pis'mó/ n. letter
питание /pitánie/ n. feeding
питательный /pitatel'nyi/ adj. nutritious
пить /pit'/ v. drink
пихта /píkhta/ f. fir
пишущая машинка /píshushchaia mashínka/ adj. +f.
   typewriter
пища /píshcha/ f. food
пищеварение /pishchevarénie/ n. digestion
пищевод /pishchevód/ m. gullet
пиявка /piiávka/ f. leech

плавать /plávat'/ v. sail; swim
плавник /plavník/ m. fin
плавный /plávnyi/ adj. smooth
плакат /plakát/ m. poster
плакать /plákat'/ v. weep, cry
пламя /plámia/ m. flame(s)
план /plan/ m. plan
планета /planéta/ f. planet
пласт /plast/ m. layer
пластинка /plastínka/ f. plate; record; disc
пластмасса /plastmássa/ f. plastic
пластырь /plástyr'/ m. plaster
плата /pláta/ f. pay
платина /plátina/ f. platinum
платить /platít'/ v. pay
платный /plátnyi/ adj. paid
платок /platók/ m. kerchief
платформа /platfórma/ f. platform
платье /plát'e/ n. dress
плашмя /plashmiá/ adv. flat
плащ /plashch/ m. raincoat
плевать /plevát'/ v. spit
плеврит /plevrít/ m. pleurisy
племянник /plemiánnik/ m. nephew
племянница /plemiánnitsa/ f. niece
плен /plen/ m. captivity
пленка /pliónka/ f. film; tape
пленник /plénnik/ m. prisoner
плесень /plésen'/ f. mould

плескать /pleskát'/ v. splash

плести /plestí/ v. weave

плеть /plet'/ f. lash

плечо /plechó/ n. shoulder

плита /plitá/ f. slab; stove

плитка /plítka/ f. tile

пловец /plovéts/ m. swimmer

плод /plod/ m. fruit

пломба /plómba/ f. filling (in tooth); seal

пломбир /plombír/ m. ice-cream

плоский /plóskii/ adj. flat

плоскогубцы /ploskogúbtsy/ pl. pliers

плот /plot/ m. raft

плотина /plotína/ f. dam

плотник /plótnik/ m. carpenter

плотный /plótnyi/ adj. tense; thick; tight; hearty (dinner)

плохой /plokhói/ adj. bad

площадка /ploshchádka/ f. ground

площадь /plóshad'/ f. square; area

плуг /plug/ m. plough

плыть /plyt'/ v. swim; sail

плюс /pliús/ m. plus

пляж /pliázh/ m. beach

плясать /pliasát'/ v. dance

по /po/ prep. along; through; on

побег /pobég/ m. flight; escape; shoot

победа /pobéda/ f. victory

побеждать /pobezhdát'/ v. conquer; defeat; win

побелка /pobélka/ f. whitewashing

побережье /poberézh'e/ n. coast

повар /póvar/ m. cook, chef

поведение /povedénie/ n. behaviour

поверхность /povérkhnost'/ f. surface

повесить /povésit'/ v. hang (up)

повестка /povéstka/ f. summons

повесть /póvest'/ f. story

по-видимому /po-vídimomu/ paren. apparently, evidently

повидло /povídlo/ n. jam

повиноваться /povinovát'sia/ v. obey

повод /póvod/ m. occasion; ground

поворачивать /povoráchivat'/ v. turn

повреждать /povrezhdát'/ v. damage

повседневный /povsednévnyi/ adj. everyday

повсюду /povsiúdu/ adv. everywhere

повторять /povtoriát'/ v. repeat; revise

повышать /povyshát'/ v. raise

повышение /povyshénie/ n. rise; increase; promotion

повязка /poviázka/ f. bandage

погибать /pogibát'/ v. perish

поговорка /pogovórka/ f. saying

погода /pogóda/ f. weather

погоня /pogónia/ f. chase

погреб /pógreb/ m. cellar

погружать /pogruzhát'/ v. dip; plunge

под /pod/ prep. under

подавать /podavát'/ v. give; serve

подавлять /podavliát'/ v. suppress

подагра /podágra/ f. gout

подарок /podárok/ m. present, gift

подбородок /podboródok/ m. chin

подвал /podvál/ m. basement; cellar

подвергать /podvergát'/ v. subject; expose

подвиг /pódvig/ m. exploit

подводный /podvódnyi/ adj. underwater; подводная
лодка /podvódnaia lódka/ submarine

подглядывать /podgliádyvat'/ v. peep

подготавливать /podgotávlivat'/ v. prepare (for)

подданство /póddanstvo/ n. citizenship

подделка /poddélka/ f. forgery; fake

поддельный /poddél'nyi/ adj. false, fake; artificial

поддерживать /poddérzhivat'/ v. support

подержанный /podérzhannyi/ adj. second-hand

поджог /podzhóg/ m. arson

подкова /podkóva/ f. horseshoe

подкожный /podkózhnyi/ adj. hypodermic

подкрадываться /podkrádyvat'sia/ v. creep up (to)

подкупать /podkupát'/ v. bribe

подлец /podléts/ m. scoundrel

подливка /podlívka/ f. gravy

подлинник /pódlinnik/ m. original

подлог /podlóg/ m. forgery

подметка /podmiótka/ f. sole (of shoe)

подмешивать /podméshivat'/ v. add; mix in

подмигивать /podmígivat'/ v. wink

подмышка /podmýshka/ f. armpit

поднимать /podnimát'/ v. raise; lift

поднос /podnós/ m. tray

подобный /podóbnyi/ adj. similar (to)

подогревать /podogrevát'/ v. warm up

пододеяльник /pododeiál'nik/ m. blanket, cover

подозревать /podozrevát'/ v. suspect (of)

подоконник /podokónnik/ m. window-sill

подоходный (налог) /podokhódnyi nalóg/ adj. + m. income tax

подошва /podóshva/ f. sole (of foot, shoe)

подписка /podpíska/ f. subscription

подписывать /podpísyvat'/ v. sign

подпись /pódpis'/ f. signature

подполковник /podpolkóvnik/ m. lieutenant-colonel

подрабатывать /podrabátyvat'/ v. work up; earn a little extra

подражать /podrazhát'/ v. imitate

подразумевать /podrazumevát'/ v. mean

подрезать /podrezát'/ v. cut, trim

подробность /podróbnost'/ f. detail

подросток /podróstok/ m. teenager

подруга /podrúga/ f. (girl-)friend

подряд /podriád/ m. contract; adv. in succession

подсказывать /podskázyvat'/ v. prompt; suggest

подследственный /podslédstvennyi/ adj. under investigation

подслушивать /podslúshivat'/ v. eavesdrop; overhear

подсознательный /podsoznátel'nyi/ adj. subconscious

подсолнечник /podsólnechnik/ m. sunflower

подставка /podstávka/ f. support; prop

подстригать /podstrigát'/ v. trim

подсудимый /podsudímyi/ m. defendant

подсчитывать /podschítyvat'/ v. count up

подтверждать /podtverzhdát'/ v. confirm

подтяжки /podtiázhki/ pl. suspenders

подушка /podúshka/ f. pillow

подходящий /podkhodiáshchii/ adj. suitable; proper

подчеркивать /podchórkivat'/ v. underline; emphasize

подчинять /podchiniát'/ v. subjugate; subordinate

подъезд /pod''ézd/ m. entrance

подъем /pod''ióm/ m. rise

поезд /póezd/ m. train

поездка /poézdka/ f. trip; journey

пожалуйста /pozháluista/ part. please

пожар /pozhár/ m. fire

пожелание /pozhelánie/ n. wish

пожертвование /pozhértvovanie/ n. donation

пожизненный /pozhíznennyi/ adj. lifelong; life

пожилой /pozhilói/ adj. elderly

пожимать /pozhimát'/ v. press; п. плечами /p. plechámi/
    shrug one's shoulders

поза /póza/ f. pose

позавчера /pozavcherá/ adv. the day before
    yesterday

позади /pozadí/ adv., prep. behind

позапрошлый /pozapróshlyi/ adj. before last

позволять /pozvoliát'/ v. allow

позвоночник /pozvonóchnik/ m. spine

поздний /pózdnii/ adj. late

поздравлять /pozdravliát'/ v. congratulate

поземельный (налог) /pozemél'nyi nalóg/ adj. + m. land
  tax

позже /pózzhe/ adv. later

позиция /pozítsiia/ f. position

позор /pozór/ m. shame

позорить /pozórit'/ v. disgrace

по-иному /po-inómu/ adv. differently

поиск /póisk/ m. search

поистине /poístine/ adv. indeed

поймать /poimát'/ v. catch

пока /poká/ adv. meanwhile, for the time being; conj. while,
  till; coll. bye-bye; so long

показание /pokazánie/ n. testimony; evidence

показатель /pokazátel'/ m. index

показывать /pokázyvat'/ v. show; demonstrate

покидать /pokidát'/ v. desert; leave

поклон /poklón/ m. bow; regards

поклонник /poklónnik/ m. admirer

покой /pokói/ m. quietness; peace

покойник /pokóinik/ m. the deceased

поколение /pokolénie/ n. generation

покорный /pokórnyi/ adj. obedient; humble

покорять /pokoriát'/ v. conquer; subjugate

покровитель /pokrovítel'/ m. patron

покрой /pokrói/ m. cut (of clothes)

покрывало /pokryválo/ n. cloth; veil

покрывать /pokryvát'/ v. cover

покупатель /pokupátel'/ m. customer

покупать /pokupát'/ v. buy

покупка /pokúpka/ f. purchase

покушаться /pokushát'sia/ v. attempt

пол /pol/ m. floor; sex

пол- /pol-/ half

полагать /polagát'/ v. think; suppose

полагаться /polagát'sia/ v. rely; depend

полдень /pólden'/ m. midday

поле /póle/ n. field; ground; margin; brim (of hat)

полезный /poléznyi/ adj. useful

полено /poléno/ n. log

полет /poliót/ m. flight

ползать /pólzat'/ v. crawl

поливать /polivát'/ v. water; pour

поликлиника /poliklínika/ f. polyclinic

полис /pólis/ m. policy (e. g. insurance)

политик /polítik/ m. politician

политика /polítika/ f. politics

полицейский /politséiskii/ m. policeman

полиция /polítsiia/ f. police

полк /polk/ m. regiment

полка /pólka/ f. shelf

полковник /polkóvnik/ m. colonel

полнеть /polnét'/ v. put on weight

полномочие /polnomóchie/ n. authority; (full) power

полностью /pólnost'iu/ adv. completely

полночь /pólnoch/ f. midnight

полный /pólnyi/ adj. full; complete; stout, plump

половина /polovína/ f. half

положение /polozhénie/ n. situation

положительный /polozhítel'nyi/ adj. positive

поломка /polómka/ f. breakage

полоса /polosá/ f. strip

полосатый /polosátyi/ adj. striped

полоскать /poloskát'/ v. rinse

полость /pólost'/ f. cavity

полотенце /poloténtse/ n. towel

полотно /polotnó/ n. linen

полоть /polót'/ v. weed

полтора /poltorá/ num. one and a half

полу- /pólu-/ semi-, half-

полузащитник /poluzashchítnik/ m. half-back (sport)

полуостров /poluóstrov/ m. peninsula

полупроводник /poluprovodník/ m. semiconductor

полуфабрикат /polufabrikát/ m. half-finished product; convenience foods

получать /poluchát'/ v. receive; obtain

полушарие /polushárie/ n. hemisphere

полчаса /polchasá/ m. half an hour

польза /pól'za/ f. use; profit

пользоваться /pól'zovat'sia/ v. make use (of)

полюс /pólius/ m. pole

поляна /poliána/ f. forest meadow

помада /pomáda/ f. lipstick

помешанный /poméshannyi/ adj. mad, crazy

помещать /pomeshchát'/ v. place, accommodate; п. капитал /p. kapitál/ invest

помещение /pomeshchénie/ n. premises

помидор /pomidór/ m. tomato

помиловать /pomílovat'/ v. pardon

помимо /pomímo/ prep. besides

поминки /pomínki/ pl. funeral repast

помнить /pómnit'/ v. remember; keep in mind

помогать /pomogát'/ v. assist; aid; help

по-моему /po-móemu/ adv. in my opinion

помощник /pomóshnik/ m. assistant

помощь /pómoshch/ f. assistance; aid; help; первая п. /pérvaia p./ first aid

понаслышке /ponaslýshke/ adv. by hearsay

понедельник /ponedél'nik/ m. Monday

понижать /ponizhát'/ v. lower, reduce

понимать /ponimát'/ v. understand, comprehend

понос /ponós/ m. diarrhoea

понятие /poniátie/ n. idea; concept; outlook

понятный /poniátnyi/ adj. clear; intelligible

поощрять /pooshchriát'/ v. encourage, stimulate

поп /pop/ m. priest

попадать /popadát'/ v. hit; get (into); reach

попарно /popárno/ adv. in pairs

поперек /poperiók/ adv. across

попеременно /popereménno/ adv. alternately

пополам /popolám/ adv. in half

пополнять /popolniát'/ v. replenish

поправлять /popravliát'/ v. correct; mend; adjust

поправляться /popravliát'sia/ v. improve; recover, get well; put on weight

по-прежнему /po-prézhnemu/ adv. as before

попугай /popugái/ m. parrot

популярный /populiárnyi/ adj. popular

попытка /popýtka/ f. attempt

пора /póra/ f. pore

пора /porá/ f. time; as pred. it is time

поражение /porazhénie/ n. defeat

поразительный /porazítel'nyi/ adj. striking, wonderful

порка /pórka/ f. flogging

поровну /pórovnu/ f. equally

порог /poróg/ m. threshold

порода /poróda/ f. breed

порок /porók/ m. vice

поросенок /porosiónok/ m. piglet

порох /pórokh/ m. (gun-)powder

порошок /poroshók/ m. powder

порт /port/ m. port

портативный /portatívnyi/ adj. portable

портвейн /portvéin/ m. port (wine)

портить /pórtit'/ v. spoil; ruin; corrupt

портниха /portníkha/ f. dressmaker

портной /portnói/ m. tailor

портрет /portrét/ m. portrait

портсигар /portsigár/ m. cigarette-case, cigar-case

потфель /portfél'/ m. brief-case; portfolio

по-русски /po-rússki/ adv. in Russian

поручение /poruchénie/ n. assignment; mission; errand

поручитель /poruchítel'/ m. guarantor; sponsor

порция /pórtsiia/ f. portion, helping

порядок /poriádok/ m. order

порядочный /poriádochnyi/ adj. decent, honest;
  considerable

посадка /posádka/ f. planting; landing; boarding; posture

по-своему /po-svóemu/ adv. in one's own way

поселять /poseliát'/ v. settle

посередине /poseredíne/ adv. in the middle (of)

посетитель /posetítel'/ m. visitor

посещать /poseshchát'/ v. visit; call; attend

поскользнуться /poskol'znút'sia/ v. slip

поскольку /poskól'ku/ conj. since; inasmuch as

после /pósle/ adv. later; prep. after

последний /poslédnii/ adj. last; latest

последователь /poslédovatel'/ m. follower

последствие /poslédstvie/ n. consequence

послезавтра /poslezávtra/ adv. the day after tomorrow

пословица /poslóvitsa/ f. proverb

послушный /poslúshnyi/ adj. obedient

пособие /posóbie/ n. grant

посол /posól/ m. ambassador

посольство /posól'stvo/ n. embassy

поспешный /pospéshnyi/ adj. hasty; abrupt

посредственный /posrédstvennyi/ adj. mediocre;
  satisfactory

пост /post/ m. post; position; fast

поставка /postávka/ f. delivery, supply

постановлять /postanovliát'/ v. resolve; decide

постель /postél'/ f. bed

постепенный /postepénnyi/ adj. gradual

постный /póstnyi/ adj. lean; vegetable (oil)

постольку /postól'ku/ conj. in so far as

посторонний /postorónnii/ adj. strange; outside; m. stranger

постоянный /postoiánnyi/ adj. constant; steady

постройка /postróika/ f. building

поступать /postupát'/ v. act; enter; join

поступок /postúpok/ m. act; action; deed

посуда /posúda/ f. plates and dishes; crockery

посылать /posylát'/ v. send; dispatch

посылка /posýlka/ f. parcel

пот /pot/ m. sweat

по-твоему /po-tvóemu/ adv. in your opinion

потенциал /potentsiál/ m. potential

потеря /potéria/ f. loss

поток /potók/ m. stream

потолок /potolók/ m. ceiling

потом /potóm/ adv. afterwards; later on

потомок /potómok/ m. descendant

потребитель /potrebítel'/ m. consumer

потребность /potrébnost'/ f. need; requirement

потрясение /potriasénie/ n. shock

похвала /pokhvalá/ f. praise

похищать /pokhishchát'/ v. steal; kidnap

поход /pokhód/ m. march; campaign

походка /pokhódka/ f. walk; gait

похожий /pokhózhii/ adj. similar (to)

поцелуй /potselúi/ m. kiss

почва /póchva/ f. soil

почему /pochemú/ adv. why

почерк /pócherk/ m. handwriting
почет /pochót/ m. honour; respect
починка /pochínka/ f. repairing
почка /póchka/ f. bud; kidney
почта /póchta/ f. post, mail; post-office
почтальон /pochtal'ón/ m. postman
почти /pochtí/ adv. almost, nearly
пошлина /póshlina/ f. duty
пошлый /póshlyi/ adj. vulgar, shallow
пощада /poshcháda/ f. mercy
поэзия /poéziia/ f. poetry
поэтому /poétomu/ adv. therefore
появление /poiavlénie/ n. emergence
появляться /poiavliát'sia/ v. appear
пояс /póias/ m. belt
поясница /poiasnítsa/ f. small of the back; loins
правда /právda/ f. truth
правило /právilo/ n. rule
правильный /právil'nyi/ adj. true
правительство /pravítel'stvo/ n. government
править /právit'/ v. rule, govern; drive; correct
право /právo/ n. right
правовой /pravovói/ adj. legal
православие /pravoslávie/ n. Orthodoxy
правосудие /pravosúdie/ n. justice
правый /právyi/ adj. right
праздник /prázdnik/ m. holiday; festival
праздновать /prázdnovat'/ v. celebrate
практика /práktika/ f. practice

практичный /praktíchnyi/ adj. practical

прах /prakh/ m. dust; remains

прачечная /práchechnaia/ f. laundry

превосходный /prevoskhódnyi/ adj. superb

превращать /prevrashchát'/ v. turn, change

преграда /pregráda/ f. obstacle

преданность /prédannost'/ f. devotion

предатель /predátel'/ m. betrayer

предварительный /predvarítel'nyi/ adj. preliminary

предел /predél/ m. limit

предлагать /predlagát'/ v. offer; propose, suggest

предлог /predlóg/ m. pretext; exuse

предложение /predlozhénie/ n. suggestion; offer; sentence

предмет /predmét/ m. object; thing; article; subject

предостерегать /predosteregát'/ v. warn

предосторожность /predostorózhnost'/ f. precaution

предполагать /predpolagát'/ v. assume; suppose

предпоследний /predposlédnii/ adj. last but one

предпочитать /predpochitát'/ v. prefer

предприниматель /predprinimátel'/ m. employer; businessman

председатель /predsedátel'/ m. chairman

предсказывать /predskázyvat'/ v. foretell; predict

представитель /predstavítel'/ m. representative; spokesman

представление /predstavlénie/ n. presentation; notion; idea; performance

представлять /predstavliát'/ v. present; produce; introduce

предупреждать /preduprezhdát'/ v. anticipate; warn; give notice (of)

предшественник /predshestvénnik/ m. predecessor;
forerunner

предыдущий /predydúshchii/ adj. previous

прежний /prézhnii/ adj. former

президент /prezidént/ m. president

президиум /prezídium/ m. presidium

презирать /prezirát'/ v. despise

презрение /prezrénie/ n. contempt

преимущество /preimúshchestvo/ n. advantage

прейскурант /preiskuránt/ m. price-list

прекрасный /prekrásnyi/ adj. beautiful, fine, lovely

прекращать /prekrashchát'/ v. stop; cease

прелестный /preléstnyi/ adj. charming

прелюбодеяние /preliubodeiánie/ n. adultery

премия /prémiia/ f. bonus

премьер /prem'ér/ m. prime minister, premier

премьера /prem'éra/ f. first night

преподаватель /prepodavátel'/ m. teacher, lecturer

препятствие /prepiátstvie/ n. obstacle; hindrance

преследовать /preslédovat'/ v. chase; persecute

пресный /présnyi/ adj. fresh (water); unsalted; insipid

пресса /préssa/ f. the press

престиж /prestízh/ m. prestige

преступление /prestuplénie/ n. crime

преступник /prestúpnik/ m. criminal

претензия /preténziia/ f. claim; complaint

преувеличивать /preuvelíchivat'/ v. exaggerate; overstate

преуменьшать /preumen'shát'/ v. underestimate

преуспевать /preuspevát'/ v. succeed (in); prosper

при /pri/ prep. by; with
прибавлять /pribavliát'/ v. add; increase
приближение /priblizhénie/ n. approach
приблизительный /priblizítel'nyi/ adj. rough
прибор /pribór/ m. device
прибрежный /pribrézhnyi/ adj. coastal
прибыль /príbyl'/ f. profit
прибытие /pribýtie/ n. arrival
привет /privét/ m. greetings
приветливый /privétlivyi/ adj. amiable
приветствовать /privétstvovat'/ v. greet; welcome; salute
прививка /privívka/ f. vaccination
привилегия /privilégiia/ f. privilege
привлекать /privlekát'/ v. attract; draw
приводить /privodít'/ v. bring; lead
привыкать /privykát'/ v. get accustomed (to)
привычка /privýchka/ f. habit
привязывать /priviázyvat'/ v. tie (to); fasten
приглашать /priglashát'/ v. invite
приговор /prigovór/ m. sentence
приготавливать /prigotávlivat'/ v. prepare; make
придумывать /pridúmyvat'/ v. invent; make up
приезжать /priezzhát'/ v. arrive; come
прием /priióm/ m. reception; admission; method
приемный /priiómnyi/ adj. reception; adopted; п. экзамен
   /p. ekzámen/ entrance examination; п. отец /p. otéts/
   foster-father
прижимать /prizhimát'/ v. press; restrict; hold tight
приз /priz/ m. prize

признавать /priznavát'/ v. recognize; admit

признаваться /priznavát'sia/ v. confess (to)

признак /príznak/ m. sign

призывать /prizyvát'/ v. call; appeal

приказывать /prikázyvat'/ v. order

прикасаться /prikasát'sia/ v. touch

приклеивать /prikléivat'/ v. stick, paste

приключение /prikliuchénie/ n. adventure

приковывать /prikóvyvat'/ v. chain

прилавок /prilávok/ m. counter

прилетать /priletát'/ v. arrive (by air); fly (in)

прилив /prilív/ m. rising tide

приличный /prilíchnyi/ adj. respectable; decent; passable

приложение /prilozhénie/ n. supplement

применение /primenénie/ n. use

применять /primeniát'/ v. apply; use

пример /primér/ m. example; instance; model

примерка /primérka/ f. fitting

примерять /primeriát'/ v. try on

примочка /primóchka/ f. lotion

принадлежать /prinadlezhát'/ v. belong (to)

принимать /prinimát'/ v. accept; receive; take over

приносить /prinosit'/ v. bring; carry

принудительный /prinudítel'nyi/ adj. compulsory

принцип /príntsip/ m. principle

приобретать /priobretát'/ v. acquire; gain

припадок /pripádok/ m. fit, attack

приправа /pripráva/ f. seasoning

природа /priróda/ f. nature

прирожденный /prirozhdiónnyi/ adj. innate

присваивать /prisváivat'/ v. appropriate; confer

присоединять /prisoediniát'/ v. joint; add; connect; annex

приспособление /prisposoblénie/ n. adjustment; device

пристальный /prístal'nyi/ adj. intent; fixed

пристань /prístan'/ f. pier

пристрастный /pristrástnyi/ adj. partial, biased

приступ /prístup/ m. storm; attack, fit

присутствие /prisútstvie/ n. presence

присылать /prisylát'/ v. send

притворяться /pritvoriát'sia/ v. feign, simulate; pretend (to be)

приток /pritók/ m. tributary; п. воздуха /p. vózdukha/ flow of air

притрагиваться /pritrágivat'sia/ v. touch

приход /prikhód/ m. arrival; receipts; parish

приходить /prikhodít'/ v. come; arrive

прихожая /prikhózhaia/ f. entrance hall, anteroom

прицеливаться /pritsélivat'sia/ v. take aim

прическа /prichóska/ f. hair-do

причесывать /prichósyvat'/ v. do smb.'s hair

причина /prichína/ f. cause; reason

причинять /prichiniát'/ v. cause; inflict

причуда /prichúda/ f. whim; caprice

пришивать /prishivát'/ v. sew (to)

прищуривать /prishchúrivat'/ v. screw up (eyes)

приютить /priiutít'/ v. shelter

приятель /priiátel'/ m. friend

приятный /priiátnyi/ adj. pleasant

про /pro/ prep. about

проба /próba/ f. test

пробел /probél/ m. gap; blank

пробивать /probivát'/ v. make a hole; pierce

пробиться /probít'sia/ v. force one's way (through)

пробка /próbka/ f. cork; traffic jam; fuse (electr.)

проблема /probléma/ f. problem

пробный /próbnyi/ adj. trial; п. камень /p. kámen'/ touchstone

пробовать /próbovat'/ v. try; taste

пробор /probór/ m. parting (of the hair)

пробуждать /probuzhdát'/ v. (a)rouse; awaken

провал /provál/ m. collapse; failure

проверять /proveriát'/ v. check; test; inspect

проветривать /provétrivat'/ v. air

провиниться /provinít'sia/ v. be guilty (of)

провинциальный /provintsiál'nyi/ adj. provincial

провод /próvod/ m. wire; wiring

проводник /provodník/ m. conductor; guide

провожать /provozhát'/ v. see off

провозглашать /provozglashát'/ v. declare; proclaim

провозить /provozít'/ v. get through; carry

проволока /próvoloka/ f. wire

проворный /provórnyi/ adj. quick, brisk

провоцировать /provotsírovat'/ v. provoke (to)

прогноз /prognóz/ m. forecast

программа /prográmma/ f. program

прогресс /progréss/ m. progress

прогулка /progúlka/ f. walk

продавать /prodavát'/ v. sell

продавец /prodavéts/ m. shop assistant

продвигаться /prodvigát'sia/ v. advance; get on; make progress

продлевать /prodlevát'/ v. prolong

продовольствие /prodovól'stvie/ n. foodstuffs; provisions

продолжать /prodolzhát'/ v. continue

продолжительный /prodolzhítel'nyi/ adj. long; protracted

продукт /prodúkt/ m. product; foodstuffs

продукция /prodúktsiia/ f. output

проезд /proézd/ m. passage, thoroughfare

проезжать /proezzhát'/ v. pass by; drive; go through

проект /proékt/ m. project; design

прожектор /prozhéktor/ m. searchlight

проживать /prozhivát'/ v. live; reside

проза /próza/ f. prose

прозрачный /prozráchnyi/ adj. transparent

проигрыватель /proígryvatel'/ m. record-player

проигрывать /proígryvat'/ v. lose

проигрыш /próigrysh/ m. loss; defeat

произведение /proizvedénie/ n. work

производительность /proizvodítel'nost'/ f. productivity

производить /proizvodít'/ v. produce

производственный /proizvódstvennyi/ adj. industrial

производство /proizvódstvo/ n. production

произвольный /proizvól'nyi/ adj. arbitrary

произношение /proiznoshénie/ n. pronunciation

происходить /proiskhodít'/ v. occur, happen

происшествие /proisshéstvie/ n. incident; accident

прокат /prokát/ m. hire; rolling

проклинать /proklinát'/ v. curse

проклятие /prokliátie/ n. curse

прокурор /prokurór/ m. public prosecutor

пролезать /prolezát'/ v. climb through; worm oneself into

пролетать /proletát'/ v. fly (past); fly by

пролив /prolív/ m. strait(s)

промах /prómakh/ m. miss; blunder

промежуток /promezhútok/ m. interval

промчаться /promchát'sia/ v. rush past

промышленность /promýshlennost'/ f. industry

пронзительный /pronzítel'nyi/ adj. piercing; shrill

проницательный /pronitsátel'nyi/ adj. acute; sharp; perspicacious

пропадать /propadát'/ v. be lost; perish; disappear

пропажа /propázha/ f. loss

пропасть /propást'/ f. precipice; abyss

прописка /propíska/ f. registration; residence permit

проповедник /propovédnik/ m. preacher

проповедь /própoved'/ f. sermon

пропорция /propórtsiia/ f. proportion

пропуск /própusk/ m. pass (document)

пропускать /propuskát'/ v. let through; miss

пророк /prorók/ m. prophet

прорубь /prórub'/ f. ice-hole

прорыв /prorýv/ m. breech; breakthrough

просвечивать /prosvéchivat'/ v. X-ray; be transparent

просвещение /prosvéshchenie/ n. enlightenment; education

просить /prosít'/ v. ask; beg; request

прослушивать /proslúshivat'/ v. listen; hear

просо /próso/ v. millet

проспект /prospékt/ m. avenue; prospectus

простительный /prostítel'nyi/ adj. excusable

простодушный /prostodúshnyi/ adj. artless, unsophisticated

простой /prostói/ adj. simple; common

простокваша /prostokvásha/ f. sour clotted milk

просторный /prostórnyi/ adj. spacious, roomy

простуда /prostúda/ f. chill, cold

проступок /prostúpok/ m. offence; misdemeanour

простывать /prostyvát'/ v. catch a chill

простыня /prostyniá/ f. sheet

просушивать /prosúshivat'/ v. dry

просыпать /prosypát'/ v. spill

просыпаться /prosypát'sia/ v. wake up

просьба /prós'ba/ f. request

протез /protéz/ m. artificial limb; зубной п. /zubnói p./ denture

протеин /proteín/ m. protein

протест /protést/ m. protest

протестант /protestánt/ m. Protestant

против /prótiv/ prep. opposite; against; contrary to

противник /protívnik/ m. opponent; enemy

противный /protívnyi/ adj. contrary; nasty

противозачаточное (средство) /protivozachátochnoe srédstvo/ adj. + n. contraceptive противоположный /protivopolózhnyi/ adj. opposite; contrary

противоречие /protivoréchie/ n. contradiction

протокол /protokól/ m. protocol

протягивать /protiágivat'/ v. extend; stretch

профессия /proféssiia/ f. profession

профиль /prófil'/ m. profile

профсоюз /profsoiúz/ m. trade union

прохладный /prokhládnyi/ adj. cool; fresh

проход /prokhód/ m. passage

проходить /prokhodít'/ v. go; pass (through, by)

прохожий /prokhózhii/ m. passer-by

процедура /protsedúra/ f. procedure

процент /protsént/ m. percentage

процесс /protséss/ m. process; trial

прочий /próchii/ adj. other

прочитывать /prochítyvat'/ v. read (through)

прочный /próchnyi/ adj. durable

прочь /proch/ adv. away; руки п.! /rúki p.!/ hands off!

прошлое /próshloe/ n. the past

прощай /proshchái/ interj. good-bye

прощать /proshchát'/ v. forgive

прощаться /proshchát'sia/ v. say good-bye (to)

пруд /prud/ m. pond

пружина /pruzhína/ f. spring

прут /prut/ m. twig

прыгать /prýgat'/ v. jump, leap; skip

прыщ /pryshch/ m. pimple

прядь /priád'/ f. lock (of hair)

пряжа /priázha/ f. yarn

пряжка /priázhka/ f. buckle

прямой /priamói/ adj. straight; direct

пряник /priánik/ m. gingerbread

прятать /priátat'/ v. hide, conceal

прятки /priátki/ pl. hide-and-seek

псевдоним /psevdoním/ m. pseudonym

психиатр /psikhiátr/ m. psychiatrist

птенец /ptenéts/ m. fledgeling

птица /ptítsa/ f. bird

публика /públika/ f. public; audience

публиковать /publikovát'/ v. publish

пугать /pugát'/ v. frighten, scare; alarm

пуговица /púguvotsa/ f. button

пудель /púdel'/ m. poodle

пудинг /púding/ m. pudding

пудра /púdra/ f. powder

пудреница /púdrenitsa/ f. powder-case

пузырь /puzýr'/ m. bubble

пульверизатор /pul'verizátor/ m. spray

пульс /pul's/ m. pulse

пульт /pul't/ m. control panel

пуля /púlia/ f. bullet

пункт /punkt/ m. point; spot; item

пуп(ок) /pup(ók)/ m. navel

пуск /pusk/ m. start

пускать /puskát'/ v. let; set in motion; start

пустыня /pustýnia/ f. desert

пустяк /pustiák/ m. trifle

путаница /pútanitsa/ f. confusion

путать /pútat'/ v. tangle; mix up; confuse

путеводитель /putevodítel'/ m. guide

путешествие /puteshéstvie/ n. journey, voyage; trip

путь /put'/ m. way; path; route; course

пух /pukh/ m. down

пучок /puchók/ m. bunch

пушистый /pushístyi/ adj. fluffy

пушка /púshka/ f. cannon; gun

пчела /pchelá/ f. bee

пшеница /pshenítsa/ f. wheat

пшено /pshenó/ n. millet

пылать /pylát'/ v. flame; blaze

пылесос /pylesós/ m. vacuum cleaner

пыль /pyl'/ f. dust

пытать /pytát'/ v. torture; torment

пышный /pýshnyi/ adj. fluffy; thick; plump; luxuriant

пьеса /p'ésa/ f. play

пьянеть /p'ianét'/ v. be (get) drunk

пьяница /p'iánitsa/ m. and f. drunkard

пятиться /plátit'sia/ v. back away; retreat

пятка /piátka/ f. heel

пятнадцать /piatnádtsat'/ num. fifteen

пятница /piátnitsa/ f. Friday

пятно /piatnó/ n. spot, stain

пять /piát'/ num. five

пятьдесят /piat'desiát/ num. fifty

пятьсот /piat'sót/ num. five hundred

Р

раб /rab/ m. slave

работа /rabóta/ f. work; job

работать /rabótat'/ v. work; operate

работоспособный /rabotosposóbnyi/ adj. able-bodied

рабочий /rabóchii/ m. worker

раввин /ravvín/ m. rabbi

равенство /rávenstvo/ n. equality

равнина /ravnína/ f. plain

равно /ravnó/ adv. equally, alike; все р. /vsió r./ it's all the
  same

равнодушие /ravnodúshie/ n. indifference

равноправие /ravnoprávie/ n. equality

равный /rávnyi/ adj. equal

ради /rádi/ prep. for the sake (of)

радио /rádio/ n. radio

радиоактивный /radioaktívnyi/ adj. radioactive

радиовещание /radioveshchánie/ n. broadcasting

радиостанция /radiostántsiia/ f. radio station

радиус /rádius/ m. radius

радоваться /rádovat'sia/ v. rejoice (at)

радостный /rádostnyi/ adj. joyful

радость /rádost'/ f. gladness; joy

радуга /ráduga/ f. rainbow

раз /raz/ m. time; one; один р. /odín r./ once; два раза /dva
  ráza/ twice

разбавлять /razbavliát'/ v. dilute

разбивать /razbivát'/ break; smash; defeat

разваливаться /razválivat'sia/ v. fall to pieces

разве /rázve/ part. really; perhaps

разведенный /razvedіónnyi/ adj. divorced

разведка /razvédka/ f. exploring; intelligence service; reconnaissance

развернутый /razvіórnutyi/ adj. unfolded; detailed; full-scale

развивать /razvivát'/ v. develop

развитие /razvítie/ n. development

развлекать /razvlekát'/ v. entertain

развод /razvód/ m. divorce

развращать /razvrashchát'/ v. corrupt

разгадка /razgádka/ f. clue

разглаживать /razglázhivat'/ v. smooth out; iron out

разговаривать /razgovárivat'/ v. talk; speak

разговор /razgovór/ m. conversation; talk

разгонять /razgoniát'/ v. disperse; drive away

разгром /razgróm/ m. crushing; defeat; devastation

раздавать /razdavát'/ v. give out

раздача /razdácha/ f. distribution

раздевалка /razdeválka/ f. cloak-room

раздевать /razdevát'/ v. undress; strip

раздел /razdél/ m. division; part

раздор /razdór/ m. discord

разлагать /razlagát'/ v. decompose; demoralize

разлад /razlád/ m. discord

разливать /razlivát'/ v. spill; pour out

различать /razlichát'/ v. make out; distinguish

различие /razlíchie/ n. difference; distinction

разлука /razlúka/ f. separation; parting

размах /razmákh/ m. scope

размахивать /razmákhivat'/ v. brandish; p. руками /r. rukámi/ wave one's hands about

разменивать /razménivat'/ v. change (money)

размер /razmér/ m. size

размещать /razmeshchát'/ v. accommodate; place

разминка /razmínka/ f. warming up; workout

размягчать /razmiagchát'/ v. soften

разнимать /raznimát'/ v. part, separate; disjoint

разница /ráznitsa/ f. difference

разнообразие /raznoobrázie/ n. variety; diversity

разноцветный /raznotsvétnyi/ adj. variegated; multi-coloured

разнузданный /raznúzdannyi/ adj. unbridled; wild

разный /ráznyi/ adj. different; varied

разоблачать /razoblachát'/ v. expose

разогревать /razogrevát'/ v. heat up; warm up

разоружать /razoruzhát'/ v. disarm

разочаровывать /razocharóvyvat'/ v. disappoint; disillusion

разрезать /razrezát'/ v. cut

разрешать /razreshát'/ v. allow; permit; let

разрешение /razreshénie/ v. permission

разрушать /razrushát'/ v. destroy; demolish; ruin, wreck

разрыв /razrýv/ m. break; rupture

разрыдаться /razrydát'sia/ v. burst into tears

разряд /razriád/ m. grade; type; category

разубеждать /razubezhdát'/ v. dissuade

разум /rázum/ m. reason; mind

разъединять /raz''ediniát'/ v. separate; disconnect

разъяснять /raz''iasniát'/ v. elucidate; make clear

рай /rai/ m. paradise

район /raión/ m. region; district; area

рак /rak/ m. crayfish; cancer

ракета /rakéta/ f. rocket; missile

ракетка /rakétka/ f. racket; bat

раковина /rákovina/ f. shell; sink

рамка /rámka/ f. frame; framework

рана /rána/ f. wound

ранг /rang/ m. rank

ранить /ránit'/ v. wound; injure

ранний /ránnii/ adj. early

раньше /rán'she/ adv. earlier

рапортовать /raportovát'/ v. report

раса /rása/ f. race

расизм /rasízm/ m. racism

раскаиваться /raskáivat'sia/ v. repent

раскаяние /raskáianie/ n. repentance

раскладывать /raskládyvat'/ v. lay out

раскрашивать /raskráshivat'/ v. paint

раскрывать /raskryvát'/ v. open; expose; reveal

распад /raspád/ m. disintegration; decay

распахивать /raspákhivat'/ v. plough up; throw open

расписание /raspisánie/ n. timetable

расписка /raspíska/ f. receipt

расписываться /raspísyvat'sia/ v. sign; register one's
  marriage

расплата /raspláta/ f. payment; punishment

распоряжение /rasporiazhénie/ n. instruction; order

расправа /raspráva/ f. reprisals

распределять /raspredeliát'/ v. distribute; allocate; assign

распродавать /rasprodavát'/ v. sell out

распродажа /rasprodázha/ f. sale

распространять /rasprostraniát'/ v. spread, distribute

распускать /raspuskát'/ v. dissolve; dismiss; undo

распутывать /raspútyvat'/ v. unravel

распятие /raspiátie/ n. crucifix; crucifixion

рассада /rassáda/ v. seedlings

рассвет /rassvét/ m. dawn

рассеянный /rasséiannyi/ adj. absent-minded

рассказ /rasskáz/ m. story, tale

рассказывать /rasskázyvat'/ v. tell; narrate

расследовать /rasslédovat'/ v. investigate; inquire

рассматривать /rassmátrivat'/ v. regard; look at; examine; consider

рассмеяться /rassmeiát'sia/ v. burst out laughing

расспрашивать /rasspráshivat'/ v. question; make enquiries

рассрочка /rassróchka/ f. instalment; купить в рассрочку /kupít' v rassróchku/ buy in instalments

расставаться /rasstavát'sia/ v. part (with); quit

расстегивать /rasstiógivat'/ v. undo; unfasten

расстояние /rasstoiánie/ n. distance

расстраивать /rasstráivat'/ v. disorganize; upset

расстреливать /rasstrélivat'/ v. shoot

рассудительный /rassudítel'nyi/ adj. sober-minded; rational

рассудок /rassúdok/ m. reason

рассуждение /rassuzhdénie/ n. reasoning

рассчитывать /rasschítyvat'/ v. calculate; count (on), plan

раствор /rastvór/ m. solution

растение /rasténie/ n. plant

растерянный /rastériannyi/ adj. bewildered; confused

расти /rastí/ v. grow (up); increase

растительный /rastítel'nyi/ adj. vegetable

растить /rastít'/ v. raise; grow

расторгать /rastorgát'/ v. cancel

растрата /rastráta/ f. embezzlement

растягивать /rastiágivat'/ v. stretch; strain

расход /raskhód/ m. expense(s); expenditure; consumption

расцветать /rastsvetát'/ v. bloom; flourish

расческа /raschóska/ f. comb

расчет /rashchót/ m. calculation; settling

расширять /rasshiriát'/ v. widen; broaden; expand

расщеплять /rasshchepliát'/ v. split

ратификация /ratifikátsiia/ f. ratification

ратуша /rátusha/ f. town hall

раунд /ráund/ m. round (sport)

рафинад /rafinád/ m. lump sugar

рвота /rvóta/ f. vomiting

реабилитировать /reabilitírovat'/ v. rehabilitate

реагировать /reagírovat'/ v. react (to); respond

реактивный /reaktívnyi/ adj. jet

реакционер /reaktsionér/ m. reactionary

реализм /realízm/ m. realism

реальный /reál'nyi/ adj. real; actual

ребенок /rebiónok/ m. child; baby; infant

ребро /rebró/ n. rib

рев /riov/ m. roar

реветь /revét'/ v. roar; howl

ревизия /revíziia/ f. revision

ревматизм /revmatízm/ m. rheumatism

ревновать /revnovát'/ v. be jealous

револьвер /revol'vér/ m. revolver

регистрация /regustrátsiia/ f. registration

регулировать /regulírovat'/ v. regulate; control

регулярный /reguliárnyi/ adj. regular

редактор /redáktor/ m. editor

редиска /redíska/ f. radish

редкий /rédkii/ adj. thin; rare

режим /rezhím/ m. regime

режиссер /rezhissiór/ m. producer

резать /rézat'/ v. cut

резерв /rezérv/ m. reserve(s)

резина /rezína/ f. rubber

резинка /resínka/ f. eraser

резкий /rézkii/ adj. sharp; harsh

результат /rezul'tát/ m. result

рейс /réis/ m. trip; voyage

река /reká/ f. river

реклама /rekláma/ f. advertisement

рекламировать /reklamírovat'/ v. advertise

рекомендация /rekomendátsiia/ f. reference

рекомендовать /rekomendovát'/ v. recommend

реконструировать /reconstruírovat'/ v. reconstruct

рекорд /rekórd/ m. record

ректор /réktor/ m. rector

религия /relígiia/ f. religion

ремень /remén'/ m. belt; р. безопасности /r. bezopásnosti/ safety belt

ремесленник /reméslennik/ m. craftsman

ремешок /remeshók/ m. strap

ремонт /remónt/ m. repair(s)

рента /rénta/ f. rent

рентген /rentgén/ m. X-ray

репа /répa/ f. turnip

репертуар /repertuár/ m. repertoire

репетиция /repetítsiia/ f. rehearsal

репортер /reportiór/ m. reporter

репрессия /représsiia/ f. repression

репродуктор /reprodúktor/ m. loudspeaker

репутация /reputátsiia/ f. reputation

ресница /resnítsa/ f. eyelash

республика /respúblika/ f. republic

реставрировать /restavrírovat'/ v. restore

ресторан /restorán/ m. restaurant

ресурс /resúrs/ m. resource

реформа /refórma/ f. reform

рецепт /retsépt/ m. prescription; recipe

речь /rech/ f. speech; talk

решать /reshát'/ v. decide; resolve

решетка /reshótka/ f. grating; bars

решительный /reshítel'nyi/ adj. resolute

ржаветь /rzhavét'/ v. rust

ржаной /rzhanói/ adj. rye

рис /ris/ m. rice

риск /risk/ m. risk

рискнуть /risknút'/ v. take a risk; venture

рисовать /risovát'/ v. draw; paint

рисунок /risúnok/ m. drawing

ритм /ritm/ m. rhythm

рифма /rífma/ f. rhyme

робкий /róbkii/ adj. shy

ров /rov/ m. ditch

ровесник /rovésnik/ m. person of the same age

ровный /róvnyi/ adj. even; level; smooth; straight

рог /rog/ m. horn

род /rod/ m. family; kin; gender; р. человеческий /r. chelovécheskii/ mankind

родильный (дом) /rodíl'nyi dom/ adj.+m. maternity home

родина /ródina/ f. homeland

родинка /ródinka/ f. birthmark

родители /rodíteli/ pl. parents

родить /rodít'/ v. give birth to

родиться /rodít'sia/ v. be born

родник /rodník/ m. spring

родной /rodnói/ adj. native

родня /rodniá/ f. relative(s); relations

родственник /ródstvennik/ m. relative

роды /ródy/ pl. childbirth; labour

рождение /rozhdénie/ n. birth; день рождения /den' rozhdéniia/ birthday рождество /rozhdestvó/ n. Christmas

рожь /rozh/ f. rye

роза /róza/ f. rose

розетка /rozétka/ f. electric socket

розничная (торговля) /róznichnaia torgóvlia/ adj. + f. retail trade

розовый /rózovyi/ adj. pink

роль /rol'/ f. role; part

ром /rom/ m. rum

роман /román/ m. novel; love affair

ромашка /romáshka/ f. camomile

ронять /roniát'/ v. drop

роса /rosá/ f. dew

рост /rost/ m. growth; height

ростбиф /róstbif/ m. roast beef

росток /rostók/ m. sprout; shoot

рот /rot/ m. mouth

рота /róta/ f. company

роща /róshcha/ f. grove

рояль /roiál'/ m. grand piano

ртуть /rtut'/ f. mercury

рубашка /rubáshka/ f. shirt

рубеж /rubézh/ m. boundary; за рубежом /za rubezhóm/ abroad

рубин /rubín/ m. ruby

рубить /rubít'/ v. chop; fell

рубленый /rúblenyi/ adj. minced

рубль /rubl'/ m. rouble

ругань /rúgan'/ f. foul language

ругать /rugát'/ v. abuse

руда /rudá/ f. ore

ружье /ruzh'ió/ n. gun

рука /ruká/ f. hand; arm

рукав /rukáv/ m. sleeve

рукавица /rukavítsa/ f. mitten

руководитель /rukovodítel'/ m. leader; head

руководить /rukovodít'/ v. lead; direct; head; guide

рукоятка /rukoiátka/ f. handle

руль /rul'/ m. steering-wheel

румяна /rumiána/ pl. rouge

румяный /rumiányi/ adj. rosy; ruddy

русалка /rusálka/ f. mermaid

русский /rússkii/ adj. Russian

ручей /ruchéi/ m. brook

ручка /rúchka/ f. pen

рыба /rýba/ f. fish

рыбак /rybák/ m. fisherman

рыжий /rýzhii/ adj. red, red-haired

рынок /rýnok/ m. market

рыть /ryt'/ v. dig

рычаг /rychág/ m. lever

рюкзак /riukzák/ m. rucksack

рюмка /riúmka/ f. wineglass

рябина /riabína/ f. rowan

ряд /riad/ m. row; line

рядовой /riadovói/ adj. ordinary; m. private (soldier)

рядом /riádom/ adv. side by side; close by

С

с /s/ prep. with

сабля /sáblia/ f. sabre

сад /sad/ m. garden

садиться /sadít'sia/ v. sit down

сажа /sázha/ f. soot

сажать /sazhát'/ v. seat; land; put under arrest

сазан /sazán/ m. carp

салака /saláka/ f. sprat

салат /salát/ m. salad

сало /sálo/ n. fat; lard

салон /salón/ m. saloon

салфетка /salfétka/ f. napkin

салют /saliút/ m. salute

сам /sam/ pron. himself

сама /samá/ pron. herself

самец /saméts/ m. male

сами /sámi/ pron. ourselves, yourselves, themselves

самка /sámka/ f. female

само /samó/ pron. itself

самодельный /samodél'nyi/ adj. homemade

самолет /samoliót/ m. aircraft, plane

самолюбивый /samoliubívyi/ adj. proud, touchy

самообслуживание /samoobslúzhivanie/ n. self-service

самоопределение /samoopredelénie/ self-determination

самоотверженный /samootvérzhennyi/ adj. selfless

самосвал /samosvál/ m. tip-up lorry

самостоятельный /samostoiátel'nyi/ adj. independent

самоубийство /samoubíistvo/ n. suicide

самоуверенный /samouvérennyi/ adj. self-confident

самоуправление /samoupravlénie/ n. self-government

самоучитель /samouchítel'/ m. teach-yourself manual

самоцвет /samotsvét/ m. semi-precious stone

самый /sámyi/ pron. (the) very; (the) most

санаторий /sanatórii/ m. sanatorium

сандалии /sandálii/ pl. sandals

санитар /sanitár/ m. medical orderly

сантиметр /santimétr/ m. centimetre

сапог /sapóg/ m. boot; top-boot

сапожник /sapózhnik/ m. shoemaker

сапфир /sapfír/ m. sapphire

сарай /sarái/ m. shed

сарделька /sardél'ka/ f. frankfurter

сардина /sardína/ f. sardine

сатана /sataná/ m. Satan

сатин /satín/ m. sateen

сатира /satíra/ f. satire

сахар /sákhar/ m. sugar

сбербанк /sberbánk/ abbr., m. savings bank

сбоку /sbóku/ adv. on one side

сборник /sbórnik/ m. collection

свадьба /svád'ba/ f. wedding

свалка /sválka/ f. scrap-heap

сведения /svédeniia/ pl. information

свежий /svézhii/ adj. fresh

свекла /sviókla/ f. beet; сахарная с. /sákharnaia s./ sugar-beet свекор /sviókor/ m. father-in-law (husband's father)

свекровь /svekróv'/ f. mother-in-law (husband's mother)

свергать /svergát'/ v. overthrow

сверкать /sverkát'/ v. sparkle

сверлить /sverlít'/ v. drill

сверток /sviórtok/ m. bundle

свертывать /sviórtyvat'/ v. roll up

сверху /svérkhu/ adv. from above

сверхъестественный /sverkh''estéstvennyi/ adj. supernatural

сверчок /sverchók/ m. cricket

свершаться /svershát'sia/ v. be fulfilled

свет /svet/ m. light; society, beau monde

светлый /svétlyi/ adj. light

светофор /svetofór/ m. traffic light(s)

свеча /svechá/ f. candle

свидание /svidánie/ n. meeting; date; до свидания /do svidániia/ good-bye

свидетель /svidétel'/ m. witness

свидетельство /svidétel'stvo/ n. evidence

свинец /svinéts/ m. lead

свинина /svinína/ f. pork

свинка /svínka/ f. mumps

свинья /svin'iá/ f. pig; swine

свирепый /svirépyi/ adj. ferocious

свисать /svisát'/ v. dangle, droop

свистеть /svistét'/ v. whistle

свитер /svíter/ m. sweater

свобода /svobóda/ f. freedom, liberty

своевременный /svoevrémennyi/ adj. timely

своеобразный /svoeobráznyi/ adj. peculiar

свой /svoi/ pron. one's own

свойство /svóistvo/ n. property, attribute

сволочь /svóloch/ f. riff-raff, rascal

свора /svóra/ f. pack

связка /sviázka/ f. bunch

связывать /sviázyvat'/ v. tie

связь /sviáz'/ f. communication(s); link; relation

святой /sviatói/ adj. holy; saint

священник /sviashchénnik/ m. priest

сгорать /sgorát'/ v. burn down

сгущенное (молоко) /sgushchónnoe molokó/ adj. + n. condensed milk

сдача /sdácha/ f. surrender; change (money)

сделка /sdélka/ f. deal

сдельный /sdél'nyi/ adj. piecework

сдерживать /sdérzhivat'/ v. hold back

сдоба /sdóba/ f. fancy bread, bun(s)

сеанс /seáns/ m. show; sitting

себестоимость /sebestóimost'/ f. cost price

себя /sebiá/ pron. oneself

себялюбивый /sebialiubívyi/ adj. selfish, self-loving

сев /sev/ m. sowing

север /séver/ m. north

северо-восток /sévero-vostók/ m. north-east

северо-запад /sévero-západ/ m. north-west

севрюга /sevriúga/ f. sturgeon

сегодня /sevódnia/ adv. today

седло /sedló/ n. saddle
седой /sedói/ adj. grey
сезон /sezón/ m. season
сейф /séif/ m. safe
сейчас /seichás/ adv. (right) now
секрет /sekrét/ m. secret
секретарь /secretár'/ m. secretary
секта /sékta/ f. sect
сектор /séktor/ m. sector
секунда /sekúnda/ f. second
селедка /seliódka/ f. herring
селезенка /seleziónka/ f. spleen
селезень /sélezen'/ m. drake
село /seló/ n. village
сельдерей /sel'deréi/ m. celery
сельский /sél'skii/ adj. rural; сельское хозяйство
   /sél'skoe khoziáistvo/ agriculture
семга /siómga/ f. salmon
семинар /seminár/ m. seminar
семнадцать /semnádtsat'/ num. seventeen
семь /sem'/ num. seven
семьдесят /sém'desiat/ num. seventy
семьсот /sem'sót/ num. seven hundred
семья /sem'iá/ f. family
семя /sémia/ n. seed; sperm
сенат /senát/ m. senate
сенатор /senátor/ m. senator
сено /séno/ n. hay
сенсация /sensátsiia/ f. sensation

сентиментальный /sentimentál'nyi/ adj. sentimental

сентябрь /sentiábr'/ m. September

сера /séra/ f. sulphur; ear-wax

сервиз /servíz/ m. service, set

сердечный /serdéchnyi/ adj. heart; cardiac; cordial

сердитый /serdítyi/ adj. angry

сердце /sérdtse/ n. heart

сердцевина /serdtsevína/ f. core

серебро /serebró/ n. silver

середина /seredína/ f. middle

сержант /serzhánt/ m. sergeant

серия /sériia/ f. series

сертификат /sertifikát/ m. certificate

серый /séryi/ adj. grey

серьга /ser'gá/ f. earring

серьезный /ser'ióznyi/ adj. serious

сессия /séssiia/ f. session

сестра /sestrá/ f. sister

сеть /set'/ f. net

сеять /séiat'/ v. sow

сжигать /szhigát'/ v. burn down

сжимать /szhimát'/ v. squeeze

сжиматься /szhimát'sia/ v. shrink

сзади /szádi/ adv. behind; from behind

сигара /sigára/ f. cigar

сигарета /sigaréta/ f. cigarette

сигнал /signál/ m. signal

сиделка /sidélka/ f. nurse

сиденье /sidén'e/ n. seat

сидеть /sidét'/ v. sit

сидр /sidr/ m. cider

сила /síla/ f. strength; power, force

сильный /síl'nyi/ adj. strong

симфония /simfóniia/ f. symphony

синагога /sinagóga/ f. synagogue

синий /sínii/ adj. blue

синица /sinítsa/ f. tomtit

синяк /siniák/ m. bruise; с. под глазом /s. pod glázom/
    black eye

сирень /sirén'/ f. lilac

сироп /siróp/ m. syrup

сирота /sirotá/ m. and f. orphan

система /sistéma/ f. system

ситец /sítets/ m. (printed) cotton; chintz

сито /síto/ n. sieve

ситуация /situátsiia/ f. situation

сиять /siiát'/ v. shine

сказка /skázka/ f. fairy-tale

скакать /skakát'/ v. jump; gallop

скала /skalá/ f. rock

скалка /skálka/ f. rolling pin

скамья /skam'iá/ f. bench

скандал /skandál/ m. scandal

скарлатина /skarlatína/ f. scarlet fever

скатерть /skátert'/ f. tablecloth

скачки /skáchki/ pl. horse race

сквер /skver/ m. public garden; park

сквозняк /skvozniák/ m. draught

сквозь /skvoz'/ prep. through

скворец /skvoréts/ m. starling

скелет /skelét/ m,. skeleton

скептик /sképtik/ m. sceptic

скидка /skídka/ f. discount

скипидар /skipidár/ m. turpentine

скисать /skisát'/ v. go sour

склад /sklad/ m. warehouse

складывать /skládyvat'/ v. put together, add; fold up

склон /sklon/ m. slope

скобка /skóbka/ f. bracket

сковорода /skovorodá/ f. frying pan

скользить /skol'zít'/ v. slide

скользкий /skól'zkii/ adj. slippery

сколько /skól'ko/ adv. how much, how many

скорлупа /skorlupá/ f. shell

скоро /skóro/ adv. quickly

скоропортящийся /skoropórtiashchiisia/ adj. perishable

скорость /skórost'/ f. speed

скот /skot/ m. cattle; beast, swine

скрепка /skrépka/ f. clip

скрипеть /skripét'/ v. creak

скрипка /skrípka/ f. violin

скромный /skrómnyi/ adj. modest

скрывать /skryvát'/ v. conceal

скука /skúka/ f. boredom

скула /skúla/ f. cheekbone

скульптор /skúl'ptor/ m. sculptor

скумбрия /skúmbriia/ f. mackerel

скупой /skupói/ adj. miserly
скучать /skuchát'/ v. be bored; miss
скучный /skúchnyi/ adj. tedious
слабительное /slabítel'noe/ n. laxative
слабый /slábyi/ adj. weak
слава /sláva/ f. fame
славянский /slaviánskii/ adj. Slav; Slavonic
сладкий /sládkii/ adj. sweet
сладкое /sládkoe/ n. dessert
слева /sléva/ adv. from the left
слегка /slegká/ adv. slightly
след /sled/ m. track; footstep; trace
следить /sledít'/ v. watch
следователь /slédovatel'/ m. investigator
следующий /sléduiushchii/ adj. following
слеза /slezá/ f. tear
слезать /slezát'/ v. climb down
слепой /slepói/ adj. blind
слесарь /slésar'/ m. fitter; locksmith
слива /slíva/ f. plum
сливки /slívki/ pl. cream
слизистый /slízistyi/ adj. mucous
слиток /slítok/ m. bar, ingot
слишком /slíshkom/ adv. too; too much
словарь /slovár'/ m. dictionary
словно /slóvno/ adv. as if
слово /slóvo/ n. word; address
слог /slog/ m. syllable; style
сложение /slozhénie/ n. addition; build, constitution

слой /sloi/ m. layer

слон /slon/ m. elephant

слуга /slugá/ m. servant

служащий /slúzhashchii/ m. employee

служить /sluzhít'/ v. serve

слух /slukh/ m. hearing; rumour

случай /slúchai/ m. case; chance; несчастный с.
/neschástnyi s./ accident

случаться /sluchát'sia/ v. happen

слушать /slúshat'/ v. listen

слушаться /slúshat'sia/ v. obey

слышать /slýshat'/ v. hear

слюна /sliúna/ f. saliva

смазка /smázka/ f. lubrication

смелый /smélyi/ adj. bold

смена /sména/ f. change; shift

смерть /smert'/ f. death

смерч /smerch/ m. sandstorm; tornado

смесь /smes'/ f. mixture

сметана /smetána/ f. sour cream

сметь /smet'/ v. dare

смех /smekh/ m. laughter

смешивать /sméshivat'/ v. blend; confuse

смешной /smeshnói/ adj. funny

смеяться /smeiát'sia/ v. laugh

смирный /smírnyi/ adj. quiet; submissive; смирно!
/smírno/ attention!

смокинг /smóking/ m. dinner-jacket

смола /smolá/ f. resin

сморкаться /smorkát'sia/ v. blow one's nose

смородина /smoródina/ f. currants

сморщенный /smórshchennyi/ adj. wrinkled

смотр /smotr/ m. review

смотреть /smotrét'/ watch; look (at); look (after)

смутный /smútnyi/ adj. vague

смущать /smushchát'/ v. embarrass

смывать /smyvát'/ v. wash off

смысл /smysl/ m. sense

смычок /smychók/ m. bow

смягчать /smiagchát'/ v. soften

смятение /smiaténie/ n. confusion

смятый /smiátyi/ adj. rumpled

снабжать /snabzhát'/ v. supply

снаружи /snarúzhi/ adv. on the outside

снаряд /snariád/ m. shell

сначала /snachála/ adv. at first

снег /sneg/ m. snow

снегирь /snegír'/ m. bullfinch

снижать /snizhát'/ v. reduce; lower

снизу /snízy/ adv. from below

снимать /snimát'/ v. take away; photograph; lease, rent; cut
   (cards)

сниться /snít'sia/ v. dream

снова /snóva/ adv. again

снотворное /snotvórnoe/ n. sleeping pills

сноха /snokhá/ f. daughter-in-law

снятое (молоко) /sniátoe molokó/ adj. + n. skim milk

собака /sobáka/ f. dog

собирать /sobirát'/ v. collect

собираться /sobirát'sia/ v. gather

соблазнять /soblazniát'/ v. tempt; seduce

соблюдать /sobliudát'/ v. observe

соболь /sóbol'/ m. sable

собор /sobór/ m. cathedral

собрание /sobránie/ n. meeting

собственник /sóbstvennik/ m. proprietor; owner

собственность /sóbstvennost'/ f. property

событие /sobýtie/ n. event

сова /sová/ f. owl

совершать /sovershát'/ v. perform

совершеннолетний /sovershennolétnii/ adj. of age

совершенный /sovershénnyi/ adj. perfect

совесть /sóvest'/ f. conscience

совет /sovét/ m. advice; council

советовать /sovétovat'/ v. advise

советоваться /sovétovat'sia/ v. consult

совещание /soveshchánie/ n. conference

совмещать /sovmeshchát'/ v. combine

современный /sovreménnyi/ adj. contemporary

совсем /sovsém/ adv. entirely

соглашение /soglashénie/ n. agreement; treaty

сода /sóda/ f. soda

содержание /soderzhánie/ n. upkeep; content(s);
  substance

соединять /soediniát'/ v. connect, join, unite

сожалеть /sozhalét'/ v. regret, deplore

создавать /sozdavát'/ v. create

сознательный /soznátel'nyi/ adj. conscious

созревать /sozrevát'/ v. mature

созывать /sozyvát'/ v. summon; convene

сок /sok/ m. juice

сокол /sókol/ m. falcon

сокращать /sokrashchát'/ v. reduce

сокровище /sokróvishche/ n. treasure

солдат /soldát/ m. soldier

соленый /soliónyi/ adj. salted, pickled

солидный /solídnyi/ adj. solid; respectable

солить /solít'/ v. salt

солнце /sóntse/ n. sun

соло /sólo/ n. solo

соловей /solovéi/ m. nightingale

солод /sólod/ m. malt

солома /solóma/ f. straw

солонина /solonína/ f. corned beef

соль /sol'/ f. salt

сомневаться /somnevát'sia/ v. doubt

сон /son/ m. sleep, dream

соображать /soobrazhát'/ v. consider; understand

сообща /soobshchá/ adv. together

сообщать /soobshchát'/ v. communicate

сообщение /soobshchénie/ n. report

сообщество /soóbshchestvo/ n. community

сообщник /soóbshchnik/ m. accomplice

соотечественник /sootéchestvennik/ m. compatriot

соперник /sopérnik/ m. rival

соперничать /sopérnichat'/ v. compete, vie

сопливый /soplívyi/ adj. snotty

сопровождать /soprovozhdát'/ v. accompany

сопротивляться /soprotivliát'sia/ v. resist

соревнование /sorevnovánie/ n. competition

сорить /sorít'/ v. litter

сорок /sórok/ num. forty

сорока /soróka/ f. magpie

сорт /sort/ m. sort; grade

сосать /sosát'/ v. suck

сосед /soséd/ m. neighbour

сосиска /sosíska/ f. sausage

соска /sóska/ (baby's) dummy

сослуживец /sosluzhívets/ m. colleague

сосна /sosná/ f. pine

сосок /sosók/ m. nipple

сосредоточенность /sosredotóchennost'/ f. concentration

состав /sostáv/ m. composition

состояние /sostoiánie/ n. condition; fortune

сострадание /sostradánie/ n. compassion

состязание /sostiazánie/ n. contest

сосуд /sosúd/ m. vessel

сотня /sótnia/ f. hundred

сотрудник /sotrúdnik/ m. staff worker; colleague;
  employee

сотрудничать /sotrúdnichat'/ v. collaborate

соты /sóty/ pl. honeycomb

соус /sóus/ m. sauce

софа /sofá/ f. sofa

сохнуть /sókhnut'/ v. dry

сохранять /sokhraniát'/ v. preserve

сохраняться /sokhraniát'sia/ v. remain (intact); last out

социализм /sotsialízm/ m. socialism

социальный /sotsiál'nyi/ adj. social

соцстрах /sotsstrákh/ abbr., m. social insurance

сочельник /sochél'nik/ m. Christmas Eve

сочинение /sochinénie/ n. composition

сочный /sóchnyi/ adj. juicy

сочувствовать /sochúvstvovat'/ v. sympathize with

союз /soiúz/ m. union

союзник /soiúznik/ m. ally

спазм /spazm/ m. spasm

спальня /spál'nia/ f. bedroom

спаржа /spárzha/ f. asparagus

спасать /spasát'/ v. save

спасибо /spasíbo/ part. thank you

спать /spat'/ v. sleep

спектакль /spektákl'/ m. performance

спектр /spektr/ m. spectrum

спекулировать /spekulírovat'/ v. speculate; profiteer

спелый /spélyi/ adj. ripe

специалист /spetsialíst/ m. specialist

специальность /spetsiál'nost'/ f. profession

спешить /speshít'/ v. hurry

спина /spiná/ f. back

спираль /spirál'/ f. spiral

спирт /spirt/ m. alcohol, spirit(s)

список /spísok/ m. list

спица /spítsa/ f. knitting needle; spoke

спичка /spíchka/ f. match
сплетничать /splétnichat'/ v. gossip
спокойный /spokóinyi/ adj. calm
спор /spor/ m. argument
спорить /spórit'/ v. dispute
спорт /sport/ m. sport
спортсмен /sportsmén/ m. sportsman
способ /spósob/ m. way
способность /sposóbnost'/ f. ability
справа /správa/ adv. from the right
справедливость /spravedlívost'/ f. justice
справедливый /spravedlívyi/ adj. fair
справка /správka/ f. information; reference; certificate
справочник /správochnik/ m. reference book
спрашивать /spráshivat'/ v. ask
спрос /spros/ m. demand
спускать /spuskát'/ v. lower; unleash
спутник /spútnik/ m. companion; satellite
сравнивать /srávnivat'/ v. compare
сражение /srazhénie/ n. battle
сразу /srázu/ adv. at once
среда /sredá/ f. Wednesday; milieu; medium
среди /sredí/ adv. among
средневековье /srednevekóv'e/ n. the Middle Ages
средний /srédnii/ adj. middle; average
средство /srédstvo/ n. means
срок /srok/ m. term
срочный /sróchnyi/ adj. urgent
срывать /sryvát'/ v. tear away; raze to the ground

ссадина /ssádina/ f. scratch
ссора /ssóra/ f. quarrel
ссуда /ssúda/ f. loan
ссужать /ssuzhát'/ v. lend
ссылать /ssylát'/ v. exile
ставить /stávit'/ v. stand; place
стадион /stadión/ m. stadium
стадия /stádiia/ f. stage
стаж /stazh/ m. length of service
стажер /stazhór/ m. probationer
стакан /stakán/ m. glass, tumbler
стандарт /standárt/ m. standard
станок /stanók/ m. machine (tool)
станция /stántsiia/ f. station
стараться /starát'sia/ v. try
стареть /starét'/ v. grow old
старик /starík/ m. old man
старинный /starínnyi/ adj. antique
старость /stárost'/ f. old age
старуха /starúkha/ f. old woman
старший /stárshii/ adj. elder; older; eldest; oldest
старый /stáryi/ adj. old
статистика /statístika/ f. statistics
статуя /státuia/ f. statue
стать /stat'/ v. become
статья /stat'iá/ v. article
стачка /stáchka/ f. strike
стая /stáia/ f. pack; flock; school; shoal
ствол /stvol/ m. trunk; barrel

стебель /stébel'/ m. stem

стекло /stekló/ m. glass

стена /stená/ f. wall

степень /stépen'/ f. degree; extent

степь /step'/ f. steppe

стеречь /steréch/ v. guard

стерильный /steríl'nyi/ adj. sterile

стерлядь /stérliad'/ f. sterlet

стиль /stil'/ m. style

стимулировать /stimulírovat'/ v. stimulate

стипендия /stipéndiia/ f. grant

стиральный /stirál'nyi/ adj. washing; стиральная машина /stirál'naia mashína/ washing mashine

стирать /stirát'/ v. wash

стих /stikh/ m. verse

стихийное (бедствие) /stikhíinoe bédstvie/ adj. + n. calamity

стихия /stikhíia/ f. element

сто /sto/ num. hundred

стог /stog/ m. stack

стоимость /stóimost'/ f. cost

стоить /stóit'/ v. cost, be worth

стойка /stóika/ f. bar

стол /stol/ m. table, desk

столб /stolb/ m. pole; pillar

столетие /stolétie/ n. century

столица /stolítsa/ f. capital

столовая /stolóvaia/ f. dining-room; canteen

столько /stól'ko/ adv. so much, so many

столяр /stoliár/ m. joiner
стонать /stonát'/ v. groan
сторожить /storozhít'/ v. watch over
сторона /storoná/ f. side
стоянка /stoiánka/ f. parking place *or* lot
стоять /stoiát'/ v. stand
страдать /stradát'/ v. suffer
стража /strázha/ f. quard(s)
страна /straná/ f. country
страница /stranítsa/ f. page
странный /stránnyi/ adj. strange
страсть /strast'/ f. passion
страус /stráus/ m. ostrich
страх /strakh/ m. fear
страхование /strakhovánie/ n. insurance
стрекоза /strekozá/ f. dragonfly
стрела /strelá/ f. arrow
стрелка /strélka/ f. hand; pointer
стрелять /streliát'/ v. shoot
стрижка /strízhka/ f. hair-cut
строгий /strógii/ adj. strict
строить /stróit'/ v. construct, build
строй /stroi/ m. system; order
стройка /stróika/ f. building-site
стройный /stróinyi/ adj. shapely
строка /stroká/ f. line
структура /struktúra/ f. structure
струна /struná/ f. string
стручок /struchók/ m. rod

струя /struiá/ f. stream

студент /studént/ m. student

студия /stúdiia/ f. studio

стужа /stúzha/ f. cold; frost

стук /stuk/ m. knock

стул /stul/ m. chair

ступенька /stupén'ka/ f. step

стучать /stuchát'/ v. knock

стыд /styd/ m. shame

стюардесса /stiuardéssa/ f. air hostess

суббота /subbóta/ f. Saturday

субсидировать /subsidírovat'/ v. subsidize

сувенир /suvenír/ m. souvenir

суверенитет /suverenitét/ m. sovereignty

сугроб /sugrób/ m. snowdrift

суд /sud/ m. court; trial

судак /sudák/ m. pike perch

судить /sudít'/ v. judge

судно /súdno/ n. ship

судорога /súdoroga/ d. cramp

судьба /sud'bá/ f. fate

судья /sud'iá/ m., f. judge; referee

суеверие /suevérie/ n. superstition

сука /súka/ f. bitch

сумасшедший /sumasshédshii/ adj. mad

сумерки /súmerki/ pl. twilight

сумка /súmka/ f. bag

сумма /súmma/ f. sum

сумочка /súmochka/ f. handbag; дамская с. /dámskaia s./ purse

сундук /sundúk/ m. trunk

суп /sup/ m. soup

супруг /suprúg/ m. husband; spouse

супруга /suprúga/ f. wife; spouse

суровый /suróvyi/ adj. severe

сустав /sustáv/ adj. joint

сутки /sútki/ pl. twenty-four hours

сутулый /sutúlyi/ adj. round-shouldered

суть /sut'/ f. essence

сухарь /sukhár'/ m. cracker; biscuit

сухой /sukhói/ adj. dry

сушить /sushít'/ v. dry

существенный /sushchéstvennyi/ adj. essential

существовать /sushchestvovát'/ v. exist

сфера /sféra/ f. sphere

схема /skhéma/ f. scheme

сцена /stséna/ f. stage; scene

сценарий /stsenárii/ m. script

счастливый /schastlívyi/ adj. happy

счастье /schást'e/ n. happiness

счет /schot/ m. account; score

счетчик /schótchik/ m. meter

считать /schitát'/ v. count

съедобный /s''edóbnyi/ adj. edible

съезд /s''ezd/ m. congress

съемка /s''iómka/ f. survey; shooting

сын /syn/ m. son

сыпать /sýpat'/ v. pour

сыпь /syp'/ f. rash

сыр /syr/ m. cheese

сырой /syrói/ adj. damp

сырье /syr'ió/ n. raw material(s)

сыщик /sýshchik/ m. detective

сюда /siudá/ adv. here

сюжет /siuzhét/ m. plot

сюрприз /siurpríz/ m. surprise

T

табак /tabák/ m. tobacco

таблетка /tablétka/ f. tablet

таблица /tablítsa/ f. table

табурет /taburét/ m. stool

таз /taz/ m. basin; pelvis

таинственный /taínstvennyi/ adj. mysterious

тайга /taigá/ f. taiga

тайна /táina/ f. mystery

тайный /táinyi/ adj. secret

так /tak/ adv. so; так как /ták kak/ since

также /tákzhe/ adv. also

такой /takói/ pron. such

такса /táksa/ f. tariff, fixed price; dachshund

такси /taksí/ n. taxi

тактика /táktika/ f. tactics

талант /talánt/ m. talent

талия /táliia/ f. waist

талон /talón/ m. coupon

тальк /tal'k/ m. talcum powder

там /tam/ adv. there

таможня /tamózhnia/ f. custom-house

танец /tánets/ m. dance

танк /tank/ m. tank

танкер /tánker/ m. tanker

танцевать /tantsevát'/ v. dance

тапочка /tápochka/ f. slipper

тара /tára/ f. packing

таракан /tarakán/ m. cockroach

тарелка /tarélka/ f. plate

тариф /taríf/ m. tariff

тащить /tashchít'/ v. drag

таять /táiat'/ v. melt

твердый /tviórdyi/ adv. hard; solid

твой /tvói/ pron. your(s)

творить /tvorít'/ v. create

творог /tvórog/ m. cottage cheese

творческий /tvórcheskii/ adj. creative

театр /teátr/ m. theatre

тезка /tiózka/ m., f. namesake

текст /tekst/ m. text

текущий /tekúshchii/ adj. current

телевидение /televídenie/ n. television

телевизор /televízor/ m. television set

телега /teléga/ f. waggon, cart

телеграмма /telegrámma/ f. telegram

телеграф /telegráf/ m. telegraph

теленок /teliónok/ m. calf

телепередача /teleperedácha/ f. telecast

телескоп /teleskóp/ m. telescope

телефон /telefón/ m. telephone

тело /télo/ n. body

телятина /teliátina/ f. veal

тема /téma/ f. theme

тембр /tembr/ m. timbre

темнеть /temnét'/ v. become dark

темнота /temnotá/ f. darkness

темп /temp/ m. tempo

температура /temperatúra/ f. temperature

тенденция /tendéntsiia/ f. tendency

теннис /ténnis/ m. tennis

тень /ten'/ f. shadow

теория /teóriia/ f. theory

теперь /tepér'/ adv. now

теплица /teplítsa/ f. hothouse

теплота /teplotá/ f. heat; warmth

теплоход /teplokhód/ m. motor ship

теплый /tióplyi/ adj. warm

терапевт /terapévt/ m. therapeutist

тереть /terét'/ v. rub

терка /tiórka/ f. grater

термометр /termómetr/ m. thermometer

термос /térmos/ m. thermos

терпеть /terpét'/ v. bear

терраса /terrása/ f. terrace

территория /territóriia/ f. territory

террор /terrór/ m. terror

терять /teriát'/ v. lose

тесный /tésnyi/ adj. tight

тесто /tésto/ n. dough

тесть /test'/ m. father-in-law (wife's father)

тетрадь /tetrád'/ f. exercise book

тетя /tiótia/ f. aunt

техник /tékhnik/ m. technician

техника /tékhnika/ f. technique; machinery

техникум /tékhnikum/ m. technical college

технология /tekhnológiia/ f. technology

течение /techénie/ n. course

течь /tech/ v. flow; leak

теща /tióshcha/ f. mother-in-law (wife's mother)

тигр /tigr/ m. tiger

тип /tip/ m. type

типичный /tipíchnyi/ adj. typical

типография /tipográfiia/ f. printing house

тираж /tirázh/ m. circulation; edition

тиран /tirán/ m. tyrant

тире /tiré/ n. dash

титул /títul/ m. title

тихий /tíkhii/ adj. quiet

ткань /tkan'/ f. cloth, fabric

ткать /tkat'/ v. weave

товар /továr/ m. commodity; goods

тогда /togdá/ adv. then

тоже /tózhe/ adv. also, too

ток /tok/ m. current

токарь /tókar'/ m. turner

толкать /tolkát'/ v. shove

толпа /tolpá/ f. crowd

толстый /tólstyi/ adj. fat

толчок /tolchók/ m. push; stimulus

только /tól'ko/ adv. only

том /tom/ m. volume

тон /ton/ m. tone; shade

тонкий /tónkii/ adj. slim; subtle

тонна /tónna/ f. ton

тоннель /tonnél'/ m. tunnel

тонуть /tonút'/ v. sink; drown

топливо /tóplivo/ n. fuel

тополь /tópol'/ m. poplar

топор /topór/ m. axe

топтать /toptát'/ v. trample

торговать /torgovát'/ v. trade

торговаться /torgovát'sia/ v. bargain

торжественный /torzhéstvennyi/ adj. solemn

тормозить /tormozít'/ v. brake

торопить /toropít'/ v. hurry

торт /tort/ m. pie; fancy cake

торф /torf/ m. peat

тоска /toská/ f. melancholy

тосковать /toskovát'/ v. pine, long

тост /tost/ m. toast; toasted sandwich

тот /tot/ pron. that

тотчас /tótchas/ adv. immediately

точить /tochít'/ v. sharpen

точно /tóchno/ adv. precisely

точный /tóchnyi/ adj. accurate

тошнить (меня тошнит) /meniá toshnít/ I feel sick

тощий /tóshchii/ adj. skinny

трава /travá/ f. grass

травма /trávma/ f. trauma

трагедия /tragédiia/ f. tragedy

традиция /tradítsiia/ f. tradition

трактор /tráktor/ m. tractor

трамвай /tramvái/ m. tram

транспорт /tránsport/ m. transport

тратить /trátit'/ v. spend

траур /tráur/ m. mourning

требовать /trébovat'/ v. demand; summon

тревога /trevóga/ f. alarm

трезвый /trézvyi/ adj. sober

тренер /tréner/ m. coach

трение /trénie/ n. friction

тренировать /trenirovát'/ v. train

треск /tresk/ m. crack

треска /treská/ f. cod

трескаться /tréskat'sia/ v. crack

третий /trétii/ num. third

треугольник /treugól'nik/ m. triangle

трещать /treshchát'/ v. crackle

трещина /tréshchina/ f. split

три /tri/ num. three

трибуна /tribúna/ f. rostrum

трибунал /tribunál/ m. tribunal

тридцать /trídtsat'/ num. thirty

трижды /trízhdy/ adv. three times, thrice

трико /trikó/ n. tights

трикотаж /trikotázh/ m. knitted fabric

тринадцать /trinádtsat'/ num. thirteen

триста /trísta/ num. three hundred

триумф /triúmf/ m. triumph

трогательный /trógatel'nyi/ adj. moving

трогать /trógat'/ v. touch

троллейбус /trolléibus/ m. trolley bus

тромб /tromb/ m. clot

трон /tron/ m. throne

тропик /trópik/ m. tropic

тропинка /tropínka/ f. path

тростник /trostník/ m. reed

тротуар /trotuár/ m. pavement

трофей /troféi/ m. trophy

труба /trubá/ f. chimney; trumpet

трубить /trubít'/ v. blow

трубка /trúbka/ f. pipe

труд /trud/ m. labour, work

трудиться /trudít'sia/ v. work

трудность /trúdnost'/ f. difficulty

труп /trup/ m. corpse

трус /trus/ m. coward

трусы /trusý/ pl. shorts; trunks

тряпка /triápka/ f. rag

трясти /triastí/ v. shake

туалет /tualét/ m. dress; toilet; lavatory

туберкулез /tuberkulióz/ m. tuberculosis

тугой /tugói/ adj. tight; taut

туда /tudá/ adv. there

туз /tuz/ m. ace

туземец /tuzémets/ m. native

туловище /túlovishche/ n. trunk; torso

туман /tumán/ m. mist

тупик /tupík/ m. blind alley

тупой /tupói/ adj. blunt; stupid

тур /tur/ m. turn; round

турист /turíst/ m. tourist

турнир /turnír/ m. tournament

тут /tut/ adv. here

туфля /tufliá/ f. shoe

тухлый /túkhlyi/ adj. rotten, bad

туча /túcha/ f. cloud

тушеный /tushónyi/ adj. stewed

тушить /tushít'/ v. stew; extinguish

тушь /tush/ f. Indian ink; mascara

ты /ty/ pron. you

тыква /týkva/ f. pumpkin

тыл /tyl/ m. rear

тысяча /týsiacha/ num. thousand

тюбик /tiúbik/ m. tube

тюк /tiuk/ m. bale

тюлень /tiulén'/ m. seal

тюль /tiul'/ m. tulle

тюльпан /tiul'pán/ m. tulip

тюрьма /tiur'má/ f. prison

тявкать /tiávkat'/ v. yap

тяжелый /tiazhólyi/ adj. heavy

тянуть /tianút'/ v. pull

У

у /u/ prep. near, by
убегать /ubegát'/ v. run away
убедительный /ubedítel'nyi/ adj. convincing
убеждать /ubezhdát'/ v. persuade
убежище /ubézhishche/ n. shelter
убивать /ubivát'/ v. kill
убийство /ubíistvo/ n. murder
убийца /ubíitsa/ f. murderer
убирать /ubirát'/ v. remove; tidy up
уборка /ubórka/ f. harvesting; tidying up
уборная /ubórnaia/ f. lavatory
уборщица /ubórshchitsa/ f. cleaner
убыток /ubýtok/ m. loss
убыточный /ubýtochnyi/ adj. unprofitable
уважать /uvazhát'/ v. respect
увеличивать /uvelíchivat'/ v. increase
уверенность /uvérennost'/ f. confidence
уверять /uveriát'/ v. assure
увечить /uvéchit'/ v. maim
увлекательный /uvlekátel'nyi/ adj. fascinating
увлечение /uvlechénie/ n. passion (for), enthusiasm
увозить /uvozít'/ v. take away
увольнять /uvol'niát'/ v. sack
увы /uvý/ int. alas!
увядать /uviadát'/ v. fade
угадывать /ugádyvat'/ v. guess (right)
угасать /ugasát'/ v. go out; die down

углевод /uglevód/ m. carbohydrate
угнетать /ugnetát'/ v. depress; oppress
уговаривать /ugovárivat'/ v. persuade
угол /úgol/ m. corner; angle
уголовный /ugolóvnyi/ adj. criminal
уголь /úgol'/ m. coal
угонять /ugoniát'/ v. drive away; steal
угорь /úgor'/ m. eel; blackhead
угощать /ugoshchát'/ v. treat
угроза /ugróza/ f. threat
угрюмый /ugriúmyi/ adj. gloomy
удав /udáv/ m. boa-constrictor
удалять /udaliát'/ v. remove; send away; dismiss
удар /udár/ m. blow; stroke; attack
ударение /udarénie/ n. stress
ударять /udariát'/ v. strike
удача /udácha/ f. good luck
удачный /udáchnyi/ adj. successful
удивлять /udivliát'/ v. surprise
удить /udít'/ v. fish
удобный /udóbnyi/ adj. comfortable; convenient
удобрение /udobrénie/ n. fertilizer
удовлетворять /udovletvoriát'/ v. satisfy
удовольствие /udovól'stvie/ n. pleasure
удостоверение /udostoverénie/ n. certificate; у. личности
  /u. líchnosti/ identity card
удостоверять /udostoveriát'/ v. certify
удочка /údochka/ f. fishing-rod
уединение /uedinénie/ n. seclusion

уезжать /uezzhát'/ v. go away

ужас /úzhas/ m. horror

ужасный /uzhásnyi/ adj. terrible

уже /uzhé/ adv. already, by now

ужин /úzhin/ m. supper

узел /úzel/ m. knot

узкий /úzkii/ adj. narrow; limited; narrow-minded

узнавать /uznavát'/ v. recognize; find out

узор /uzór/ m. pattern

указ /ukáz/ m. decree

указатель /ukazátel'/ m. index; directory

указывать /ukázyvat'/ v. show

укладывать /ukládyvat'/ v. lay; pile, stack

уклончивый /uklónchivyi/ adj. evasive

уклоняться /ukloniát'sia/ v. avoid

укол /ukól/ m. injection

укор /ukór/ m. reproach

украдкой /ukrádkoi/ adv. furtively

украшать /ukrashát'/ v. adorn; decorate

укроп /ukróp/ m. dill

укрощать /ukroshchát'/ v. tame

уксус /úksus/ m. vinegar

укус /ukús/ m. bite, sting

улей /úlei/ m. (bee)hive

улетать /uletát'/ v. fly away

улика /ulíka/ f. evidence

улитка /ulítka/ f. snail

улица /úlitsa/ f. street

улов /ulóv/ m. catch

улучшать /uluchshát'/ v. improve
улыбаться /ulybát'sia/ v. smile
ультиматум /ul'timátum/ m. ultimatum
ультразвуковой /ul'trazvukovói/ adj. supersonic
ультрафиолетовый /ul'trafiolétovyi/ adj. ultra-violet
ум /um/ m. mind, intellect
умение /uménie/ n. ability, skill
уменьшать /umen'shát'/ v. decrease
умеренный /umérennyi/ adj. moderate
уметь /umét'/ v. know how, be able
умирать /umirát'/ v. die
умножать /umnozhát'/ v. multiply
умный /úmnyi/ adj. clever, intelligent
умываться /umyvát'sia/ v. wash (oneself)
умышленный /umýshlennyi/ adj. intentional
универмаг /univermág/ m. department store
универсальный /universál'nyi/ adj. universal; у. магазин
   /u. magazín/ supermarket
университет /universitét/ m. university
унижать /unizhát'/ v. humiliate
уникальный /unikál'nyi/ adj. unique
унитаз /unitáz/ m. lavatory pan
уничтожать /unichtozhát'/ v. destroy
уносить /unosít'/ v. take away
унция /úntsiia/ f. ounce
унылый /unýlyi/ adj. depressed
упаковывать /upakóvyvat'/ v. pack
упоминать /upominát'/ v. mention
упорный /upórnyi/ adj. stubborn

употреблять /upotrebliát'/ v. use
управление /upravlénie/ n. administration
управлять /upravliát'/ v. direct
упражнение /uprazhnénie/ n. exercise
упражняться /uprazhniát'sia/ v. practise
упрашивать /upráshivat'/ v. entreat
упрекать /uprekát'/ v. reproach
упрощать /uproshchát'/ v. simplify
упругий /uprúgii/ adj. elastic; resilient
упрямый /upriámyi/ adj. stubborn
ура /urá/ int. hurrah
уравнение /uravnénie/ n. equation
ураган /uragán/ m. hurricane
уран /urán/ m. uranium
урна /úrna/ f. urn; ballot-box; litter-bin
уровень /úroven'/ m. level
уродливый /uródlivyi/ adj. ugly
урожай /urozhái/ m. harvest
урожденная /urozhdiónnaia/ adj. née
урок /urók/ m. lesson
урон /urón/ m. loss
усадьба /usád'ba/ f. country estate
усердный /usérdnyi/ adj. zealous
усилие /usílie/ n. effort
ускорять /uskoriát'/ v. speed up
условие /uslóvie/ n. condition
услуга /uslúga/ f. service
усмехаться /usmekhát'sia/ v. grin
уснуть /usnút'/ v. go to sleep

усовершенствование /usovershénstvovanie/ n. improvement

успеваемость /uspeváemost'/ f. progress

успех /uspékh/ m. success

успокаивать /uspokáivat'/ v. quiet

устав /ustáv/ m. regulation

уставать /ustavát'/ v. get tired

усталый /ustályi/ adj. weary

устанавливать /ustanávlivat'/ v. install; establish

устарелый /ustarélyi/ adj. obsolete

устный /ústnyi/ adj. verbal, oral

устойчивый /ustóichivyi/ adj. stable

устраивать /ustráivat'/ v. arrange

устранять /ustraniát'/ v. remove

устрица /ústritsa/ f. oyster

устройство /ustróistvo/ n. arrangement; construction

уступать /ustupát'/ v. yield

уступка /ustúpka/ f. concession

усы /usý/ pl. moustache

утвердительный /utverdítel'nyi/ adj. affirmative

утверждение /utverzhdénie/ n. assertion

утешать /uteshát'/ v. console

утка /útka/ f. duck

утолять /utoliát'/ v. quench

утомительный /utomítel'nyi/ adj. tiresome

уточнять /utochniát'/ v. specify

утрата /utráta/ f. loss

утро /útro/ n. morning

утюг /utiúg/ m. iron

уха /ukhá/ f. fish soup

ухаживать /ukházhivat'/ v. nurse; make advances to

ухо /úkho/ n. ear

уход /ukhód/ m. departure; nursing

уходить /ukhodít'/ v. go away

ухудшать /ukhudshát'/ v. make worse

уцелеть /utselét'/ v. survive

участвовать /uchástvovat'/ v. participate

участник /uchástnik/ m. participant

участок /uchástok/ m. plot; section

учащийся /ucháshchiisia/ m. student; pupil

учеба /uchóba/ f. studies

учебник /uchébnik/ m. textbook

учение /uchénie/ n. doctrine

ученый /uchónyi/ m. scholar, scientist

учитель /uchítel'/ m. teacher

учить /uchít'/ v. learn; teach

учиться /uchít'sia/ v. learn, study

учреждение /uchrezhdénie/ n. establishment

ушиб /ushíb/ m. injury

ущерб /ushchérb/ m. damage

уют /uiút/ m. comfort

уязвимый /uiazvímyi/ adj. vulnerable

Ф

фабрика /fábrika/ f. factory

фаза /fáza/ f. phase

фазан /fazán/ m. pheasant

факел /fákel/ m. torch

факт /fakt/ m. fact

фактический /faktcheskii/ adj. real

фактор /fáktor/ m. factor

факультет /fakul'tét/ m. faculty

фальшивый /fal'shvyi/ adj. false

фамилия /famliia/ f. surname

фанатизм /fanatzm/ fanaticism

фанера /fanéra/ f. plywood

фантазия /fantáziia/ f. fantasy

фара /fára/ f. headlight

фармацевт /farmatsévt/ m. pharmaceutist

фартук /fártuk/ m. apron

фарфор /farfór/ m. china; porcelain

фарш /farsh/ m. stuffing

фасад /fasád/ m. façade

фасоль /fasól'/ f. bean(s)

фасон /fasón/ m. fashion

фашизм /fashzm/ m. fascism

фаянс /faiáns/ m. pottery

февраль /fevrál'/ m. February

фейерверк /feiervérk/ m. firework(s)

феномен /fenómen/ m. phenomenon

феодализм /feodalzm/ f. feudalism

ферма /férma/ f. farm

фермер /férmer/ m. farmer

фестиваль /festivál'/ m. festival

фея /féia/ f. fairy

фиалка /fiálka/ f. violet

фигура /figra/ f. figure

фигурист /figuríst/ m. figure-skater
физика /fízika/ f. physics
физкультура /fizkul'túra/ f. gymnastics
филантроп /filantróp/ m. philantropist
филе /filé/ n. sirloin; fillet
филиал /filiál/ m. branch
философия /filosófiia/ f. philosophy
фильм /fil'm/ m. film
фильтр /fil'tr/ m. filter
финал /finál/ m. final; finale
финансировать /finansírovat'/ v. finance
финансы /finánsy/ pl. finance(s)
финик /fínik/ m. date
финиш /fínish/ m. finish
фиолетовый /fiolétovyi/ adj. violet
фирма /fírma/ f. firm
флаг /flag/ m. flag
флакон /flakón/ m. (scent-)bottle
фланель /flanél'/ f. flannel
флейта /fléita/ f. flute
флиртовать /flirtovát'/ v. flirt
флот /flot/ m. fleet
флюс /fliús/ m. gumboil
фойе /foié/ n. foyer
фокус /fókus/ m. focus; trick
фольга /fol'gá/ f. foil
фольклор /fol'klór/ m. folklore
фон /fon/ m. background
фонарь /fonár'/ m. lantern

фонд /fond/ m. fund

фонтан /fontán/ m. fountain

форель /forél'/ f. trout

форма /fórma/ f. form; mould; uniform

формальность /formál'nost'/ f. formality

формула /fórmula/ f. formula

фортепьяно /fortep'iáno/ n. piano

форточка /fórtochka/ f. (window-)pane

фосфор /fósfor/ m. phosphorus

фотоаппарат /fotoapparát/ m. camera

фотография /fotográfiia/ f. photograph

фраза /fráza/ f. phrase

фракция /fráktsiia/ f. faction

французский /frantsúzskii/ adj. French

фрахт /frakht/ m. freight

фронт /front/ m. front

фрукт /frukt/ m. fruit

фундамент /fundáment/ m. foundation

фунт /funt/ m. pound

фуражка /furázhka/ f. peaked cap

футбол /futból/ m. football; soccer

фыркать /fýrkat'/ v. snort

X

халат /khalát/ m. dressing-gown

хам /kham/ m. boor

хаос /kháos/ m. chaos

характер /kharákter/ m. character

характеристика /kharakterístika/ f. reference; description

хвалить /khvalít'/ v. praise
хвастаться /khvástat'sia/ v. boast
хватать /khvatát'/ v. grasp; be sufficient
хвойный /khvóinyi/ adj. coniferous
химия /khímiia/ f. chemistry
химчистка /khimchístka/ f. dry cleaning
хирург /khirúrg/ m. surgeon
хитрость /khítrost'/ f. cunning
хитрый /khítryi/ adj. sly, crafty
хищник /khíshchnik/ m. beast (bird) of prey
хищный /khíshchnyi/ adj. predatory
хлам /khlam/ m. rubbish
хлеб /khleb/ m. bread
хлестать /khlestát'/ v. lash
хлопать /khlópat'/ v. bang; clap
хлопок /khlópok/ m. cotton
хлопотать /khlopotát'/ v. bustle; petition (for)
хлопчатобумажный /khlopchatobumázhnyi/ adj. cotton
хлопья /khlóp'ia/ pl. flakes
хлыст /khlyst/ m. whip
хмуриться /khmúrit'sia/ v. frown
хмурый /khmúryi/ adj. gloomy
хна /khna/ f. henna
хобот /khóbot/ m. trunk
ход /khod/ m. move; motion; course
ходатайствовать /khodátaistvovat'/ v. petition, apply
ходить /khodít'/ v. go, walk
ходьба /khod'bá/ f. walking
хозяин /khoziáin/ m. master; host; landlord

хозяйка /khoziáika/ f. proprietress, hostess; landlady

хозяйство /khoziáistvo/ n. economy

хоккей /khokkéi/ m. hockey; ice-hockey

холера /kholéra/ m. cholera

холм /kholm/ m. hill

холод /khólod/ m. cold

холодильник /kholodíl'nik/ m. refrigerator

холодный /kholódnyi/ adj. cold

холостяк /kholostiák/ m. bachelor

холст /kholst/ m. canvas; linen

хор /khor/ m. choir; chorus

хоронить /khoronít'/ v. bury

хорошенький /khoróshen'kii/ adj. pretty

хороший /khoróshii/ adj. good

хотеть /khotét'/ v. want

хотя /khotiá/ adv. although

хохот /khókhot/ m. laughter

храбрый /khrábryi/ adj. valiant

храм /khram/ m. temple

хранить /khranít'/ v. preserve; store

храпеть /khrapét'/ n. snore

хребет /khrebét/ m. spine; (mountain) range; ridge

хрипеть /khripét'/ v. be hoarse

христианин /khristianín/ m. Christian

христианство /khristiánstvo/ n. Christianity

хромать /khromát'/ v. limp

хромой /khromói/ adj. lame

хроника /khrónika/ f. chronicle

хронология /khronológiia/ f. chronology

хрупкий /khrúpkii/ adj. fragile
хруст /khrust/ m. crackle
хрусталь /khrustál'/ m. cut glass; crystal
хрустеть /khrustét'/ v. crunch
худеть /khudét'/ v. grow thin
художественный /khudózhestvennyi/ adj. artistic
художник /khudózhnik/ m. artist; painter
хуже /khúzhe/ adv. worse
хулиган /khuligán/ m. hooligan

Ц

цапля /tsáplia/ f. heron
царапина /tsarápina/ f. scratch
царь /tsar'/ m. tsar
цвести /tsvestí/ v. blossom
цвет /tsvet/ m. colour
цветной /tsvetnói/ adj. coloured
цветок /tsvetók/ m. flower
целиком /tselikóm/ adv. entirely; wholly
целовать /tselovát'/ v. kiss
целый /tsélyi/ adj. whole; intact
цель /tsel'/ f. aim, target
цемент /tsemént/ m. cement
цена /tsená/ f. price
ценз /tsenz/ m. qualification
цензура /tsenzúra/ f. censorship
ценить /tseni't'/ v. value; appreciate
ценный /tsénnyi/ adj. valuable
центр /tsentr/ m. centre

центральный /tsentrál'nyi/ adj. central

цепь /tsep'/ f. chain; series; circuit

церемония /tseremóniia/ f. ceremony

церковь /tsérkov'/ f. church

цех /tsekh/ m. workshop

цивилизация /tsivilizátsiia/ f. civilization

цикл /tsikl/ m. cycle

циклон /tsiklón/ m. cyclone

цинга /tsingá/ f. scurvy

цинизм /tsinízm/ m. cynicism

цинк /tsink/ m. zinc

цирк /tsirk/ m. circus

циркуль /tsírkul'/ m. (pair of) compasses

цистерна /tsistérna/ f. cistern

цитата /tsitáta/ f. quotation

цитрус /tsítrus/ m. citrus

циферблат /tsiferblát/ m. dial, face

цифра /tsífra/ f. number, figure

цыган /tsygán/ m. Gypsy

цыпленок /tsypliónok/ m. chicken

цыпочки (на цыпочках) /natsýpochkakh/ prep.+pl. on tiptoe

Ч

чаевые /chaevýe/ pl. tip

чайка /cháika/ f. gull

чайник /cháinik/ m. teapot

час /chas/ m. hour

частная (собственность) /chástnaia sóbstvennost'/ adj. +
   f. private property

частный /chástnyi/ adj. private

часто /chásto/ adv. often

частый /chástyi/ adj. frequent

часть /chast'/ f. part

часы /chasý/ pl. clock, watch

чашка /cháshka/ f. cup

чаща /cháshcha/ f. thicket

чаще /cháshche/ adv. more often

чей /chéi/ pron. whose

чек /chek/ m. cheque

человек /chelovék/ m. man

человечество /chelovéchestvo/ n. mankind

человечный /chelovéchnyi/ adj. humane

челюсть /chéliust'/ f. jaw

чем /chem/ conj. than

чемодан /chemodán/ m. suitcase

чемпион /chempión/ m. champion

чепуха /chepukhá/ f. nonsense

червь /cherv'/ m. worm

чердак /cherdák/ m. garret

чередоваться /cheredovát'sia/ v. alternate

через /chérez/ prep. over; through; via

черемуха /cheriómukha/ f. bird cherry

череп /chérep/ m. skull

черепаха /cherepákha/ f. turtle

чересчур /chereschúr/ adv. too; too much

черешня /cheréshnia/ f. cherry (-tree)

чернила /cherníla/ pl. ink

черновик /chernovík/ m. rough copy

чернозем /chernozióm/ m. black earth
чернокожий /chernokózhii/ m. Negro, Black
чернорабочий /chernorabóchii/ m. unskilled worker
черный /chórnyi/ adj. black
черствый /chórstvyi/ adj. stale; callous
черт /chort/ m. devil
черта /chertá/ f. line
чертеж /chertiózh/ m. sketch
чертить /chertít'/ v. draw
чесать /chesát'/ v. comb; scratch
чесаться /chesát'sia/ v. itch
чеснок /chesnók/ m. garlic
честный /chéstnyi/ adj. honest
честолюбивый /chestoliubívyi/ adj. ambitious
честь /chest'/ f. honour
чета /chetá/ f. married couple; match
четверг /chetvérg/ m. Thursday
четверть /chétvert'/ f. quarter
четкий /chótkii/ adj. clear
четный /chótnyi/ adj. even
четыре /chetýre/ num. four
четырехугольник /chetyriókhugól'nik/ m. quadrangle
чехол /chekhól/ m. cover
чешуя /cheshuiá/ f. scales
чиновник /chinóvnik/ m. official
чирикать /chiríkat'/ v. chirp
численность /chíslennost'/ f. numbers; strength
число /chisló/ n. number; date
чистить /chístit'/ v. clean

чистка /chístka/ f. cleaning; purge

чистый /chístyi/ adj. clean

читать /chitát'/ v. read

член /chlen/ m. member; limb

чрезвычайный /chrezvycháinyi/ adj. extraordinary

чтение /chténie/ n. reading

что /chto/ pron. what; conj. that

что-либо, что-нибудь /chtó-libo, chtó-nibud'/ pron. something

чувство /chúvstvo/ n. feeling

чувствовать /chúvstvovat'/ v. feel

чугун /chugún/ m. cast iron

чудак /chudák/ m. crank

чудесный /chudésnyi/ adj. wonderful

чудо /chúdo/ n. miracle

чудовище /chudóvishche/ n. monster

чужак /chuzhák/ m. stranger

чужой /chuzhói/ adj. foreign; alien

чулок /chulók/ m. stocking

чума /chumá/ f. plague

чурбан /churbán/ m. block; blockhead

чуткий /chútkii/ adj. sensitive; tactful

чуть /chut'/ adv. hardly; ч.-чуть /ch.-chut'/ a tiny bit; ч. не /ch. ne/ almost, nearly

чутье /chut'ió/ n. scent; instinct (for)

чушь /chush/ f. nonsense

чуять /chúiat'/ v. scent, smell

Ш

шаблон /shablón/ m. pattern

шаг /shag/ m. step

шагать /shagát'/ v. step

шайба /sháiba/ f. puck

шайка /sháika/ f. gang; tub

шалить /shalít'/ v. be naughty

шалфей /shalféi/ m. sage

шаль /shal'/ f. shawl

шампанское /shampánskoe/ n. champagne

шампунь /shampún'/ m. shampoo

шанс /shans/ m. chance

шантаж /shantázh/ m. blackmail

шапка /shápka/ f. hat

шар /shar/ m. ball; воздушный ш. /vozdúshnyi sh./ balloon

шариковая (ручка) /shárikovaia rúchka/ adj. + f. ball-point pen

шарф /sharf/ m. scarf

шасси /shassí/ pl. chassis

шататься /shatát'sia/ v. stagger

шатен /shatén/ m. person with dark brown hair

шаткий /shátkii/ adj. unsteady

шахматы /shákhmaty/ pl. chess

шахтер /shakhtiór/ m. miner

шашка /sháshka/ f. sabre; pl. draughts

шашлык /shashlýk/ m. shashlik

шевелить /shevelít'/ v. move, stir

шедевр /shedévr/ m. masterpiece

шелк /sholk/ m. silk

шептать /sheptát'/ v. whisper

шерсть /sherst'/ f. wool

шерстяной /sherstianói/ adj. wool(len)

шест /shest/ m. pole

шестнадцать /shestnádtsat'/ num. sixteen

шесть /shest'/ num. six

шестьдесят /shest'desiát/ num. sixty

шестьсот /shest'sót/ num. six hundred

шеф /shef/ m. chief

шея /shéia/ f. neck

шикарный /shikárnyi/ adj. smart

шина /shína/ f. tyre

шипеть /shipét'/ v. hiss

шиповник /shipóvnik/ m. dog-rose

ширина /shiriná/ f. breadth, width

ширма /shírma/ f. screen

широкий /shirókii/ adj. wide

широта /shirotá/ f. latitude

ширпотреб /shirpotréb/ m. consumer goods

шить /shit'/ v. sew

шишка /shíshka/ f. bump; cone

шкала /shkalá/ f. scale

шкатулка /shkatúlka/ f. box, casket

шкаф /shkaf/ m. cupboard; wardrobe

школа /shkóla/ f. school

школьник /shkól'nik/ m. schoolboy

школьница /shkól'nitsa/ f. schoolgirl

шкура /shkúra/ f. hide

шланг /shlang/ m. hose

шлепать /shliópat'/ v. smack

шляпа /shliápa/ f. hat
шмель /shmel'/ bumble-bee
шнур /shnur/ m. cord
шнурок /shnurók/ m. lace
шов /shov/ m. stitch
шовинизм /shovinízm/ m. chauvinism
шок /shok/ m. shock
шоколад /shokolád/ m. chocolate
шорох /shórokh/ m. rustle
шоссе /shossé/ n. highway
шофер /shofiór/ m. driver
шпилька /shpíl'ka/ f. hairpin
шпинат /shpinát/ m. spinach
шпион /shpión/ m. spy
шприц /shprits/ m. syringe
шпрот /shprot/ m. sprat
шрам /shram/ m. scar
шрифт /shrift/ m. print, type
штаб /shtab/ m. staff; headquarters
штамп /shtamp/ m. stamp; cliché
штаны /shtaný/ pl. trousers
штат /shtat/ m. state; staff
штепсель /shtépsel'/ m. plug
штопать /shtópat'/ v. darn
штопор /shtópor/ m. corkscrew
штора /shtóra/ f. blind
шторм /shtorm/ m. gale
штраф /shtraf/ f. fine
штрих /shtrikh/ m. trait; hatching

штука /shtúka/ f. piece

штукатурить /shtukatúrit'/ v. plaster

штурм /shturm/ storm, assault

шуба /shúba/ f. fur-coat

шуметь /shumét'/ v. make a noise

шурин /shúrin/ m. brother-in-law (wife's brother)

шутка /shútka/ f. joke

Щ

щавель /shchavél'/ m. sorrel

щадить /shchadít'/ v. spare; have mercy on

щегол /shchegól/ m. goldfinch

щедрый /shchédryi/ adj. generous

щека /shcheká/ f. cheek

щекотать /shchekotát'/ v. tickle

щелкать /shchólkat'/ v. click

щелчок /shchelchók/ m. flick; fillip

щель /shchel'/ f. crack; голосовая щ. /golosováia shch./
  glottis

щенок /shchenók/ m. pup, cub

щепка /shchépka/ f. splinter, chip

щетка /shchótka/ f. brush

щи /shchi/ pl. cabbage soup

щиколотка /shchíkolotka/ f. ankle

щипать /shchipát'/ v. pinch

щипцы /shchiptsý/ pl. pincers

щит /shchit/ m. shield

щука /shchúka/ f. pike

щупальце /shchúpal'tse/ n. tentacle

щупать /shchúpat'/ v. feel; probe

щуриться /shchúrit'sia/ v. screw up one's eyes

Э

эвакуация /evakuátsiia/ f. evacuation

эволюция /evoliútsiia/ f. evolution

эгоизм /egoízm/ m. egoism

экватор /ekvátor/ m. equator

эквивалент /ekvivalént/ m. equivalent

экзамен /ekzámen/ m. exam

экземпляр /ekzempliár/ m. copy

экипаж /ekipázh/ m. crew

экономика /ekonómika/ f. economics

экономист /ekonomíst/ m. economist

экономить /ekonómit'/ v. save

экран /ekrán/ m. screen

экскаватор /ekskavátor/ m. excavator

экскурсия /ekskúrsiia/ f. excursion

экспедиция /ekspedítsiia/ f. expedition

эксперимент /eksperimént/ m. experiment

эксперт /ekspért/ m. expert

эксплуатация /ekspluatátsiia/ f. exploitation

экспорт /éksport/ m. export

экспортер /eksportiór/ m. exporter

экспресс /ekspréss/ m. express

экстренный /ékstrennyi/ adj. extraordinary; emergency

элеватор /elevátor/ m. elevator

элегантный /elegántnyi/ adj. elegant

электрический /elektrícheskii/ adj. electric

элемент /elemént/ m. element

эмаль /emál'/ f. enamel

эмблема /embléma/ f. emblem

эмигрант /emigránt/ m. emigrant

эмиграция /emigrátsiia/ f. emigration

эмоциональный /emotsionál'nyi/ adj. emotional

энергичный /energíchnyi/ adj. energetic; vigorous

энтузиазм /entuziázm/ m. enthusiasm

энциклопедия /entsiklopédiia/ f. encyclopedia

эпидемия /epidémiia/ f. epidemic

эпизод /epizód/ m. episode

эпилог /epilóg/ m. epilogue

эпоха /epókha/ f. epoch

эскалатор /eskalátor/ m. escalator

эскиз /eskíz/ m. sketch

эссенция /esséntsiia/ f. essence

эстафета /estaféta/ f. relay race

эстрада /estráda/ f. variety

этаж /etázh/ m. storey

этап /etáp/ m. stage

этика /étika/ f. ethics

этикетка /etikétka/ f. label

этнический /etnícheskii/ adj. ethnic

этот /étot/ pron. this

этюд /etiúd/ m. study; sketch

эффект /effékt/ m. effect

эхо /ékho/ n. echo

эшелон /eshelón/ m. echelon

Ю

юбилей /iubiléi/ m. jubilee

юбка /iúbka/ f. skirt

ювелир /iuvelír/ m. jeweller

юг /iúg/ m. south

юго-восток /iúgo-vostók/ m. south-east.

юго-запад /iúgo-západ/ m. south-west

южный /iúzhnyi/ adj. south(ern)

юмор /iúmor/ m. humour

юность /iúnost'/ f. youth

юноша /iúnosha/ m. youth

юридический /iuridícheskii/ adj. legal

юрист /iuríst/ m. lawyer

Я

я /iá/ pron. I

яблоко /iábloko/ n. apple

явный /iávnyi/ adj. evident

ягненок /iagniónok/ m. lamb

ягода /iágoda/ f. berry

ягодица /iagodítsa/ f. buttock

яд /iád/ m. poison

ядерный /iádernyi/ adj. nuclear

ядовитый /iadovítyi/ adj. poisonous

ядро /iadró/ n. nucleus; shot

язва /iázva/ f. ulcer

язык /iazýk/ m. tongue; language

яичник /iaíchnik/ m. ovary

яичница /iaíchnitsa/ f. fried eggs

яйцо /iaitsó/ n. egg

якобы /iákoby/ conj. allegedly

якорь /iákor'/ m. anchor

яма /iáma/ f. pit; hole

январь /ianvár'/ m. January

янтарь /iantár'/ m. amber

яркий /iárkii/ adj. bright

ярмарка /iármarka/ f. fair

ярость /iárost'/ f. fury

ясли /iásli/ pl. manger; day nursery

ясновидец /iasnovídets/ m. clairvoyant

ясный /iásnyi/ adj. clear

ястреб /iástreb/ m. hawk

яхта /iákhta/ f. yacht

ячейка /iachéika/ f. cell

ячмень /iachmén'/ m. barley

яшма /iáshma/ f. jasper

ящерица /iáshcheritsa/ f. lizard

ящик /iáshchik/ m. box; drawer; мусорный я. /músornyi ia./ dustbin

GEOGRAPHICAL NAMES

Абхазия /abkháziia/ Abkhazia

Австралия /avstrálila/ Australia

Австрия /ávstriia/ Austria

Аддис-Абеба /addís-abéba/ Addis Ababa

Аден /áden/ Aden

Адриатическое море /adriatícheskoe móre/ the Adriatic Sea

Азербайджан /azerbaidzhán/ Azerbaijan

Азия /áziia/ Asia

Аккра /ákkra/ Accra

Албания /albánia/ Albania

Алжир /alzhír/ Algeria; Algiers

Альпы /ál'py/ the Alps

Аляска /aliáska/ Alaska

Амазонка /amazónka/ the Amazon

Америка /amérika/ America

Амман /ammán/ Amman

Амстердам /amsterdám/ Amsterdam

Англия /ángliia/ England

Ангола /angóla/ Angola

Анкара /ankará/ Ankara

Антарктида /antarktída/ the Antarctic continent, Antarctica

Антарктика /antárktika/ the Antarctic

Антверпен /antvérpen/ Antwerp

Антигуа и Барбуда /antígua i barbúda/ Antigua and
   Barbuda
Аравийское море /aravíiskoe móre/ the Arabian Sea
Аравия /aráviia/ Arabia
Аргентина /argentína/ Argentina
Арктика /árktika/ the Arctic
Армения /arméniia/ Armenia
Атлантический океан /atlantícheskii okeán/ the Atlantic
   (Ocean)
Афганистан /afganistán/ Afghanistan
Афины /afíny/ Athens
Африка /áfrika/ Africa

Бавария /baváriia/ Bavaria
Багамские острова /bagámskie ostrová/ the Bahamas
Багдад /bagdád/ Bag(h)dad
Базель /bázel'/ Basel or Basle
Байкал /baikál/ (Lake) Baikal
Балканский п-ов /balkánskii poluóstrov/ the Balkan
   Peninsula
Балканы /balkány/ the Balkan states, the Balkans
Балтийское море /baltíiskoe móre/ the Baltic Sea
Балтимор /baltimór/ Baltimore
Бангкок /bangkók/ Bangkok
Бангладеш /bangladésh/ Bangladesh
Бандунг /bandúng/ Bandung
Барбадос /barbádos/ Barbados
Баренцево море /bárentsevo móre/ the Barents Sea
Барселона /barselóna/ Barcelona

Бахрейн /bakhréin/ Bahrain

Бейрут /beirút/ Beirut *or* Beyrouth

Белград /belgrád/ Belgrade

Белое море /béloe móre/ the White Sea

Белоруссия /belorússiia/ Byelorussia, Belarus

Белуджистан /beludzhistán/ Baluchistan

Бельгия /bél'giia/ Belgium

Бенгалия /bengáliia/ Bengal

Бенин /benín/ Benin

Берингов пролив /béringov prolív/ the Bering Strait

Берлин /berlín/ Berlin

Бермудские о-ва /bermúdskie ostrová/ Bermuda

Берн /bern/ Berne

Бирма /bírma/ Birma

Бирмингем /bírmingem/ Birmingham

Бисау /bisáu/ Bissau

Бискайский залив /biskáiskii zalív/ the Bay of Biscay

Богота /bogotá/ Bogota

Болгария /bolgáriia/ Bulgaria

Боливия /bolíviia/ Bolivia

Бомбей /bombéi/ Bombay

Бонн /bonn/ Bonn

Борнео /bornéo/ Borneo; see Калимантан

Босния /bósniia/ Bosnia

Бостон /bóston/ Boston

Босфор /bosfór/ the Bosp(h)orus

Ботсвана /botsvána/ Botswana

Браззавиль /brazzavíl'/ Brazzaville

Бразилиа /brazília/ Brasilia

Бразилия /brazíliia/ Brazil
Братислава /bratisláva/ Bratislava
Бретань /bretán'/ Brittany
Бриджтаун /bridzhtáun/ Bridgetown
Бристоль /bristól'/ Bristol
Бруней /brunéi/ Brunei
Брюссель /briussél'/ Brussels
Будапешт /budapésht/ Budapest
Буркина-Фасо /burkína-fasó/ Burkina Faso
Бурунди /burúndi/ Burundi
Бутан /bután/ Bhutan
Бухарест /bukharést/ Bucharest
Буэнос-Айрес /buénos-áires/ Buenos Aires

Ванкувер /vankúver/ Vancouver
Варшава /varsháva/ Warsaw
Ватикан /vatikán/ Vatican City
Вашингтон /vashingtón/ Washington
Везувий /vezúvii/ Vesuvius
Великобритания /velikobritániia/ Great Britain
Вена /véna/ Vienna
Венгрия /véngriia/ Hungary
Венесуэла /venesuéla/ Venezuela
Венеция /venétsiia/ Venice
Виктория /viktóriia/ Victoria
Виндхук /víndkhuk/ Windhoek
Виннипег /vínnipeg/ Winnipeg
Виргинские о-ва /virgínskie ostrová/ the Virgin Islands
Волга /vólga/ the Volga

Восточное Самоа /vostóchnoe samóa/ Eastern Samoa
Вьентьян /v'ent'ián/ Vientiane
Вьетнам /v'etnám/ Vietnam

Гаага /gaága/ The Hague
Габон /gabón/ Gabon
Гавайи /gaváii/ Hawaii
Гавайские о-ва /gaváiskie ostrová/ the Hawaiian Islands
Гавана /gavána/ Havana
Гаити /gaíti/ Haiti
Гайана /gaiiána/ Guyana
Галапагос /galapagós/ the Galapagos Islands
Галлиполи /gallípoli/ Gallipoli
Гамбия /gámbiia/ Gambia
Гамбург /gámburg/ Hamburg
Гана /gána/ Ghana
Ганг /gang/ the Ganges
Гваделупа /gvadelúpa/ Guadeloupe
Гватемала /gvatemála/ Guatemala
Гвиана /gviána/ Guiana
Гвинея-Бисау /gvinéia-bisáu/ Guinea-Bissau
Гент /gent/ Ghent
Генуя /génuia/ Genoa
Германия /germániia/ Germany
Герцеговина /gertsegovína/ Herzegovina
Гибралтарский пролив /gibraltárskii prolív/ the Strait of Gibraltar
Гималаи /gimalái/ the Himalaya(s)
Глазго /glázgo/ Glasgow
Гоби /góbi/ the Gobi

Голландия /gollándiia/ Holland

Гольфстрим /gol'fstrím/ the Gulf Stream

Гондурас /gondurás/ Honduras

Гонконг /gonkóng/ Hong Kong

Гонолулу /gonolúlu/ Honolulu

Гренада /grenáda/ Grenada

Гренландия /grenlándiia/ Greenland

Греция /grétsiia/ Greece

Гринвич /grínvich/ Greenwich

Грузия /grúziia/ Georgia

Гуам /guám/ Guam

Гудзон /gudzón/ the Hudson

Гудзонов залив /gudzónov zalív/ Hudson Bay

Дакар /dakár/ Dakar

Дакка /dákka/ Dacca

Дамаск /damásk/ Damascus

Дания /dániia/ Denmark

Дарданеллы /dardanélly/ the Dardanelles

Дар-эс-Салам /dar-es-salám/ Dar es Salaam

Дели /déli/ Delhi

Детройт /detróit/ Detroit

Джакарта /dzhakárta/ Jakarta

Джеймстаун /dzheimstáun/ Jamestown

Джомолунгма /dzhomolúngma/ Chomolungma

Джорджтаун /dzhordzhtáun/ Georgetown

Доминиканская республика /dominikánskaia respúblika/
   the Dominican Republic

Дрезден /drézden/ Dresden

Дублин /dúblin/ Dublin
Дувр /duvr/ Dover
Дунай /dunái/ the Danube

Европа /evrópa/ Europe
Египет /egípet/ Egypt
Енисей /eniséi/ the Yenisei

Женева /zhenéva/ Geneva

Заир /zaír/ Zaire
Замбези /zambézi/ the Zambezi *or* Zambesi
Замбия /zámbiia/ Zambia
Западное Самоа /západnoe samóa/ Western Samoa
Зимбабве /zimbábve/ Zimbabwe

Иерусалим /ierusalím/ Jerusalem
Израиль /izráil'/ Israel
Индийский океан /indíiskii okeán/ the Indian Ocean
Индия /índiia/ India
Индокитай /indokitái/ Indochina
Индонезия /indonéziia/ Indonesia
Индостан /indostán/ Hindustan
Иоганнесбург /iogánnesburg/ Johannesburg
Иордания /iordániia/ Jordan
Ирак /irák/ Iraq
Иран /irán/ Iran
Ирландия /irlándiia/ Ireland
Исламабад /islamabád/ Islamabad

Исландия /islándiia/ Iceland

Испания /ispániia/ Spain

Италия /itáliia/ Italy

Йемен /iémen/ Yemen

Йокогама /iokogáma/ Yokohama

Кабо-Верде /kábo-vérde/ Cape Verde

Кабул /kabúl/ Kabul

Кавказ /kavkáz/ the Caucasus

Кадис /kadís/ Cadiz

Казахстан /kazakhstán/ Kazakhstan

Казбек /kazbék/ Kazbek

Каир /kaír/ Cairo

Кале /kalé/ Calais

Калимантан /kalimantán/ Kalimantan

Калькутта /kal'kútta/ Calcutta

Камбоджа /kambódzha/ Cambodia

Камерун /kamerún/ Cameroon

Камчатка /kamchátka/ Kamchatka

Канада /kanáda/ Canada

Канарские о-ва /kanárskie ostrová/ the Canary Islands

Канберра /kanbérra/ Canberra

Каракас /karakás/ Caracas

Карачи /karáchi/ Karachi

Кардифф /kardíff/ Cardiff

Карибское море /karíbskoe móre/ the Caribbean Sea

Карпаты /karpáty/ the Carpathians

Каспийское море /kaspíiskoe móre/ the Caspian Sea

Кашмир /kashmír/ Kashmir

Квебек /kvebék/ Quebec

Квинсленд /kvínslend/ Queensland

Кейптаун /keiptáun/ Cape Town *or* Capetown

Кельн /kiól'n/ Cologne

Кембридж /kémbridzh/ Cambridge

Кения /kéniia/ Kenya

Киев /kíev/ Kiev

Килиманджаро /kilimandzháro/ Kilimanjaro

Киншаса /kinshása/ Kinshasa

Киото /kióto/ Kyoto *or* Kioto

Кипр /kipr/ Cyprus

Киргизия /kirgíziia/ Kirghizia

Китай /kitái/ China

Коломбо /kolómbo/ Colombo

Колумбия /kolúmbiia/ Colombia

Конго /kóngo/ Congo; the Congo

Копенгаген /kopengágen/ Copenhagen

Кордильеры /kordil'éry/ the Cordilleras

Корейская Народно-Демократическая Республика
/koréiskaia naródno-demokratícheskaia respublika/ the
Democratic People's Republic of Korea

Корсика /kórsika/ Corsica

Корфу /kórfu/ Corfu

Коста-Рика /kósta-ríka/ Costa Rica

Кот-д'Ивуар /kot-d''ivuár/ Cote d'Ivoire

Краков /krákov/ Cracow

Крым /krym/ the Crimea

Куба /kúba/ Cuba
Кувейт /kuvéit/ Kuwait
Курильские о-ва /kurĺl'skie ostrová/ the Kuril(e) Islands

Лагос /lágos/ Lagos
Ла-Манш /la-mánsh/ the English Channel
Лаос /laós/ Laos
Латвия /látviia/ Latvia
Лахор /lakhór/ Lahore
Лесото /lesóto/ Lesotho
Либерия /libériia/ Liberia
Ливан /liván/ Lebanon
Ливия /líviia/ Libya
Лима /líma/ Lima
Лион /lión/ Lyons
Лиссабон /lissabón/ Lisbon
Литва /litvá/ Lithuania
Лихтенштейн /likhtenshtéin/ Liechtenstein
Лондон /lóndon/ London
Лос-Анжелес /los-ánzheles/ Los Angeles
Лотарингия /lotaríngiia/ Lorraine
Луанда /luánda/ Luanda
Лусака /lusáka/ Lusaka
Люксембург /liuksembúrg/ Luxemb(o)urg

Мадагаскар /madagaskár/ Madagascar
Мадрас /madrás/ Madras
Мадрид /madríd/ Madrid
Македония /makedóniia/ Macedonia

Малайзия /maláiziia/ Malaysia
Малая Азия /málaia áziia/ Asia Minor
Мальта /mál'ta/ Malta
Манила /maníla/ Manila
Мекка /mékka/ Mecca
Мексика /méksika/ Mexico
Мехико /mékhiko/ Mexico City
Молдова /moldóva/ Moldova
Монголия /mongóliia/ Mongolia
Москва /moskvá/ Moscow
Мюнхен /miúnkhen/ Munich

Нева /nevá/ the Neva
Неман /néman/ the Niemen
Нигер /níger/ Niger
Нигерия /nigériia/ Nigeria
Нидерланды /niderlándy/ the Netherlands
Никарагуа /nikarágua/ Nicaragua
Никосия /nikosíia/ Nicosia
Новая Зеландия /nóvaia zelándiia/ New Zealand
Норвегия /norvégiia/ Norway
Нюрнберг /niúrnberg/ Nuremberg

Объединенная Арабская Республика /ob''ediniónnaia
  arábskaia respúblika/ United Arab Republic
Объединенные Арабские Эмираты /ob''ediniónnye
  arábskie emiráty/ United Arab Emirates
Ольстер /ól'ster/ Ulster
Осло /óslo/ Oslo

Пакистан /pakistán/ Pakistan

Палестина /palestína/ Palestine

Памир /pamír/ the Pamirs

Панама /panáma/ Panama

Парагвай /paragvái/ Paraguay

Париж /parízh/ Paris

Пекин /pekín/ Bejing

Пенджаб /pendzháb/ the Punjab

Персидский залив /persídskii zalív/ the Persian Gulf

Перу /perú/ Peru

Польша /pól'sha/ Poland

Португалия /portugáliia/ Portugal

Прага /prága/ Prague

Рейкьявик /reik'iávik/ Reykjavik

Рим /rim/ Rome

Россия /rossíia/ Russia

Румыния /rumýniia/ R(o)umania

Санкт-Петербург (б. Ленинград) /sánkt peterbúrg/
  St. Petersburg (Leningrad)

Сан-Сальвадор /san-sal'vadór/ San Salvador

Саудовская Аравия /saúdovskaia aráviia/ Saudi Arabia

Сахалин /sakhalín/ Sakhalin

Северная Америка /sévernaia amérika/ North America

Северное море /sévernoe móre/ the North Sea

Северный Ледовитый океан /sévernyi ledovítyi okeán/
  the Arctic Ocean

Сеул /seúl/ Seoul

Сибирь /sibír'/ Siberia

Сирия /síriia/ Syria

Словакия /slovákiia/ Slovakia

Соединенное Королевство Великобритании и Северной Ирландии /soediniónnoe korolévstvo velikobritánii i sévernoi irlándii/ United Kingdom of Great Britain and Northern Ireland

Соединенные Штаты Америки /США/ /soediniónnye shtáty amériki, sé shé á / United States of America /USA/

Сомали /somalí/ Somali(a)

София /sofíia/ Sofia

Средиземное море /sredizémnoe móre/ the Mediterranean (Sea)

Стамбул /stambúl/ Istanbul

Стокгольм /stokgól'm/ Stockholm

Судан /sudán/ the Sudan

Суэцкий канал /suétskii kanál/ the Suez Canal

Таджикистан /tadzhikistán/ Tajikistan

Танжер /tanzhér/ Tangier

Танзания /tanzániia/ Tanzania

Тегеран /tegerán/ Teh(e)ran

Тель-Авив /tel'-avív/ Tel Aviv

Тибет /tibét/ Tibet, Thibet

Тихий океан /tíkhii okeán/ the Pacific (Ocean)

Токио /tókio/ Tokyo

Тунис /tunís/ Tunisia; Tunis

Туркмения /turkméniia/ Turkmenia

Турция /túrtsiia/ Turkey

Тянь-Шань /tian'-shán'/ Tien Shan

Уганда /ugánda/ Uganda
Узбекистан /uzbekistán/ Uzbekistan
Украина /ukraína/ the Ukraine
Улан-Батор /ulán-bátor/ Ulan-Bator
Урал /urál/ Urals
Уругвай /urugvái/ Uruguay

Федеративная Республика Германия (ФРГ) /federatívnaia respúblika germániia, fé ér gé/ Federal Republic of Germany (FRG)
Филиппины /filippíny/ the Philippines
Финляндия /finliándiia/ Finland
Фолклендские Острова /folkléndskie ostrová/ the Folkland Islands
Франция /frántsiia/ France

Ханой /khanói/ Hanoi
Хельсинки /khél'sinki/ Helsinki
Хиросима /khirosíma/ Hiroshima

Черное море /chórnoe móre/ the Black Sea
Чехо-Словакия /chékho-slovákiia/ Czechoslovakia
Чили /chíli/ Chile

Швейцария /shveitsáriia/ Switzerland
Швеция /shvétsiia/ Sweden
Шотландия /shotlándiia/ Scotland

Шри-Ланка /shri-lanká/ Sri Lanka

Эдинбург /edinbúrg/ Edinburgh
Эквадор /ekvadór/ Ecuador
Эстония /estóniia/ Estonia
Эфиопия /efiópiia/ Ethiopia

Югославия /iugosláviia/ Yugoslavia
Южная Америка /iúzhnaia amérika/ South America
Южная Корея /íuzhnaia koréia/ South Korea
Южно-Африканская Республика /íuzhno-afrikánskaia
   respúblika/ Republic of South Africa
Ютландия /iutlándiia/ Jutland

Ява /iáva/ Java
Якутия /iakútiia/ Yakutia
Ямайка /iamáika/ Jamaica
Япония /iapóniia/ Japan
Японское море /iapónskoe móre/ the Sea of Japan

ENGLISH-RUSSIAN
DICTIONARY
АНГЛО-РУССКИЙ
СЛОВАРЬ

LIST OF ABBREVIATIONS
ENGLISH

adj — имя прилагательное
adv —наречие
conj — союз
interj — междометие
n — имя существительное
num — числительное
pl — множественное число
poss. (pron) — притяжательное
(местоимение)

predic. — предикативное
употребление
prep — предлог
pron — местоимение
v — глагол
vi — непереходный глагол
vt — переходный глагол

RUSSIAN

ав. — авиация
анат. — анатомия
воен. — военное дело
вчт. — вычислительная
техника
грам. — грамматика
ед. ч. — единственное
число
ж.-д. — железнодорожный
транспорт
ист. — история
мат. — математика
мед. — медицина
мн. ч. — множественное
число
муз. — музыка
о-в(а) — остров(а)
оз. — озеро
п. — падеж

перен. — в переносном
значении
п-ов — полуостров
прил. — имя прилагательное
разг. — разговорное слово,
выражение
рел. — религия
см. — смотри
сущ. — имя существительное
с.-х. — сельское хозяйство
тех. — техника
физ. — физика
фото — фотография
хим. — химия
церк. — церковное слово,
выражение
шахм. — шахматы

Предисловие

Перед вами не совсем обычный словарь. Он предназначен для тех, кто еще недостаточно хорошо овладел английским языком и испытывает затруднения при чтении транскрипций. Поэтому в этом словаре произношение английских слова дается в русской транслитерации. Как известно, не существует точного соответствия между английскими и русскими звуками. Особое затруднение вызывают следующие звуки:

1. Глухой и звонкий межзубные звуки, которые на письме передаются сочетанием букв th; в данном словаре они обозначаются русскими буквами з, с, т, ф.

2. Т.н. "нейтральный" звук — в большинстве случаев гласный звук, на который не падает ударение. У нас в словаре он передан буквами э, е.

3. Долгий "нейтральный" звук, особенно в начале слова — early, urgent и т.п. Для его обозначения в русском языке более всего подходит буква ё. Однако следует помнить, что произносить этот звук надо без напряжения, т.е. как что-то среднее между о и ё.

Что касается ударений, то в односложных словах они опущены; кроме того, ударение не проставлено в тех случаях, когда оно падает на букву ё. Многие слова имеют два или даже три ударения.

В английском языке гласные звуки различаются по долготе звучания. Мы пользовались удвоенной буквой для обозначения долгого ударного звука; в безударных слогах долгота не указывается.

Словарь содержит около 6500 слов и сочетаний, снабженных краткими грамматическими пояснениями. В конце приведен список географических названий.

Мы надеемся, что этот словарь поможет вам быстрее адаптироваться в новой языковой среде. Желаем успеха!

A

A, a /эй/ (муз.) ля; (A) высшая оценка, "отлично"; from A to Z /фром эй ту зэд/ от а до я

a, an /эй, э, эн/ неопределенный артикль (на русский не переводится)

aback /эбэ́к/ adv: taken ~ /тэйкн ~/ застигнутый врасплох

abandon /эбэ́ндэн/ vt оставлять, покидать

abate /эбэ́йт/ vi стихать, успокаиваться

abbey /э́би/ n аббатство

abbot /э́бэт/ n аббат

abbreviation /эбри́ивиэ́йшн/ n сокращение

abdomen /э́бдэмен/ n брюшная полость; живот

abduct /эбда́кт/ vt похищать

ability /эби́лити/ n способность

able /эйбл/ adj способный; be ~ /би ~/ мочь, быть в состоянии

aboard /эбо́рд/ adv на борту

abolish /эбо́лиш/ vt отменять

abortion /эбо́ршн/ n аборт

abortive /эбо́ртив/ adj неудавшийся

abound /эба́унд/ vi изобиловать

about /эба́ут/ prep о; вокруг; adv приблизительно

above /эба́в/ prep над; более; выше

abridge /эбри́дж/ vt сокращать

abroad /эбро́од/ adv за границей

abrupt /эбра́пт/ adj отрывистый; резкий

absent /э́бсент/ adj отсутствующий

absent-minded /э́бсентма́йндыд/ adj рассеянный

absolute /э́бсэлют/ adj абсолютный

absorb /эбсо́рб/ vt поглощать, впитывать

abstain /эбстэ́йн/ vi воздерживаться

abstract /э́бстрэкт/ adj абстрактный

absurd /эбсёрд/ adj нелепый

abundant /эба́ндэнт/ adj обильный;

abuse /эбью́юс/ n брань; злоупотребление

academic /э́кэдэ́мик/ adj академический

academy /экэ́деми/ n академия

accelerate /экса́лерэйт/ vti ускорять(ся)

accent /э́ксент/ n ударение; акцент

accept /экса́пт/ vt принимать

acceptable /экса́птэбл/ adj приемлемый, допустимый

accessible /экса́сибл/ adj доступный

accident /э́ксидэнт/ n несчастный случай

accidental /э́ксидэ́нтл/ adj случайный

acclaim /эклэ́йм/ vt приветствовать

accommodation /эко́мэдэ́йшн/ n жилье

accompany /эка́мпэни/ vt сопровождать; аккомпанировать

accomplish /эко́мплиш/ vt завершать; исполнять

accordingly /эко́рдингли/ adv соответственно

according to /эко́рдингтэ/ prep согласно

account /эка́унт/ n счет; отчет; settle ~s /сэтл ~c/ сводить счеты; take into ~ /тэйк и́нту ~/ принимать во внимание

accountant /эка́унтэнт/ n бухгалтер

accredited /экрэ́дитыд/ adj аккредитованный

accumulate /экью́юмьюлэйт/ vt накапливать

accurate /э́кьюрит/ adj точный

accuse /экьюз/ vt обвинять

accustomed /экáстэмд/ adj привыкший

ace /эйс/ n (карты) туз; ас

ache /эйк/ n боль; vi болеть

achieve /эчи́ив/ vt достигать

achievement /эчи́ивмент/ n достижение

acid /э́сид/ adj кислый; n кислота

acknowledge /экнóлидж/ vt признавать; подтверждать получение (письма)

acoustic /экýустик/ adj акустический

acquaintance /эквэ́йнтэнс/ n знакомый; знакомство

acquire /эквáйе/ vt приобретать, полу-чать

acquit /экви́т/ vt оправдывать

acquittance /экви́тэнс/ n расписка об уплате долга

acre /э́йкэ/ n акр

across /экрóс/ adv поперек; на той стороне; крест-накрест

act /экт/ n поступок; акт; vti действовать; исполнять (роль)

action /экшн/ n действие

activity /экти́вити/ n деятельность

actor /э́ктэ/ n актер

actual /э́кчюэл/ adj действительный

actually /э́кчюэли/ adv на самом деле, фактически

acute /экьью́ют/ adj острый; проницательный

adapt /эдэ́пт/ vt приспособлять; переделывать

add /эд/ vt добавлять; складывать

addendum /эдэ́ндэм/ n приложение (к книге, договору и т.п.)

addict /э́дикт/ n наркоман

additional /эди́шнл/ adj дополнительный

address /эдрэ́с/ n адрес; обращение; vt адресовать; обращаться к

addressee /э́дрэси́и/ n адресат

adequate /э́диквит/ adj соответствующий

adhere /эдхи́э/ vi прилипать; твердо держаться (принципов и т.п.)

adjective /э́джиктив/ n (грам.) имя прилагательное

adjourn /эджёрн/ vt отсрочивать; объявлять перерыв (в работе)

adjust /эджа́ст/ vt поправлять; регулировать

administration /эдми́нистрэ́йшн/ n управление; администрация; правительство

admirable /э́дмэрэбл/ adj восхитительный; похвальный

admiral /э́дмэрл/ n адмирал

admire /эдма́йе/ vt восхищаться, любоваться

admission /эдми́шн/ n признание; вход

admit /эдми́т/ vt впускать; допускать

adolescent /э́доле́снт/ adj подростковый; n юноша; девушка; подросток

adopt /эдо́пт/ vt усыновлять, удочерять; принимать

adorable /эдо́орэбл/ adj восхитительный

adorn /эдо́рн/ vt украшать

adult /э́далт/ n, adj взрослый

advance /эдва́анс/ n наступление; успех; (фин.) аванс; vt продвигать; платить авансом; vi делать успехи

advanced /эдва́анст/ adj передовой; пожилой; успевающий

advantage /эдва́антыдж/ n преимущество

adventure /эдве́нче/ n приключение; авантюра

adverb /э́двёрб/ n наречие

advertisement, сокр. ad /эдве́ртисмент, эд/ n реклама

advice /эдва́йс/ n совет

advise /эдва́йз/ vt советовать

advocate /э́двэкит/ n адвокат; сторонник; /э́двэкейт/ vt защищать; отстаивать

aeroplane /э́эрэплэйн/ n самолет

aesthetics /исте́тикс/ n эстетика

affair /эфэ́э/ n дело; love ~/лав ~/ роман, связь

affect /эфе́кт/ vt влиять на; затрагивать (интересы)

affiliate /эфи́лиэйт/ vt присоединять в качестве филиала

affirm /эфёрм/ vt утверждать

afford /эфо́рд/ vt позволять себе

afraid /эфрэ́йд/ pred adj испуганный

after /а́афтэ/ prep за; после; adv позади; потом; ~ all /~p оол/ в конце концов

afternoon /а́афтэну́ун/ n время после полудня

afterwards /а́афтэвэдз/ adv потом

again /эге́н/ adv опять

against /эге́йнст/ prep против

age /эйдж/ n возраст; век

aged /э́йджид/ adj пожилой

agency /э́йдженси/ n агентство

agent /э́йджент/ n агент

aggravate /э́грэвэйт/ vt ухудшать

aggressive /эгре́сив/ adj агрессивный

ago /эго́у/ adv тому назад; long ~ /лонг ~/ давно

agony /э́гэни/ n мука

agree /эгри́и/ vt согласовывать; vi соглашаться

agreement /эгри́имент/ n договор

agriculture /э́грикалче/ n сельское хозяйство

ahead /эхе́д/ adv вперед, впереди

aid /эйд/ n пособие; помощь

ailment /э́йлмент/ n болезнь

aim /эйм/ n цель

air /ээ/ n воздух; adj воздушный

air-conditioning /э́экэнди́шнинг/ n кондиционирование воздуха

airline /э́элайн/ n авиалиния

airmail /э́эмэйл/ n авиапочта

alarm /эла́рм/ n тревога

alarm clock /эла́рмклок/ n будильник

alas /эла́ас/ interj увы

album /э́лбэм/ n альбом

alcohol /э́лкэхол/ n алкоголь

alert /эле́рт/ adj бдительный

algebra /э́лджибрэ/ n алгебра

alibi /э́либай/ n алиби

alien /э́йльен/ adj иностранный; чуждый; n иностранец, иностранка

alike /эла́йк/ adj схожий; adv одинаково

alimony /э́лимэни/ n алименты

alive /эла́йв/ adj живой

all /оол/ adj весь, все, вся; всякий; ~ the same /~ зэ сэйм/ все равно; ~ right /~ райт/ хорошо; pron все, всё; not at ~ /нот эт ~/ ничуть, пожалуйста allergic /элёрджик/ adj аллергический

alliance /эла́йенс/ n союз

allotment /элóтмент/ n участок земли

allow /эла́у/ vt позволять, допускать

allowance /эла́уэнс/ n пособие; деньги на расходы; travelling ~ /трэ́велинг ~/ командировочные

ally /э́лай/ n союзник

almost /óолмоуст/ adv почти

alone /элóун/ adj один; adv только

along /элóнг/ prep вдоль; по; ~ the road /~ зэ рóуд/ по дороге

aloud /эла́уд/ adv вслух, громко

alphabet /э́лфэбит/ n алфавит, азбука

already /олрэ́ди/ adv уже

also /óолсоу/ adv также, тоже

alter /óолтэ/ vt изменять, переделывать

alternative /олтёрнэтив/ adj альтернативный; n альтернатива

although /олзóу/ conj хотя

altogether /óолтэгéзэ/ adv в целом; всего

always /óолвэз/ adv всегда

ambassador /эмбáсэдэ/ n посол

ambiguous /эмби́гьюэс/ adj двусмысленный

ambition /эмби́шн/ n честолюбие

ambulance /э́мбьюлэнс/ n карета скорой помощи

amiable /э́ймьебл/ adj любезный

among /эмáнг/ prep среди; между

amount /эмáунт/ n сумма; количество

amplifier /э́мплифайе/ n (радио) усилитель

amusing /эмью́юзинг/ adj забавный

analyse /э́нэлайз/ vt анализировать

analysis /эна́лэсис/ n анализ

anatomy /эна́тэми/ n анатомия

ancestor /э́нсистэ/ n предок

anchovy /э́нчэви/ n анчоус

ancient /эйншнт/ adj древний

and /энд/ conj и

angel /э́йнжел/ n ангел

anger /э́нгэ/ n гнев, ярость; vt сердить

angle /энгл/ n угол

angry /э́нгри/ adj сердитый

animal /э́нимэл/ n животное

animated /э́нимэйтыд/ adj оживленный; ~ cartoon(s) /~ карту́ун(з)/ мультипликация

ankle /энкл/ n лодыжка

anniversary /э́нивёсри/ n годовщина

announce /эна́унс/ vt объявлять

annoy /эно́й/ vt раздражать

annual /э́ньюэл/ adj ежегодный, годовой

annul /эна́л/ vt аннулировать

anonymous /эно́нимэс/ adj анонимный

another /эна́зэ/ pron, adj другой, еще один

answer /а́ансэ/ n ответ; vt отвечать

ant /энт/ n муравей

ante meridiem, сокр. a.m. /э́нтимири́диэм, эй эм/ до полудня

antibiotic /э́нтибайо́тик/ n антибиотик

anticipate /энти́сипэйт/ vt предчувствовать

antidote /э́нтидоут/ n противоядие

antiquity /энти́квити/ n античность; древность, глубокая старина

antiseptic /э́нтисе́птик/ n антисептическое средство; adj антисептический

anus /э́йнэс/ n (анат.) задний проход

anxious /э́нкшес/ adj озабоченный; be ~ /би~/ страстно желать

any /э́ни/ adj любой, всякий; pron кто-нибудь что-нибудь; adv несколько

anybody, anyone /э́нибо́ди, э́ниван/ pron кто-нибудь

anyhow /э́нихау/ adv как-нибудь; так или иначе

anything /э́нифинг/ pron что-нибудь

anyway /э́нивэй/ adv где-нибудь, где/куда угодно

apart /эпа́рт/ adv отдельно

apartment /эпа́ртмент/ n квартира

ape /эйп/ n обезьяна; vt подражать, обезьянничать

apologize /эпо́лэджайз/ vi извиняться

appalling /эпо́олинг/ adj ужасный

apparatus /э́пэрэ́йтэс/ n аппарат;

apparent /эпэ́рэнт/ adj явный

appeal /эпи́ил/ n призыв; vi обращаться; подавать апелляционную жалобу

appear /эпи́э/ vi появляться; казаться

appearance /эпи́эрэнс/ n появление; вид; видимость

appendicitis /эпе́ндиса́йтис/ n аппендицит

appetite /э́питайт/ n аппетит

applaud /эпло́од/ vt аплодировать

apple /эпл/ n яблоко

applicant /э́пликэнт/ n кандидат; абитуриент

application /эпликéйшн/ n заявление; ~ form /~ форм/ анкета

apply /эплáй/ vt применять; vi ~ to /~ ту/ обращаться к

appointment /эпóйнтмент/ n назначение; должность; встреча; прием (у врача)

appraisal /эпрэ́йзл/ n оценка

appreciate /эпри́ишиэйт/ vt ценить

approach /эпрóуч/ vi приближаться к; обращаться к; n подход

appropriate /эпрóуприит/ adj подходящий; /эпрóуприэйт/ vt присваивать, красть; ассигновывать

approve /эпрýув/ vt одобрять

approximate /эпрóксимит/ adj приблизительный

apricot /э́йприкот/ n абрикос

April /эйпрл/ n апрель

apt /эпт/ adj подходящий; способный

aquarium /эквэ́риэм/ n аквариум

Arabic /эрэ́бик/ n арабский язык; adj арабский

arable /э́рэбл/ adj пахотный

arbiter /а́рбитэ/ n арбитр

arc /арк/ n дуга

arch /арч/ n арка

archaeology /а́ркиóлэджи/ n археология

archaic /аркéйик/ adj устарелый

archbishop /а́рчби́шэп/ n архиепископ

archipelago /а́ркипéлигоу/ n архипелаг

architecture /а́ркитэкче/ n архитектура

ardent /а́рдэнт/ adj горячий, пылкий

area /э́эриэ/ n площадь; зона

argue /áргью/ vt обсуждать; vi спорить

argument /áргьюмент/ n аргумент; спор

arise /эрáйз/ vi возникать

aristocratic /э́ристэкра́тик/ adj аристократический

arithmetic /эри́фметик/ n арифметика

arm /арм/ n рука; pl оружие; vti вооружать(ся)

armament /а́рмэмент/ n вооружение

armchair /а́рмчеэ/ n кресло

armpit /а́рмпит/ n подмышка

army /а́рми/ n армия; join the ~ /джойн зы ~/ поступить
на военную службу

around /эра́унд/ prep вокруг; adv всюду; кругом

arrange /эрэ́йндж/ vt устраивать; приводить в порядок;
(муз.) аранжировать

arrest /эрéст/ n арест; vt арестовывать

arrival /эра́йвл/ n прибытие

arrive /эра́йв/ vi приезжать

arrogant /э́рэгэнт/ adj надменный

arsenic /арсéник/ n мышьяк

arson /арсн/ n поджог

art /арт/ n искусство

article /а́ртикл/ n статья; предмет; (грам.) артикль

artificial /а́ртифи́шл/ adj искусственный

artillery /арти́лери/ n артиллерия

artist /а́ртист/ n художник

as /эз/ adv как, в качестве; ~ a rule /~ э руул/ как
правило; ~ if /~ иф/ как будто

ascend /эсэ́нд/ vi подниматься; vt подниматься на

ash(es) /эш(из)/ n pl зола; n ясень

ashamed /эшéймд/ adj пристыженный

ashore /эшóр/ adv на берег, на берегу

ash-tray /э́штрэй/ n пепельница

Asian /эйшн/ n азиат, азиатка; adj азиатский

ask /ааск/ vt спрашивать; просить; ~ a question /~ э квесчн/ задавать вопрос

asleep /эслйип/ adj спящий; be ~ /би ~/ спать; fall ~ /фоол ~/ засыпать

asparagus /эспэ́рэгэс/ n спаржа

aspect /э́спект/ n аспект; сторона

aspiration /э́спэрэ́йшн/ n стремление

aspirin /э́спэрин/ n аспирин

ass /эс/ n осел

assassin /эсэ́син/ n убийца

assault /эсóолт/ n нападение; vt нападать

assemble /эсэ́мбл/ vt собирать; монтировать; vi собираться

assent /эсэ́нт/ n согласие; vi соглашаться

assert /эсёрт/ vt утверждать

assess /эсэ́с/ vt оценивать; облагать (налогом)

assets /э́сэтс/ n pl (фин.) актив; имущество

assignment /эсáйнмент/ n назначение; ассигнование

assimilate /эсúмилэйт/ vt ассимилировать; усваивать

assistance /эсúстэнс/ n помощь

association /эсóусиэ́йшн/ n ассоциация

assortment /эсóртмент/ n ассортимент

assume /эсъю́юм/ vt брать на себя; предполагать

assure /эшуэ́/ vt уверять

asthma /э́смэ/ n астма

astonish /эстóниш/ vt удивлять

astrology /эстрóлэджи/ n астрология

astronomy /эстрóнэми/ n астрономия

asylum /эсáйлэм/ n приют; психиатрическая больница

at /эе/ в; на; ~ first /~ фёрст/ сначала; ~ home /~ хóум/ дома; ~ last /~ лааст/ наконец; ~ least /~ лиист/ по крайней мере; ~ night /~ найт/ ночью; ~ once /~ ванс/ сразу

athlete / э́тлиит/ n спортсмен, атлет

atmosphere /э́тмэсфиэ/ n атмосфера

atom /э́тэм/ n атом

attach /этэ́ч/ vt прикреплять; придавать

attack /этэ́к/ n атака; припадок

attain /этэ́йн/ vt достигать

attempt /этэ́мпт/ n попытка; vt пытаться

attend /этэ́нд/ vt посещать (лекции); ухаживать (за больным)

attention /этэ́ншн/ n внимание

attitude /э́титьюд/ n отношение

attract /этрэ́кт/ vt привлекать; пленять

attractive /этрэ́ктив/ adj привлекательный

attribute /э́трибьют/ n свойство, атрибут; /этри́бьют/ vt приписывать

auction /бóкшн/ n аукцион; vt продавать с аукциона

audience /бóдьенс/ n публика

audit /бóдит/ n ревизия; vt проверять (счета)

auditor /бóдитэ/ n ревизор

augment /огмéнт/ vti увеличивать(ся)

August /бóгэст/ n август

aunt /аант/ n тетя

Australian /острэ́йлияэн/ n австралиец, австралийка; adj австралийский

author /о́осэ/ n автор

authority /осо́рити/ n авторитет; pl власти

automatic /бо́тэмэ́тик/ adj автоматический

autonomy /ото́нэми/ n автономия

autumn /о́отэм/ n осень

auxiliary /огзи́льери/ adj вспомогательный

available /эвэ́йлэбл/ adj имеющийся; доступный

avenue /э́винью/ n авеню

average /э́вэридж/ adj средний

aviation /э́йвиэ́йшн/ n авиация

avoid /эво́йд/ vt избегать

awake /эвэ́йк/ adj бодрствующий

award /эво́рд/ n награда

aware /эвэ́э/ adj сознающий; be ~ of /би ~ ов/ сознавать

away /эвэ́й/ adj отсутствующий; adv прочь; far ~ /фар ~/ далеко

awful /о́офул/ adj ужасный

awkward /о́оквэд/ adj неуклюжий

axe /экс/ n топор

B

babble /бэбл/ vti бормотать; журчать

baby /бэ́йби/ n младенец

bachelor /бэ́челэ/ n холостяк

back /бэк/ n спина; защитник (футбол); adj задний; adv назад; vt поддерживать background /бэ́кграунд/ n фон; подготовка, образование; происхождение

backward /бэ́квэд/ adj обратный; отсталый; adv назад; задом наперед

bacon /бэйкн/ n грудинка, бекон

bad /бэд/ adj плохой

badge /бэдж/ n значок; эмблема

bag /бэг/ n мешок; сумка

baggage /бэ́гидж/ n багаж

bake /бэйк/ vt печь

baker's shop /бэ́йкэзшо́п/ n булочная

balance /бэ́лэнс/ n равновесие; баланс; vt взвешивать

balcony /бэ́лкэни/ n балкон

bald /боолд/ adj лысый

ball /боол/ n шар; мяч; бал

ballet /бэ́лей/ n балет

balloon /бэлу́ун/ n воздушный шар

ballot /бэ́лэт/ n баллотировка

ballot-paper /бэ́лэтпэ́йпэ/ n избирательный бюллетень

ban /бэн/ n запрещение; vt запрещать

banana /бэна́анэ/ n банан

band /бэнд/ n оркестр; банда; лента

bandage /бэ́ндыдж/ n бинт, повязка

bang /бэнг/ n удар; vti ударять(ся)

banish /бэ́ниш/ vt изгонять

bank /бэнк/ n берег; банк

bankrupt /бэ́нкрэпт/ n банкрот; go ~ /го́у ~/ обанкротиться

banquet /бэ́нквит/ n банкет

bar /бар/ n полоска (металла); брусок; преграда; бар

barber /бáрбэ/ n парикмахер

bare /бээ/ adj голый; vt обнажать

bargain /бáргин/ n сделка; into the ~ /йнту зэ ~/ к тому же; vi торговаться

barley /бáрли/ n ячмень

barrier /бэ́риэ/ n барьер

barter /бáртэ/ n меновая торговля; vt обмениваться (товарами)

base /бэйс/ n основа; база

baseball /бэ́йсбол/ n бейсбол

basement /бэ́йсмент/ n фундамент; (полу)подвальный этаж

basic /бэ́йсик/ adj основной

basin /бэйсн/ n таз; водоем

basis /бэ́йсис/ n основание; база

basket /бáаскит/ n корзина

bastard /бáстэд/ adj незаконнорожденный; n внебрачный ребенок

bath /баас/ n ванна

bathe /бэйз/ n купание; vti купать(ся)

battery /бэ́тэри/ n батарея; аккумулятор

battle /бэтл/ n битва

bay /бэй/ n залив

bazaar /бэзáр/ n базар

be /бии/ vi быть; how are you? /хáу ар ю/ как вы поживаете?; how much is it? /хáу мач из ит/ сколько это стоит?; ~ off /~ оф/ уезжать

beach /биич/ n пляж

bean /биин/ n боб

bear /бээ/ n медведь

bear /бээ/ vt носить; рожать; терпеть, выносить; vi
держаться; ~ in mind /~ ин майнд/ помнить

beard /бйэд/ n борода

beast /биист/ n зверь

beat /биит/ vt ударять

beautiful /бьютэфул/ adj красивый

because /бикоз/ conj потому что; ~ of /~ ов/ из-за

become /бикам/ vi становиться

bed /бед/ n постель; клумба; русло; go to ~ /гоу ту ~/
ложиться спать

bedroom /бедрум/ n спальня

bee /бии/ n пчела

beef /бииф/ n говядина

beefsteak /биифстэйк/ n бифштекс

beer /бйэ/ n пиво

beetroot /биитрут/ n свекла

before /бифор/ adv раньше; long ~ /лонг ~/ задолго; prep
перед; the day ~ /зэ дэй ~/ позавчера

beggar /бегэ/ n нищий

begin /бигин/ vti начинать(ся)

beginning /бигининг/ n начало

behaviour /бихейвье/ n поведение

behind /бихайнд/ adv позади; prep за, сзади

being /биинг/ n существо; бытие; human ~ /хьюмэн ~/
человек

believe /билиив/ vt верить

bell /бел/ n колокол; звонок

belong /билонг/ vi принадлежать

belongings /билóнгингз/ n pl пожитки

below /билóу/ adv внизу; prep ниже, под

belt /белт/ n пояс; ремень

bench /бенч/ n скамья

beneath /бинúис/ adv внизу; prep под, ниже

benefit /бéнифит/ n польза; пособие

bent /бент/ adj изогнутый

berry /бéри/ n ягода

beside /бисáйд/ prep рядом с, около

besides /бисáйдз/ adv кроме того

best /бест/ adj самый лучший

bestseller /бéстсéлэ/ n бестселлер

bet /бет/ n пари; make a ~ /мэйк э ~/ заключать пари

betray /битрэ́й/ vt выдавать

better /бéтэ/ adj лучший; be ~ off /би ~ роф/ жить лучше; adv лучше

between /битвúин/ adv между

beware /бивэ́э/ vi остерегаться; ~ of trains! /~ ов трэйнз/
    берегись поезда!

beyond /бийóнд/ prep по ту сторону; выше; ~ doubt /~
    дáут/ вне сомнения

bias /бáйес/ n пристрастие

Bible /байбл/ n библия

bicycle /бáйсикл/ n велосипед

bid /бид/ n заявка; make a ~ /мэйк э ~/ предлагать цену

big /биг/ adj большой

bike /байк/ n велосипед

bill /бил/ n законопроект; счет; банкнота; ~ of entry /~
    ов э́нтри/ таможенная декларация; 10 dollar ~ /тен
    дóлэ ~/ десятидолларовая купюра

billion /би́льен/ n миллиард

bin /бин/ n мусорное ведро

bind /байнд/ vt связывать

biography /байо́грэфи/ n биография

biology /байо́лэджи/ n биология

birch /бёрч/ n береза

bird /бёрд/ n птица

birth /бёрс/ n рождение; ~ certificate /~ сети́фикит/ метрика; ~ control /~ кэнтро́ул/ противозачаточные меры

birthday /бёрсдэй/ n день рождения

biscuit /би́скит/ n печенье

bit /бит/ n частица; a ~ /э ~/ немного; not a ~ /нот э ~/ ничуть

bitch /бич/ n сука

bite /байт/ n укус; have a ~ /хэв э ~/ перекусить; vt кусать

bitter /би́тэ/ adj горький

black /блэк/ adj черный

blackmail /блэ́кмэйл/ n шантаж

bladder /блэ́дэ/ n мочевой пузырь

blade /блэйд/ n лезвие

blame /блэйм/ n вина; vt порицать

blanket /блэ́нкит/ n одеяло

blast /блааст/ n взрыв

blazer /блэ́йзэ/ n блейзер; куртка

bleach /блиич/ vt белить, отбеливать

blend /бленд/ n смесь; vt смешивать

bless /блес/ vt благословлять

blind /блайнд/ adj слепой

block /блок/ n квартал

blond(e) /блонд/ n блондин, блондинка

blood /блад/ n кровь; ~ pressure /~ пре́ше/ кровяное давление

blouse /бла́уз/ n кофточка

blow /бло́у/ n удар

blue /блюю/ adj синий, голубой

blunder /бла́ндэ/ n ошибка

blunt /блант/ adj тупой; vt притуплять

blush /блаш/ n краска стыда; vt краснеть

board /борд/ n доска; правление; on ~ /он ~/ на борту; vt садиться (на самолет и т.д.)

boarding /бо́рдинг/ n пансион, интернат

boast /бо́уст/ vti хвастаться, гордиться

boat /бо́ут/ n лодка; пароход

bobsleigh /бо́бслей/ n бобслей

body /бо́ди/ n тело; корпус; орган, ассоциация

boil /бойл/ vti кипятить(ся)

boiled /бойлд/ adj вареный; кипяченый

bold /бо́улд/ adj смелый; наглый

bolt /бо́улт/ n болт; vt запирать на засов (дверь)

bomb /бом/ n бомба; atom ~ /э́тэм ~/ атомная бомба; vt бомбить

bond /бонд/ n связь; облигация

bone /бо́ун/ n кость

bonus /бо́унэс/ n премиальные

book /бук/ n книга; vt заказывать (билеты и т.п.)

booking-office /бу́кингфис/ n билетная касса

book-keeper /бу́ккиипэ/ n бухгалтер

boom /буум/ n гул; большой спрос

boot /буут/ n ботинок; багажник; high ~ /хай ~/ сапог

border /бо́рдэ/ n граница

boredom /бо́одэм/ n скука

born /борн/ adj (при)рожденный; be ~ /би ~/ родиться

borrow /бо́роу/ vt брать взаймы

bosom /бу́зэм/ n грудь

boss /бос/ n хозяин, босс

botany /бо́тэни/ n ботаника

both /бо́ус/ adj, pron оба

bother /бо́зэ/ vt беспокоить, надоедать

bottle /ботл/ n бутылка

bottom /бо́тэм/ n дно; зад

bound /ба́унд/ n прыжок; adj связанный, обязанный

boundary /ба́ундэри/ n граница

bow /бо́у/ n лук; смычок; бант

bow /ба́у/ n поклон; vi кланяться

bowels /ба́уэлз/ n pl кишечник

bowl /бо́ул/ n чаша, ваза; шар

box /бокс/ n коробка, ящик

box-office /бо́ксо́фис/ n театральная касса

boxer /бо́ксэ/ n боксер

boy /бой/ n мальчик

brain /брэйн/ n мозг

brain-drain /брэ́йндрэйн/ n утечка мозгов

brainwash /брэ́йнвош/ vt "промывать мозги"

brake /брэйк/ n тормоз; vt тормозить

branch /браанч/ n ветка; отрасль; филиал

brand /брэнд/ n клеймо, марка, сорт

brandy /брэнди/ n коньяк

brass /браас/ n желтая медь, латунь; top ~ /топ ~/ руководящая верхушка

brassiere /брэсиэ/ n бюстгальтер

brave /брэйв/ adj храбрый

Brazilian /брэзильен/ n бразилец, бразильянка; adj бразильский

breach /бриич/ n пролом; нарушение (закона)

bread /брэд/ n хлеб

bread-winner /брэдвинэ/ n кормилец

break /брэйк/ n поломка; lunch ~ /ланч ~/ перерыв на обед; vt ломать

breakfast /брэкфэст/ n завтрак

breast /брэст/ n грудь

breathe /брииз/ vi дышать

bribe /брайб/ n взятка

brick /брик/ n кирпич

bride /брайд/ n невеста

bridegroom /брайдгрум/ n жених

bridge /бридж/ n мост; бридж

brief /брииф/ adj краткий

brigade /бригейд/ n бригада

bright /брайт/ adj яркий

brilliant /брильент/ adj блестящий

bring /бринг/ vt приносить, привозить; ~ to life /~ ту лайф/ приводить в чувство; ~ up /~ ап/ воспитывать

British /бритиш/ adj британский, английский

broad /броод/ adj широкий

broadcast /бро́одкаст/ vt передавать по радио

broiler /бро́йлэ/ n бройлер

broken /бро́укн/ adj разбитый

broker /бро́укэ/ n маклер

bronchitis /бронка́йтис/ n бронхит

bronze /бронз/ n бронза

brooch /бро́уч/ n брошь

broth /брос/ n суп

brother /бра́зэ/ n брат

brother-in-law /бра́зэринлоо/ n зять, шурин, деверь

brow /бра́у/ n бровь

brown /бра́ун/ adj коричневый, карий

brush /браш/ n щетка, кисть

bucket /ба́кит/ n ведро

bud /бад/ n почка (растения)

budget /ба́джит/ n бюджет

buffet /буфе́й/ n буфет, буфетная стойка

bug /баг/ n клоп

build /билд/ vt строить

building /би́лдинг/ n здание

bulb /балб/ n электрическая лампочка

bulk /балк/ n бо́льшая часть; sell in ~ /сел ин ~/
   продавать оптом

bull-dog /бу́лдог/ n бульдог

bullet /бу́лит/ n пуля

bulletin /бу́литин/ n бюллетень

bunch /банч/ n пучок; связка

burden /бёдн/ n бремя; vt обременять

bureau /бьюрóу/ n бюро

bureaucratic /бьюэрокрáтик/ adj бюрократический

burglary /бёглэри/ n кража со взломом

burn /бён/ n ожог; vt жечь; vi гореть

burst /бёст/ n взрыв; vi взрываться; ~ open /~ óупэн/
распахиваться

bury /бэри/ vt хоронить

bus /бас/ n автобус

bush /буш/ n куст

business /бúзнис/ n дело, коммерческое предприятие

businessman /бúзнисмэн/ n бизнесмен

bust /баст/ n бюст, грудь

busy /бúзи/ adj занятый

but /бат/ conj но, а; adv только; prep кроме; anything ~
/энифинг ~/ далеко не

butter /бáтэ/ n масло

butterfly /бáтэфлай/ n бабочка

buttock /бáтэк/ n ягодица

button /батн/ n пуговица

buy /бай/ vt покупать

buyer /бáйе/ n покупатель

by /бай/ pron у, около, мимо, посредством; ~ airmail /~
эмэйл/ авиапочтой; ~ law /~ лоо/ по закону; ~ no
means /~ нóу миинз/ ни в коем случае; ~ 5 o'clock /~
файв оклóк/ к пяти часам; ~ the way /~ зэ вэй/ между
прочим; adv близко; мимо

by-election /бáйилéкшн/ n дополнительные выборы

byte /байт/ n (вчт.) байт, слог

C

cab /кэб/ n такси

cabbage /кэ́бидж/ n капуста

cabinet /кэ́бинит/ n кабинет

cable /кейбл/ n кабель; телеграмма

cafe /кэ́фей/ n кафе

cage /кейдж/ n клетка

cake /кейк/ n торт, пирожное

calculate /кэ́лкьюлэйт/ vt вычислять

calendar /кэ́линдэ/ n календарь

call /коол/ n зов, призыв; (телефонный) вызов; vt звать;
~ for /~ фо/ требовать;~ off /~ оф/ отзывать; ~ on /~
он/ навещать

calm /каам/ adj спокойный

camel /кэ́мэл/ n верблюд

camera /кэ́мерэ/ n фотоаппарат

camp /кэмп/ n лагерь

campaign /кэмпэ́йн/ n кампания

can /кэн/ n бидон; банка консервная

can /кэн/ v aux мочь, уметь

Canadian /кэнэ́йдьен/ n канадец, канадка; adj
канадский

cancel /кэнсл/ vt отменять

cancer /кэ́нсэ/ n рак

candidate /кэ́ндидит/ n кандидат

candle /кэндл/ n свеча

cap /кэп/ n шапка, фуражка

capable /кэ́йпэбл/ adj одаренный; ~ of /~ ов/ способный
на

capacity /кэпэсити/ n емкость; способность; (тех.)
мощность

capital /кэпитл/ n капитал; столица; adj главный; ~ letter
/~ лэтэ/ заглавная буква; ~ punishment /~ панишмент/
смертная казнь

capitalism /кэпитэлизм/ n капитализм

captain /кэптин/ n капитан

capture /кэпче/ vt захватывать

car /кар/ n автомобиль (легковой); вагон

card /кард/ n карта; билет (членский,
пригласительный)

care /кээ/ n забота, внимание; take ~ of /тэйк ~ ов/
заботиться о; vi заботиться; I don't ~ /ай доунт ~/ мне
все равно

career /кэриэ/ n карьера; быстрый бег

careful /кээфул/ adj заботливый

careless /кээлис/ adj беззаботный

carpet /карпит/ n ковер

carriage /кэридж/ n повозка; вагон; перевозка

carrot /кэрэт/ n морковь

carry /кэри/ vt везти, нести; ~ on /~ он/ продолжать; ~
out /~ аут/ выполнять

cartoon /катуун/ n карикатура; мультфильм

carve /карв/ vt вырезать, ваять

case /кейс/ n случай; (судебное) дело; чемодан; падеж;
in any ~ /ин эни ~/ во всяком случае

cash /кэш/ n наличные деньги; ~ on delivery /~ он
диливэри/ наложенным платежом; vt: ~ out the cheque
/~ аут зэ чек/ получать деньги по чеку

cassette /кэсе́т/ n кассета; video ~ /ви́деоу ~/ видеокассета

cast /кааст/ n бросок; форма для отливки; (театр.) состав; ~ of mind /~ ов майнд/ склад ума; vt бросать; отливать

castle /каасл/ n за́мок

casual /кэ́жьюэл/ adj случайный; небрежный

cat /кэт/ n кот, кошка

catarrh /кэта́р/ n катар, простуда

catastrophe /кэта́стрэфи/ n катастрофа

catch /кэч/ vt ловить; ~ cold /~ ко́улд/ простужаться

category /кэ́тигэри/ n категория

cater /ке́йтэ/ vi обслуживать

Catholic /кэ́фэлик/ adj католический

cattle /кэтл/ n скот

cauliflower /ко́лифла́уэ/ n цветная капуста

cause /кооз/ n причина

cautious /ко́ошес/ adj осторожный

caviar /кэ́виа/ n икра

cavity /кэ́вити/ n дупло (в зубе)

cease /сиис/ vti прекращать(ся)

ceiling /си́илинг/ n потолок

celebrate /се́либрэйт/ vt праздновать

celery /се́лери/ n сельдерей

cell /сел/ n тюремная камера; (биол.) клетка

cemetery /се́митри/ n кладбище

cent /сэнт/ n цент; per ~ /пер ~/ процент

central /се́нтрэл/ adj центральный

centre /се́нтэ/ n центр

century /сэ́нчури/ n столетие, век

cereal /си́эриэл/ n крупа

certain /сётн/ adj определенный; некий; I'm ~ /айм ~/ я уверен(а)

certainly /сётнли/ adv непременно

certificate /сэти́фикит/ n удостоверение; ~ of health /~ ов хелф/ справка о состоянии здоровья

chain /чейн/ n цепь

chair /чээ/ n стул; кафедра

chairman /че́эмэн/ n председатель

challenge /ча́линдж/ n вызов

chamber /че́ймбэ/ n комната; палата

champagne /шэмпе́йн/ n шампанское

champion /че́мпиэн/ n чемпион

chance /чаанс/ n случайность; by ~ /бай ~/ случайно

change /чейндж/ n перемена, here's your ~ /хи́эз йо ~/ вот ваша сдача; vt менять; делать пересадку; one's mind /~ ванз майнд/ передумывать

channel /чэнл/ n пролив; канал (телевизионный)

chapter /ча́птэ/ n глава (книги)

character /кэ́риктэ/ n характер; буква; персонаж

charge /чардж/ n заряд; обвинение; поручение; цена; pl расходы

charity /че́рити/ n благотворительность

charming /ча́рминг/ adj прелестный

charter /ча́ртэ/ n устав

chatter /ча́тэ/ vi болтать

chauffeur /шо́уфэ/ n шофер

cheap /чиип/ adj дешевый

cheat /чиит/ n обман; vti обманывать

check /чек/ vt проверять; сдерживать

cheek /чиик/ n щека; наглость

cheer /чи́э/ vt ободрять; ~ up /~ ап/ не унывай!

cheerful /чи́эфл/ adj веселый

cheese /чииз/ n сыр

chemical /ке́микл/ adj химический

chemist /ке́мист/ n химик; аптекарь

cheque /чек/ n чек

chess /чес/ n шахматы

chest /чест/ n сундук; грудная клетка

chewing-gum /чу́ингам/ n жевательная резинка

chicken /чи́кин/ n курица

chief /чииф/ adj главный; n глава

child /чайлд/ n ребенок

children /чи́лдрн/ n pl дети

chilli (chilly) /чи́ли/ n красный острый перец

chin /чин/ n подбородок

china /ча́йнэ/ n фарфор

Chinese /чайна́из/ n китаец, китаянка; adj
  китайский

chocolate /чо́кэлит/ n шоколад

choice /чойс/ n выбор

choose /чууз/ vt выбирать

chop /чоп/ n удар; отбивная котлета

chorus /ко́орэс/ n хор

Christ /крайст/ n Христос

Christian /кри́стьен/ adj христианский; n христианин;
  ~ name /~ нэйм/ имя

Christmas /крисмс/ n Рождество; Merry C.! /мéри ~/ с
Рождеством!; C. tree /~ трии/ рождественская елка

chronic /крóник/ adj хронический

church /чёрч/ n церковь

cigar /сигáр/ n сигара

cigarette /сѝгэрéт/ n сигарета

cinema /сѝнимэ/ n кино

cinnamon /сѝнэмэн/ n корица

circle /сёркл/ n круг

circulate /сёркьюлэйт/ vi циркулировать

circumstance /сёркемстэнс/ n обстоятельство

circus /сёркес/ n цирк

cite /сайт/ vt цитировать

citizen /сѝтизн/ n гражданин

citizenship /сѝтизншип/ n подданство

city /сѝти/ n (большой) город

civil /сивл/ adj гражданский

civilization /сѝвилайзéйшн/ n цивилизация

claim /клэйм/ n претензия; (юр.) иск; vt требовать

clan /клэн/ n клан

clap /клэп/ vti хлопать (в ладоши)

clarify /клэ́рифай/ vt вносить ясность в

clash /клэш/ n столкновение; vi сталкиваться

clasp /клаасп/ n застежка

class /клаас/ n класс; сорт

classical /клэ́сикл/ adj классический

clause /клооз/ n статья; (грам.) предложение

clay /клэй/ n глина

clean /клиин/ adj чистый; vt чистить

clear /клиэ/ adj ясный, светлый; четкий

clerk /клаак/ n клерк

clever /клэвэ/ adj умный, искусный

client /клайент/ n клиент, покупатель

climate /клаймит/ n климат

climb /клайм/ vt взбираться на

clinic /клиник/ n клиника

clip /клип/ n приколка (для волос); скрепка (канцелярская)

cloak-room /клоукрум/ n раздевалка

clock /клок/ n часы; at five o'~ /эт файв оклок/ в пять часов

close /клоус/ adj тесный; близкий; /клоуз/ vti закрывать(ся), заканчивать(ся)

clothes /клоувз/ n pl одежда

cloud /клауд/ n облако

clown /клаун/ n клоун

club /клаб/ n дубинка; (спорт.) клюшка; клуб

clue /клуу/ n ключ (к разгадке)

clumsy /кламзи/ adj неуклюжий

cluster /кластэ/ n гроздь; пучок

clutch /клач/ vt зажимать

coach /коуч/ n (ж/д) вагон; тренер

coal /коул/ n уголь

coarse /коос/ adj грубый

coast /коуст/ n побережье

coat /коут/ n пальто; пиджак

cock /кок/ n петух; курок (пистолета)

cockroach /кокроуч/ n таракан

cocktail /кóктэйл/ n коктейль

cocoa /кóукоу/ n какао

cod /код/ n треска

code /кóуд/ n кодекс; код

coercion /коуёршн/ n насилие

coffee /кóфи/ n кофе

coffee-pot /кóфипот/ n кофейник

coffin /кóфин/ n гроб

coil /койл/ n кольцо; (эл.) катушка

coin /койн/ n монета

coincide /кóуинсáйд/ vi совпадать

coke /кóук/ n кокс; кока-кола

cold /кóулд/ adj холодный; I am ~ /айм ~/ мне холодно; n холод, простуда

colic /кóлик/ n колика, резкая боль

collapse /кэлэ́пс/ n крах; vi терпеть крах; терять сознание

collar /кóлэ/ n воротник

colleague /кóлииг/ n коллега

collect /кэлéкт/ vt собирать

college /кóлидж/ n колледж

colloquial /кэлóуквиэл/ adj разговорный

colonel /кёнэл/ n полковник

colour /кáлэ/ n цвет, краска; колорит

colourful /кáлэфул/ adj красочный

column /кóлэм/ n колонна; столб; столбец (газеты); графа

columnist /кóлэмнист/ n фельетонист

comb /кóум/ n расческа

combine /кэмбáйн/ vt объединять; vi смешиваться

combustible /кэмбáстэбл/ adj горючий

come /кам/ vi приходить, приезжать; ~ back /~ бэк/ возвращаться; ~ in! /~ ин/ войди(те)!; ~ to /~ ту/ приходить в себя; ~ what may /~ вот мэй/ будь что будет!

comedy /кóмиди/ n комедия

comet /кóмит/ n комета

comfortable /кáмфэтэбл/ adj удобный

comic /кóмик/ adj комический; n pl комиксы

coming /кáминг/ adj наступающий

comma /кóмэ/ n запятая; inverted ~s /инвёртыд ~з/ кавычки

command /кэмáанд/ n приказ; vt приказывать

commander /кэмáандэ/ n командир; ~-in-chief /~-ин-чииф/ главнокомандующий

commend /кэмéнд/ vt хвалить

commentary /кóментэри/ n комментарий

commerce /кóмес/ n торговля

commercial /кемёршэл/ adj коммерческий

commission /кэмúшн/ n поручение; комиссия; комиссионное вознаграждение

commit /кэмúт/ vt совершать (преступление, самоубийство); ~ oneself /~ вансéлф/ обязаться

commitment /кэмúтмент/ n обязательство

committee /кэмúти/ n комитет

commodity /кэмóдити/ n товар

common /кóмэн/ adj общий; обыкновенный; ~ sense /~ сэнс/ здравый смысл; have nothing in ~ /хэв нáфинг ин ~/ не иметь ничего общего commonplace /ко́мэнплэйс/ n банальность

commonwealth /ко́мэнвэлф/ n государство; the British C. /зэ бри́тиш ~/ Британское Содружество Наций

communication /кэмьюдьюникейшн/ n связь; means of ~ /миинз ов ~/ средства связи

communism /ко́мьюнизм/ n коммунизм

community /кэмью́юнити/ n община

companion /кэмпэ́ньен/ n компаньон(ка)

company /ка́мпэни/ n компания; рота; труппа

compare /кэмпэ́э/ vt сравнивать

comparison /кэмпэ́рисн/ n сравнение

compartment /кэмпа́ртмент/ n отделение; купе

compassion /кэмпэ́шн/ n сострадание

compatible /кэмпэ́тэбл/ adj совместимый

compatriot /кэмпэ́триэт/ n соотечественник

compel /кэмпе́л/ vt заставлять

compensate /ко́мпенсэйт/ vt компенсировать

competent /ко́мпитэнт/ adj компетентный

competition /ко́мпити́шн/ n конкуренция

competitive /кэмпе́титив/ adj конкурирующий

competitor /кэмпе́титэ/ n конкурент

compile /кэмпа́йл/ vt составлять

complain /кэмплэ́йн/ vi жаловаться

complete /кэмпли́ит/ adj полный, законченный; vt завершать

completely /кэмпли́итли/ adv совершенно

complex /ко́мплекс/ adj сложный; n комплекс

complicated /ко́мпликейтыд/ adj сложный

complicity /кэмпли́сити/ n соучастие (в преступлении)

compliment /кómплимент/ n комплимент; pl поздравление

comply /кэмплáй/ vi уступать; ~ with /~ виз/ соглашаться с

component /кэмпóунент/ adj составной; n компонент

compose /кэмпóуз/ vti составлять; сочинять (музыку)

composer /кэмпóузэ/ n композитор

composition /кóмпэзúшн/ n состав; сочинение

compound /кómпаунд/ adj составной, сложный

comprehend /кóмприхéнд/ vt постигать

comprehensive /кóмприхéнсив/ adj исчерпывающий

comprise /кэмпрáйз/ vt заключать в себе

compromise /кómпрэмайз/ n компромисс

compulsory /кэмпáлсэри/ adj обязательный

computer /кэмпьюютэ/ n компьютер

conceal /кэнсúил/ vt скрывать

concentrate /кóнсентрэйт/ vti сосредоточивать (ся)

concept /кóнсэпт/ n понятие

concern /кэнсёрн/ n интерес; беспокойство; концерн; it is no ~ of mine /ит из нóу ~ ов майн/ это меня не касается; vt касаться

concerning /кэнсёрнинг/ prep относительно

concert /кóнсэт/ n концерт

concession /кэнсэ́шн/ n уступка; концессия

concise /кэнсáйс/ adj краткий

conclude /кэнклýуд/ vti заканчивать (ся)

conclusion /кэнклýужн/ n вывод

concrete /кóнкриит/ adj конкретный; бетонный; n бетон

condemn /кэндэ́м/ vt осуждать

condition /кэнди́шн/ n условие; состояние

conduct /ко́ндэкт/ n поведение; /кэнда́кт/ vt руководить; вести

confectioner /кэнфе́кшенэ/ n кондитер; ~'s shop /~з шоп/ кондитерская

confederacy /кэнфе́дэрэси/ n конфедерация

confer /кэнфёр/ vt присуждать (звание, степень)

conference /ко́нференс/ n конференция

confess /кэнфе́с/ vti признавать(ся); исповедовать(ся)

confidence /ко́нфидэнс/ n доверие

confident /ко́нфидэнт/ adj уверенный

confine /кэнфа́йн/ vt ограничивать; be confined to bed /би кэнфа́йнд ту бед/ быть прикованным к постели

confinement /кэнфа́йнмент/ n тюремное заключение

confirm /кэнфёрм/ vt подтверждать

confiscate /ко́нфискейт/ vt конфисковать

confiscation /ко́нфиске́йшн/ n конфискация

conflict /ко́нфликт/ n конфликт

confront /кэнфра́нт/ vt стоять лицом к лицу с

confuse /кэнфью́юз/ vt спутывать; смущать

confusion /кэнфью́южн/ n беспорядок

congratulate /кэнгрэ́тьюлейт/ vt поздравлять

congratulation /кэнгрэ́тьюлейшн/ n поздравление

congress /ко́нгрес/ n конгресс, съезд

conjecture /кэнджекче/ n предположение

connect /кэнэ́кт/ vti соединять(ся)

connection, connexion /кэнэ́кшн/ n связь; родство; have good ~s /хэв гуд ~з/ иметь хорошие связи

conquer /ко́нкэ/ vt завоевывать

conscience /кóншенс/ n совесть

conscious /кóншес/ adj сознательный

conscription /кэнскрúпшн/ n воинская повинность

consent /кэнсэ́нт/ n согласие; vi соглашаться

consequence /кóнсиквенс/ n последствие

conservative /кэнсēветив/ n консерватор

consider /кэнсúдэ/ vt рассматривать; vi полагать

considerable /консúдэрэбл/ adj значительный

consideration /кэнсúдэрэ́йшн/ n рассмотрение; take into
  ~ /тэйк úнту ~/ принимать во внимание

consign /кэнсáйн/ vt отправлять (товары)

consignee /кóнсайнúи/ n грузополучатель

consist (of) /кэнсúст ов/ vi состоять из

consistent /кэнсúстэнт/ adj последовательный

console /кэнсóул/ vt утешать

constant /кóнстэнт/ adj постоянный

constituency /кэнстúтьюэнси/ n избирательный
  округ

constitution /кóнститью́юшн/ n конституция

construction /кэнстрáкшен/ n строительство

consul /консл/ n консул

consult /кэнсáлт/ vt советоваться с

consume /кэнсью́юм/ vt потреблять

consumer /кэнсью́юмэ/ n потребитель; ~ goods /~ гудз/
  ширпотреб

consumption /кэнсáмпшн/ n потребление

contact /кóнтэкт/ n соприкосновение, контакт;
  /кэнтэ́кт/ vt устанавливать контакт

contain /кэнтэ́йн/ vt содержать, вмещать

contemporary /кэнтэ́мпэрэри/ adj современный; n
современник

contempt /кэнтэ́мпт/ n презрение

content /кэнтэ́нт/ adj довольный

contents /ко́нтэнтс/ n pl содержимое

contest /ко́нтэст/ n соревнование, конкурс

continent /ко́нтинент/ n материк

continue /кэнти́нью/ vt продолжать

contraceptive /ко́нтрэсэ́птив/ n противозачаточное
средство

contract /ко́нтрэкт/ n контракт; /кэнтрэ́кт/ vt заключать
договор; сжимать

contractor /кэнтрэ́ктэ/ n подрядчик

contradiction /ко́нтрэди́кшн/ n противоречие

contrary /ко́нтрэри/ adj противоположный

contrast /ко́нтрэст/ n контраст

contribute /кэнтри́бьют/ vt способствовать; жертвовать
(деньги)

control /кэнтро́ул/ n контроль, проверка; vt управлять

controversial /ко́нтрэвё́шл/ adj спорный

convalescent /ко́нвэлэ́снт/ adj выздоравливающий

convenience /кэнви́иньенс/ n удобство

convenient /кэнви́иньент/ adj удобный

convention /кэнвэ́ншн/ n съезд; договор; конвенция

conventional /кэнвэ́ншенл/ adj общепринятый

conversation /ко́нвесэ́йшн/ n разговор

convertible /кэнвё́ртэбл/ adj ~ currency /~ ка́рэнси/
конвертируемая валюта

conviction /кэнви́кшн/ n убеждение; (юр.) осуждение

convince /кэнвинс/ vt убеждать

convoke /кэнвоук/ vt созывать

cook /кук/ n повар; vt готовить

cool /куул/ adj прохладный; vti охлаждать(ся)

co-operate /кооперэйт/ vi сотрудничать

co-operative /кооперэтив/ adj кооперативный; ~ society /~ сэсайети/ кооператив

cope /коуп/ vi: ~ with /~ виз/ справляться с

copper /копэ/ n медь

copy /копи/ n копия, экземпляр; rough ~ /раф ~/ черновик; vt копировать

copyright /копирайт/ n авторское право

cordial /кордьел/ adj сердечный

corduroy /кордерой/ n вельвет

cork /корк/ n пробка

corkscrew /коркскру/ n штопор

corn /корн/ n кукуруза

corn-flour /корнфлауэ/ n кукурузная мука

corned beef /корндбииф/ n солонина

corner /корнэ/ n угол

corporation /корпэрэйшн/ n корпорация

corps /кор/ n (воен.) корпус

correct /кэрект/ adj правильный; vt исправлять

correspondence /кориспондэнс/ n соответствие; переписка; ~ courses /~ корсыз/ заочные курсы

corridor /коридор/ n коридор

corrupt /кэрапт/ adj продажный

cosmetics /козметикс/ n pl косметика

cosmic /козмик/ adj космический

cost /кост/ n стоимость; pl издержки; ~ of living /~ ов
ли́винг/ стоимость жизни; ~ price /~ прайс/
себестоимость; at all ~s /эт оол ~с/ любой ценой; vi
стоить

costume /ко́стьюм/ n костюм

cottage /ко́тыдж/ n коттедж

cotton /котн/ n хлопок; ~ wool /~ вул/ вата

cough /коф/ n кашель; vi кашлять

council /ка́унсл/ n совет

count /ка́унт/ n счет; vt считать

counter /ка́унтэ/ n прилавок

counterbalance /ка́унтэба́лэнс/ n противовес

counterfeit /ка́унтэфит/ adj поддельный; n подделка,
подлог; vt подделывать

countless /ка́унтлис/ adj бесчисленный

country /ка́нтри/ n страна; родина; the ~ /зэ ~/ сельская
местность

countryman /ка́нтримэн/ n соотечественник; сельский
житель

county /ка́унти/ n графство (в Англии); округ (в США)

couple /капл/ n пара; married ~ /ма́рид ~/ супруги;
vt соединять

courage /ка́ридж/ n мужество

courageous /кэре́йджес/ adj храбрый

course /корс/ n курс; ход (событий); течение (времени);
in due ~ /ин дью ~/ в свое время; of ~ /ов ~/ конечно

court /корт/ n двор; суд; (спорт.) корт

cousin /казн/ n двоюродный брат; двоюродная
сестра

cover /кáвэ/ n покрывало; укрытие; vt покрывать; прикрывать

cow /кáу/ n корова

coward /кáуэд/ n трус

cowboy /кáубой/ n ковбой

crab /крэб/ n краб

crack /крэк/ n трещина, треск; vi раскалываться

crackle /крэкл/ n треск; vi хрустеть

cradle /крэйдл/ n колыбель

craft /краафт/ n ремесло, искусность

craftsman /крáафтсмэн/ n мастер; ремесленник

cramp /крэмп/ n судорога; (тех.) скоба

cranberry /крэнбери/ n клюква

crane /крэйн/ n журавль; (тех.) кран

crash /крэш/ n грохот; авария; vi падать с грохотом; терпеть аварию

crawl /кроол/ vi ползать

crazy /крэйзи/ adj сумасшедший

creak /криик/ n скрип; vi скрипеть

cream /криим/ n сливки, крем

cream-cheese /криимчииз/ n плавленый сыр

crease /криис/ n складка

create /кризйт/ vt творить, создавать

creation /кризйшн/ n создание; произведение (искусства)

creature /крииче/ n живое существо

credit /кредит/ n доверие; кредит

creeper /криипэ/ n ползучее растение

crime /крайм/ n преступление

criminal /кри́минл/ adj преступный; n преступник

cripple /крипл/ n калека; vt калечить

crisis /кра́йсис/ n кризис

crisp /крисп/ adj хрустящий

critical /кри́тикэл/ adj критический

crocodile /кро́кэдайл/ n крокодил

crook /крук/ n крюк; мошенник

crop /кроп/ n урожай

cross /крос/ n крест; vt пересекать; ~ out /~ а́ут/ вычеркивать; ~ oneself /~ вансэ́лф/ креститься

crossing /кро́синг/ n переход

cross-road /кро́сроуд/ n перекресток

crow /кро́у/ n ворона

crowd /кра́уд/ n толпа; vi толпиться

crown /кра́ун/ n корона; крона; коронка (зубная)

crucial /кру́ушьел/ adj решающий

crude /крууд/ adj сырой; грубый

cruel /кру́эл/ adj жестокий

cruise /круу́з/ n плавание, круиз

cruiser /кру́узэ/ n крейсер

crumb /крам/ n крошка, крупица

crush /краш/ vt давить, сокрушать

crust /краст/ n корка; земная кора

cry /край/ n крик, плач; vi кричать, плакать

crystal /кристл/ adj хрустальный; n хрусталь

cube /кьюю́б/ n куб

cucumber /кьюю́кэмбэ/ n огурец

cuddle /кадл/ n объятие; vi ласково прижиматься

cue /кьюю/ n намек

cuff-links /ка́флинкс/ n pl запонки

culinary /ка́линэри/ adj кулинарный

cultivate /ка́лтивэйт/ vt возделывать

culture /ка́лче/ n культура

cunning /ка́нинг/ adj коварный

cup /кап/ n чашка

cupboard /ка́бэд/ n шкаф, буфет

curb /кёрб/ vt обуздывать

curd /кёрд/ n творог

cure /кью́э/ n лечение; vt исцелять

curious /кью́эриэс/ adj любопытный

curl /кёрл/ n локон; vi виться (о волосах)

currant /карнт/ n: black (red) ~ /блэк (ред) ~/ черная
    (красная) смородина

currency /ка́рнси/ n валюта

current /карнт/ adj текущий (о времени, событии),
    общепринятый; ~ affairs /~ эфэ́эз/ текущие события;
    n поток; (эл.) ток

curse /кёрс/ n проклятие; vt проклинать

curt /кёрт/ adj краткий

curtail /кёртэ́йл/ vt сокращать

curtain /кёртн/ n занавес; штора

curve /кёрв/ n кривая линия, изгиб

cushion /кушн/ n подушка (диванная)

custom /ка́стэм/ n обычай; привычка

customer /ка́стэмэ/ n покупатель

customs /ка́стэмз/ n pl таможня; ~ officer /~ о́фисэ/
    таможенник

cut /кат/ n разрез, порез; покрой (платья); снижение (цен); vt резать; сокращать (дорогу, расходы)

cute /кьюют/ adj умный; прелестный

cutlery /ка́тлэри/ n ножевые изделия

cutlet /ка́тлит/ n отбивная котлета

cycle /сайкл/ n цикл; велосипед

cynical /си́никл/ adj циничный

cyst /сист/ n киста

Czechoslovak /че́кослóувэк/ adj чехословацкий

D

dab /дэб/ n мазок (кистью)

dad(dy) /дэ́д(и)/ n папа, папочка

daily /дэ́йли/ adj ежедневный

dairy /дэ́эри/ n молочная, маслодельня

dam /дэм/ n дамба, плотина

damage /дэ́мидж/ n повреждение, ущерб; vt повреждать, наносить ущерб

damn /дэм/ n проклятие; vt проклинать

damp /дэмп/ adj сырой; n сырость

dance /даанс/ n танец; vi танцевать

danger /дэ́йндже/ n опасность

dangerous /дэ́йнджрес/ adj опасный

dangle /дэнгл/ vt покачивать; vi свисать

dare /дээ/ vi сметь, отважиться

dark /дарк/ adj темный; it is getting ~ /ит из ге́тинг ~/ темнеет; n темнота

darling /да́рлинг/ adj дорогой, милый

dash /дэш/ n стремительное движение, порыв; тире; примесь; vodka with a ~ of lemon /вóдка виз э ~ ов лéмэн/ водка с кусочком лимона; vt швырять; vi мчаться

data /дéйтэ/ n pl данные, факты

date /дэйт/ n дата; свидание; out of ~ /áут ов ~/ устаревший; up to ~ /ап ту ~/ современный

daughter /дóотэ/ n дочь

daughter-in-law /дóотэринлоо/ n невестка; сноха

dawn /доон/ n рассвет, заря

day /дэй/ n день; all ~ long /оол ~ лонг/ весь день; ~ off /~ оф/ выходной день; the ~ after tomorrow /зэ ~ áафтэ тумóроу/ послезавтра; the ~ before yesterday /зэ ~ бифóр йéстэди/ позавчера; some ~ /сам ~/ когда-нибудь; the other ~ /зы áзэ ~/ на днях

daylight /дéйлайт/ n дневной свет; in broad ~ /ин броод ~/ средь бела дня

dead /дэд/ adj мертвый

dead-end /дэ́дэ́нд/ n тупик

deaf /дэф/ adj глухой

deal /диил/ n количество; сделка; a good ~ /э гуд ~/ много; make a ~ with /мэйк э ~ виз/ заключать сделку с; vi: ~ with /~ виз/ иметь дело с; ~ in /~ ин/ торговать

dealer /ди́илэ/ n торговец

dear /ди́э/ adj дорогой, милый; ~ me! /~ ми/ боже мой! D. Sir /~ сёр/ уважаемый господин (в письмах)

death /дес/ n смерть

death-rate /дéсрейт/ n смертность

debit /дéбит/ n (бухг.) дебет

debt /дет/ n долг; run into ~ /ран и́нту ~/ влезать в долг

debtor /де́тэ/ n должник

decade /дэ́кейд/ n десятилетие

decay /дикэ́й/ vi приходить в упадок; n разложение, упадок

deceive /диси́ив/ vt обманывать

December /дисэ́мбэ/ n декабрь

decent /ди́иснт/ adj приличный

decide /диса́йд/ vti решать

decision /диси́жн/ n решение

declare /дикла́ээ/ vt объявлять, заявлять; предъявлять (вещи, облагаемые пошлиной на таможне)

decline /дикла́йн/ n упадок

decorate /дэ́кэрэйт/ vt украшать; награждать

decrease /дикри́ис/ vt уменьшать

dedicate /дэ́дикейт/ vt посвящать

deep /диип/ adj глубокий

deer /ди́э/ n олень

defeat /дифи́ит/ n поражение

defect /дифе́кт/ n дефект; vi дезертировать

defence /дифе́нс/ n оборона, защита

defend /дифе́нд/ vt защищать

deficiency /дифи́шнси/ n недостаток

define /дифа́йн/ vt определять

definition /дэ́фини́шн/ n определение

deflate /дифла́йт/ vt выпускать воздух из; сокращать выпуск денежных знаков

deform /дифо́рм/ vt деформировать

degenerate /дидже́нерэйт/ vi вырождаться, ухудшаться

degree /дигри́и/ n степень; градус

delay /дилэ́й/ n задержка; vt задерживать, отсрочивать

delegation /дэлигэ́йшн/ n делегация

delicate /дэ́ликит/ adj щекотливый (о сиуации); слабый (о здоровье)

delicious /дили́шес/ adj вкусный

delight /дила́йт/ n восторг, наслаждение; vt приводить в восторг; ~ed to meet you /~ыд ту миит ююю/ очень рад познакомиться с вами

delightful /дила́йтфул/ adj очаровательный

deliver /дили́вэ/ vt доставлять, разносить (письма); произносить (речь)

delivery /дили́вэри/ n доставка

demand /дима́анд/ n требование; great ~ for /грэйт ~ фор/ большой спрос на; vt требовать

democracy /димо́крэси/ n демократия

democratic /дэмэкрэ́тик/ adj демократический

demonstrate /дэ́мэнстрэйт/ vt демонстрировать; доказывать

demonstration /дэ́мэнстрэ́йшн/ n демонстрация; доказательство

denim /дэ́ним/ n джинсовая ткань

dense /денс/ adj плотный, густой

dental /дентл/ adj зубной

dentist /дэ́нтист/ n зубной врач

deny /дина́й/ vt отрицать; отказывать в

department /дипа́ртмент/ n министерство; департамент; факультет; ~ store /~ стор/ универмаг

departure /дипа́рче/ n отправление

depend /дипэ́нд/ vi зависеть; it ~s /ит ~з/ смотря по обстоятельствам dependant /дипéндэнт/ n иждивенец, иждивенка

dependent /дипéндэнт/ adj зависимый, подчиненный; be ~ on /би ~ он/ зависеть от

deportation /ди́ипотэ́йшн/ n высылка

deposit /дипóзит/ n вклад в банке; задаток; месторождение; vt класть в банк; давать задаток

depositor /дипóзитэ/ n вкладчик

depreciation /дипри́иши́зйшн/ n обесценение

depression /дипрéшн/ n депрессия; (экон.) застой

deprive /дипрáйв/ vt лишать

depth /депс/ n глубина

deputy /дéпьюти/ n депутат; заместитель

derive /дирáйв/ vt извлекать

descendant /дисэ́ндэнт/ n потомок

descent /дисэ́нт/ n происхождение

describe /дискрáйб/ vt описывать

description /дискри́пшн/ n описание

desert /дéзет/ adj необитаемый; n пустыня; /дизэ́рт/ vi дезертировать

deserve /дизэ́рв/ vt заслуживать

design /дизáйн/ n замысел, проект; узор; vt замышлять; проектировать

designation /дéзигнэ́йшн/ n назначение на должность; знак, обозначение

desire /дизáйе/ n желание; желать

desk /деск/ n письменный стол

despair /диспэ́э/ n отчаяние

despatch /диспэ́ч/ n депеша; vt посылать

despite /диспáйт/ prep вопреки

dessert /дизёрт/ n десерт

destination /дёстинэйшн/ n место назначения

destiny /дёстини/ n судьба

destroy /дистрóй/ vt разрушать

destruction /дистрáкшн/ n разрушение

detached /дитэ́чт/ adj обособленный; semi-~ house /сэ́ми~ хáус/ один из двух особняков, имеющих общую стену

detail /дийтэйл/ n подробность; in ~ /ин ~/ подробно

detective /дитéктив/ n сыщик; adj детективный; ~ story /~ стóори/ детектив

deteriorate /дитú:эриэрэ́йт/ vti ухудшать(ся)

determination /дитёрминэ́йшн/ n решительность

determine /дитёрмин/ vt определять

detestable /дитéстэбл/ adj отвратительный

detrimental /дéтриментл/ adj вредный

devaluation /дийивэльюэ́йшн/ n девальвация

develop /дивéлоп/ vt развивать

development /дивéлэпмент/ n развитие

device /дивáйс/ n приспособление

devil /дéвл/ n дьявол

devoid (of) /дивóйд ов/ adj лишенный (чего-л.)

devote /дивóут/ vt посвящать

dew /дьюю/ n роса

diabetes /дáйэбúитиз/ n сахарный диабет

diagnosis /дáйэгнóусис/ n диагноз

dial /дáйэл/ n диск набора (тел.); циферблат; vt набирать (номер)

dialect /дáйэлект/ n диалект, говор

dialogue /да́йэлог/ n диалог, разговор

diameter /дайэ́митэ/ n диаметр

diamond /да́йэмэнд/ n алмаз, бриллиант; pl бубны (карты)

diarrhoea /да́йэри́э/ n понос

diary /да́йэри/ n дневник

dictate /дикта́йт/ vt диктовать

dictatorship /дикта́йтэшип/ n диктатура

dictionary /ди́кшенри/ n словарь

die /дай/ vi умирать; очень хотеть

diet /да́йэт/ n диета, пища

differ /ди́фэ/ vi различаться

difference /ди́фрэнс/ n разница

different /ди́фрэнт/ adj различный, иной

difficult /ди́фикэлт/ adj трудный

dig /диг/ vti копать, рыть

digest /да́йджест/ n обзор, дайджест

dignity /ди́гнити/ n достоинство, сан

dilapidated /дила́пидэйтыд/ adj ветхий

dimension /диме́ншн/ n измерение

diminish /дими́ниш/ vti уменьшать(ся)

dine /дайн/ vi обедать

dinner /ди́нэ/ n обед

diphtheria /дифти́эриэ/ n дифтерия

diploma /дипло́умэ/ n диплом

diplomat /ди́плэмэт/ n дипломат

direct /дире́кт/ adj прямой; vt направлять, руководить

direction /дире́кшн/ n направление, управление

dirty /дёрти/ adj грязный; неприличный

disabled /дисэ́йблд/ adj нетрудоспособный

disadvantage /ди́сэдва́антыдж/ n невыгодное положение, ущерб, вред

disagree /ди́сэгри́и/ vi не соглашаться

disappear /ди́сэпи́э/ vi исчезать

disappoint /ди́сэпо́йнт/ vt разочаровывать

disapproval /ди́сэпру́увл/ n неодобрение

disarmament /диса́рмэмент/ n разоружение

disaster /диза́астэ/ n бедствие

disband /дисбэ́нд/ vt распускать

discard /диска́рд/ vt отбрасывать

discern /дисёрн/ vt распознавать

discharge /дисча́рдж/ освобождать (от обязанностей)

disciple /диса́йпл/ n последователь

discipline /ди́сиплин/ n дисциплина

disclose /дискло́уз/ vt раскрывать

disconnect /ди́скэнэ́кт/ vt разъединить

discontent /ди́скэнтэ́нт/ n недовольство

discord /диско́рд/ n разногласие

discount /диска́унт/ n скидка; vt учитывать векселя; снижать; сбавлять

discover /диска́вэ/ vt обнаруживать

discreet /дискри́ит/ adj осмотрительный

discrimination /дискри́мине́йшн/ n дискриминация

discuss /диска́с/ vt обсуждать

disdain /дисдэ́йн/ n презрение

disease /дизи́из/ n болезнь

disentagle /ди́синтэ́нгл/ vt распутывать

disfigure /дисфи́гэ/ vt обезображивать

disgrace /дисгрэ́йс/ n позор

disguise /дисга́йз/ n маскировка

disgust /дисга́ст/ n омерзение

dish /диш/ n блюдо

dishwasher /ди́швóше/ n машина для мытья посуды

dishonest /дисо́нист/ adj нечестный

dishonour /дисо́нэ/ n бесчестие; vt позорить

disillusion /ди́силю́южн/ vt разочаровывать

disinherit /ди́синхе́рит/ vt лишать наследства

disintegrate /диси́нтегрэйт/ vti разлагать(ся)

disinterested /диси́нтристыд/ adj бескорыстный;
незаинтересованный

disk /диск/ n магнитный диск, дискета

dislike /дисла́йк/ n неприязнь; vt не любить

dismantle /дисмэ́нтл/ vt демонтировать

dismiss /дисми́с/ vt увольнять

disorder /дисо́рдэ/ n беспорядок

disorganize /дисо́ргэнайз/ vt дезорганизовывать

dispassionate /диспэ́шнит/ adj бесстрастный

dispel /диспе́л/ vt разгонять

dispense /диспе́нс/ vt раздавать; ~ with /~ виз/
обходиться без

disperse /диспе́рс/ vt разгонять

displace /диспплэ́йс/ vt перемещать, смещать; ~ed person
/~т пёрсн/ перемещенное лицо

display /дисппле́й/ n выставка; дисплей

disposable /диспо́узэбл/ adj одноразового пользования

disposal /диспо́узл/ n: at your ~ /эт йо ~/ в вашем
распоряжении

disqualify /дисквóлифай/ vt дисквалифицировать

disregard /дисригáрд/ vt игнорировать

dissatisfaction /дúссэ́тисфэ́кшн/ n недовольство

disseminate /дисéминэйт/ vt распространять

dissertation /дúсэтэ́йшн/ n диссертация

dissipate /дúсипейт/ vt рассеивать; проматывать (деньги)

dissolve /дизóлв/ vt расторгать, распускать; vi растворяться

distance /дúстэнс/ n расстояние

distant /дúстэнт/ adj дальний, далекий

distil /дистúл/ vt дистиллировать

distinct /дистúнкт/ adj отчетлиеый

distinction /дистúнкшн/ n отличие

distinguish /дистúнгвиш/ vt различать

distinguished /дистúнгвишт/ adj выдающийся, известный

distort /дистóрт/ vt искажать

distrain /дистрэ́йн/ vt описывать (имущество)

distress /дистрéс/ n беда, бедствие; vt огорчать

distribute /дистрúбьют/ vt распределять, раздавать

district /дúстрикт/ n район, округ

distrust /дистрáст/ n недоверие

disturbance /дистёрбэнс/ n волнение; pl беспорядки

dive /дайв/ n прыжок (в воду)

diverse /дайвёрс/ adj разнообразный

divert /дайвёрт/ vt отвлекать; развлекать

divide /дивáйд/ vti разделять(ся)

dividend /ди́виденд/ n делимое; дивиденд

divine /дива́йн/ adj божественный

division /диви́жн/ n деление; отдел; дивизия

divorce /диво́рс/ n развод; vt разводиться с

dizzy /ди́зи/ adj головокружительный

do /ду/ vt поступать, делать; ~ a room /~ э руум/ убирать комнату; that will ~! /зэт вил ~/ довольно; ~ away with /~ эвэ́й виз/ покончить с; ~ without /~ виза́ут/ обходиться без; how do you ~? /ха́у ду ю ~ / здравствуйте; well-to-~ /вэл ту ~/ зажиточный

dockyard /до́къярд/ n верфь

doctor /до́ктэ/ n врач, доктор

document /до́кьюмент/ n документ

dog /дог/ n собака

doll /дол/ n кукла

dollar /до́лэ/ n доллар

domestic /дэме́стик/ adj домашний; внутренний; ручной

donate /донэ́йт/ vt передавать в дар

done /дан/ adj сделанный

donkey /до́нки/ n осел

doom /дуум/ n рок

door /дор/ n дверь

doorway /до́рвэй/ n дверной проем

dose /до́ус/ n доза

dot /дот/ n точка

double /дабл/ adj двойной; ~ bed /~ бед/ двуспальная кровать; ~ room /~ руум/ номер на двоих; adv вдвойне, вдвое; n двойник, дубликат; vti удваивать(ся)

double-dealing /да́блдйилинг/ n двурушничество

doubt /да́ут/ n сомнение; vt сомневаться в

doubtful /да́утфул/ adj сомнительный

doubtless /да́утлис/ adv несомненно

dough /до́у/ n тесто

doughnut /до́унат/ n пончик

dove /дав/ n голубь

down /да́ун/ n спуск, падение; prop вниз; adv внизу; ~ with /~ виз/ долой!; vt опускать

downfall /да́унфол/ n падение, гибель

downstairs /да́унстэ́эз/ adv внизу

dozen /дазн/ n дюжина

draft /драфт/ n черновик, набросок; чек; (воен.) набор

drag /дрэг/ vti тащить(ся)

dragon /дрэгн/ n дракон

drain /дрэйн/ vt дренировать, осушать (почву)

drainpipe /дрэ́йнпайп/ n водосточная труба

dramatic /дрэмэ́тик/ adj драматический

drastic /дрэ́стик/ adj суровый, крутой; радикальный

draught /драафт/ n тяга, сквозняк; pl шашки

draw /дроо/ n жеребьёвка; ничья (в игре); vt тянуть; рисовать; выписывать (чек); выводить (заключение); кончать (игру) вничью; привлекать (внимание)

drawback /дро́обэк/ n недостаток

drawer /дроо/ n (выдвижной) ящик; pl кальсоны

drawing /дро́оинг/ n рисунок, чертёж

dreadful /дрэ́дфул/ adj ужасный

dream /дриим/ n сон; мечта; vt видеть во сне; мечтать о

dress /дресс/ n платье, одежда; vt одевать; перевязывать (рану); приправлять (салат); vi одеваться

dressing √дрéсинг/ n одевание; перевязка; приправа, соус

dress rehearsal /дрéсрихёёсл/ n генеральная репетиция

dried /драйд/ adj сушеный

drift /дрифт/ n дрейф; vi дрейфовать

drink /дринк/ n напиток; soft ~s /софт ~с/ безалкогольные напитки; vt пить

drip /дрип/ n капля; vi капать

drive /драйв/ n поездка; (тех.) привод; vt гнать; вбивать (гвоздь); водить (автомобиль)

driver /дрáйвэ/ n шофер

driving /дрáйвинг/ n вождение (автомобиля); ~ licence /~ лáйсенс/ водительские права

drizzle /дризл/ n мелкий дождь; vi моросить

drop /дроп/ n капля; pl (мед.) капли; vt ронять; подвозить (до дома)

drought /дрáут/ n засуха

drown /дрáун/ vt топить; vi тонуть

drug /драг/ n лекарство; наркотик; ~ addict /~ э́дикт/ наркоман

drugstore /дрáгстор/ n аптека

drunk /дранк/ adj пьяный; get ~ /гет ~/ напиться

dry /драй/ adj сухой; vti сушить (ся)

dry-cleaning /дрáйклúининг/ n химчистка

dual /дьюъэл/ adj двойственный

dubious /дьюбьес/ adj сомнительный

duck /дак/ n утка; vi окунаться

due /дьюю/ adj должный, надлежащий; ~ to /~ ту/ благодаря; in ~ time /ин ~ тайм/ в свое время; n должное; pl сборы, пошлины; членские взносы

duet /дьюэ́т/ n дуэт

dull /дал/ adj тупой, скучный

dumb /дам/ adj немой; deaf and ~ /дэф энд ~/ глухонемой

dummy /да́ми/ adj подставной; учебный; n манекен; макет

dump /дамп/ n свалка; vt сваливать

dumping /да́мпинг/ n демпинг

dupe /дьююп/ n простофиля; vt надувать

duplicate /дьююпликит/ n дубликат

durable /дьюэрэбл/ adj прочный; длительного пользования

during /дьюэ́ринг/ prep в течение

dusk /даск/ n сумерки

dust /даст/ n пыль

dustbin /да́стбин/ n мусорный ящик

Dutch /дач/ adj голландский; n голландский язык

duty /дьюю́ти/ n долг, обязанность; пошлина; be on ~ /би он ~/ дежурить; ~-free /~ фрии/ не подлежащий обложению пошлиной; do one's ~ /ду ванз ~/ исполнять долг

dwell /двел/ vi жить, обитать

dwelling /две́линг/ n жилище; ~ house /~ ха́ус/ жилой дом

dye /дай/ n краситель; vt красить

dynamic /дайнэ́мик/ adj динамический

dysentery /ди́снтри/ n дизентерия

E

each /иич/ adj, pron каждый; ~ other /~ а́зэ/ друг друга
eager /и́игэ/ adj страстно стремящийся
eagle /иигл/ n орел
ear /и́э/ n ухо; колос
early /ёрли/ adj ранний; adv рано
earn /ёрн/ vt зарабатывать; заслуживать
earnest /ёрнист/ adj серьезный
earnings /ёрнингз/ n pl заработок
earring /и́эринг/ n серьга
earth /ёрс/ n земля, земной шар
earthquake /ёрсквэйк/ n землетрясение
easily /и́изили/ adv легко
Easter /и́истэ/ n пасха
eastern /и́истэн/ adj восточный
easy /и́изи/ adj легкий
easy-going /и́изигбуинг/ adj добродушный, покладистый
eat /иит/ vt есть
eau-de-Cologne /бỳдэкэлбун/ n одеколон
echo /э́коу/ n эхо
ecology /икóлэджи/ n экология
economic /и́икэнóмик/ adj экономический
economy /икóнэми/ n хозяйство
edge /эдж/ n край; лезвие
edible /э́дибл/ adj съедобный
edit /э́дит/ vt редактировать
edition /иди́шн/ n издание

editorial /эдитóориэл/ n передовица

education /эдьюкéйшн/ n образование

effect /ифéкт/ n действие; эффект

effective /ифéктив/ adj эффективный

efficient /ифúшент/ adj умелый, эффективный

e.g. /úджú/ abbr например

egg /эг/ n яйцо; fried ~s /фрайд ~з/ глазунья; scrambled ~s /скрэмблд ~з/ яичница

egoism /эгóизм/ n эгоизм

eight /эйт/ num восемь

eighteen /эйтúин/ num восемнадцать

eighty /эйти/ num восемьдесят

either /áйзэ/ adj один из двух; тот или другой; любой; ~ ... or ... /~ ... op .../ или... или...; ~ way /~ вэй/ и так и этак

elaborate /илэбрит/ adj подробный

elastic /илэстик/ adj эластичный

elbow /элбоу/ n локоть; vt толкать локтями

elder /элдэ/ adj старший; n старец

elderly /элдэли/ adj пожилой

elect /илéкт/ vt избирать

election /илéкшн/ n выборы

electric /илéктрик/ adj электрический

electricity /илектрúсити/ n электричество

elegant /элигэнт/ adj элегантный

element /элимент/ n элемент; стихия

elementary /элимéнтэри/ adj элементарный

elephant /элифэнт/ n слон

elevate /эливэйт/ vt поднимать

eleven /илéвн/ num одиннадцать

eliminate /илúмэнейт/ vt ликвидировать

elite /эйлúит/ n элита

else /элс/ adv еще; кроме; what ~ /вот ~/ что еще?;
nobody ~ /нóубэди ~/ больше никто; or ~ /ор ~/ а то

emancipate /имáнсипейт/ vt освобождать

embankment /имбáнкмент/ n набережная

embark /имбáрк/ vti грузить(ся); ~ upon /~ эпóн/
браться (за что-л.)

embarrass /имбáрэс/ vt смущать; затруднять

embassy /эмбэси/ n посольство

emblem /эмблем/ n эмблема

embodiment /имбóдимент/ n воплощение

embrace /имбрéйс/ n объятия; vt обнимать; охватывать

embroidery /имбрóйдэри/ n вышивка

emerald /эмерлд/ n изумруд

emerge /имёёдж/ vi всплывать, возникать

emergency /имёёдженси/ n крайность; in case of ~ /ин кейс
ов ~/ при крайней необходимости; ~ brake /~ брэйк/
запасной тормоз; ~ exit /~ эксит/ запасный выход

emigrant /эмигрэнт/ n эмигрант

emigrate /эмигрэйт/ vi эмигрировать

eminent /эминент/ adj выдающийся

emit /имúт/ vt испускать; выпускать (деньги)

emotional /имóушенл/ adj эмоциональный

emphasis /эмфэсис/ n ударение

empire /эмпайе/ n империя

employ /имплóй/ n служба; vt нанимать; применять; be
~ed by /би ~д бай/ работать у

employee /эмплойи́и/ n служащий

employer /имплойе́/ n наниматель

employment /имплой́мент/ n служба; использование; full ~ /фул ~/ полная занятость

emporium /эмпо́ориэм/ n большой магазин

empty /э́мти/ adj пустой; vt опорожнять

enable /инэ́йбл/ vt давать возможность

enchanting /инча́антинг/ adj прелестный

enclose /инкло́уз/ vt огораживать; прилагать (к письму, документу)

encounter /инка́унтэ/ n (неожиданная) встреча; vt наталкиваться на

encourage /инка́ридж/ vt ободрять

encroach on /инкро́уч он/ vi покушаться на

encyclopaedia /энса́йклопи́идье/ n энциклопедия

end /энд/ n конец; in the ~ /ин зы ~/ в конце концов; make both ~s meet /мэйк бо́ус ~з миит/ сводить концы с концами; vti кончать(ся)

endless /э́ндлис/ adj бесконечный

endure /индью́э/ vt выдерживать

enema /э́нимэ/ n клизма

enemy /э́ними/ n враг

energy /э́нэджи/ n энергия

engaged /инге́йджд/ adj занятый; помолвленный

engender /индже́ндэ/ vt порождать

engine /э́нджин/ n мотор, двигатель

engineer /э́нджини́э/ n инженер

English /и́нглиш/ n английский язык; adj английский; the ~ /зы ~/ n pl англичане engraving /ингрэ́йвинг/ n гравюра

enhance /инха́анс/ vt повышать

enjoy /инджо́й/ vt наслаждаться

enjoyment /инджо́ймент/ n удовольствие

enlarge /инла́рдж/ vti увеличивать(ся)

enlist /инли́ст/ vi поступать на военную службу

enormous /ино́рмэс/ adj громадный

enough /ина́ф/ adj достаточный; adv довольно

enquiry /инква́йери/ n наведение справок; расследование; ~ office /~ о́фис/ справочное бюро

enrich /инри́ч/ vt обогащать; удобрять

enrol(l) /инро́ул/ vt вербовать; вносить в список

ensure /иншу́э/ vt обеспечивать

entail /интэ́йл/ vt влечь за собой

entangle /интэ́нгл/ vt запутывать

enter /э́нтэ/ vti входить (в); поступать (в институт); вносить (в книгу)

enterprise /э́нтэпрайз/ n предприятие; предпринимательство

entertainment /э́нтэтэ́йнмент/ n развлечение; прием (гостей); банкет

enthusiasm /инфью́юзиэзм/ n энтузиазм

entire /инта́йе/ adj полный, весь

entitle /инта́йтл/ vt озаглавливать

entrance /э́нтрэнс/ n вход; ~ exam /~ игзэ́м/ вступительный экзамен

entrust /интра́ст/ vt поручать

entry /э́нтри/ n вход; запись; заявка

enumerate /инью́юмерейт/ vt перечислять

envelope /энвилоуп/ n конверт

envious /энвиэс/ adj завистливый

environment /инвáйерэнмент/ n среда, окружение

envy /энви/ n зависть; vt завидовать

epidemic /эпидéмик/ adj эпидемический; n эпидемия

episode /эписоуд/ n эпизод

epoch /úипок/ n эпоха

equal /úиквэл/ adj равный; n ровня; vt равняться

equality /иквóлити/ n равенство

equator /иквэ́йтэ/ n экватор

equipment /иквúпмент/ n оборудование

equivalent /иквúвэлэнт/ n эквивалент

era /úэрэ/ n эра

erect /ирэ́кт/ adj прямой; vt воздвигать

erosion /ирóужн/ n эрозия

erotic /ирóтик/ adj эротический

erroneous /ирóуньес/ adj ошибочный

error /э́рэ/ n ошибка

eruption /ирáпшн/ n извержение; сыпь

escape /искéйп/ n побег; vt избегать, избавляться от; vi
    бежать (из тюрьмы)

especial /испéшл/ adj специальный

especially /испéшели/ adv особенно

essay /э́сэй/ n очерк

essence /эснс/ n сущность; эссенция

essential /исэ́ншл/ adj существенный

establish /истэ́блиш/ vt устанавливать; учреждать

establishment /истэ́блишмент/ n учреждение; the ~ /зы
    ~/ правящие круги

estate /истэ́йт/ n имение; имущество; personal ~ /пёрснл ~/ движимость; real ~ /ри́эл ~/ недвижимость

estimate /э́стимит/ n оценка, смета; /э́стимэйт/ vt оценивать

etcetera, etc. /итсэ́трэ/ и так далее (и т.д.)

eternal /итёрнл/ adj вечный

ethics /э́тикс/ n этика

ethnic /э́тник/ adj этнический

European /юэрэпи́эн/ n европеец; adj европейский

evacuate /ивэ́кьюэйт/ vt эвакуировать

evade /ивэ́йд/ vt уклоняться от

evaluate /ивэ́льюэйт/ vt оценивать

evasive /ивэ́йсив/ adj уклончивый

eve /иив/ n канун; on the ~ /он зы ~/ накануне; Christmas ~ /кри́смэс ~/ сочельник

even /и́ивэн/ adj ровный; одинаковый; четный (число); adv даже; vt выравнивать

evening /и́ивнинг/ n вечер; good ~! /гуд ~/ добрый вечер!

event /ивэ́нт/ n событие; случай; at all ~s /эт оол ~с/ во всяком случае

ever /э́вэ/ adv когда-либо; ~ since /~ синс/ с тех пор; for ~ /фор ~/ навсегда; hardly ~ /ха́рдли ~/ очень редко

every /э́ври/ adj каждый; ~ now and then /~ на́у энд зэн/ то и дело; ~ other day /~ а́зэ дэй/ через день

everybody /э́врибоди/ pron каждый, всякий; все

everything /э́врисинг/ pron всё

everywhere /э́вривзэ/ adv повсюду, везде

evict /иви́кт/ vt выселять

evidence /э́видэнс/ n свидетельство; улика

evident /э́видэнт/ adj очевидный

evidently /э́видэнтли/ adv ясно

evil /иивл/ adj злой, дурной

evolution /йивэлю́юшн/ n эволюция

evolve /иво́лв/ vti развивать(ся)

exact /игзэ́кт/ adj точный; vt взыскивать

exactly /игзэ́ктли/ adv точно

exaggerate /игзэ́джерейт/ vt преувеличивать

examination /игзэ́мине́йшн/ n экзамен; осмотр

example /игза́ампл/ n пример; for ~ /фор ~/ например

excellent /э́ксклэнт/ adj отличный

except /иксэ́пт/ prep за исключением; кроме

exception /иксэ́пшн/ n исключение

excerpt /э́ксэрпт/ n отрывок

excess /иксэ́с/ n излишек; ~ luggage /~ ла́гидж/ багаж
  выше нормы

excessive /иксэ́сив/ adj чрезмерный

exchange /иксче́йндж/ n обмен; биржа; bill of ~ /бил ов
  ~/ вексель; ~ rate /~ рэйт/ валютный курс; vt
  обменивать

exciting /икса́йтинг/ adj захватывающий

exclaim /иксклэ́йм/ vi восклицать

exclusive /иксклу́усив/ adj исключительный

excursion /икскёршн/ n экскурсия

excuse /икскьюос/ n извинение; отговорка;
  /икскьюоз/ vt прощать; ~ me! /~ ми/ извините!

execute /э́ксикьют/ vt исполнять; казнить

executive /игзэ́кьютив/ n исполнительная власть; adj
  исполнительный

exempt /игзэ́мт/ adj освобожденный; tax ~ /тэкс ~/ освобожденный от налогов

exercise /э́ксэсайз/ n упражнение; vti упражнять(ся)

exhale /эксхэ́йл/ vt выдыхать

exhausted /игзо́остыд/ adj изнуренный

exhibition /э́ксиби́шн/ n выставка

exile /э́ксайл/ n ссылка; изгнанник; vt ссылать

exist /игзи́ст/ vi существовать

existence /игзи́стэнс/ n существование

exit /э́ксит/ n выход; ~ visa /~ ви́изэ/ выездная виза

expand /икспэ́нд/ vti расширять(ся)

expanse /икспэ́нс/ n пространство

expect /икспе́кт/ vt ожидать

expedient /икспи́идьент/ adj целесообразный; n средство для достижения цели

expel /икспе́л/ vt исключать

expenditure /икспе́ндиче/ n расходование; трата

expense /икспе́нс/ n расход; at our ~ /эт а́уэ ~/ за наш счет

expensive /икспе́нсив/ adj дорогой

experience /икспи́эриэнс/ n (жизненный) опыт, переживание; vt переживать

experiment /икспе́римент/ n эксперимент

expert /э́кспёт/ adj опытный; n эксперт

expire /икспа́йе/ vi истекать (о сроке)

explain /испплэ́йн/ vt объяснять

explanation /э́ксплэнэ́йшн/ n объяснение

explode /иксплбуд/ vt взрывать; vi взрываться, разражаться (смехом и т.п.)

exploit /э́ксплойт/ n подвиг; /иксплóйт/ vt эксплуатировать

explore /иксплóр/ vt исследовать

explosion /иксплóужн/ n взрыв

export /э́кспорт/ n экспорт; /экспóрт/ vt экспортировать

exporter /экспóртэ/ n экспортер

expose /икспóуз/ vt выставлять; подвергать; разоблачать; давать выдержку

express /икспрэ́с/ n ж.-д. экспресс; federal ~ /фéдэрэл ~/ срочная почта; adj срочный; недвусмысленный; vt выражать

expression /икспрэ́шн/ n выражение

extension /икстэ́ншн/ n протяжение; продление; пристройка; добавочный номер (телефона)

extensive /икстэ́нсив/ adj обширный

extent /икстэ́нт/ n протяжение; to what ~ /ту вот ~/ до какой степени

external /экстёрнл/ adj внешний

extinguish /иксти́нгвиш/ vt тушить; уничтожать

extinguisher /иксти́нгвише/ n огнетушитель

extra /э́кстрэ/ adj добавочный; особый; ~ charge /~ чардж/ доплата; adv дополнительно

extract /э́кстрэкт/ n отрывок; экстракт; /икстрэ́кт/ vt удалять (зуб); добывать

extradition /э́кстрэди́шн/ n выдача (преступника)

extraordinary /икстрóоднри/ adj чрезвычайный, внеочередной; необычный

extravagant /икстрэ́вигент/ adj расточительный; экстравагантный extreme /икстри́им/ adj крайний; n крайность

extremely /икстри́имли/ adv чрезвычайно

eye /ай/ n глаз; глазок (в двери); ушко (иглы); keep an ~ on /киип эн ~ он/ следить за; vt рассматривать

eyebrow /а́йбрау/ n бровь

eyesight /а́йсайт/ n зрение

eyewitness /а́йви́тнис/ n очевидец

F

fable /фэйбл/ n басня

fabric /фа́брик/ n ткань; структура

fabricate /фа́брикейт/ vt фабриковать

face /фэйс/ n лицо; внешний вид; лицевая сторона; фасад; циферблат; make ~s /мэйк ~ыз/ гримасничать; vt стоять лицом к, смело встречать; ~ the facts /~ зэ фэктс/ смотреть правде в глаза

facilitate /фэси́литэйт/ vt содействовать

facility /фэси́лити/ n легкость; pl удобства

fact /фэкт/ n факт; in ~ /ин ~/ на самом же деле...

factory /фа́ктэри/ n фабрика, завод

factual /фа́ктьюел/ adj действительный

faculty /фа́кэлти/ n способность; факультет

fade /фэйд/ vi увядать

fail /фэйл/ vt обманывать ожидания, подводить; vi потерпеть неудачу; проваливаться (на экзаменах)

failure /фэ́йлье/ n неудача, провал; неудачник

faint /фэйнт/ adj слабый, тусклый; n потеря сознания; vi падать в обморок

fair /фээ/ adj красивый; справедливый; белокурый; ~ copy /~ко́пи/ чистовик; play ~ /плэй ~/ играть честно; n ярмарка

fairy /фэ́эри/ n фея; adj волшебный; ~ tale /~ тэйл/ сказка

faith /фэйф/ n вера, доверие; in good ~ /ин гуд ~/ честно

faithfully /фэ́йсфули/ adv честно; yours ~ /йооз ~/ с искренним уважением (в конце письма)

fake /фэйк/ n фальшивка

fall /фоол/ n падение; осень; водопад; vi падать, понижаться; ~ asleep /~ эсли́ип/ засыпать; ~ behind /~ биха́йнд/ отставать; ~ in love with /~ ин лав виз/ влюбляться в; ~ sick /~ сик/ заболевать

false /фоолс/ n ложный; фальшивый; искусственный

fame /фэйм/ n слава

familiar /фэми́лье/ adj знакомый; близкий

family /фэ́мили/ n семья

famous /фэ́ймэс/ adj знаменитый

fan /фэн/ n веер; вентилятор; болельщик

fancy /фэ́нси/ n воображение, фантазия; каприз; take a ~ to /тэйк э ~ ту/ увлекаться

fantastic /фэнтэ́стик/ adj фантастический

fantasy /фэ́нтэси/ n фантазия

far /фар/ adj далекий; adv далеко; by ~ /бай ~/ намного; ~ better /~ бе́тэ/ гораздо лучше; ~ from it /~ фром ит/ отнюдь нет; in so ~ as /ин со́у ~ эз/ поскольку; go too ~ /го́у туу ~/ заходить слишком далеко

fare /фээ/ n плата за проезд; bill of ~ /бил ов ~/ меню

farewell /фэ́эвэл/ n прощание

farm /фарм/ n ферма

farmer /фа́рмэ/ n фермер

farther /фа́азэ/ adv дальше

fascinating /фэ́синэйтинг/ adj очаровательный

fascism /фэ́шизм/ n фашизм

fashion /фэшн/ n мода; out of ~ /аут ов ~/ старомодный

fashionable /фэ́шнэбл/ adj модный

fast /фааст/ adj быстрый, скорый; adv крепко, прочно; be ~ asleep /би ~ эсли́ип/ крепко спать; vt поститься; n пост

fasten /фаасн/ vt прикреплять; застегивать

fat /фэт/ adj жирный, толстый; n жир

fate /фэйт/ n судьба, рок

father /фа́азэ/ n отец

father-in-law /фа́азэринло/ n свекор; тесть

fatherland /фа́азэлэнд/ n отчизна

fatigue /фэти́иг/ n утомление; vt изнурять

fault /фоолт/ n недостаток; ошибка

favour /фэ́йвэ/ n расположение, милость; in ~ of /ин ~ ов/ в пользу

favourable /фэ́йвэрэбл/ adj благоприятный

favourite /фэ́йвэрит/ adj излюбленный

fear /фи́э/ n страх; vt бояться

feasible /фи́изэбл/ adj выполнимый

feast /фиист/ n пир, праздник

feather /фе́зэ/ n перо

feature /фи́иче/ n особенность, черта; ~ film /~ филм/ художественный фильм

February /фе́бруэри/ n февраль

federal /фе́дэрл/ adj федеральный

fee /фии/ n гонорар; членский взнос; плата (за учение)

feeble /фиибл/ adj хилый

feed /фиид/ n питание, корм; vi питаться; I am fed up /ай эм фед ап/ надоело

feel /фиил/ n чутье, ощущение; vt чувствовать, ощущать; vi чувствовать себя; I ~ cold /ай ~ ко́улд/ мне холодно; I ~ like sleeping /ай ~ лайк сли́ипинг/ мне хочется спать

feeling /фи́илинг/ n чувство

fellow /фе́лоу/ n товарищ; собрат; парень; nice ~ /найс ~/ славный малый

fellow-countryman /фе́лоука́нтримэн/ n соотечественник

female /фи́имэйл/ adj женский; n женщина; (зоол.) самка

fence /фенс/ n забор, изгородь

ferment /фе́рмент/ n брожение

ferocious /феро́ушес/ adj свирепый

ferry /фе́ри/ n паром

fertile /фе́ртайл/ adj плодородный

fervent /фе́рвент/ adj пылкий

festival /фе́стивл/ n фестиваль

fetch /феч/ vt принести, сходить за

fetters /фе́тэз/ n pl оковы

feudal /фью́юдл/ adj феодальный

fever /фи́ивэ/ n лихорадка

few /фью́ю/ adj немногие, мало; a ~ /э ~/ немного; quite a ~ /квайт э ~/ много fiancé /фиа́ансэй/ n жених

fiancée /фиа́ансэй/ n невеста

fiction /фи́кшн/ n вымысел; беллетристика

fidgety /фи́джити/ adj беспокойный

field /фии́лд/ n поле; область, сфера деятельности

fierce /фи́эс/ adj свирепый; неистовый, сильный

fiery /фа́йери/ adj огненный; пламенный

fifteen /фи́фти́ин/ num пятнадцать

fifty /фи́фти/ num пятьдесят; ~ fifty /~ фи́фти/ пополам

fight /файт/ n бой, драка; борьба; vt драться, бороться с

fighter /фа́йтэ/ n борец; (авиа) истребитель

figure /фи́гэ/ n фигура; цифра; рисунок

file /файл/ n напильник; папка; подшивка (газет);
    картотека; досье; ряд; шеренга; (вчт.) файл

fill /фил/ vt заполнять; пломбировать (зуб); ~ in /~ ин/
    заполнять (бланк)

film /филм/ n фильм; (фото)пленка; ~ star /~ стар/
    кинозвезда

filthy /фи́лфи/ adj грязный; непристойный

final /файнл/ adj финальный; окончательный

finance /файнэ́нс/ n финансы; vt финансировать

find /файнд/ vt находить; ~ out /~ а́ут/ разузнать

fine /файн/ adj превосходный; тонкий; изящный;
    мелкий; ~ arts /~ артс/ изящные искусства; that's ~!
    /зэтс ~/ прекрасно!; n штраф; vt штрафовать

finger /фи́нгэ/ n палец; index/middle/fourth ~ /и́ндэкс,
    мидл, форс ~/ указательный/средний/безымянный
    палец; little ~ /литл ~/ мизинец

finish /фи́ниш/ n конец; vt кончать

fir /фёр/ n пихта; ель

fire /фа́йе/ n огонь, пожар; vt зажигать; увольнять; vi стрелять

fire alarm /фа́йерэла́рм/ n пожарная тревога

fireproof /фа́йепруф/ adj огнеупорный

firm /фёрм/ adj твердый; прочный; n фирма

first /фёрст/ adj первый; adv сначала; ~ of all /~ ов оол/ прежде всего

first aid /фёрстэйд/ n скорая помощь

first floor /фёрстфлор/ n второй этаж

first-hand /фёрстхэнд/ adj из первых рук

first-rate /фёрстрэйт/ adj первоклассный

fiscal /фи́скэл/ adj финансовый

fish /фиш/ n рыба; vi ловить рыбу

fist /фист/ n кулак

fit /фит/ adj годный, подходящий; n припадок; a ~ of coughing /э ~ ов ко́финг/ приступ кашля; vt прилаживать

fitness /фи́тнис/ n (при)годность

five /файв/ num пять; n пятерка

fix /фикс/ n дилемма; vt прикреплять; устанавливать

fixed /фикст/ adj неподвижный; установленный

flag /флэг/ n флаг

flake /флэйк/ n снежинка; pl хлопья

flame /флэйм/ n пламя

flash /флэш/ n вспышка

flat /флэт/ adj плоский; ровный

flatter /флэ́тэ/ vt льстить

flavour /флэ́йвэ/ n привкус, аромат

flaw /флоо/ n изъян; трещина

flee /флии/ vti спасаться бегством

fleet /флиит/ n флот

flesh /флеш/ n мясо; плоть; мякоть

flexible /флéксэбл/ adj гибкий

flight /флайт/ n полет; стая (птиц); бегство

float /флóут/ vi плыть

flock /флок/ n стадо (овец); стая (птиц)

flog /флог/ vt пороть, сечь

flood /флад/ n наводнение; прилив; vt наводнять

floor /флор/ n пол; этаж; ground ~ /грáунд ~/ первый
  этаж; take the ~ /тэйк зэ ~/ брать слово

flounder /флáундэ/ n камбала

flour /флáуэ/ n мука

flourish /флáриш/ vi процветать

flow /флóу/ n течение, поток; vi течь

flower /флáуэ/ n цветок; vi цвести

fluent /флюóэнт/ adj беглый, плавный

fluid /флюóид/ adj жидкий; n жидкость

fly /флай/ n муха; ширинка (в брюках); vi летать

foam /фóум/ n пена; vi пениться

fodder /фóдэ/ n корм

fog /фог/ n туман

fold /фóулд/ n складка; vt складывать

folk /фóук/ n народ

follow /фóлоу/ vt следовать, идти за

following /фóлоуинг/ adj следующий

fond /фонд/ adj любящий; be ~ of /би ~ ов/ любить

food /фууд/ n пища, съестное

foodstuffs /фу́удстафс/ n pl еда, продукты

fool /фуул/ n дурак, глупец; шут

foolish /фу́улиш/ adj глупый

foot /фут/ n нога; фут (мера); подножие холма; from head to ~ /фром хед ту ~/ с головы до ног; by ~ /бай ~/ пешком

football /футбо́л/ n футбол

footwear /фу́твээ/ n обувь

for /фор/ prep для, за, к, вместо; as ~ me /эз ~ ми/ что касается меня; ~ good /~ гуд/ навсегда; what ~? /вот ~/ зачем?; conj ибо

forbid /фэби́д/ vt запрещать

force /форс/ n сила; pl (воен.) вооруженные силы; vt заставлять, принуждать

forecast /фо́ркаст/ n прогноз; weather ~ /вэ́зэ ~/ прогноз погоды

forehead /фо́рид/ n лоб

foreign /фо́рин/ adj иностранный, чужой; ~ policy /~ по́лиси/ внешняя политика; ~ trade /~ трэйд/ внешняя торговля

foreigner /фо́ринэ/ n иностранец

forest /фо́рист/ n лес

foretell /фоттэ́л/ vt предсказывать

foreword /фо́рвёд/ n предисловие

forget /фэгéт/ vt забывать

forgive /фэги́в/ vt прощать

fork /форк/ n вилка

form /форм/ n форма; бланк; класс (в школе); vt формировать, образовывать

formal /фо́рмэл/ adj формальный

former /фо́рмэ/ adj прежний; the ~ /зэ ~/ первый (из двух)

formula /фо́рмьюлэ/ n формула

forth /форс/ adv вперед; and so ~ /энд со́у ~/ и так далее

fortify /фо́ртифай/ vt укреплять

fortnight /фо́ртнайт/ n две недели

fortress /фо́ртрис/ n крепость

fortunate /фо́рчнит/ adj счастливый, удачный

fortune /фо́рчен/ n счастье, удача; судьба; состояние; tell ~s /тэл ~з/ гадать; make a ~ /мэйк э ~/ разбогатеть

forty /фо́рти/ num сорок

forward /фо́рвэд/ adj передовой; adv вперед; vt пересылать; способствовать, ускорять

foster-mother /фо́стэма́зэ/ n приемная мать

foul /фа́ул/ adj скверный, непристойный; ~ language /~ лэ́нгвидж/ сквернословие; ~ play /~ плэй/ нечестная игра; n (спорт.) нарушение правил

found /фа́унд/ vt основывать

foundation /фаундэ́йшн/ n основание, фундамент; фонд

fountain /фа́унтин/ n фонтан

four /фор/ num четыре

fourteen /фо́рти́ин/ num четырнадцать

fowl /фа́ул/ n домашняя птица; дичь

fox /фокс/ n лиса, лисица

fraction /фрэкшн/ n дробь; частица

fragile /фрэ́джайл/ adj хрупкий

fragment /фрэ́гмент/ n осколок; фрагмент

fragrant /фрэ́йгрэнт/ adj благоухающий

frail /фрэйл/ adj хрупкий, тщедушный

frame /фрэйм/ n рама; остов; телосложение; vt обрамлять

framework /фрэ́ймвёк/ n рамки

franchise /фрэ́нчайз/ n право участия в выборах

frank /фрэнк/ adj откровенный

fraternal /фрэтёрнл/ adj братский

fraud /фроод/ n обман; обманщик

freckle /фрекл/ n веснушка

free /фрии/ adj свободный; бесплатный; ~ trade /~ трэйд/ беспошлинная торговля; vt освобождать

freedom /фри́идэм/ n свобода

freelance /фри́илáанс/ adj работающий внештатно; vi работать внештатно

freeze /фрииз/ vt замораживать; ~ wages /~ вэ́йджиз/ замораживать заработную плату

freezer /фри́изэ/ n морозильник

freight /фройт/ n груз; ~ train /~ трэйн/ товарный поезд

French /фрэнч/ n французский язык; adj французский

frenzy /фрэ́нзи/ n бешенство, неистовство

frequent /фри́иквэнт/ adj частый

fresh /фреш/ adj свежий; ~ water /~ во́отэ/ пресная вода

friction /фрикшн/ n трение

Friday /фрáйди/ n пятница

friend /френд/ n друг; girl ~ /гёрл ~/ подруга

friendship /фрéндшип/ n дружба

frighten /фрайтн/ vt пугать

frigid /фри́джид/ adj холодный

fringe /фриндж/ n бахрома; челка; ~ benefits /~ бе́нифитс/ дополнительные льготы

frog /фрог/ n лягушка

from /фром/ prep от, из, с; ~ above /~ эба́в/ сверху; ~ behind /~ бихайнд/ из-за; ~ now on /~ на́у он/ отныне

front /франт/ n передняя сторона, фасад; (воен.) фронт; in ~ of /ин ~ ов/ перед; adj передний

frontier /фра́нтье/ n граница

frost /фрост/ n мороз

frown /фра́ун/ n хмурый взгляд; vi хмуриться

frozen /фро́узн/ adj замороженный; замерзший

frugal /фруугл/ adj скудный

fruit /фруут/ n плод, фрукт(ы); tinned ~ /тинд ~/ консервированные фрукты

fruitful /фру́утфул/ adj плодотворный

frustrate /фрастрэ́йт/ vt расстраивать, срывать

frustration /фрастрэ́йшн/ n срыв; крах; разочарование

frying pan /фра́йингпэн/ n сковорода с ручкой

fuel /фью́эл/ n топливо, горючее

fulfil /фулфи́л/ vt выполнять, осуществлять

fulfilment /фулфи́лмент/ n исполнение

full /фул/ adj полный; сытый; целый

full stop /фу́лстоп/ n точка

full time /фу́лтайм/ n полный рабочий день

fully /фу́ли/ adv вполне, полностью

fume /фьююм/ n дым; pl испарения

fun /фан/ n потеха, забава; have ~ /хэв ~/ веселиться; for ~ /фо ~/ в шутку; make ~ of /мэйк ~ ов/ высмеивать

function /фанкшн/ n функция; vi функционировать

functionary /фа́нкшнэри/ n должностное лицо

fund /фанд/ n фонд; pl денежные средства

fundamental /фа́ндэме́нтл/ adj основной

funeral /фью́юнэрл/ n похороны; ~ service /~ сёрвис/ панихида

funny /фа́ни/ adj забавный, чудной

fur /фёр/ n мех; накипь (в чайнике); ~ coat /~ ко́ут/ шуба

furious /фью́эриэс/ adj взбешенный, яростный

furnace /фёрнис/ n печь, горн

furnish /фёрниш/ vt снабжать; меблировать

furniture /фёрниче/ n мебель

further /фёрзэ/ adj дальнейший; adv далее, затем; vt продвигать

furthermore /фёрзэмо́р/ adv кроме того

fury /фью́эри/ n ярость

fuse /фью́юз/ n взрыватель; (эл.) предохранитель; vt плавить; vi соединяться; перегорать

fuss /фас/ n суета; make a ~ (about) /мэйк э ~ (эба́ут)/ поднимать шум (вокруг)

futile /фью́ютайл/ adj тщетный

future /фью́юче/ adj будущий; n будущее; in ~ /ин ~/ в будущем

G

gadget /га́джит/ n приспособление

gaily /га́йли/ adv весело; ярко

gain /гейн/ n прибыль, выигрыш; pl доходы; vt выигрывать, достигать; ~ time /~ тайм/ выигрывать время gala /гáалэ/ n празднество

galaxy /гэ́лэкси/ n галактика

gall /гоол/ n желчь; желчный пузырь

gallery /гэ́лери/ n галерея

gallon /гэ́лэн/ n галлон

gallop /гэ́лэп/ n галоп; vi нестись галопом

game /гейм/ n игра; дичь

gang /гэнг/ n банда; (разг.) компания

gap /гэп/ n брешь; пробел (в знаниях)

garage /гэ́раж/ n гараж

garbage /гáрбидж/ n мусор

garden /гардн/ n сад; kitchen ~ /кúчин ~/ огород

garlic /гáрлик/ n чеснок

gas /гэс/ n газ; (US) бензин

gas cooker /гэ́скýкэ/ n газовая плита

gas meter /гэ́смúитэ/ n газовый счетчик

gasolene /гэ́сэлин/ n газолин; (US) бензин

gasp /гаасп/ n удушье; vi задыхаться

gastric /гэ́стрик/ adj желудочный

gate /гейт/ n ворота; застава

gather /гэ́зэ/ vt собирать; ~ strength /~ стренгс/ копить силы; vi собираться

gauge /гейдж/ n измерительный прибор; vt измерять

gay /гэй/ adj веселый; (разг.) гомосексуальный

gaze /гейз/ n пристальный взгляд; vi смотреть

gear /гиэ/ n прибор; передача; ~ box /~ бокс/ коробка скоростей; change ~ /чейндж ~/ переключать передачу

general /дже́нэрэл/ adj общий, всеобщий; обычный; ~ election /~ иле́кшн/ всеобщие выборы; in ~ /ин ~/ вообще; n генерал

generation /дженэре́йшн/ n поколение

generator /дже́нэрэйтэ/ n генератор

generous /дже́нэрэс/ adj щедрый, великодушный

genitals /дже́нитлз/ n pl половые органы

genius /джи́иньес/ n гений

gentle /джентл/ adj мягкий, нежный, кроткий

gentleman /дже́нтлмэн/ n джентльмен

genuine /дже́ньюин/ adj подлинный, настоящий; искренний

geography /джио́грэфи/ n география

geology /джио́лэджи/ n геология

geometry /джио́митри/ n геометрия

germ /джёрм/ n микроб; зародыш

German /джёрмэн/ n немец, немка; немецкий язык; adj немецкий, германский

gesture /дже́сче/ n жест

get /гет/ vt получать; добиваться; vi становиться; ~ marrried /~ мэ́рид/ жениться; выйти замуж; ~ on /~ он/ преуспевать; ~ out of order /~ а́ут ов о́рдэ/ портиться; ~ ready /~ ре́ди/ готовить(ся); ~ rid of /~ рид ов/ избавляться от; ~ up /~ ап/ вставать

ghost /го́уст/ n привидение

giant /джа́йент/ n великан, гигант

giddy /ги́ди/ adj головокружительный; легкомысленный

gift /гифт/ n подарок; дар, талант

gigantic /джайгэ́нтик/ adj гигантский

gin /джин/ n джин

ginger /джи́нже/ n имбирь; ~ bread /~ брэд/ имбирный
пряник

gipsy /джи́пси/ цыган(ка); adj цыганский

girl /гёрл/ n девочка, девушка

gist /джист/ n суть

give /гив/ vt давать; ~ away /~ эвэ́й/ выдавать; ~ birth to
/~ бёрф ту/ родить; ~ in /~ ин/ уступать; ~ up /~ ап/
отказываться от, бросать

glad /глэд/ adj довольный, радостный; I am ~ /ай эм ~/
я рад(а)

glamorous /глэ́мэрэс/ adj шикарный

glance /глаанс/ n (быстрый) взгляд; at first ~ /эт фёрст
~/ с первого взгляда; vi взглянуть; ~ through /~ фру/
бегло просматривать

gland /глэнд/ n железа

glass /глаас/ adj стеклянный; n стекло; стакан; рюмка;
зеркало; pl очки

glide /глайд/ n скольжение; vi скользить

glimmer /гли́мэ/ n мерцание, тусклый свет; vi мерцать

glimpse /глимпс/ n быстрый взгляд; vt видеть мельком

glitter /гли́тэ/ vi сверкать

globe /глоуб/ n земной шар; глобус

gloomy /глу́уми/ adj угрюмый

glory /глоо́ри/ n слава

glossary /гло́сэри/ n словарь

glove /глав/ n перчатка

glow /глоу/ n заря; румянец; свечение; vi сиять, пылать

glue /глюю/ n клей; vt приклеивать

gnat /нэт/ n комар

gnaw /ноо/ vt глодать

go /róy/ vi идти, ходить, ехать, ездить; ~ ahead /~ эхéд/
двигаться вперед; ~ away /~ эвэ́й/ уходить, уезжать; ~
back /~ бэк/ возвращаться; ~ by /~ бай/ проходить
мимо; ~ on /~ он/ продолжать; let ~ /лет ~/
освобождать; n попытка; have a ~ at /хэв э ~ эт/
попытаться

go-ahead /róyэхед/ adj (разг.) предприимчивый

goal /róyл/ n цель; (спорт.) гол; score a ~ /скор э ~/
забивать гол

goal-keeper /róyлкийипэ/ n вратарь

goat /róyт/ n коза, козел

go-between /róyбитвийин/ n посредник

god /год/ n бог; my G.! /май ~/ Боже мой!; thank G.!
/сэнк ~/ слава Богу!

godchild /róдчайлд/ n крестник, крестница

godfather /róдфáазэ/ n крестный отец

godmother /róдмáзэ/ n крестная мать

gold /róyлд/ n золото

golden /róyлдэн/ adj золотой

goldsmith /róyлдсмит/ n ювелир

golf /голф/ n гольф

good /гуд/ adj хороший, добрый; ~ morning /~ мóрнинг/
доброе утро!; ~ night /~ найт/ спокойной ночи; ~
afternoon (evening)! /~ áафтэнýун (йивнинг)/ добрый
день (вечер)!; ~ bye /~ бай/ до свидания!; n благо,
польза; it is no ~ /ит из нóу ~/ бесполезно

goods /гудз/ n pl товары

goose /гуус/ n гусь, гусыня

gorgeous /го́рджес/ adj великолепный

gospel /госпл/ n евангелие; ~ truth /~ труус/ истинная правда

gossip /го́сип/ n сплетня; сплетник; vi сплетничать

govern /гавн/ vt управлять, править

government /га́вэнмент/ n правительство; правление

governor /га́вэнэ/ n губернатор

grab /грэб/ vt хватать, захватывать

graceful /грэ́йсфул/ adj грациозный, изящный

grade /грэйд/ n степень; сорт; класс

gradual /грэ́дьюэл/ adj постепенный

graduate /грэ́дьюит/ n выпускник; /грэ́дьюэйт/ vt оканчивать университет

grain /грэйн/ n зерно; against the ~ /эгэ́йнст зэ ~/ против шерсти

grammer /грэ́мэ/ n грамматика

gram(me) /грэм/ n грамм

grandchild /грэ́нчайлд/ n внук, внучка

grandfather /грэ́нфа́азэ/ n дедушка

grandmother /грэ́нма́зэ/ n бабушка

granny /грэ́ни/ n бабушка

grant /граант/ n субсидия; стипендия; vt дарить; предоставлять; допускать; take for ~ed /тэйк фо ~ыд/ считать само собой разумеющимся

grape /грэйп/ n виноград

grapefruit /грэ́йпфрут/ n грейпфрут

graphic /грэ́фик/ adj наглядный

grasp /грaасп/ n хватка; понимание; beyond one's ~ /бийо́нд ванз ~/ выше чьего-либо понимания; vt схватывать; понимать

grass /грaас/ n трава

grateful /грэ́йтфул/ adj благодарный

grater /грэ́йтэ/ n терка

gratis /грэ́йтис/ adv бесплатно

gratitude /грэ́титьюд/ n благодарность

gratuity /грэтью́ити/ n денежное пособие; чаевые

grave /грэйв/ adj серьезный, важный; n могила

gravity /грэ́вити/ n сила тяжести; specific ~ /спесйфик ~/ удельный вес

grease /гриис/ n жир, смазка; /грииз/ vt смазывать

great /грэйт/ adj великий, большой; a ~ many /э ~ мэ́ни/ множество

greatcoat /грэ́йткоут/ n пальто (мужское)

greed, greediness /гриид, грии́динис/ n жадность

greedy /грии́ди/ adj алчный

Greek /гриик/ n грек, гречанка; греческий язык; adj греческий

green /гриин/ adj зеленый

greengrocer /грии́нгроусэ/ n зеленщик

greet /гриит/ vt приветствовать

greeting /грии́тинг/ n приветствие

grey /грэй/ adj серый; седой

grief /грииф/ n горе

grim /грим/ adj угрюмый; жестокий

grin /грин/ n ухмылка; vi ухмыляться

grip /грип/ n хватка; сжатие; vt схватывать

groan /гро́ун/ n стон; vi стонать

grocer /гро́усэ/ n бакалейщик

grocery /гро́усэри/ n бакалея

groin /гройн/ n пах

grope /гро́уп/ vi идти ощупью

gross /грос/ adj грубый; крупный; валовой; ~ income /~ и́нкэм/ валовой доход; ~ weight /~ вэйт/ вес брутто

ground /гра́унд/ n земля; почва; причина, мотив; on the ~s of /он зэ ~з ов/ на основании; vt обосновывать

ground floor /гра́ундфло́р/ n первый этаж

group /грууп/ n группа; vti группировать (ся)

grow /гро́у/ vt выращивать, отращивать; vi расти, становиться; ~ little /~ литл/ уменьшаться; ~ old /~ о́улд/ стареть

grown-up /гро́унап/ n, adj взрослый

growth /гро́ус/ n рост

grumble /грамбл/ n ворчание; vi ворчать

guarantee /гэ̀рэнти́и/ n гарантия; vt гарантировать

guarantor /гэ̀рэнто́р/ n поручитель, гарант

guard /гард/ n охрана; стража; часовой; гвардия; advance ~ /эдва́анс ~/ авангард; be on ~ /би он ~/ быть начеку; vt охранять

guess /гес/ n догадка; vt отгадывать

guest /гест/ n гость, гостья

guide /гайд/ n гид, проводник; vt руководить

guilt /гилт/ n вина

guilty /ги́лти/ adj виновный

guise /гайз/ n вид, личина, маска; предлог; under the ~ of /а́ндэ зэ ~ ов/ под видом guitar /гита́р/ n гитара

gulf /галф/ n залив

gull /гал/ n чайка

gulp /галп/ n глоток; at one ~ /эт ван~/ залпом; vt глотать с жадностью или поспешностью

gum /гам/ n десна; клей; vt склеивать

gun /ган/ n ружье, винтовка; пушка

gunpowder /га́нпа́удэ/ n порох

gust /гаст/ n порыв (ветра)

gut /гат/ n кишка; pl внутренности

guy /гай/ n парень

gymnastics /джимнэ́стикс/ n гимнастика

gynaecologist /га́йнико́лэджист/ n гинеколог

H

haberdashery /хэ́бэдэ́шери/ n галантерея

habit /хэ́бит/ n привычка; обычай

habitual /хэби́чьюэл/ adj обычный, привычный

hack /хэк/ vt рубить

hackneyed /хэ́книд/ adj банальный, избитый

haemorrhage /хэ́мэридж/ n кровотечение

hair /хээ/ n волос(ы); шерсть (животного)

haircut /хэ́экат/ n стрижка

hairdo /хэ́эду/ n прическа

hairdresser /хэ́эдрéсэ/ n парикмахер

hair-drier /хэ́эдра́йе/ n сушилка для волос

half /ха́аф/ n половина; adv наполовину; ~ an hour /~ эн а́уэ/ полчаса; at ~ price /эт ~ прайс/ за полцены

halfway /хáафвэй/ adj лежащий на полпути; компромиссный; meet smb. ~ /миит сáмбэди ~/ идти на компромисс

hall /хоол/ n зал, холл

hallo /хэлбу/ interj алло!; привет!

halt /хоолт/ n остановка, привал; interj стой!

ham /хэм/ n ветчина, окорок

hamper /хэ́мпэ/ vt мешать, затруднять

hand /хэнд/ n рука, кисть руки; стрелка (часов); работник; at ~ /эт ~/ наготове; by ~ /бай ~/ от руки; ~ in ~ /~ ин ~/ рука об руку; on ~ /он ~/ в наличии; ~s off! /~з оф/ руки прочь!; ~s up! /~з ап/ руки вверх!; get the upper ~ /гет зы áпэ ~/ брать верх; vt передавать, вручать

handbag /хэ́ндбэг/ n сумка

handful /хэ́ндфул/ n горсть

handicap /хэ́ндикэп/ n гандикап; помеха

handicraft /хэ́ндикрафт/ n ремесло; ручная работа

handkerchief /хэ́нкэчиф/ n носовой платок; косынка

handle /хэндл/ n рукоятка; vt трогать рукой; обращаться с; иметь дело с

handmade /хэ́ндмэйд/ adj ручной работы

handshake /хэ́ндшейк/ n рукопожатие

handsome /хэ́нсэм/ adj красивый

handwriting /хэ́ндрáйтинг/ n почерк

hang /хэнг/ vt вешать; vi висеть

haphazard /хэ́пхэ́ззэд/ adj случайный; adv случайно; at ~ /эт ~/ наудачу

happen /хэпн/ vi случаться; whatever ~s /вотэ́вэ ~з/ что бы ни случилось

happiness /хэ́пинис/ n счастье

happy /хэ́пи/ adj счастливый; удачный

harass /хэ́рэс/ vt беспокоить; изматывать

harbour /ха́рбэ/ n гавань

hard /хард/ adj твердый; жесткий; тяжелый; трудный; ~ cash /~ кэш/ наличные деньги; adv твердо; крепко; упорно; drink ~ /дринк ~/ сильно пить; work ~ /вёрк ~/ много работать

hard-boiled /ха́рдбо́йлд/ adj сваренный вкрутую (о яйце)

hardly /ха́рдли/ adv едва, едва ли

hardware /ха́рдвээ/ n металлические изделия; (вчт.) аппаратное обеспечение (в отличие от программного)

hare /хээ/ n заяц

harm /харм/ n вред; vt вредить; обижать

harmony /ха́рмэни/ n гармония

harsh /харш/ adj суровый; грубый

harvest /ха́рвист/ n урожай; vt собирать урожай

haste /хейст/ n спешка, торопливость

hasten /хейсн/ vti торопить(ся)

hat /хэт/ adj шляпа, шапка

hate /хейт/ vt ненавидеть

hatred /хе́йтрид/ n ненависть

haughty /хо́оти/ adj надменный

have /хэв/ vt иметь; I ~ /ай ~/ у меня есть...; I ~ not /ай ~ нот/ у меня нет...; I ~ to /ай ~ ту/ я должен....; you had better... /ю хэд бе́тэ/ вам лучше бы...

hazardous /хэ́зэдэс/ adj рискованный

he /хи/ pron он; n мужчина; самец

head /хед/ n голова; верхняя часть; руководитель; hit the
  nail on the ~ /хит зэ нэйл он зэ ~/ попадать в точку; vt
  возглавлять; озаглавливать

headache /хéдэйк/ n головная боль

heading /хéдинг/ n заглавие

headline /хéдлайн/ n заголовок

headphones /хéдфоунз/ n pl наушники

headquarters /хéдквóотэз/ n pl штаб

heal /хиил/ vt излечивать; vi заживать

health /хелф/ n здоровье

heap /хиип/ n куча; vt нагромождать

hear /хи́э/ vt слышать; слушать; ~ from /~ фром/ получать известия от

heart /харт/ n сердце; сущность; by ~ /бай ~/ наизусть;
  take to ~ /тэйк ту ~/ принимать близко к сердцу

heat /хиит/ n жара; пыл; vti нагревать(ся), топить(ся)

heaven /хевн/ n небо; рай

heavy /хéви/ adj тяжелый; сильный (дождь); ~ traffic /~
  трéфик/ сильное движение

hedgehog /хéджхог/ n еж

heed /хиид/ n внимание; vt обращать внимание на

heel /хиил/ n пятка; каблук

height /хайт/ n высота; рост

heir /ээ/ n наследник

hell /хел/ n ад

hello /хелóу/ interj алло!; здравствуйте!

help /хелп/ n помощь; vt помогать; ~ yourself /~ йосэлф/
  угощайтесь; I can't ~ it /ай кант ~ ит/ я ничего не могу
  поделать

helpless /хέлплис/ adj беспомощный

hemisphere /хέмисфиэ/ n полушарие

hen /хен/ n курица

her /хέ/ pron ee, ей

herb /хέрб/ n трава; целебное растение

here /хйэ/ adv здесь, тут, сюда, вот; ~ goes /~ гоуз/ начнем!; ~'s to you! /~з ту ю/ ваше здоровье!; look ~ /лук ~/ послушай(те)!

heredity /хирέдити/ n наследственность

heritage /хέритыдж/ n наследство

hero /хйэроу/ n герой

herring /хέринг/ n сельдь

hers /хέрз/ pron ee, принадлежащий ей; this book is ~ /зыс бук из ~/ эта книга принадлежит ей

herself /хέсέлф/ pron себя, себе, собой

hesitate /хέзитэйт/ vi колебаться

hi /хай/ interj эй!, привет!

hiccup /хйкап/ n икота; vi икать

hide /хайд/ n шкура; vti прятать(ся)

high /хай/ adj высокий, высший; сильный (ветер); большой (о скорости); ~ school /~ скуул/ средняя школа; ~ sea /~ сии/ открытое море; adv высоко

highway /хάйвэй/ n шоссе

hijack /хάйджек/ vt угонять (самолет)

hill /хил/ n холм

him /хим/ pron его, ему

himself /химсέлф/ pron себя, себе, собой

hinder /хйндэ/ vt мешать

hint /хинт/ n намек; vt: ~ at /~ эт/ намекать на

hip /хип/ n бедро

hire /хáйе/ n наем; прокат; vt нанимать; брать напрокат; снимать

hire-purchase /хáйепёчес/ n покупка в рассрочку

his /хиз/ pron его, свой

historic(al) /хистóрик(л)/ adj исторический

history /хи́стэри/ n история

hit /хит/ n удар; попадание; успех; гвоздь сезона, популярная песня, пластинка; make a ~ /мэйк э ~/ производить сенсацию; vt ударять, попадать в цель

hitch /хич/ n помеха; without a ~ /визáут э ~/ как по маслу; vti зацеплять(ся)

hitchhike /хи́чхайк/ vi "голосовать" на дороге

hoarse /хоорс/ adj хриплый

hobby /хóби/ n любимое занятие, конек

hockey /хóки/ n хоккей

hold /хóулд/ n захват; vt держать; владеть; вмещать; проводить; ~ on /~он/ подожди!; ~ one's tongue /~ванз танг/ держать язык за зубами; ~ up /~ап/ задерживать

holding /хóулдинг/ n владение

hole /хóул/ n дыра, нора

holiday /хóлидэй/ n праздник; отпуск; выходной день; pl каникулы

hollow /хóлоу/ adj полый; впалый

holy /хóули/ adj священный, святой

home /хóум/ n дом, жилище; родина; at ~ /эт ~/ дома; adj домашний; родной (город и т.п.); внутренний (торговля и т.п.); adv домой; make yourself at ~ /мэйк йосáлф эт ~/ будьте как дома!

honest /óнист/ adj честный

honey /хáни/ n мед; (разг.) дорогой, голубчик

honeymoon /хáнимун/ n медовый месяц

honour /óнэ/ n честь; pl почести

hook /хук/ n крючок, крюк; by ~ or by crook /бай ~ о бай крук/ не мытьем, так катаньем

hop /хоп/ vi скакать; n прыжок

hope /хóуп/ n надежда; vi надеяться

horizon /хэрáйзн/ n горизонт

horizontal /хóризóнтл/ adj горизонтальный

horn /хорн/ n рог; гудок

horoscope /хóрэскоуп/ n гороскоп

horrible /хóрэбл/ adj ужасный

horror /хóрэ/ n ужас

horse /хоос/ n лошадь, конь

horse-power /хóоспáуэ/ n (тех.) лошадиная сила

horse-race /хóосрэйс/ n скачки, бега

hosiery /хóужери/ n чулочные изделия; трикотажное белье

hospitable /хóспитэбл/ adj гостеприимный

hospital /хóспитл/ n больница

host /хóуст/ n хозяин (дома)

hostage /хóстыдж/ n заложник

hostess /хóустыс/ n хозяйка (дома)

hostile /хóстайл/ adj враждебный

hot /хот/ adj горячий, острый

hotel /хоутэ́л/ n гостиница

hour /áуэ/ n час

house /хáус/ n дом; династия

household /хáусхóулд/ n домочадцы; домашнее хозяйство

housewife /хáусвайф/ n домашняя хозяйка

housing /хáузинг/ n жилищное строительство; ~ problem /~ прóблем/ жилищная проблема

how /хáу/ adv как, каким образом; ~ far /~ фар/ как далеко; ~ long /~ лонг/ как долго; ~ much (many)? /~ мач (мэ́ни)/ сколько?; ~ do you do? /~ ду ю ду/ здравствуйте!

however /хáуэ́вэ/ adv как бы ни; conj однако

hue /хьюю/ n оттенок

huge /хьююдж/ adj громадный

hull /хал/ n кожура; корпус (корабля)

human /хьбюмэн/ adj человеческий

humane /хьюмэ́йн/ adj гуманный

humanity /хьюмэ́нити/ n человечество

humble /хамбл/ adj смиренный

humid /хьбюмид/ adj влажный

humiliate /хьюми́лиэйт/ vt унижать

humour /хьбюмэ/ n юмор; настроение

hundred /хáндрэд/ n сто

hundredweight /хáндрэдвэйт/ n центнер

hunger /хáнгэ/ n голод

hunger-strike /хáнгэстрайк/ n голодовка

hungry /хáнгри/ adj голодный

hunt /хант/ n охота; vt охотиться на

hurrah /хурáа/ interj ура!

hurricane /хáрикэн/ n ураган

hurry /хáри/ n спешка; in a ~ /ин э ~/ второпях; vti торопить (ся); ~ up /~ ап/ скорее!

hurt /хёрт/ n вред; боль; vt ушибать; vi болеть

husband /хáзбэнд/ n муж

hush /хаш/ n тишина; vti успокаивать(ся); ~ up /~ ап/ замалчивать; interj тише!

husk /хаск/ n шелуха, оболочка

hustle /хасл/ vti толкать(ся), теснить(ся)

hydrogen /хáйдрэджен/ n водород

hygiene /хáйджин/ n гигиена

hymn /хим/ n гимн (церковный)

hypocrisy /хипóкрэси/ n лицемерие

hypodermic /хáйпэдёрмик/ adj подкожный; ~ syringe /~ сирúндж/ шприц

hysterical /хистéрикл/ adj истерический

I

I /ай/ pron я

ice /айс/ n лед; мороженое

iceberg /áйсбёрг/ n айсберг

ice-cream /áйскрúим/ n мороженое

icon /áйкон/ n икона

idea /айдúэ/ n идея, мысль, понятие; bright ~ /брайт ~/ блестящая идея

ideal /айдúэл/ adj идеальный; n идеал

identical /айдéнтикл/ adj тождественный

identification /айдéнтификéйшн/ n опознание; ~ card /~ кард/ удостоверение личности

ideology /áйдиолэджи/ n идеология

idiocy /úдиэси/ n идиотизм, идиотство

idiom /úдиэм/ n идиома; диалект, говор

idle /айдл/ adj праздный, ленивый; тщетный, пустой

idol /айдл/ n кумир

if /иф/ conj если, если бы, ли; as ~ /эз ~/ как будто; even ~ /иивн ~/ если даже

ignition /игнишн/ n зажигание

ignore /игнóр/ vt игнорировать

ill /ил/ adj больной; дурной; ~ feeling /~ фѝилинг/ неприязнь; n зло, вред; fall ~ /фоол ~/ заболевать

illegal /илѝигл/ adj незаконный

illegitimate /ѝлиджѝтимит/ adj незаконный

illiterate /илѝтэрит/ adj неграмотный

illness /ѝлнис/ n болезнь

illuminate /ильюминэйт/ vt освещать

illusion /илюóжн/ n иллюзия

illustrate /ѝлэстрэйт/ vt иллюстрировать

ill-will /ѝлвѝл/ n недоброжелательство

image /ѝмидж/ n образ, подобие

imagination /имэ́джинэ́йшн/ n воображение

imagine /имэ́джин/ vt воображать, представлять себе

imitate /ѝмитэйт/ vt имитировать

immature /ѝмэтьюэ/ adj незрелый

immediate /имиѝдьет/ adj непосредственный, немедленный

immense /имéнс/ adj безмерный, необъятный

immigrant /ѝмигрэнт/ n иммигрант

immigrate /ѝмигрэйт/ vi иммигрировать

immobile /имóубайл/ adj неподвижный

immoral /имóрл/ adj безнравственный

immovable /имýувэбл/ adj неподвижный; n pl недвижимость

immunity /имьююнити/ n иммунитет

impact /ѝмпэкт/ n удар, влияние

impair /импѝэ/ vt повреждать

impartial /импáршл/ adj беспристрастный

impatient /импѐйшнт/ adj нетерпеливый

impeachment /импѝичмент/ n привлечение к суду; импичмент

impede /импѝид/ vt препятствовать

impel /импéл/ vt побуждать, приводить в движение

impending /импéндинг/ adj предстоящий, надвигающийся

imperative /импéрэтив/ adj повелительный

imperialism /импѝэриэлизм/ n империализм

impersonal /импѐрснл/ adj безличный

implement /ѝмплимент/ n орудие; vt выполнять, осуществлять

implore /имплóр/ vt умолять

imply /имплáй/ vt подразумевать

impolite /ѝмпэлáйт/ adj невежливый

import /импóрт/ vt ввозить, импортировать; /ѝмпорт/ n ввоз, импорт; ~ duty /~ дьюти/ ввозная пошлина

important /импóртэнт/ adj значительный

impossible /импóсэбл/ adj невозможный

impotent /ѝмпэтэнт/ adj бессильный

impoverish /импóвериш/ vt доводить до нищеты

impression /импрéшн/ n впечатление; оттиск

impressive /импрéсив/ adj внушительный, производящий впечатление

imprint /и́мпринт/ n отпечаток, след; printer's ~ /при́нтэз ~/ выходные данные

imprison /импри́зн/ vt заключать в тюрьму

improbable /импро́бэбл/ adj невероятный

improve /импру́ув/ vti улучшать (ся)

improvement /импру́увмент/ n улучшение

impudent /и́мпьюдент/ adj дерзкий

impulse /и́мпалс/ n побуждение, импульс

impunity /импью́юнити/ n безнаказанность; with ~ /виз ~/ безнаказанно

in /ин/ prep в, на, во время, через; ~ all /~ оол/ всего; ~ a week /~ э виик/ за неделю; ~ due course /~ дью корс/ в свое время; ~ the morning /~ зэ мо́рнинг/ утром; ~ my opinion /~ май эпи́ньен/ по моему мнению; ~ the sun /~ зэ сан/ на солнце; ~ time /~ тайм/ вовремя; ~ writing /~ ра́йтинг/ в письменной форме; adv внутри, внутрь

inability /и́нэби́лити/ n неспособность

inaccessible /и́нэксе́сэбл/ adj недоступный

inaccurate /инэ́кьюрит/ adj неточный

inadequate /инэ́диквит/ adj недостаточный

inasmuch as /и́нэзмáчэз/ conj поскольку

incalculable /инкэ́лкьюлэбл/ adj неисчислимый

incapable /инке́йпэбл/ adj неспособный

incentive /инсе́нтив/ n побуждение, стимул

incessant /инсе́снт/ adj непрерывный

inch /инч/ n дюйм

incident /и́нсидент/ n происшествие, инцидент

incidental /и́нсиде́нтл/ adj случайный

inclination /и́нклинэ́йшн/ n склонность

include /инклю́юд/ vt включать

including /инклю́юдинг/ prep в том числе

income /и́нкэм/ n доход; ~ tax /~ тэкс/ подоходный налог

incompatible /и́нкэмпэ́тэбл/ adj несовместимый

incompetent /инко́мпитент/ adj неспособный, некомпетентный

incomplete /и́нкэмпли́ит/ adj неполный, незавершенный

inconsistent /и́нкэнси́стент/ adj непоследовательный

inconvenient /и́нкэнви́иньент/ adj неудобный

incorrect /и́нкэрéкт/ adj неправильный

increase /и́нкрис/ n увеличение; /инкри́ис/ vt увеличивать

increment /и́нкримент/ n прибавка; увеличение

incur /инкёр/ vt навлекать на себя, подвергаться; ~ losses /~ лóсыз/ терпеть убытки

indebted /индэ́тыд/ adj находящийся в долгу, обязанный

indecent /инди́иснт/ adj неприличный

indeed /инди́ид/ adv в самом деле, действительно

indefinite /индéфинит/ adj неопределенный

indemnity /индэ́мнити/ n компенсация

independent /и́ндипéндэнт/ adj независимый

index /и́ндэкс/ n указатель; показатель

Indian /и́ндьен/ n индиец, индеец, индианка; adj индийский, индейский; ~ summer /~ сáмэ/ бабье лето

indicate /и́ндикейт/ vt указывать

indicator /и́ндикейтэ/ n индикатор

indictment /индáйтмент/ n обвинительный акт

indifferent /индúфрэнт/ adj безразличный

indigestion /úндиджéсчн/ n расстройство желудка

indignant /индúгнэнт/ adj возмущенный

indirect /úндирéкт/ adj косвенный, непрямой

indispensable /úндиспéнсэбл/ adj незаменимый

indistinct /úндистúнкт/ adj неясный

individual /úндивúдьюэл/ adj личный; n индивидуум, человек

indivisible /úндивúзэбл/ adj неделимый

Indo-European /úндоюóэрэпúэн/ adj индо европейский

indoors /úндóрз/ adv в помещении

induce /индьюóюс/ vt побуждать

indulge /индáлдж/ vt баловать, потакать; ~ in /~ ин/ предаваться

industrial /индáстриэл/ adj промышленный

industrious /индáстриэс/ adj трудолюбивый

industry /úндэстри/ n промышленность

inefficient /úныфúшнт/ adj неспособный; неэффективный

inequality /úныквóлити/ n неравенство

inevitable /инэ́витэбл/ adj неизбежный

inexhaustible /úнызгóостэбл/ adj неистощимый

inexpensive /úныкспéнсив/ adj недорогой

inexperience /úныкспúэриэнс/ n неопытность

infant /úнфэнт/ n младенец

infantry /úнфэнтри/ n пехота

infection /инфéкшн/ n инфекция

inferior /инфи́эриэ/ adj низший, худший; n подчиненный

inferiority /инфи́эрио́рити/ n неполноценность; ~ complex /~ ко́мплекс/ комплекс неполноценности

infinite /и́нфинит/ adj бесконечный

inflame /инфлэ́йм/ vt воспламенять

inflate /инфлэ́йт/ vt надувать; вздувать (цены)

inflexible /инфле́ксэбл/ adj негибкий; непреклонный

influence /и́нфлуэнс/ n влияние; vt влиять на

influenza /и́нфлуэ́нзэ/ n грипп

inform /инфо́рм/ vt сообщать; ~ against /~ эге́йнст/ доносить на

informal /инфо́рмл/ adj неофициальный

information /и́нфэмэ́йшн/ n информация, сведения

infringement /инфри́нджмент/ n нарушение

ingenious /инджи́иньес/ adj изобретательный

inglorious /ингло́ориэс/ adj бесславный

inhabitant /инхэ́битэнт/ n житель

inhale /инхэ́йл/ vt вдыхать

inheritance /инхе́ритэнс/ n наследство

inhuman /инхью́юмэн/ adj бесчеловечный

initial /ини́шел/ adj первоначальный; n начальная буква; pl инициалы

initiative /ини́шиэтив/ n инициатива

inject /инджéкт/ vt впрыскивать

injection /инджéкшн/ n укол

injury /и́нджери/ n ранение

injustice /инджа́стис/ n несправедливость

ink /инк/ n чернила; printer's ~ /принтэз ~/ типографская краска

inmate /инмэйт/ n жилец; заключенный (в тюрьме)

inn /ин/ n гостиница

inner /инэ/ adj внутренний

innocence /инэснс/ n невиновность

innovation /иновэйшн/ n нововведение

innumerable /иньюмэрэбл/ adj бесчисленный

inoculate /инокьюлэйт/ vt делать прививку

in-patient /инпэйшнт/ n стационарный больной

inquest /инквэст/ n (юр.) следствие

insane /инсэйн/ adj душевнобольной

insect /инсект/ n насекомое

insecure /инсикьюэ/ adj небезопасный

inseparable /инсэпрэбл/ adj неотделимый

insert /инсёрт/ vt вставлять; помещать (в газете)

inside /инсайд/ adj внутренний; n внутренняя часть; adv внутри, внутрь; ~ out /~ аут/ наизнанку; prep внутри, в

insist /инсист/ vi настаивать

insoluble /инсолюбл/ adj неразрешимый

insomnia /инсомниэ/ n бессонница

inspect /инспект/ vt осматривать, инспектировать

inspector /инспектэ/ n инспектор

inspiration /инспэрэйшн/ n вдохновение

instability /инстэбилити/ n неустойчивость

installation /инстэлэйшн/ n монтаж; pl сооружения

instalment /инстолмент/ n очередной взнос; pay by ~s /пэй бай ~c/ выплачивать в рассрочку; очередной выпуск

instance /и́нстэнс/ n пример; for ~ /фор ~/ например

instant /и́нстэнт/ adj немедленный; n мгновение

instead /инстэ́д/ adv вместо; вместо того, чтобы

instinct /и́нстинкт/ n инстинкт

institute /и́нститьют/ n институт; vt учреждать, устанавливать

institution /и́нститьбюшн/ n учреждение

instruct /инстра́кт/ vt обучать

instruction /инстра́кшн/ n обучение; pl указания

instructive /инстра́ктив/ adj поучительный

instrument /и́нструмент/ n инструмент, прибор, орудие (также образн.)

insufficient /и́нсэфи́шент/ adj недостаточный

insulin /и́нсъюлин/ n инсулин

insult /и́нсалт/ n оскорбление; /инса́лт/ vt оскорблять

insurance /иншу́эрэнс/ n страхование; fire ~ /фа́йе ~/ страхование от пожара; ~ policy /~ по́лиси/ страховой полис

integral /и́нтигрл/ adj неотъемлемый; цельный; (матем.) интегральный

intellect /и́нтилект/ n интеллект, ум

intellectual /и́нтиле́ктьюэл/ adj умственный; n интеллигент; pl интеллигенция

intelligent /инте́лиджент/ adj умный, разумный

intend /интэ́нд/ vt намереваться

intense /интэ́нс/ adj напряженный, сильный

intensify /интэ́нсифай/ vti усиливать (ся)

intention /интэ́ншн/ n намерение

interchangeable /и́нтэчэ́йнджебл/ adj взаимо-заменяемый

intercourse /и́нтэко́рс/ n общение; сношения

interdependence /и́нтэдипэ́ндэнс/ n взаимозависимость

interest /и́нтрист/ n интерес; процент; bear ~ /бээ ~/ приносить прибыль; in your ~ /ин йо ~/ в ваших интересах; rate of ~ /рэйт ов ~/ норма процента; vt интересовать

interesting /и́нтристинг/ adj интересный

interfere /и́нтэфи́э/ vi вмешиваться; ~ with /~ виз/ мешать

interior /инти́эриэ/ adj внутренний; n интерьер

internal /интёрнл/ adj внутренний

international /и́нтэнэ́шнл/ adj международный

interpret /интёрприт/ vt переводить (устно)

iinterpreter /интёрпритэ/ n переводчик (устный)

interrogate /интэ́рэгэйт/ vt допрашивать

interrupt /и́нтэра́пт/ vt прерывать

interval /и́нтэвл/ n перерыв; (театр.) антракт

interview /и́нтэвьюю/ n беседа, интервью; vt интервьюировать

intestine /интэ́стин/ n кишка

intimate /и́нтимит/ adj близкий; интимный

into /и́нту/ prep в, во, на; ~ the bargain /~ зэ ба́ргин/ в придачу

intolerable /инто́лэрэбл/ adj невыносимый

intolerant /инто́лэрэнт/ adj нетерпимый

intoxicate /инто́ксикейт/ vt опьянять

intricate /и́нтрикит/ adj запутанный

introduce /и́нтрэдьюю́с/ vt представлять; вводить; ~ oneself /~ ванса́лф/ представиться introduction /интрэда́кшн/ n представление; предисловие

intrude /интру́уд/ vi вторгаться; vt навязывать

intuition /и́нтьюйшн/ n интуиция

invade /инвэ́йд/ vt вторгаться

invalid /и́нвэлид/ adj больной; n инвалид

invalid /инва́лид/ adj несостоятельный; недействительный

invaluable /инва́льюэбл/ adj бесценный

invariable /инвэ́эриэбл/ adj неизменный

invention /инве́ншен/ n изобретение

inventory /и́нвентри/ n инвентаризация, опись имущества

invest /инве́ст/ vt вкладывать, помещать (капитал)

investigation /инве́стигэ́йшн/ n (юр.) следствие; исследование

investment /инве́стмент/ n капиталовложение

investor /инве́стэ/ n вкладчик

invisible /инви́зэбл/ adj невидимый

invitation /и́нвитэ́йшн/ n приглашение

invite /инва́йт/ vt приглашать

invoice /и́нвойс/ n накладная

involuntary /инво́лэнтри/ adj невольный

involve /инво́лв/ vt вовлекать, запутывать; включать в себя

inward /и́нвэд/ adj внутренний

iodine /а́йэдин/ n йод

I.O.U. /а́йоую́ю/ n долговая расписка

Irish /а́йэриш/ n ирландский язык; adj ирландский

iron /áйен/ n железо, утюг; pl кандалы; adj железный; vt гладить

ironic(al) /айрóник(л)/ adj иронический

iron-ore /áйеноо/ n железная руда

irony /áйерэни/ n ирония

irrational /ирáшенл/ adj нерациональный

irregular /ирáгьюлэ/ adj нерегулярный; неправильный

irrelevant /ирáливэнт/ adj неуместный; несоответствующий

irrespective /ирисп
éктив/ adj независимый (от), безотносительный

irresponsible /ириспóнсэбл/ adj безответственный

irrigation /ириг
éйшн/ n ирригация

irritable /ирритэбл/ adj раздражительный

Islam /úзлаам/ n ислам

island /áйлэнд/ n остров

isolation /áйсэлэ́йшн/ n изоляция

Israelite /úзриэлайт/ n израильтянин, израильтянка; adj израильский

issue /úсью/ n выпуск; предмет обсуждения; vi выходить; vt выпускать

it /ит/ pron он, она, оно; what is ~ /вот из ~/ что это?; ~ rains /~ рэйнз/ идет дождь

Italian /итáльен/ n итальянец, итальянка; итальянский язык; adj итальянский

item /áйтэм/ n пункт; статья; предмет

its /итс/ poss pron его, ее, свой

itself /итсéлф/ pron себя, сам, сама, само; she is virtue ~ /ши из вёртью ~/ она сама добродетель

ivory /áйври/ n слоновая кость

J

jacket /джэ́кит/ n жакет, куртка, пиджак; суперобложка (книги)

jail /джейл/ n тюрьма

jam /джэм/ n джем; traffic ~ /трэ́фик ~/ затор; vt загромождать; (радио) заглушать; vi останавливаться, заедать

January /джэ́ньюэри/ n январь

Japanese /джэ́пэни́из/ n японец, японка; японский язык; adj японский

jar /джар/ n банка, кувшин

jaundice /джо́ондис/ n желтуха

jaw /джоо/ n челюсть

jazz /джэз/ n джаз

jealous /джэ́лэс/ adj ревнивый

jeans /джиинз/ n pl джинсы

jelly /джэ́ли/ n желе

jerk /джэ́рк/ n толчок, подергивание

jersey /джёёзи/ n свитер; ~ dress /~ дрэс/ вязаное платье

Jesus /джи́изэс/ n Иисус

Jew /джуу/ n еврей

jewel /джу́уэл/ n драгоценный камень

jewellery /джу́уэлри/ n ювелирные изделия

Jewish /джу́уиш/ adj еврейский

jingle /джингл/ n звяканье; vi звякать

job /джоб/ n работа

jog /джог/ vt подталкивать; vi бежать мелкой рысцой; n толчок jogging /джо́гинг/ n бег трусцой

join /джойн/ vt соединять; вступать; ~ the army /~ зы а́рми/ вступать в армию; vi соединяться

joint /джойнт/ n сустав; часть разрубленной туши; out of ~ /а́ут ов ~/ вывихнутый; adj совместный

joint-stock /джо́йнсток/ n акционерный капитал; ~ company /~ ка́мпэни/ акционерное общество

joke /джо́ук/ n шутка, анекдот; practical ~ /прэ́ктикэл ~/ грубая шутка; vi шутить

jolly /джо́ли/ adj веселый

journal /джёрнэл/ n журнал; дневник

journalist /джёрнэлист/ n журналист

journey /джёрни/ n путешествие, поездка

joy /джой/ n радость

jubilee /джу́убили/ n юбилей, годовщина

judge /джадж/ n судья, ценитель; vti судить, решать

jug /джаг/ n кувшин; vt тушить (мясо)

juice /джуус/ n сок

juicy /джу́уси/ adj сочный; пикантный

July /джула́й/ n июль; adj июльский

jump /джамп/ n прыжок; vti прыгать

jumper /джа́мпэ/ n прыгун; джемпер

junction /джанкшн/ n соединение; (ж/д) узел

June /джуун/ n июнь

junior /джу́унье/ n, adj младший

junk-shop /джа́нкшоп/ n лавка старьевщика

jurisprudence /джу́ериспру́уденс/ n юриспруденция

jurist /джу́ерист/ n юрист

jury /джу́ери/ n суд присяжных; жюри

just /джаст/ adj справедливый; adv точно, как раз, только что

justify /джáстифай/ vt оправдывать

justly /джáстли/ adv справедливо

juvenile /джýувинайл/ adj юный; n подросток

K

keep /киип/ vti держать; хранить; соблюдать (правило); содержать ~ silence /~ сáйленс/ молчать; ~ them waiting /~ зэм вэйтинг/ заставлять их ждать; ~ a secret /~ э сúикрит/ хранить тайну; ~ up /~ ап/ поддерживать; ~ well /~ вэл/ обладать хорошим здоровьем; ~ one's word /~ ванз вёрд/ держать слово

kennel /кеппл/ n конура; pl собачий питомник

kerb /кёрб/ n край тротуара, обочина

kerchief /кёрчиф/ n платок, косынка

kettle /кетл/ n чайник

key /кии/ n ключ (также образн.); клавиша

keyboard /кúиборд/ n клавиатура

keyhole /кúихоул/ n замочная скважина

kid /кид/ n козленок; ребенок

kidnap /кúднэп/ vt похищать (людей)

kill /кил/ vti убивать; резать (скот)

killer /кúлэ/ n убийца

kin /кин/ n родственники; next of ~ /нэкст ов ~/ ближайший родственник

kind /кайнд/ adj добрый, любезный; how ~ of you /хáу ~ ов ю/ как мило с вашей стороны!; ~ regards /~ ригáрдз/ сердечный привет; n сорт; порода; in ~ /ин ~/ натурой

kindergarten /ки́ндэга́ртн/ n детский сад

king /кинг/ n король; дамка (в шашках)

kiss /кис/ n поцелуй; vt целовать

kit /кит/ n комплект инструментов

kitchen /ки́чин/ n кухня; ~ unit /~ ю́нит/ набор кухонной мебели

kitchenette /ки́чинéт/ n маленькая кухня/ниша, используемая в качестве кухни

knapsack /нэ́псэк/ n рюкзак

knee /нии/ n колено; vi становиться на колени

knife /найф/ n нож; vt ударять ножом

knit /нит/ vti вязать

knitwear /ни́твээ/ n трикотажные изделия

knock /нок/ n стук, удар; vt бить, ударять; vi стучаться; ~ down /~ да́ун/ сбивать; ~ out /~ а́ут/ (спорт.) нокаутировать; ~ together /~ тэгéзэ/ сколачивать

knot /нот/ n узел; бант

know /но́у/ vt знать; n знание; be in the ~ /би ин зэ ~/ быть в курсе дела

know-how /но́уха́у/ n умение; "ноу-хау", научная или техническая информация

knowledge /но́лидж/ n знание; to my ~ /ту май ~/ насколько мне известно

known /но́ун/ adj известный

L

label /лэ́йбл/ n ярлык; vt наклеивать ярлык

laboratory /лэбо́рэтри/ n лаборатория

labour /лэ́йбэ/ n труд, работа; ~ pains /~ пэйнз/ родовые схватки; L. Party /~ па́рти/ лейбористская партия; vi трудиться

labourer /лэ́йбэрэ/ n рабочий

lace /лэйс/ n кружево; шнурок (ботинок); vt шнуровать

lack /лэк/ n недостаток, отсутствие; vti нуждаться в; he ~s courage /хи ~с ка́ридж/ ему недостает смелости

lad /лэд/ n парень

ladder /лэ́дэ/ n (приставная) лестница

lading /лэ́йдинг/ n фрахт; bill of ~ /бил ов ~/ накладная, коносамент

lady /лэ́йди/ n дама, леди; young ~ /янг ~/ девушка; Our L. /а́уэ ~/ Богоматерь

lag /лэг/ n отставание; vi отставать

lake /лэйк/ n озеро

lame /лэйм/ adj хромой

lament /лэмэ́нт/ n жалоба; vti оплакивать

lamentable /лэ́ментэбл/ adj печальный

lamp /лэмп/ n лампа, фонарь; фара

lampoon /лэмпу́ун/ n пасквиль

land /лэнд/ n земля; страна; by ~ /бай ~/ по суше; vi высаживаться на берег, приземляться

landing /лэ́ндинг/ n приземление, (авиа)посадка; лестничная площадка

landlady /лэ́нлэйди/ n домовладелица, сдающая квартиры; хозяйка гостиницы

landlord /лэ́ндлорд/ n домовладелец, сдающий квартиры; хозяин гостиницы

lane /лэйн/ n тропинка; переулок; проход

language /лэ́нгвидж/ n язык

lapel /лэпе́л/ n лацкан

lapse /лэпс/ n недосмотр, ляпсус; vi истекать, проходить

lard /лард/ n смалец; vt шпиговать

large /лардж/ adj большой, крупный; at ~ /эт ~/ на свободе; подробно; в целом

largely /ла́рджли/ adv в значительной степени

last /лааст/ adj последний; прошлый; ~ but one /~ бат ван/ предпоследний; ~ night /~ найт/ вчера вечером/ночью; ~ week /~ виик/ на прошлой неделе; at ~ /эт ~/ наконец; vi длиться

lasting /ла́астинг/ adj прочный

late /лэйт/ adj поздний; покойный; it is ~ /ит из ~/ поздно; be ~ for a train /би ~ фор э трэйн/ опаздывать на поезд

lately /лэ́йтли/ adv недавно

lateral /лэ́тэрл/ adj боковой

lather /ла́азэ/ n (мыльная) пена; vt намыливать

latter /лэ́тэ/ adj последний

laud /лоод/ vt хвалить

laugh /лааф/ n смех; vi смеяться; burst out ~ing /бёрст а́ут ~инг/ расхохотаться; ~ing-stock /ла́афингсток/ посмешище

laughter /ла́афтэ/ n смех

launch /лоонч/ n запуск; спуск (на воду); vt запускать (ракету); vti начинать

laundry /ло́ондри/ n прачечная

lavatory /лэ́ветри/ n уборная

lavish /лэ́виш/ adj щедрый, обильный; vt расточать

law /лоо/ n закон, право; by ~ /бай ~/ по закону; go to ~ /гоу ту ~/ подавать в суд

law-court /лóокот/ n суд

lawful /лóофул/ adj законный

lawless /лóолис/ adj беззаконный

lawn /лоон/ n газон

lawn-mower /лóонмóэ/ n газонокосилка

lawsuit /лóосьют/ n процесс, тяжба

lawyer /лóойе/ n адвокат; юрист

lay /лэй/ vt класть, закладывать (основание, фундамент); накрывать (на стол); vi ~ aside /~ эсáйд/ откладывать; ~ by /~ бай/ запасать

layette /лэйéт/ n приданое новорожденного

laziness /лэ́йзинис/ n лень

lazy /лэ́йзи/ adj ленивый

lead /лиид/ n руководство; пример; главная роль; первое место; vt вести, водить; ~ a good life /~ э гуд лайф/ вести хорошую жизнь

leader /лии́дэ/ n вождь; передовая статья

leadership /лии́дэшип/ n руководство

leaf /лииф/ n лист

leaflet /лии́флит/ n листовка

league /лииг/ n лига, союз

leakage /лии́кэдж/ n утечка (также образн.)

lean /лиин/ adj тощий; постный (о мясе); vti наклонять(ся), прислонять(ся)

leap /лиип/ n прыжок; vi прыгать

leap-year /лии́пйе/ n високосный год

learn /лёрн/ vt учить, узнавать; vi учиться

lease /лиис/ n аренда; vt сдавать, брать в аренду

leaseholder /ли́исхо́улдэ/ n арендатор

leash /лииш/ n поводок; on the ~ /он зэ ~/ на поводке

least /лиист/ adj наименьший; adv менее всего; at ~ /эт ~/ по крайней мере

leather /ле́зэ/ n кожа

leave /лиив/ n разрешение; отпуск; on ~ /он ~/ в отпуске; take one's ~ /тэйк ванз ~/ прощаться; vt оставлять; vi уходить, уезжать

lecture /ле́кче/ n лекция; vi читать лекцию; преподавать; vt читать нотацию

lecturer /ле́кчерэ/ n преподаватель; лектор

left /лефт/ adj левый; n левая сторона; on the ~ /он зэ ~/ налево; to the ~ /ту зэ ~/ слева

left-handed /ле́фтхэ́ндыд/ n левша

left-overs /ле́фто́увэз/ n pl остатки

leg /лег/ n нога; ножка (стула и т.п.)

legacy /ле́гэси/ n наследство

legal /лиигл/ adj законный, юридический, правовой; ~ adviser /~ эдва́йзэ/ юрисконсульт; take ~ action /тэйк ~ экшн/ возбуждать судебное дело

leggings /ле́гингз/ n pl ползунки (для ребенка)

legislation /ле́джислэ́йшн/ n законодательство

legitimate /лиджи́тимит/ adj законный

leisure /ле́же/ n досуг; at ~ /эт ~/ на досуге

lend /ленд/ vt давать взаймы; одалживать

length /ленгс/ n длина, долгота; at ~ /эт ~/ подробно

lengthen /ле́нгсен/ vti удлинять(ся)

lens /ленз/ n линза; contact ~ /ко́нтэкт ~/ контактная линза

less /лес/ adj меньший; adv меньше; more or ~ /мо́ро ~/ более или менее

lessen /лесн/ vti уменьшать(ся)

lesson /лесн/ n урок

let /лет/ vt позволять, пускать; сдавать внаем; ~ him talk /~ хим тоок/ пусть говорит!; house to ~ /ха́ус тэ ~/ дом сдается; ~ go /~ го́у/ освобождать; ~ out /~ а́ут/ выпускать

letter /ле́тэ/ n буква, письмо; ~ of credit /~ ов кре́дит/ аккредитив

letter-box /ле́тэбокс/ n почтовый ящик

lettuce /ле́тис/ n салат

level /левл/ adj ровный; n уровень; vt выравнивать

lever /ли́ивэ/ n рычаг

liability /ла́йеби́лити/ n ответственность, обязательство

liable /ла́йебл/ adj ответственный; подверженный; подлежащий

libel /лайбл/ n клевета; vt клеветать

liberal /ли́берэл/ adj либеральный; щедрый; n либерал

liberation /ли́бере́йшн/ n освобождение

liberty /ли́бети/ n свобода, вольность; at ~ /эт ~/ на свободе

library /ла́йбрэри/ n библиотека

licence /лайснс/ n лицензия; driving ~ /дра́йвинг ~/ водительские права

lick /лик/ vt лизать

lid /лид/ n крышка

lie /лай/ vi лежать; ~ down /~ да́ун/ ложиться; ~ in wait /~ ин вэйт/ подстерегать

life /лайф/ n жизнь; from ~ /фром ~/ с натуры

life-annuity /ла́йфэньюити/ n пожизненная рента

life-insurance /ла́йфиншу́эрнс/ n страхование жизни

life-interest /ла́йфи́нтрист/ n право на пожизненное владение

lifelong /ла́йфлонг/ adj пожизненный

light /лайт/ n свет, освещение; pl светофор; throw ~ on /сро́у ~ он/ проливать свет на; adj светлый, легкий; vti освеща(ся), зажигать(ся); please, give me a ~ /плииз гив ми э ~/ разрешите прикурить

lighter /ла́йтэ/ n зажигалка

like /лайк/ adj похожий, подобный; adv как; be ~ /би ~/ быть похожим на; vt любить; as you ~/эз ю ~/ как вам угодно; I should ~ /ай шуд ~/ я хотел бы

likely /ла́йкли/ adj вероятный; adv вероятно

likewise /ла́йквайз/ adv подобно

limb /лим/ n конечность

lime /лайм/ n известь; лимон

limit /ли́мит/ n граница, предел; vt ограничивать

limitation /ли́митэ́йшн/ n ограничение

limited /ли́митыд/ adj ограниченный; ~ company /~ ка́мпэни/ акционерная компания с ограниченной ответственностью

line /лайн/ n линия; строка; леска (удочки); очередь; vt линовать; ставить подкладку; ~ up /~ ап/ занимать очередь

linen /ли́нин/ n полотно; белье

liner /ла́йнэ/ n рейсовый пароход/самолет

link /линк/ n звено, pl узы; vt соединять; связывать

lip /лип/ n губа; край

lipstick /ли́пстык/ n губная помада

liquid /ли́квид/ adj жидкий; n жидкость

liquor /ли́кэ/ n (спиртной) напиток, выпивка; hard ~ /хард ~/ крепкий напиток

list /лист/ n список; vt вносить в список

listen /лисн/ vi слушать; ~ in /~ ин/ слушать радио

literate /ли́тэрит/ adj грамотный

literature /ли́триче/ n литература

little /литл/ adj маленький; ~finger /~фи́нгэ/ мизинец; adv мало

live /лайв/ adj живой

live /лив/ vi жить

livelihood /ла́йвлихуд/ n средства к существованию

liver /ли́вэ/ n печень; печенка

living /ли́винг/ adj живой; современный; n образ жизни; earn a ~ /ёрн э ~/ зарабатывать на жизнь

living-room /ли́вингрум/ n столовая, гостиная

load /ло́уд/ n груз; vt грузить; заряжать (оружие)

loaf /ло́уф/ n каравай, буханка хлеба; vi слоняться

loan /ло́ун/ n заем; vt давать взаймы

local /ло́укл/ adj местный; ~ train /~ трэйн/ пригородный поезд

locality /лоука́лити/ n местность

location /лоуке́йшн/ n местожительство

lock /лок/ n локон (волос); замок; шлюз; under ~ and key /а́ндэ ~ энд кии/ под замком; vt запирать на замок; ~ out /~ а́ут/ объявлять локаут locksmith /лóксмит/ n слесарь

lock-up /лóкап/ n тюрьма

lodge /лодж/ vt временно поселять; давать на хранение; vi снимать квартиру

lodger /лóдже/ n квартирант(ка)

lodging /лóджинг/ n жилье; board and ~ /борд энд ~/ пансион

loft /лофт/ n чердак, сеновал

loin /лойн/ n филейная часть; pl поясница

lollipop /лóлипоп/ n леденец

lonely /лóунли/ adj одинокий

long /лонг/ adj длинный; долгий; in the ~ run /ин зэ ~ ран/ в конце концов; adv долго; ~ ago /~ эгóу/ давно; all day ~ /оол дэй ~/ целый день

long-distance /лóнгди́стнс/ adj дальний; ~ call /~ коол/ междугородный/международный телефонный разговор

longing /лóнгинг/ n страстное желание

long-term /лóнгтём/ adj долгосрочный

look /лук/ vi смотреть; выглядеть; ~ after /~ áафтэ/ заботиться о; ~ for /~ фо/ искать; ~ here! /~ хúэ/ послушай(те)!; ~ like /~ лайк/ быть похожим на; ~ out /~ áут/ разыскивать; ~ out! /~ áут/ берегись!; ~ round /~ páунд/ оглядываться; ~ through /~ сруу/ просматривать; ~ well /~ вэл/ выглядеть хорошо; n взгляд, вид, внешность; good ~s /гуд ~с/ красота; take a ~ at /тэйк э ~ эт/ посмотреть на

looking-glass /лýкинглас/ n зеркало

look-out /лýкаут/ n бдительность; наблюдение; перспективы; be on the ~ /би он зэ ~/ быть настороже loose /луус/ adj свободный, просторный; неприкрепленный; распущенный

lose /лууз/ vt терять; проигрывать; ~ one's way /~ ванз вэй/ заблудиться

loss /лос/ n потеря; проигрыш; at a ~ /эт э ~/ в затруднении

lost /лост/ adj утраченный; ~ and found /~ энд фáунд/ бюро находок

loud /лáуд/ adj громкий; кричащий (о цвете)

loudspeaker /лáудспииикэ/ n громкоговоритель

love /лав/ n любовь; возлюбленный, возлюбленная; (спорт.) нуль; fall in ~ /фоол ин ~/ влюбляться в; ~ affair /~ эфэ́э/ роман; vt любить

lovely /лáвли/ adj прелестный; вкусный

lover /лáвэ/ n любовник; любитель

low /лóу/ adj низкий (также образн.); тихий; adv низко; ~ neck /~ нэк/ глубокий вырез; ~ pressure /~ прэ́ше/ низкое давление; ~ water /~ вóотэ/ отлив

lubricate /льюбрикейт/ vt смазывать

luck /лак/ n счастье, удача; good ~! /гуд ~/ в добрый путь!; try one's ~ /трай ванз ~/ попытать счастья

lucky /лáки/ adj счастливый; удачный

luggage /лáгидж/ n багаж; excess ~ /иксэ́с ~/ багаж выше нормы

lumber /лáмбэ/ n хлам, лесоматериалы

lump /ламп/ n кусок; глыба; опухоль; ~ sum /~ сам/ крупная сумма

luxurious /лагзьюэриэс/ adj роскошный

lying-in /лáйингиин/ n роды

M

machine /мэшйин/ n машина; **adding ~** /э́динг ~/ счетная машина

machinery /мэшйинэри/ n машины, машинное оборудование

mad /мэд/ adj сумасшедший; бешеный (о собаке); **go ~** /гóу ~/ сходить с ума

made /мэйд/ adj сделанный; **~ in USA (Japan)** /~ ин ююэ́сэ́й (джепэ́н)/ изготовлено в США (Японии); **~ to order** /~ ту óрдэ/ сделанный на заказ

made-up /мэ́йдáп/ adj составной; вымышленный

madhouse /мэ́дхаус/ n сумасшедший дом

madness /мэ́днис/ n сумасшествие

magazine /мэ́гэзйин/ n журнал

magic /мэ́джик/ adj волшебный; **~ wand** /~ вонд/ волшебная палочка; n волшебство; **as if by ~** /эз иф бай ~/ как по волшебству

magistrate /мэ́джистрит/ n судья

magnificent /мэгнйфиснт/ adj великолепный

maid /мэйд/ n девица; служанка

mail /мэйл/ n почта; vt посылать почтой

mail-box /мэ́йлбокс/ n почтовый ящик

mailman /мэ́йлмэн/ n почтальон

main /мэйн/ adj главный; **~ road** /~ póуд/ шоссе; **~ street** /~ стриит/ главная улица; **the ~ thing** /зэ ~ синг/ главное; **in the ~** /ин зэ ~/ в основном

maintain /мэнтэ́йн/ vt поддерживать; содержать

maintenance /мэ́йнтинэнс/ n содержание; (тех.) ремонт

major /мэ́йдже/ adj больший, главный; n майор

majority /мэджо́рити/ n большинство

make /мэйк/ n производство; модель; тип; vt делать, производить; ~ a bed /~ э бед/ стелить постель; ~ enquiries /~ инква́йериз/ наводить справки; ~ money /~ ма́ни/ "делать" деньги; ~ up one's mind /~ ап ванз майнд/ решать(ся); ~ use of /~ ююс ов/ использовать

make-up /мэ́йкап/ n грим

male /мэйл/ adj мужской; n мужчина

malicious /мэли́шес/ adj злобный

malignant /мэли́гнент/ adj злокачественный

malnutrition /мэ́лнъютри́шн/ n недоедание

man /мэн/ n человек, мужчина; ~ and wife /~ энд вайф/ муж и жена; ~ in the street /~ ин зэ стриит/ рядовой человек

manage /мэ́нидж/ vt управлять; vi справляться с

management /мэ́ниджмент/ n управление; администрация

manager /мэ́нидже/ n управляющий

manhood /мэ́нхуд/ n мужество; зрелость

maniac /мэ́йниэк/ n маньяк

manifest /мэ́нифест/ adj явный; vt проявлять

manifestation /мэ́нифестэ́йшн/ n проявление

manifold /мэ́нифо́улд/ adj разнообразный

manipulate /мэни́пьюлэйт/ vt манипулировать

mankind /мэнка́йнд/ n человечество

manner /мэ́нэ/ n способ, образ; pl манеры

manual /мэ́ньюэл/ adj ручной; n справочник

manufacture /мэ́ньюфэ́кче/ n производство; изделие; vt производить

manufacturer /мэ́ньюфо́кчерэ/ n фабрикант; изготовитель

many /мэ́ни/ adj много, многие; how~? /ха́у ~/ сколько?

map /мэп/ n карта, план

March /марч/ n март

marine /мэри́ин/ adj морской; n флот; морской пехотинец

marital /мэра́йтл/ adj брачный

mark /марк/ n знак; метка; след; балл; марка (монета); up to the ~ /ап ту зэ ~/ на должной высоте; vt отмечать, метить; ставить балл

market /ма́ркит/ n рынок; сбыт; adj рыночный; money ~ /ма́ни ~/ денежный рынок; vt продавать на рынке, сбывать

marketing /ма́ркитинг/ n маркетинг

marriage /мэ́ридж/ n брак, свадьба; ~ licence /~ ла́йснс/ свидетельство о браке

married /мэ́рид/ adj женатый, замужняя; ~ couple /~ капл/ супружеская чета; newly-~ couple /нью́юли ~ капл/ чета новобрачных; get~ (to) /гет ~ ту/ жениться на, выйти замуж за

marry /мэ́ри/ vt женить, выдавать замуж; жениться на, выходить замуж за

martial /ма́ршел/ adj военный; ~ law /~ лоо/ военное положение

Martian /ма́ршьен/ n марсианин

marvellous /ма́рвилэс/ adj чудесный

masculine /ма́аскьюлин/ adj мужской

mash /мэш/ n пюре; vt разминать; ~ed potatoes /~т пэтэ́йтоуз/ картофельное пюре mason /мэйсн/ n каменщик; масон

mass /мэс/ n масса; ~ production /~ прэда́кшн/ серийное производство

massive /мэ́сив/ adj массивный, крупный

master /ма́астэ/ n хозяин; мастер; учитель; vt овладевать, справляться с

master-key /ма́астэки/ n отмычка

mastermind /ма́астэмайнд/ n руководитель; вдохновитель

masterpiece /ма́астэпис/ n шедевр

mat /мэт/ n мат, циновка; подстилка (под блюдо)

match /мэч/ n спичка; ровня; матч; a good ~ /э гуд ~/ хорошая партия; vt подбирать под пару, гармонировать с; состязаться с

match-box /мэ́чбокс/ n спичечная коробка

material /мэти́эриэл/ n материал, материя; adj существенный

maternity /мэтёрнити/ n материнство; ~ home /~ хо́ум/ родильный дом

matrimony /мэ́тримени/ n супружество

matter /мэ́тэ/ n вещество; дело; what's the ~ with you? /вотс зэ ~ виз ю/ что с вами?; as a ~ of fact /эз э ~ офэ́кт/ фактически; it's a ~ of taste /итс э ~ ов тэйст/ это дело вкуса; vi иметь значение; it doesn't ~ /ит дазнт ~/ неважно

matter-of-course /мэ́тэрэвко́ос/ adj само собой разумеющийся

maturity /мэтью́эрити/ n зрелость

May /мэй/ n май

may /мэй/ v aux мочь, иметь возможность; ~ I say /~ ай сэй/ могу я сказать...; I ~ come /ай ~ кам/ может быть я приду; ~ I come in? /~ ай кам ин/ можно войти?

maybe /мэ́йби/ adv может быть

mayor /мээ/ n мэр

me /мии/ pron меня, мне и т.д.

meadow /мéдоу/ n луг

meal /миил/ n еда

mealtime /мѝилтайм/ n время еды

mean /миин/ adj подлый; средний; n середина; vt подразумевать

means /миинз/ n способ, средства; by all ~ /бай оол ~/ конечно; by ~ of /бай ~ ов/ при помощи; by ~ /бай нóу ~/ никоим образом

meeting /мѝитинг/ n встреча, собрание; hold a ~ /хóулд э ~/ проводить собрание

melon /мéлэн/ n дыня

member /мэ́мбэ/ n член; full ~ /фул ~/ полноправный член

membership /мэ́мбэшип/ n членство; ~ card /~ кард/ членский билет

memory /мéмэри/ n память

menace /мéнэс/ n угроза; vt угрожать

mend /менд/ vt чинить, штопать; vi поправляться

mending /мéндинг/ n починка, штопка

mental /ментл/ adj умственный; ~ patient /~ пэйшнт/ душевнобольной

mention /мéншен/ n упоминание; vt упоминать; don't ~ it /дóунт ~ ит/ не стоит благодарности

merchandise /мёёчендайз/ n товары

merchant /мёёчент/ n купец; adj торговый

mere /миэ/ adj простой

merely /миэли/ adv только

merge /мёрдж/ vti сливать(ся)

merger /мёрдже/ n объединение

merit /мёрит/ n заслуга; vt заслуживать

merry /мёри/ adj веселый

mess /мес/ n беспорядок, путаница; столовая (в учебном заведении)

message /мёсидж/ n сообщение

messenger /мёсиндже/ n посыльный, курьер

metal /метл/ n металл; щебень; adj металлический

metallurgy /метэлёджи/ n металлургия

meter /миитэ/ n счетчик

method /мёсэд/ n метод, способ

metre /миитэ/ n метр

metropolis /митрóпэлис/ n столица

metropolitan /мéтрополитн/ adj столичный

mid /мид/ adj средний; in ~ winter /ин ~ винтэ/ в
  середине зимы

midday /миддэй/ n полдень

middle /мидл/ n середина; adj средний

middle-aged /мидлэйджд/ adj средних лет

middle-sized /мидлсáйзд/ adj среднего размера

midnight /миднайт/ n полночь

midwife /мидвайф/ n акушерка

might /майт/ n могущество, мощь

mighty /мáйти/ adj могучий, мощный; adv
  чрезвычайно

migration /майгрэ́йшн/ n миграция, переселение

mild /майлд/ adj мягкий, слабый (на вкус)

mile /майл/ n миля

military /ми́литри/ adj военный, воинский; the ~ /зэ ~/ военные

milk /милк/ n молоко; vt доить

Milky Way /ми́лкивэ́й/ n Млечный Путь

mill /мил/ n мельница; завод

milliard /ми́льард/ n миллиард; (амер.) биллион

million /ми́льен/ n миллион

millionaire /ми́льенэ́э/ n миллионер

mince /минс/ n фарш; vt крошить; ~d meat /~т миит/ мясной фарш

mind /майнд/ n ум; мнение; bear in ~ /бээр ин ~/ иметь в виду; change one's ~ /чейндж ванз ~/ передумать; keep in ~ /киип ин ~/ помнить; of sound ~ /ов са́унд ~/ здравомыслящий; vt возражать; I don't ~ /ай до́унт ~/ я не против; never ~ /нэ́вэ ~/ не беспокойтесь!

mine /майн/ poss pron мой, моя, мое, мои; this car is ~ /зыс кар из ~/ это мой автомобиль; a friend of ~ /э фрэнд ов ~/ мой друг

mine /майн/ n шахта; (воен.) мина; vt добывать; минировать

miner /ма́йнэ/ n шахтер

minister /ми́нистэ/ n министр; посланник; священник

ministry /ми́нистри/ n министерство

mink /минк/ n норка; норковый мех

minor /ма́йнэ/ adj меньший; незначительный; n несовершеннолетний minority /майно́рити/ n меньшинство

minute /ми́нит/ n минута

minute-hand /ми́нитхэнд/ n минутная стрелка

miraculous /мирэ́кьюлэс/ adj сверхъестественный, чудесный

mirror /ми́рэ/ n зеркало; vt отражать

miscarriage /миска́ридж/ n выкидыш

mischievous /ми́счивэс/ adj озорной

miserable /ми́зэрбл/ adj несчастный, убогий

misery /ми́зэри/ n нищета

misfortune /мисфо́рчен/ n несчастье, неудача

misgiving /мисги́винг/ n опасение

mishap /ми́схэп/ n неудача

mislead /мисли́ид/ vt вводить в заблуждение

miss /мис/ vi промахнуться; vt упускать, опаздывать на; избегать; скучать по; be ~ing /би ~инг/ отсутствовать, недоставать; n промах

missile /ми́сайл/ n ракета

missing /ми́синг/ adj отсутствующий, недостающий; без вести пропавший

mission /ми́шен/ n миссия, поручение

mistake /мистэ́йк/ n ошибка

mistaken /мистэ́йкен/ adj ошибочный; be ~ /би ~/ ошибаться

mister /ми́стэ/ n мистер, господин

mistrust /мистра́ст/ n недоверие; vt не доверять

misunderstanding /ми́сандэстэ́ндинг/ n недоразумение

misuse /ми́сьююс/ n злоупотребление; /ми́сьююз/ vt злоупотреблять mitten /митн/ n рукавица

mix /микс/ vt смешивать; ~ up /~ ап/ путать

moan /моун/ n стон; vi стонать

mobile /моубайл/ adj передвижной; подвижный

mobility /мобилити/ n подвижность

mocking /мокинг/ adj насмешливый

mode /моуд/ n способ; мода, обычай

model /модл/ adj образцовый; n модель, образец;
   натурщик, натурщица; vt моделировать

moderate /модрит/ adj умеренный; /модэрэйт/ vt
   умерять

moderation /модэрэйшн/ n умеренность

modern /модэн/ adj современный; ~ languages /~
   лэнгвиджиз/ новые языки

modest /модист/ adj скромный

modify /модифай/ vt (видо)изменять

mohair /моухээ/ n ангорская шерсть, мохер

moisture /мойсче/ n влага

momentous /моуменптэс/ adj важный

Monday /манди/ n понедельник

money /мани/ n деньги

money-changer /маничейндже/ n меняла

money order /маниордэ/ n денежный перевод

monkey /манки/ n обезьяна

monopoly /мэнопэли/ n монополия

monotonous /мэнотнэс/ adj однообразный

monstrous /монстрэс/ adj чудовищный

month /манс/ n месяц

monthly /мансли/ adj ежемесячный; n ежемесячник

monument /мóньюмент/ n памятник

mood /мууд/ n настроение; (грам.) наклонение

moon /муун/ n луна, месяц

mop /моп/ n швабра; vt мыть шваброй

moral /морл/ adj моральный, нравственный; n мораль; pl нравственность

morbid /мóрбид/ adj болезненный

more /мор/ adv больше, еще; once ~ /ванс ~/ еще раз

moreover /моорóувэ/ adv кроме того

morning /мóрнинг/ n утро; good ~ /гуд ~/ доброе утро!

morsel /мóрсэл/ n кусочек

mortal /мортл/ adj смертный; смертельный

mortality /мотэ́лити/ n смертность

mortgage /мóогидж/ n закладная; vt закладывать

Moslem /мóзлем/ n мусульманин, мусульманка; adj мусульманский

mosquito /мэскúитоу/ n комар, москит

most /мóуст/ adj наибольший; adv больше всего; at the ~ /эт зэ ~/ самое большее

mostly /мóустли/ adv главным образом

mother /мáзэ/ n мать; ~'s day /~з дэй/ (амер.) День матери; ~ tongue /~ танг/ родной язык

motherhood /мáзэхуд/ n материнство

mother-in-law /мáзэринлóо/ n теща, свекровь

motherland /мáзэлэнд/ n родина

motion /мóушн/ n движение; предложение; ~ picture /~ пúкче/ кинофильм

motor /мóутэ/ n мотор, двигатель; ~ car /~ кар/ автомобиль

mountain /ма́унтин/ n гора

mournful /мо́рнфул/ adj траурный

mouse /ма́ус/ n (pl mice) мышь

mousetrap /ма́устрэп/ n мышеловка

moustache /мэста́аш/ n усы

mouth /ма́ус/ n рот; устье (реки)

move /муув/ n движение; ход (в игре); (образн.) шаг; vt двигать; трогать, волновать; vi двигаться

movement /му́увмент/ n движение; (тех.) ход

movies /му́увиз/ n pl кино

moving /му́увинг/ adj движущийся; трогательный

much /мач/ adj много; adv очень; how ~ ? /ха́у ~/ сколько?; too ~ /туу ~/ слишком много

muffler /ма́флэ/ n кашне

mug /маг/ n кружка

multicoloured /ма́лтика́лэд/ adj цветной

multi-millionaire /ма́лтими́льенээ/ n мультимиллионер

multiple /ма́лтипл/ adj многочисленный; составной

multiply /ма́лтиплай/ vt умножать

multitude /ма́лтитьюд/ n множество

municipal /мьюни́сипл/ adj городской, муниципальный

murder /мёрдэ/ n убийство; vt убивать

murderer /мёрдэрэ/ n убийца

muscle /масл/ n мускул, мышца

muscular /ма́скьюлэ/ adj мускульный, мускулистый

museum /мьюзи́эм/ n музей

mushroom /ма́шрум/ n гриб

music /мьйю́юзик/ n музыка; ноты

musical /мьюю́зикл/ adj музыкальный; ~ comedy /~ ко́миди/ оперетта; n мьюзикл

music-hall /мьюю́зикхол/ n мюзик-холл

musician /мьюзи́шен/ n музыкант

musk /маск/ n мускус

must /маст/ v aux должен, должна и т.д.; I ~ /ай ~/ я должен; he ~ have gone /хи ~ хэв гон/ должно быть, он ушел

mustard /ма́стэд/ n горчица; ~ plaster /~ пла́астэ/ горчичник

mutton /матн/ n баранина

mutual /мьюю́тьюэл/ adj взаимный; ~ relations /~ рилэ́йшнз/ взаимоотношения

mutually /мьюю́тьюэли/ adv взаимно

my /май/ poss adj мой, моя, мое, мои

myself /майсэ́лф/ pron себя, себе, сам, сама

mystery /ми́стэри/ n тайна

N

nail /нэйл/ n ноготь; гвоздь

naked /нэ́йкид/ adj голый, нагой; ~ eye /~ ай/ невооруженный глаз

name /нэйм/ n имя, фамилия; название; репутация; in God's ~ /ин годз ~/ ради бога!; call ~s /коол ~з/ обзывать; vt называть

nameless /нэ́ймлис/ adj безымянный

namely /нэ́ймли/ adv именно

nap /нэп/ n короткий сон; have a ~ /хэв э ~/ вздремнуть

napkin /нэ́пкин/ n салфетка; пеленка

narrow /нэ́роу/ adj узкий

narrowness /нэ́роунис/ n узость, ограниченность

nasty /на́асти/ adj гадкий, отвратительный

nation /нэйшн/ n нация, народ; государство

national /на́шенл/ n подданный; adj национальный; ~ economy /~ икóнэми/ народное хозяйство

nationalism /на́шнэлизм/ n национализм

nationalist /на́шнэлист/ n националист

nationality /нэшенэ́лити/ n национальность; подданство

native /нэ́йтив/ adj родной; местный; ~ tongue /~ танг/ родной язык; n туземец, уроженец

natural /нэчрл/ adj естественный

naturalization /нэ́чрэлизэ́йшн/ n натурализация

naturally /нэ́чрэли/ adv конечно

nature /нэ́йче/ n природа; характер

naught /ноот/ n ничто; ноль

naughty /нóоти/ adj непослушный, шаловливый

naval /нэ́йвл/ adj военно-морской

navigation /нэ́вигéйшн/ n навигация

navy /нэ́йви/ n военно-морской флот; ~ blue /~ блюю/ темно-синий

Nazi /на́аци/ n нацист

near /ниэ/ adj близкий; adv близко; prep возле, около, у, близко от

nearly /ни́эли/ adv почти

near-sighted /ни́эса́йтыд/ adj близорукий

neat /ниит/ adj опрятный

necessary /не́сисри/ adj необходимый; n (самое) необходимое

necessity /нисэ́сити/ n необходимость; предмет первой необходимости

neck /нек/ n шея; горлышко (бутылки)

necklace /нéклис/ n ожерелье

need /ниид/ n нужда, надобность, потребность; if ~ be /иф ~ би/ в случае нужды; vt нуждаться в

needle /ниидл/ n игла, иголка; спица (вязальная); стрелка (компаса)

needless /нúидлис/ adj ненужный

needy /нúиди/ n нуждающийся

negative /нéгэтив/ adj отрицательный

neglect /ниглéкт/ n пренебрежение, vt пренебрегать

negotiable /нигбóушьебл/ adj реализуемый

negotiation /нигбóушиэйшн/ n переговоры

Negro /нúигроу/ n негр, негритянка; adj негритянский

neighbour /нэ́йбэ/ n сосед(ка); love one's ~ /лав ванз ~/ любить ближнего своего

neighbourhood /нэ́йбэхуд/ n округа, район

neither /на́йзэ/ adj, pron никакой; ни тот, ни другой; ~ of us /ов ас/ никто из нас

neo- /нúио/ prefix нео-

nephew /нéвью/ n племянник

nervous /нёрвэс/ adj нервный; be ~ about /би ~ эба́ут/ волноваться о

net /нет/ n сеть; adj нетто; ~ cost /~ кост/ себестоимость; ~ profit /~ прóфит/ чистый доход; ~ weight /~ вейт/ вес нетто

network /нéтвёрк/ n сеть (железнодорожная, телевизионная и т.д.)

neurotic /ньюэрóтик/ adj нервный

neutral /ньютрэл/ adj нейтральный

never /нэ́вэ/ adv никогда; ~ mind /~ майнд/ ничего, неважно

nevertheless /нэвээзэлес/ adv тем не менее

new /ньюю/ adj новый; свежий

new-born /ньююборн/ adj новорожденный

newcomer /ньююкáмэ/ n приезжий, новичок

news /ньююз/ n новость, известие

newspaper /ньююспэ́йпэ/ n газета

news-stand /ньююзстэнд/ n газетный киоск

next /нэкст/ adj следующий, ближайший

next-door /нэ́кстдóр/ adj соседний

nice /найс/ adj хороший, приятный, милый, деликатный

nickel /никл/ n никель; монета в 5 центов

niece /ниис/ n племянница

night /найт/ n ночь; вечер; good ~! /гуд ~/ спокойной ночи!

nine /найн/ num девять

nineteen /нáйнтиин/ num девятнадцать

nineteenth /нáйнтиинс/ ord num девятнадцатый

ninetieth /нáйнтис/ ord num девяностый

ninety /нáйнти/ num девяносто

ninth /найнс/ ord num девятый

no /нóу/ adv нет; adj никакой; ~ admittance /~ эдмѝтнс/ вход воспрещен; ~ doubt /~ дáут/ несомненно; ~ matter

/~ мэ́тэ/ неважно; ~ one /~ ван/ никто; ~ smoking /~
сму́кинг/ курить воспрещается

nobody /но́убоди/ pron никто

nocturnal /нокте́рнл/ adj ночной

noise /нойз/ n шум

noiseless /но́йзлис/ adj бесшумный

noisy /но́йзи/ adj шумный

nominate /но́минэйт/ vt выставлять кандидатом;
назначать

nominee /но́минии/ n кандидат

non- /нон/ prefix не-, без-

nonalcoholic /но́нэлкэхо́лик/ adj безалкогольный

none /нан/ pron никто, ничто; ~ of that! /~ов зэт/
хватит!; adv нисколько

nonetheless /но́нзэлес/ adv тем не менее, все же

non-existent /но́нигзи́стнт/ adj несуществующий

non-payment /но́нпэ́ймент/ n неплатеж

nonsense /но́нсэнс/ n вздор, глупости

noon /нуун/ n полдень; adj полуденный

nor /нор/ conj и не, также не, ни

normal /нормл/ adj нормальный

north /норс/ n север; adv на север; adj северный

northern /но́рзэн/ adj северный

nose /но́уз/ n нос; vt: ~ out /~ а́ут/ разнюхивать

nostril /но́стрил/ n ноздря

not /нот/ adv не, ни; ~ at all /~ эт оол/ не стоит
(благодарности), нисколько

notary /но́утэри/ n нотариус

note /но́ут/ n записка, заметка; нота

note-book /нóутбук/ n записная книжка

noted /нóутыд/ adj знаменитый

noteworthy /нóутвёзи/ adj достопримечательный

nothing /нáсинг/ pron ничто, ничего; for ~ /фо~/ зря; даром

notice /нóутис/ n объявление; внимание; give ~ /гив ~/ предупреждать (об увольнении); vt замечать

noticeable /нóутисэбл/ adj заметный

notice-board /нóутисбод/ n доска для объявлений

notification /нóутификéйшн/ n извещение

notify /нóутифай/ vt уведомлять

notorious /нотóориэс/ adj пресловутый

nourishment /нáришмент/ n питание, пища

novel /новл/ n роман; adj новый, необычный

November /новéмбэ/ n ноябрь

now /нáу/ adv теперь; from ~ on /фром ~ он/ впредь

nowadays /нáуэдэйз/ adv нынче

nowhere /нóувээ/ adv нигде; никуда

nuclear /ньюóюклиэ/ adj ядерный

null /нал/ adj недействительный; ~ and void /~ энд войд/ не имеющий законной силы

number /нáмбэ/ n число, номер; a ~ of /э ~ ов/ ряд; vt нумеровать; насчитывать

numerous /ньюóюмрэс/ adj многочисленный

nurse /нёёс/ n медицинская сестра, сиделка; няня; vt ухаживать за; нянчить, лелеять

nursery /нёёсри/ n детская, ясли, питомник; ~ school /~ скуул/ детский сад

nursing /нёёсинг/ n уход, выкармливание; ~ home /~ хóум/ частная лечебница nutrition /ньютри́шн/ n питание; диететика

O

oats /о́утс/ n pl овес

oatmeal /о́утмил/ n овсянка

obedient /эби́идьент/ adj послушный

obituary /эби́тьюэри/ n некролог

object /о́бджикт/ n предмет; /эбджéкт/ vi возражать

objection /эбджéкшн/ n возражение

objective /обджéктив/ adj объективный; n цель

obligation /о́блигэ́йшн/ n обязательство

obliging /эбла́йджинг/ adj услужливый

obscene /обси́ин/ adj непристойный

obscure /эбскью́э/ adj темный, смутный, неясный; vt затемнять, делать неясным

observation /о́бзэвэ́йшн/ n замечание

observer /эбзё́ёвэ/ n наблюдатель

obsolete /о́бсэлит/ adj устарелый

obstacle /о́бстэкл/ n препятствие

obtain /эбтэ́йн/ vt получать

obvious /о́бвиэс/ adj очевидный, явный

occasion /экéйжн/ n случай, (удобный) повод; festive ~ /фéстив ~/ праздник

occasional /экéйжнл/ adj случайный

occupation /о́кьюпэ́йшн/ n профессия; оккупация

ocean /о́ушн/ n океан

o'clock /экло́к/: at one ~ /эт ван ~/ в час

October /экто́убэ/ n октябрь

odd /од/ adj нечетный; странный; ~ job /~ джоб/ случайная работа

odour /óудэ/ n запах

of /ов/ prep: ~ course /~ корс/ конечно; one ~ them /ван ~ зэм/ один из них

off /оф/ adj дальний; незанятый; adv: be ~ /би ~/ уходить; a mile ~ /э майл ~/ в одной миле от; ~ and on /~ энд он/ время от времени; prep с, от

offence /эфéнс/ n преступление; обида

offend /эфéнд/ vt обижать

offer /óфэ/ n предложение; vt предлагать

office /óфис/ n контора, ведомство; good ~s /гуд ~ыз/ услуги; ~ hours /~ áуэз/ служебные часы

officer /óфисэ/ n офицер

official /эфúшл/ adj официальный; ~ duties /~ дьюютиз/ служебные обязанности; n чиновник

often /офн/ adv часто

oil /ойл/ n масло; нефть; pl масляные краски; ~ cloth /~ клос/ клеенка

ointment /óйнтмент/ n мазь

old /óулд/ adj старый; how ~ are you? /хáу ~ а ю/ сколько вам лет?; ~ man /~ мэн/ старик; ~ woman /~ вýмэн/ старуха

old-age /óулдэ́йдж/ adj старческий; ~ pension /~ пеншн/ пенсия по старости

olive /óлив/ n маслина; ~ oil /~ ойл/ оливковое масло

on /он/ prep на, в, о; ~ Monday /~ мáнди/ в понедельник; ~ sale /~ сэйл/ в продаже; go ~ /гóу ~/ продолжайте!

once /ванс/ adv раз; ~ more /~ мор/ еще раз; at ~ /эт ~/ сейчас же

one /ван/ num один; ~ another /~ эна́зэ/ друг друга; ~ day /~ дэй/ однажды; ~ of us /~ эв ас/ один из нас; no ~ /но́у ~/ никто

oneself /вансэ́лф/ pron себя; be ~ /би ~/ быть самим собой

one-way /ва́нвэй/ adj односторонний; ~ street /~ стриит/ улица с односторонним движением

only /о́унли/ adv только; adj единственный

open /о́упн/ vti открывать(ся); adj открытый, откровенный

opener /о́упэнэ/ n открывалка

operate /о́перэйт/ vt управлять; vi действовать; делать операцию

operation /о́перэйшн/ n действие; операция (также хирург.)

opinion /эпи́ньен/ n мнение

opponent /эпо́унент/ n противник, оппонент; adj противоположный

opportunity /о́пэтью́юнити/ n удобный случай

opposite /о́пэзит/ adj противоположный; prep против; adv напротив

opposition /о́пэзи́шн/ n сопротивление; оппозиция

oppression /эпре́шн/ n гнет

oppressive /эпре́сив/ adj гнетущий

optician /опти́шн/ n оптик

option /о́пшн/ n выбор

or /ор/ conj или; ~ else /~ элс/ иначе

orange /о́ринж/ n апельсин; adj оранжевый

order /о́рдэ/ n порядок; приказ; заказ; money ~ /ма́ни ~/ денежный перевод; out of ~ /а́ут ов ~/ неисправный; ~ form /~ форм/ бланк заказа; vt приказывать; заказывать

orderly /о́рдэли/ adj опрятный; n ординарец; санитар

organization /о́ргэниза́йшн/ n организация

organize /о́ргэнайз/ vt организовывать

orientation /о́ориента́йшн/ n ориентация

origin /о́риджин/ n происхождение

original /эри́джинл/ adj первоначальный; оригинальный; n подлинник

orthopaedy /о́рсопи́ди/ n ортопедия

other /а́зэ/ adj другой, иной

otherwise /а́зэвайз/ adv иначе

ought /оот/ v aux должен, следовало бы

ounce /а́унс/ n унция (=28,35 г)

our, ours /а́уэ, а́узз/ poss pron наша, наш и т.д.; свой, своя и т.д.

ourselves /а́уэсэ́лвз/ pron себя; сами

out /а́ут/ adv наружу, из; go ~ /го́у ~/ выходить

outbreak /а́утбрэйк/ n взрыв, вспышка

outcome /а́уткам/ n исход, результат

outdoor /а́утдо/ adj на открытом воздухе

outer /а́утэ/ adj наружный

outline /а́утлайн/ n очертание, набросок; vt описывать в общих чертах

outlook /а́утлук/ n вид; перспектива; точка зрения

outnumber /аутна́мбэ/ vt превосходить численно

out of /аут ов/ prep из, вне, за; ~ date /~ дэйт/ устаревший

out-patient /а́утпэ́йшнт/ n амбулаторный больной

output /а́утпут/ n выпуск; продукция

outrageous /аутрэ́йджес/ adj неистовый; оскорбительный

outright /а́утрайт/ adj прямой; adv сразу

outset /а́утсет/ n начало

outside /а́утса́йд/ adj наружный, крайний; prep вне, за

outskirts /а́утскётс/ n pl окраина

outstanding /аутстэ́ндинг/ adj выдающийся; неуплаченный

outward /а́утвэд/ adj внешний

oven /авн/ n печь, духовка

over /о́увэ/ prep над, через, по, за, более, свыше; adv сверх; all ~ /оол ~/ повсюду; it is all ~ /ит из оол ~/ все кончено

overall /о́уверол/ adj общий; n pl комбинезон

overcharge /о́увэчадж/ vt дорого запрашивать

overcoat /о́увэкоут/ n пальто, шинель

overcome /о́увэка́м/ vt преодолевать

overdo /о́увэду́у/ vt утрировать; пережаривать

overdraw /о́увэдро́о/ vt превышать кредит (в банке)

overdue /о́увэдью́ю/ adj запоздалый; просроченный

overestimate /о́увэрэ́стимейт/ vt переоценивать

overhear /о́увэхи́э/ vt подслушивать

overheat /о́увэхи́ит/ vti перегревать(ся)

overlook /óувэлу́к/ vt не замечать, проглядеть; выходить на (об окнах)

overnight /óувэна́йт/ adv накануне вечером; вдруг; stay ~ /стэй ~/ ночевать

overpay /óувэпэ́й/ vt переплачивать

overproduction /óувэпрэда́кшн/ n перепроизводство

overseer /óувэсиэ́/ n надзиратель; мастер; контролер

oversleep /óувэсли́ип/ vi просыпа́ть

overstate /óувэстэ́йт/ vt преувеличивать

overtime /óувэтайм/ adv сверхурочно; work ~ /вёрк ~/ работать сверхурочно

overturn /óувэтёрн/ vti опрокидывать(ся)

overweight /óувэвэ́йт/ adj тяжелее обычного; ~ luggage /~ ла́гидж/ оплачиваемый излишек багажа; n излишек веса

overwork /óувэвэ́рк/ vti переутомлять(ся)

owe /óу/ vt быть должным, быть обязанным; I ~ him 5 dollars /ай ~ хим файв до́ларз/ я должен ему пять долларов

own /óун/ adj собственный; vt владеть

owner /óунэ/ n владелец

ownership /óунэшип/ n собственность, владение; право собственности

P

pacific /пэси́фик/ adj мирный

package /пэ́кидж/ n пакет; посылка

packed /пэкт/ adj набитый

packer /пэ́кэ/ n упаковщик

packet /пэ́кит/ n пакет, пачка (сигарет)

packing /пэ́кинг/ n упаковка

packing-case /пэ́кингкейс/ n ящик для упаковки

padding /пэ́динг/ n набивка

padlock /пэ́длок/ n висячий замо́к

page /пэйдж/ n страница

pail /пэйл/ n ведро

pain /пэйн/ n боль; vt причинять боль

painful /пэ́йнфул/ adj болезненный

painstaking /пэ́йнзтэ́йкинг/ adj старательный

paint /пэйнт/ n краска; vt красить

painter /пэ́йнтэ/ n художник

painting /пэ́йнтинг/ n живопись; картина

pair /пээ/ n пара

pajamas /пэджа́амез/ n pl пижама

pal /пэл/ n приятель

palace /пэ́лис/ n дворец

pan /пэн/ n сковорода

pancake /пэ́нкейк/ n блин

pane /пэйн/ n оконное стекло

pants /пэнтс/ n pl штаны; трусы

papa /пэпа́а/ n папа

paper /пэ́йпэ/ n бумага; газета; документ; adj бумажный; ~ money /~ ма́ни/ ассигнации

paper-back /пэ́йпэбэк/ n книга в бумажной обложке

paralyze /пэ́рэлайз/ vt парализовать

paralysis /пэрэ́лисис/ n паралич

parcel /па́рсэл/ n пакет; посылка; участок

pardon /пардн/ n прощение; (юр.) помилование; I beg
     your ~! /ай бег йо ~/ извините!; ~? что вы сказали?

parent /пэ́эрэнт/ n родитель

parish /пэ́риш/ n церковный приход; ~ register /~
     ре́джистэ/ метрическая книга

parishioner /пэри́шенэ/ n прихожанин, прихожанка

parking /па́ркинг/ n стоянка; no ~ any time /но́у ~ э́ни
     тайм/ стоянка категорически запрещена

parliament /па́рлэмент/ n парламент

parlour /па́рлэ/ n гостиная, приемная

part /парт/ n часть; vti разделять(ся), разлучать(ся)

participate /пати́сипейт/ vi участвовать

particle /па́ртикл/ n частица

particular /пэти́кьюлэ/ adj особенный, определенный

particularly /пэти́кьюлэли/ adv в частности

partition /пати́шн/ n раздел, перегородка; vt разделять

partner /па́ртнэ/ n партнер(ша), супруг(а)

part-owner /па́ртбу́нэ/ n совладелец

part-timer /па́ртта́ймэ/ n рабочий, занятый неполный
     рабочий день

party /па́рти/ n партия; группа; вечеринка; (юр.)
     сторона; interested ~ /и́нтристыд ~/ заинтересованная
     сторона

pass /паас/ vt передавать; выносить (решение);
     принимать (закон); выдерживать (экзамен);
     проводить (время); проходить/проезжать мимо;
     переходить через; обгонять; n пропуск; разрешение

passage /пэ́сидж/ n проход, проезд; отрывок

passenger /пэ́синдже/ n пассажир

passer-by /па́асэбай/ n прохожий

pass-key /па́аски/ n отмычка

passport /па́аспорт/ n паспорт

past /пааст/ adj прошлый; n прошлое; adv мимо; half ~ one /хааф ~ ван/ половина второго

paste /пэйст/ n паста; тесто; клейстер; vt наклеивать

pastime /па́астайм/ n времяпрепровождение

pastor /па́астэ/ n пастырь; пастор

pastry /пэ́йстри/ n печенье, пирожное

pastry-shop /пэ́йстришо́п/ n кондитерская

patchwork quilt /пэ́чвёккви́лт/ n стеганое одеяло из лоскутов

patent /пэ́йтент/ adj явный; патентованный

path /пааф/ n тропинка, дорожка

patience /пэ́йшенс/ n терпение

patient /пэ́йшент/ adj терпеливый; n пациент

patriot /пэ́йтриэт/ n патриот

patrol /пэтро́ул/ n патруль, vt патрулировать

patron /пэ́йтрэн/ n покровитель, патрон

patronize /пэ́трэнайз/ vt покровительствовать

patronymic /пэ́трэни́мик/ n отчество

pattern /пэ́тэн/ n образец; выкройка; узор

patty /пэ́ти/ n пирожок

pause /пооз/ n пауза; vi делать паузу/перерыв

pavement /пэ́йвмент/ n тротуар, мостовая

paw /поо/ n лапа

pawnshop /по́оншоп/ n ломбард

pay /пэй/ n плата; зарплата, жалованье; vt платить, оплачивать; ~ attention /~ этэ́ншн/ обращать внимание; ~ in cash /~ ин кэш/ платить наличными pay-day /пэ́йдэй/ n день зарплаты

payment /пэ́ймент/ n уплата, платеж; ~ in advance /~ ин эдва́анс/ плата вперед

pay-office /пэ́йо́фис/ n касса

pay-roll /пэ́йроул/ n платежная ведомость

pea /пии/ n горошина; pl горох

peace /пиис/ n мир

peach /пиич/ n персик

peanut /пи́инат/ n арахис, земляной орех

pear /пээ/ n груша

pearl /пёрл/ n жемчуг, жемчужина, перл

peasant /пезнт/ n крестьянин

pedestal /пе́дистл/ n пьедестал

pedestrian /пиде́стриан/ n пешеход

pedigree /пе́дигрии/ n родословная

peel /пиил/ n кожица, кожура; vt чистить, шелушить

peels /пиилз/ n pl очистки

peep /пиип/ n взгляд украдкой; vi подглядывать; пищать

pen /пен/ n перо, ручка

penalize /пи́инэлайз/ vt наказывать

penalty /пе́нлти/ n штраф (также спорт.)

pencil /пенсл/ n карандаш

pendant /пе́ндэнт/ n кулон

penetrate /пе́нитрэйт/ vt пронизывать, проникать

peninsula /пени́нсьюлэ/ n полуостров

pension /пеншн/ n пенсия, пансион

pensioner /пе́ншенэ/ n пенсионер

penthouse /пе́нтхаус/ n роскошная квартира на верхнем этаже, выходящая окнами на крышу

people /пиипл/ n народ, люди; young ~ /янг ~/ молодежь; vt населять

pepper /пéпэ/ n перец; мятная лепешка; vt перчить

perambulator /прэ́мбьюлэйтэ/ n детская коляска

perception /песéпшн/ n восприятие

perfect /пéрфикт/ adj совершенный; /пефéкт/ vt совершенствовать

perfectly /пéрфиктли/ adv вполне; превосходно

perform /пефóрм/ vt выполнять (обязанности); исполнять (роль)

performance /пефóрмэнс/ n выполнение; (театр.) представление

perfume /пéрфьюм/ n духи

perhaps /пехэ́пс, прэпс/ adv может быть

period /пи́эриэд/ n период; точка

periodical /пи́эриóдикл/ n журнал, периодическое издание

perishable /пéришебл/ adj скоропортящийся

permanent /пéрмэнент/ adj постоянный

permission /пеми́шн/ n разрешение

permit /пéрмит/ n пропуск, разрешение; /пеми́т/ vt разрешать, позволять

perpetual /пепéтьюэл/ adj вечный, бесконечный

persecute /пéрсикьют/ vt преследовать

persistent /песи́стэнт/ adj упорный, настойчивый

person /пéрсн/ n человек; лицо, особа; in ~ /ин ~/ лично

personage /пéрснидж/ n выдающаяся личность; персонаж

personal /пéрснл/ adj личный

perspiration /пёрсперэ́йшн/ n пот

persuade /песвэ́йд/ vt убеждать

pertinent /пёртинент/ adj уместный

pet /пет/ n любимое животное; баловень, любимец

petitioner /пити́шнэ/ n проситель

petrol /пе́трэл/ n бензин; ~ tank /~ тэнк/ бензобак

petroleum /питро́ульем/ n нефть

petticoat /пе́тикоут/ n нижняя юбка

petty /пе́ти/ adj мелкий; мелочный; маловажный

pharmacy /фа́рмэси/ n аптека

physical /фи́зикл/ adj физический

physician /физи́шн/ n врач

physicist /фи́зисист/ n физик

piano /пьэ́ноу/ n рояль; upright ~ /а́прайт ~/ пианино

pick /пик/ n выбор; лучшая часть; кирка; vt выбирать; рвать; собирать; ~ up /~ ап/ поднимать; выздоравливать

picked /пикт/ adj отборный

picket /пи́кит/ n пикет; vt пикетировать

pickle /пикл/ n рассол; vt мариновать

pickpocket /пи́кпо́кит/ n карманный вор

picture /пи́кче/ n картина; фильм

picturesque /пи́кчерэск/ adj живописный

picture-theatre /пи́кчеси́этэ/ n кинотеатр

pie /пай/ n пирог; apple ~ /эпл ~/ яблочный пирог

piece /пиис/ n кусок, часть; штука; ~ of ground /~ ов гра́унд/ участок земли

piece-work /пи́исвёрк/ n сдельная работа

pig /пиг/ n свинья

pigeon /пи́джин/ n голубь

pile /пайл/ n куча, груда, кипа (бумаги); vt: ~ up /~ ап/
нагромождать; накоплять

pill /пил/ n пилюля, таблетка

pillar box /пи́лэбокс/ n почтовый ящик

pillow /пи́лоу/ n подушка

pillow-case /пи́лоукейс/ n наволочка

pilot /па́йлэт/ n (авиа)пилот, летчик; (мор.) лоцман; vt
вести, пилотировать

pimple /пимпл/ n прыщик

pin /пин/ n булавка, шпилька; vt прикалывать
булавкой

pincers /пи́нсэз/ n pl щипцы, клещи

pinch /пинч/ n щипок; щепотка (соли и т.п.); vt щипать;
жать (об обуви); красть

pine /пайн/ n сосна

pineapple /па́йнэпл/ n ананас

pink /пинк/ adj розовый; n гвоздика

pint /пайнт/ n пинта (= 0,57 литра)

pipe /пайп/ n труба; (курительная) трубка; дудка,
свирель; pl (муз.) волынка

pipe-line /па́йплайн/ n трубопровод

pistol /пистл/ n пистолет

pit /пит/ n яма; шахта; партер

pitiable, pitiful /пи́тиэбл, пи́тифул/ adj жалкий;
жалостливый

pitiless /пи́тилис/ adj безжалостный

pity /пи́ти/ n жалость; for ~'s sake! /фо ~з сэйк/ ради
Бога!; what a ~! /вот э ~/ как жалко!; vt жалеть

place /плэйс/ n место, положение; take ~ /тэйк ~/ состояться; out of ~ /áут ов ~/ неуместный; vt класть, ставить

plaid /плэд/ n плед

plain /плэйн/ adj простой, ясный; некрасивый; одноцветный; ~ clothes /~ клóувз/ штатское платье

plaint /плэйнт/ n иск

plaintiff /плэ́йнтиф/ n истец

plait /плэт/ n коса; vt заплетать

plane /плэйн/ n плоскость; самолет; (тех.) рубанок; vt строгать

planet /плэ́нит/ n планета

plane-tree /плэ́йнтрии/ n платан

plank /плэнк/ n доска, планка; vt выстилать досками

plant /плаант/ n (бот.) растение; завод; vt сажать; (образн.) насаждать

plaster /плáастэ/ n (мед.) пластырь; (строит.) штукатурка

plastic /плэ́стик/ adj пластический; пластмассовый

plate /плэйт/ n тарелка

plate-rack /плэ́йтрэк/ n сушилка для посуды

play /плэй/ n игра; пьеса; vt играть

player /плэ́йе/ n актер; игрок

playful /плэ́йфул/ adj игривый

plead /плиид/ vi умолять; ~ not guilty /~ нот ги́лти/ не признавать себя виновным; vt: ~ a case /~ э кейс/ защищать дело

pleasant /плезнт/ adj приятный

please /плииз/ vi хотеть, изволить; ~ ! пожалуйста!; vt нравиться pleased /плиизд/ adj довольный; ~ to meet you /~ ту миит ю/ приятно познакомиться

pleasure /пле́же/ n удовольствие

pleat /плиит/ n складка; ~ed skirt /~ыд скёрт/ юбка в складку

plentiful /пле́нтифул/ adj обильный

plenty /пле́нти/ n изобилие; ~ of /~ ов/ много

pliers /пла́йез/ n щипцы, плоскогубцы

plot /плот/ n заговор; фабула; участок земли; vi устраивать заговор

plug /плаг/ n затычка; (эл.) штепсель; vt затыкать

plum /плам/ n слива

plumber /пла́мэ/ n водопроводчик

plump /пламп/ adj полный, пухлый

plunder /пла́ндэ/ n грабеж

plush /плаш/ n плюш; adj плюшевый

pneumonia /ньюмо́унье/ n воспаление легких

pocket /по́кит/ n карман; vt класть в карман, прикарманивать

pocket-money /по́китма́ни/ n карманные деньги

point /пойнт/ n точка; пункт; острие; очко; ~ of view /~ ов вьюю/ точка зрения

pointless /по́йнтлис/ adj бессмысленный

poison /пойзн/ n яд; vt отравлять

poisoning /по́йзнинг/ n отравление

police /пэли́ис/ n полиция; ~ station /~ стэйшн/ полицейский участок

policeman /пэли́исмэн/ n полицейский

policy /по́лиси/ n политика; страховой полис

polish /по́лиш/ n политура; крем для обуви; vt полировать; чистить (обувь)

polite /пэла́йт/ adj вежливый

politician /по́литишн/ n политик

politics /по́литикс/ n политика

poll /по́ул/ n баллотировка; опрос населения; vi голосовать; vt получать голоса

polling-booth /по́улингбу́ус/ n кабина для голосования

polling-station /по́улингстэ́йшн/ n избирательный пункт

pollute /пэлью́ют/ vt загрязнять

pond /понд/ n пруд

ponder /по́ндэ/ vt обдумывать; vi размышлять

pool /пуул/ n лужа; бассейн; фонд

poor /пу́э/ adj бедный, плохой; ~ thing /~ синг/ бедняжка; the ~ /зэ ~/ беднота

pop /поп/ n отрывистый звук; ~ art /~ арт/ поп-арт; ~ music /~ мью́юзик/ поп-музыка; vti хлопать

pop-corn /по́пкорн/ n кукурузные хлопья

popular /по́пьюлэ/ adj популярный, народный

populate /по́пьюлэйт/ vt заселять

population /по́пьюлэ́йшн/ n население

porcelain /по́ослин/ n фарфор

porch /порч/ n крыльцо

pork /порк/ n свинина

porridge /по́ридж/ n каша

port /порт/ n порт; портвейн

portable /по́ртэбл/ adj портативный

porter /по́ртэ/ n швейцар; носильщик; портер (черное пиво)

portion /поршн/ n часть, доля, порция; vt делить на части, разделять

pose /поуз/ n поза; vi позировать; ~ as /~ эз/ выдавать себя за

position /пэзишн/ n позиция; должность

positive /позетив/ adj положительный

possess /пэзéс/ vt владеть, обладать

possession /пэзéшн/ n владение, обладание; pl имущество

possessor /пэзéсэ/ n владелец

possibility /посэбилити/ n возможность

possible /посэбл/ adj возможный

post /поуст/ n почта; должность; (воен.) пост; столб; ~ office /~ офис/ почта, почтамт

postage /поустыдж/ n почтовые расходы

postal /поустэл/ adj почтовый; ~ order /~ брдэ/ почтовый перевод

postcard /поусткард/ n открытка

poste restante /поустрéстаант/ adv до востребования

poster /поустэ/ n афиша, плакат

postgraduate /поустгрэдьюит/ n аспирант

posthumous /постьюмэс/ adj посмертный

postman /поустмэн/ n почтальон

post meridiem, p.m. /поустмеридиэм, пииэм/ adv после полудня

postpone /поустпоун/ vt откладывать

pot /пот/ n горшок

potato /пэтэйтоу/ n картофелина; pl картофель

potential /пэтэншл/ adj потенциальный; n потенциал

potion /поушн/ n микстура

pottery /потэри/ n керамика

poultry /поултри/ n домашняя птица

pound /паунд/ n фунт

pour /поор/ vt лить(ся), сыпать(ся); it's ~ing /итс ~инг/ идет проливной дождь

poverty /повэти/ n бедность

powder /паудэ/ n порох; порошок; пудра; vt пудрить

powder-room /паудэруум/ n дамская туалетная комната

powdered milk /паудэдмилк/ n порошковое молоко

power /пауэ/ n сила, мощность; власть; держава

powerful /пауэфул/ adj сильный, могущественный

powerless /пауэлис/ adj бессильный

practicable /практикэбл/ adj осуществимый

practical /практикл/ adj практический; ~ joke /~ джоук/ грубая шутка

practice /практис/ n практика; in ~ /ин ~/ на деле; put into ~ /пут инту ~/ осуществлять

practitioner /прэктишнэ/ n практикующий врач/юрист

praise /прэйз/ n похвала; vt хвалить

pram /прэм/ n детская коляска

prawn /проон/ n креветка

pray /прэй/ vi молиться

preacher /приче/ n проповедник

precaution /прикоошн/ n предосторожность

precede /присиид/ vt предшествовать

precinct /приисинкт/ n избирательный/полицейский участок

precious /прэшес/ adj драгоценный

precise /присáйс/ adj точный

precisely /присáйсли/ adv точно

precocious /прикóушес/ adj скороспелый

predict /придúкт/ vt предсказывать

prediction /придúкшн/ n предсказание

predominant /придóминэнт/ adj преобладающий

prefer /прифёр/ vt предпочитать

preferable /прéфрэбл/ adj предпочтительный

pregnancy /прéгнэнси/ n беременность

pregnant /прéгнэнт/ adj беременная

prejudice /прéджудис/ n предрассудок, предубеждение;
vt наносить ущерб

preliminary /прилúминэри/ adj предварительный

premature /прéмэтьюэ/ adj преждевременный

premise /прéмис/ n (пред)посылка; pl помещение

premium /прúимьем/ n награда, премия

premonition /прúимэнúшн/ n предчувствие

preoccupation /приóкьюпэ́йшн/ n озабоченность

preparation /прéпэрэ́йшн/ n приготовление

prepare /припэ́э/ vti готовить(ся)

prepay /прúипэ́й/ vt платить вперед

prescription /прискрúпшн/ n предписание; (мед.)
рецепт

presence /прéзнс/ n присутствие, наличие

present /прéзнт/ adj присутствующий; нынешний; at ~
/эт ~/ в настоящее время; n подарок; настоящее время
(также грам.); /призéнт/ vt дарить; подавать
(петицию)

preservative /призёрвэтив/ n предохраняющее средство

preserve /призёрв/ vt сохранять; консервировать; n заповедник

press /прес/ n (тех.) пресс; печать; пресса; типография; ~ conference /~ кóнферэнс/ пресс-конференция; vt жать, нажимать, давить

pressman /прéсмэн/ n журналист

pressure /прéше/ n давление, нажим

presumably /призьюю́юмэбли/ adv предположительно

presumption /призáмшн/ n предположение

pressupose /прúисэпóуз/ vt предполагать

pretence /притéнс/ n притворство

pretend /притéнд/ vi притворяться; ~ to /~ ту/ претендовать на

pretty /прúти/ adj хорошенький; adv довольно

prevent /привéнт/ vt предотвращать, препятствовать

preventive /привéнтив/ adj предупредительный; профилактический

previous /прúивьес/ adj предыдущий

price /прайс/ n цена; vt назначать цену

priceless /прáйслис/ adj бесценный

price-list /прáйслист/ n прейскурант

pride /прайд/ n гордость

priest /приист/ n священник

primary /прáймэри/ adj первичный; (перво)начальный; ~ school /~ скуул/ начальная школа

prime /прайм/ adj главный; ~ minister /~ мúнистэ/ премьер-министр

primer /прáймэ/ n букварь

primitive /прúмитив/ adj первобытный; примитивный

primrose /пра́мроуз/ n примула

principal /пра́нсэпл/ adj главный; n глава

principally /пра́нсэпэли/ adv главным образом

principle /пра́нсэпл/ n принцип

print /принт/ n отпечаток; шрифт; печать; in ~ /ин ~/ в
продаже; out of ~ /а́ут ов ~/ распроданный; vt печатать

printed /пра́нтыд/ adj печатный; набивной

priority /прайо́рити/ n приоритет, срочность

prison /призн/ n тюрьма

prisoner /пра́знэ/ n пленный; заключенный

privacy /пра́йвэси/ n уединение

private /пра́йвит/ adj частный; ~ secretary /~ се́кретри/
личный секретарь

privation /прайве́йшн/ n лишение

privilege /пра́вилидж/ n привилегия

prize /прайз/ n приз; award a ~ /эво́рд э ~/ присуждать
премию; vt высоко ценить

probable /про́бэбл/ adj вероятный

probably /про́бэбли/ adv вероятно

probation /прэбе́йшн/ n испытание, стажировка

probationary /прэбе́йшнэри/ adj испытательный; ~
sentence /~ се́нтэнс/ условный приговор

probationer /прэбе́йшнэ/ n стажер; послушник

problem /про́блем/ n проблема, задача

procedure /прэси́идже/ n процедура

proceeding /прэси́идинг/ n поступок; судебная
процедура; pl протокол

proceeds /про́усидз/ n pl выручка

process /про́усэс/ n процесс

proclaim /прэклэ́йм/ vt провозглашать

produce /про́дьюс/ n продукция; /прэдью́ос/ vt производить; ставить (пьесу, кинокартину)

producer /прэдью́юсэ/ n производитель; продюсер

product /про́дэкт/ n продукт

production /прэда́кшн/ n производство

productive /прэда́ктив/ adj производительный

productivity /про́дакти́вити/ n производительность

profession /прэфе́шн/ n профессия

professional /прэфе́шенл/ adj профессиональный; n профессионал

proficient /прэфи́шент/ adj умелый

profit /про́фит/ n прибыль, доход; vi приносить пользу

profitable /про́фитэбл/ adj прибыльный

profiteer /про́фити́э/ n спекулянт

profound /прэфа́унд/ adj глубокий

profuse /прэфью́юс/ adj обильный

prohibit /прэхи́бит/ vt запрещать

prohibition /про́иби́шн/ n запрещение; "сухой закон"

project /про́джект/ n проект; /прэдже́кт/ vt проектировать; vi выдаваться

prominent /про́минэнт/ adj выдающийся

promise /про́мис/ n обещание; vt обещать

promising /про́мисинг/ adj многообещающий

promote /прэмо́ут/ vt повышать в чине или звании; содействовать

promotion /прэмо́ушн/ n повышение

prompt /промт/ adj немедленный; ~ payment /~ пэ́ймент/ наличный расчет promptly /прóмтли/ adv быстро

pronounce /прэнáунс/ vt провозглашать; произносить

proof /прууф/ n доказательство; испытание; корректура

proper /прóпэ/ adj пристойный, правильный

property /прóпэти/ n собственность, имущество

prophecy /прóфиси/ n пророчество

proportional /прэпóршнл/ adj пропорциональный

proposal /прэпóузл/ n предложение

propose /прэпóуз/ vt предлагать; vi делать предложение (о браке)

proposition /прóпэзúшн/ n предложение; заявление

proprietor /прэпрáйетэ/ n собственник

prose /прóуз/ n проза; ~ writer /~ рáйтэ/ прозаик

prosecute /прóсикьют/ vt преследовать судебным порядком

prosecutor /прóсикьютэ/ n обвинитель; public ~ /нáблик ~/ прокурор

prospect /прóспект/ n перспектива, вид; pl виды на будущее

prosperity /просперúти/ n благосостояние

prosperous /прóсперэс/ adj процветающий

protect /прэтéкт/ vt защищать, охранять; покровительствовать

protection /прэтéкшн/ n защита

protective /прэтéктив/ adj защитный

protest /прóутест/ n протест; /прэтéст/ vi протестовать

protrude /прэтрýуд/ vti высовывать(ся)

proud /прáуд/ adj гордый

prove /пруув/ vt доказывать; vi оказываться

provide /прэвáйд/ vt снабжать; ~ for /~ фо/ обеспечивать

provident /прóвидэнт/ adj предусмотрительный

province /прóвинс/ n провинция, область

provision /прэвúжн/ n обеспечение; условие; pl запасы, провизия; vt снабжать продовольствием

provisional /прэвúжнл/ adj временный

provoke /прэвóук/ vt провоцировать

proxy /прóкси/ n полномочие, доверенность; by ~ /бай ~/ по доверенности

prudent /прýудэнт/ adj благоразумный

psychiatrist /сайкáйетрист/ n психиатр

psychic /сáйкик/ adj психический

psycho-analysis /сáйкоэнэ́лэсис/ n психоанализ

psychological /сáйкэлóджикл/ adj психологический

psychology /сайкóлэджи/ n психология

pub /паб/ n пивная

public /пáблик/ adj общественный; общедоступный; государственный; национальный; ~ health /~ хелф/ здравоохранение; ~ service /~ сёрвис/ коммунальное обслуживание; n публика, общественность; in ~/ин~/ публично

publication /пáбликéйшн/ n опубликование; издание

publicity /паблúсити/ n гласность, реклама

publicize /пáблисайз/ vt рекламировать

publish /пáблиш/ vt издавать, опубликовывать

publisher /пáблише/ n издатель

pudding /пýдинг/ n пудинг

pull /пул/ n тяга, рывок; vt тянуть; грести; ~ oneself together /~ вансэ́лф тэгéзэ/ брать себя в руки pulse /палс/ n пульс, биение

pumpkin /пáмкин/ n тыква

pun /пан/ n каламбур

punctual /пáнктьюэл/ adj пунктуальный

punctuality /пáнктьюэ́лити/ n пунктуальность

puncture /пáнкче/ n прокол; vt прокалывать (шины)

punish /пáниш/ vt наказывать

punishment /пáнишмент/ n наказание

punitive /пьюнитив/ adj карательный

pupil /пьюупл/ n ученик; зрачок

puppet /пáпит/ n марионетка; ~ show /~ шóу/
кукольный театр

puppy /пáпи/ n щенок

purchase /пёрчсс/ n покупка; vt покупать

purchaser /пёрчесэ/ n покупатель

pure /пьюэ/ n чистый

purify /пьюэрифай/ vt очищать

purity /пьюэрити/ n чистота

purple /пёрпл/ adj пурпурный, фиолетовый, лиловый

purpose /пёрпэс/ n цель

purposeful /пёрпэсфул/ adj целенаправленный;
преднамеренный

purse /пёрс/ n кошелек; дамская сумочка; the public ~
/зэ пáблик ~/ казна

pursue /пэсьюю/ n гнаться за, преследовать; проводить
(политику)

pursuit /пэсьюют/ n погоня; занятие

push /пуш/ n толчок; vt толкать

pusher /пýше/ n (разг.) торговец наркотиками

puss(y) /пу́с(и)/ n кошечка, киска

put /пут/ vt класть, ставить; задавать (вопросы); излагать, формулировать; ~ by /~ бай/ откладывать (на черный день); ~ down /~ да́ун/ подавлять; записывать; снижать; ~ off /~ оф/ отсрочивать: ~ on /~ он/ надевать; ~ out /~ а́ут/ высовывать, выпячивать; тушить, гасить; ~ through /~ сруу/ соединять (по телефону); ~ together /~ тэгэ́зе/ соединять; ~ up /~ ап/ поднимать; приютить

puzzle /пазл/ n загадка; vt ставить в тупик

pyjamas /пэджа́амэз/ n pl пижама

Q

qualification /кво́лификейшн/ n квалификация; оговорка; ограничение

qualify /кво́лифай/ vi квалифицировать

quality /кво́лити/ n качество

quantity /кво́нтити/ n количество

quarrel /кворл/ n ссора; vi ссориться

quart /кворт/ n кварта (в Англии = 1,14 л; в Америке = 0,95 л)

quarter /кво́ртэ/ n четверть; квартал; a ~ past five /э ~ пааст файв/ четверть шестого

queen /квиин/ n королева; (карты) дама; (шахм.) ферзь

queer /кви́э/ adj странный

quest /квест/ n поиски

question /квесчн/ n вопрос; beyond ~ /бийо́нд ~/ вне сомнения; vt спрашивать, (д)опрашивать; сомневаться в questionable /квéсченэбл/ adj сомнительный

questionaire /квéстиэнзэ/ n анкета

queue /кьюю/ n очередь; jump the ~ /джамп зэ ~/ пролезть без очереди; vi стоять в очереди

quick /квик/ adj быстрый, проворный

quickly /квúкли/ adv быстро

quick-tempered /квúктэмпэд/ adj вспыльчивый

quick-witted /квúквúтыд/ adj остроумный

quiet /квáйет/ adj тихий; interj тише!

quietly /квáйетли/ adv тихо

quilt /квилт/ n стеганое одеяло

quinsy /квúнзи/ n ангина

quit /квит/ vt покидать; ~ the job /~ зэ джоб/ уйти с работы

quite /квайт/ adv совсем, вполне; ~ so /~ сóу/ именно так

quiz /квиз/ n опрос; викторина

quotation /квотэ́йшн/ n цитата

quote /квóут/ vt цитировать; назначать цену

R

rabbit /рэ́бит/ n кролик

race /рэйс/ n раса; гонка; pl бега, скачки; arms ~ /армз ~/ гонка вооружений; vi состязаться в скорости, мчаться

race-course /рэ́йскос/ n ипподром

racial /рэйшл/ adj расовый

rack /рэк/ n вешалка

racket /рэ́кит/ n шум; вымогательство, рэкет; ракетка

radiation /рэ́йдиэ́йшн/ n радиация

radiator /рэ́йдиэ́йтэ/ n радиатор

radical /рэ́дикэл/ adj коренной; радикальный

radish /рэ́диш/ n редиска

raffle /рэфл/ n лотерея

rag /рэг/ n тряпка

rage /рэйдж/ n гнев, ярость; vi свирепствовать (об эпидемии и т.п.)

raglan /рэ́глэн/ n пальто-реглан

raid /рэйд/ n облава; рейд; vt делать налет на

rail /рэйл/ n перила; рельс; by ~ /бай ~/ по железной дороге

railway /рэ́йлвэй/ n железная дорога; ~ timetable /~ та́ймтэйбл/ расписание поездов; ~ car /~ кар/ вагон; ~ station /~ стэйшн/ вокзал

rain /рэйн/ n дождь; vti лить(ся)

rainbow /рэ́йнбоу/ n радуга

rainy /рэ́йни/ adj дождливый

raise /рэйз/ vt поднимать; воспитывать (детей); выращивать (растения); повышать (плату)

raisin /рэйзн/ adj изюмина; pl изюм

ram /рэм/ n баран

ranch /раанч/ n ранчо, ферма

random /рэ́ндэм/ adj случайный; n: at ~ /эт ~/ наугад

rank /рэнк/ n ряд; шеренга; чин

ransom /рэ́нсэм/ n выкуп

rape /рэйп/ n изнасилование; vt насиловать

rapid /рэ́пид/ adj быстрый

rare /рээ/ adj редкий; недожаренный

rascal /páаскэл/ n негодяй

raspberry /páазбери/ n малина

rat /рэт/ n крыса

rate /рэйт/ n ставка, норма; ~ of exchange /~ ов иксчéйндж/ валютный курс; at any ~ /эт эни ~/ во всяком случае; vt оценивать

rather /páазэ/ adv скорее; довольно; лучше; interj еще бы!; конечно, да!

ratification /рэтификéйшн/ n ратификация

ratify /рэтифай/ vt ратифицировать

ratio /рэ́йшиоу/ n соотношение, коэффициент

rational /рэ́шенл/ adj рациональный

rat-trap /рэ́ттрэп/ n крысоловка

raw /роо/ adj сырой; ~ material /~ мэтúриэл/ сырье

ray /рэй/ n луч

razor /рэ́йзэ/ n бритва

reach /риич/ n предел досягаемости; охват; протяжение; out of ~ /áут ов ~/ вне досягаемости; vti протягивать(ся); дотягиваться до, доходить до

react /риэ́кт/ vi реагировать

reaction /риэ́кшн/ n реакция

read /риид/ vt читать

readable /рúидэбл/ adj удобочитаемый, хорошо написанный

reader /рúидэ/ n читатель

readily /рéдили/ adv охотно

readiness /рéдинис/ n готовность

reading /рúидинг/ n чтение; ~ room /~ руум/ читальный зал

ready /ре́ди/ adj готовый

real /ри́эл/ adj настоящий, действительный; подлинный; недвижимый (о собственности)

reality /риэ́лити/ n действительность

realization /ри́элизэ́йшн/ n осуществление

realize /ри́элайз/ vt осуществлять; понимать

really /ри́эли/ adv действительно

rear /ри́э/ n тыл; задняя сторона; in the ~ /ин зэ ~/ в тылу; adj задний

reason /ри́изн/ n разум; причина; vi рассуждать

reasonable /ри́изнэбл/ adj (благо)разумный

reassure /ри́иэшю́э/ vt успокаивать, заверять

rebellious /рибе́льес/ adj мятежный

rebuff /риба́ф/ n отпор; vt давать отпор

rebuke /рибью́юк/ n упрек; vt упрекать

rebut /риба́т/ vt опровергать

recall /рико́ол/ n отзыв (депутата и т.п.); vt вспоминать; отзывать; отменять

receipt /риси́ит/ n квитанция; расписка; получение; pl денежные поступления; выручка

receive /риси́ив/ vt получать, принимать

receiver /риси́ивэ/ n получатель; телефонная трубка; радиоприемник

recent /ри́иснт/ adj недавний

recently /ри́иснтли/ adv недавно

reception /рисэ́пшн/ n прием; восприятие; ~ room /~ руум/ приемная

recess /рисэ́с/ n перерыв; ниша; in the secret ~es /ин зэ си́икрэт ~ыз/ в тайниках

recipe /ре́сипи/ n рецепт

recipient /риси́пиэнт/ n получатель

reciprocal /риси́прэкл/ adj взаимный

reciprocate /риси́прэкэйт/ vt отвечать взаимностью

reciprocity /ре́сипро́сити/ n взаимность

recite /риса́йт/ vt декламировать

reckless /ре́клис/ adj безрассудный; ~ driving /~ дра́йвинг/ лихачество

reckon /рекн/ vi думать; считать, подсчитывать; ~ with /~ виз/ считаться с

reclaim /рикле́йм/ vt требовать обратно; осваивать (заброшенные земли)

recline /рикла́йн/ vi полулежать

recognition /ре́кэгни́шн/ n узнавание; признание

recognize /ре́кэгнайз/ vt узнавать; признавать

recoil /рико́йл/ n отдача (о ружье); vi отдавать (о ружье); отпрянуть

recollect /ре́кэле́кт/ vt вспоминать

recollection /ре́кэле́кшн/ n воспоминание

recommend /ре́кэме́нд/ vt рекомендовать

recommendation /ре́кэменда́йшн/ n рекомендация

recompense /ре́кэмпенс/ n вознаграждение; vt вознаграждать

reconcile /ре́кэнсайл/ vt примирять

reconciliation /ре́кэнсилиа́йшн/ n примирение

reconnaissance /рико́нисэнс/ n разведка

reconnoitre /ре́коно́йтэ/ vt разведывать

reconsider /ри́икэнси́дэ/ vt пересматривать

reconstruct /ри́икэнстра́кт/ vt перестраивать

reconstruction /рйикэнстра́кшн/ n перестройка, реконструкция

record /ре́код/ n запись; протокол; (граммофонная) пластинка; личное дело; (спорт.) рекорд; off the ~ /оф зэ ~/ неофициально; ~ player /~ пле́йе/ проигрыватель; /рико́рд/ vt записывать; регистрировать

recount /рика́унт/ vt пересказывать; /рйика́унт/ пересчитывать

recover /рика́вэ/ vt получать обратно; vi выздоравливать

recovery /рика́вэри/ n выздоровление

recreation /ре́криэ́йшн/ n отдых

rectum /ре́ктэм/ n прямая кишка

recuperate /рикьюю́прэйт/ vti выздоравливать; поправить (здоровье)

red /ред/ adj красный; turn ~ /тёрн ~/ краснеть; R. Cross /~ крос/ Красный крест

redeem /риди́им/ vt выкупать, избавлять

red-haired /ре́дхе́эд/ adj рыжеволосый

red-letter day /ре́длэтэдэ́й/ n праздник

red-tape /ре́дтэ́йп/ n бюрократизм

reduce /ридью́юс/ vt снижать (цену); сокращать

reduction /рида́кшн/ n снижение; сокращение

reel /риил/ n катушка, шпулька; vi кружиться; пошатываться

refer /рифёр/ vt отсылать, направлять; ~ to /~ ту/ ссылаться на

reference /ре́фрэнс/ n ссылка, упоминание; рекомендация

refined /рифа́йнд/ adj очищенный; утонченный

reflect /рифле́кт/ vt отражать; vi размышлять

reflection /рифле́кшн/ n отражение; размышление

reform /рифо́рм/ n реформа; vti исправлять(ся)

reformer /рифо́рмэ/ n преобразователь, реформатор

refreshment /рифре́шмент/ n отдых; pl закуски

refrigerator /рифри́джерэ́йтэ/ n холодильник

refuge /ре́фьюдж/ n убежище

refugee /ре́фьюджи́и/ n беженец

refusal /рифью́юзл/ n отказ

refuse /рифью́юз/ vt отвергать, отказываться от; /ре́фьюс/ n отбросы, мусор

refute /рифью́ют/ vt опровергать

regard /рига́рд/ n уважение; отношение; pl привет; with ~ to /виз ~ ту/ относительно; vt рассматривать, считать; as ~s /эз ~з/ что касается

region /ри́иджн/ n область, район

register /ре́джистэ/ n журнал; список; vt регистрировать, записывать

registered /ре́джистэд/ adj зарегистрированный; ~ letter /~ ле́тэ/ заказное письмо

regret /ригре́т/ n сожаление; vt сожалеть

regular /ре́гьюлэ/ adj регулярный; правильный

regulation /ре́гьюлэ́йшн/ n регулирование; правило; pl устав

rehabilitation /ри́иэби́лите́йшн/ n реабилитация

reinforce /ри́инфо́рс/ vt усиливать

reject /ридже́кт/ vt отвергать

rejection /ридже́кшн/ n отказ, отклонение

rejoice /риджо́йс/ vti радовать(ся)

relapse /риле́пс/ n рецидив

relate /риле́йт/ vt рассказывать; vi относиться к

relation /риле́йшн/ n родственник, родственница; отношение, связь

relationship /риле́йшншип/ n родство; взаимоотношение

relative /ре́лэтив/ adj относительный; n родственник, родственница

relax /риле́кс/ vti расслаблять(ся)

release /рили́ис/ vt освобождать; выпускать (фильм и т.п.)

relevant /ре́ливэнт/ adj уместный, относящийся к делу

reliable /рила́йебл/ adj надежный

relic /ре́лик/ n остаток; pl останки; реликвии

relief /рили́иф/ n облегчение; пособие; помощь; рельеф

relieve /рили́ив/ vt облегчать; сменять

religion /рили́джн/ n религия

religious /рили́джес/ adj религиозный

reluctant /рила́ктэнт/ adj неохотный

remain /риме́йн/ vi оставаться

remainder /риме́йндэ/ n остаток

remark /рима́рк/ n замечание; vt замечать

remarkable /рима́ркэбл/ adj замечательный

remedy /ре́миди/ n средство, лекарство; vt исправлять; вылечивать

remember /риме́мбэ/ vt помнить, вспоминать

remind /рима́йнд/ vt напоминать

remittance /реми́тэнс/ n денежный перевод

remnant /ре́мнэнт/ n остаток

remodel /рйимо́дл/ vt переделывать

remote /римо́ут/ adj отдаленный

removal /риму́увл/ n перемещение, переезд; ~ van /~ вэн/ фургон для перевозки мебели

remove /риму́ув/ vt перемещать; удалять; устранять; vi переезжать

remunerate /римью́юнэрэйт/ vt вознаграждать

renaissance /рэнэ́йсэнс/ n возрождение

render /ре́ндэ/ vt воздавать; оказывать (помощь)

renew /ринью́ю/ vt возобновлять, продлевать

renewal /ринью́эл/ n обновление; возобновление

rent /рент/ n квартирная плата; vt нанимать; сдавать в аренду; брать напрокат

rental /рентл/ n арендная плата

repair /рипэ́э/ n починка, ремонт; vt чинить, ремонтировать

repay /рипэ́й/ vt отплачивать, возмещать

repayment /рипэ́ймент/ n выплата (долга), возмещение

repeal /рипи́ил/ n отмена; vt отменять

repeat /рипи́ит/ vti повторять(ся)

repeatedly /рипи́итыдли/ adv неоднократно

replacement /рипдэ́йсмент/ n замена

reply /рипла́й/ n ответ; ~ paid /~ пэйд/ с оплаченным ответом; vt отвечать

report /рипо́рт/ n доклад; vt докладывать, сообщать; vi являться

reporter /рипо́ртэ/ n докладчик; репортер

represent /ре́призе́нт/ vt представлять, изображать

repress /рипрéс/ vt подавлять

reprimand /рéприманд/ n выговор; vt делать выговор

reproachful /рипрóучфул/ adj укоризненный

reproduce /рйипрэдьююс/ vt воспроизводить

reprove /рипрýув/ vt порицать

republic /рипáблик/ n республика

repulse /рипáлс/ n отпор; vt отражать

repulsive /рипáлсив/ adj отталкивающий

reputation /рéпьютэ́йшн/ n репутация

request /риквéст/ n просьба; vt просить

requirement /риквáйемент/ n требование

rescue /рéскью/ n спасение; vt спасать

research /рисéрч/ n исследование; ~ worker /~ вёркэ/
  научный работник

resemblance /ризэ́мблэнс/ n сходство

resemble /ризэ́мбл/ vt походить на

reservation /рéзэвэ́йшн/ n оговорка; предварительный
  заказ

reserve /ризёрв/ n резерв; заповедник; with ~ /виз ~/ с
  оговоркой; vt сберегать; бронировать; ~ the right /~ зэ
  райт/ сохранять право

reserved /ризёёвд/ adj сдержанный; заказанный
  заранее

reside /ризáйд/ vi проживать

residence /рéзидэнс/ n местожительство

resident /рéзидэнт/ n постоянный житель

resign /ризáйн/ vi уходить в отставку

resignation /рéзигнэ́йшн/ n отставка; смирение,
  покорность

resist /ризи́ст/ vt сопротивляться

resistance /ризи́стэнс/ n сопротивление

resolute /ре́зэлют/ adj решительный

resolution /ре́зэлю́шн/ n решение; резолюция; решительность

resolve /ризо́лв/ n решимость; vt решать

resort /ризо́рт/ n прибежище; курорт; last ~ /лааст ~/ последнее средство; vi: ~ to прибегать к

resource /рисо́рс/ n ресурс; средство

resourceful /рисо́рсфул/ adj находчивый

respect /риспе́кт/ n уважение; in all ~s /ин оол ~с/ во всех отношениях; vt уважать

respectable /риспе́ктэбл/ adj почтенный, порядочный

respective /риспе́ктив/ adj соответственный

respiration /ре́спэрэ́йшн/ n дыхание

respite /ре́спайт/ n передышка, отсрочка

respond /риспо́нд/ vi отвечать; отзываться

responsibility /риспо́нсэби́лити/ n ответственность

responsible /риспо́нсэбл/ adj ответственный

rest /рест/ n отдых; покой; остаток; остальные; vi отдыхать

restaurant /ре́стэрон/ n ресторан

restore /ристо́р/ vt реставрировать, восстанавливать

restriction /ристри́кшн/ n ограничение

result /риза́лт/ n результат

resume /ризьюю́м/ vt возобновлять

retail /ри́итэйл/ n розничная продажа; ~ price /~ прайс/ розничная цена; /рите́йл/ vt продавать в розницу

retailer /рите́йлэ/ n розничный торговец

retain /ритэ́йн/ vt сохранять, удерживать

retard /рита́рд/ vt задерживать

retire /рита́йе/ vt уходить в отставку; уединяться

retirement /рита́йемент/ n отставка

retreat /ритри́ит/ n отступление; vi отступать

return /ритёрн/ n возвращение; прибыль; in ~ /ин ~/ в обмен; tax ~ /тэкс ~/ налоговая декларация; many happy ~s /мэ́ни хэ́пи ~з/ с днем рождения; ~ ticket /~ ти́кит/ обратный билет, билет в оба конца; vti возвращать(ся)

reunion /рии́ню́юньен/ n воссоединение; примирение

reveal /риви́ил/ vt обнаруживать

revenue /ре́винью/ n (государственный) доход; pl доходные статьи; tax ~ /тэкс ~/ доход от налогов

review /ривью́ю/ n обзор, обозрение; рецензия; (юр.) пересмотр; vt рецензировать; проверять; (юр.) пересматривать

revive /рива́йв/ vt приводить в чувство, оживлять; vi приходить в чувство

revolt /рибу́лт/ n восстание; vi восставать

revolting /рибу́лтинг/ adj отвратительный

revolution /ре́взлю́юшн/ n революция; вращение; оборот

revolver /рибо́лвэ/ n револьвер

reward /рибо́рд/ n награда; vt награждать

rheumatism /ру́умэтизм/ n ревматизм

rib /риб/ n ребро

ribbon /ри́бэн/ n лента, тесьма

rice /райс/ n рис

rich /рич/ adj богатый

rid /рид/ vt избавлять; get ~ of /гет ~ ов/ отделываться от

ridge /ридж/ n горный хребет

ridiculous /риди́кьюлэс/ adj смехотворный

rifle /райфл/ n винтовка

right /райт/ n право; справедливость; правая сторона; civil ~s /си́вил ~с/ гражданские права; human ~s /хью́юмэн ~с/ права человека; ~s and duties /~с энд дью́ютиз/ права и обязанности; adj правый; справедливый; правильный; adv правильно; направо; all ~ /ол ~/ ладно; ~ away /~ эвэ́й/ немедленно; interj хорошо!

rightful /ра́йтфул/ adj законный

rigid /ри́джид/ adj жесткий, непреклонный

rim /рим/ n обод(ок); оправа (очков)

ring /ринг/ n круг; кольцо; ринг; звонок; vt звонить в; vi звучать; ~ up /~ ап/ звонить по телефону

ring-finger /ри́нгфи́нгэ/ n безымянный палец

rink /ринк/ n каток

rinse /ринс/ vt полоскать

ripe /райп/ adj зрелый, спелый

rise /райз/ n подъем, повышение; восход (солнца); vi подниматься; повышаться, вставать

rival /райвл/ n соперник; vt соперничать

rivalry /ра́йвэлри/ n соперничество, конкуренция

river /ри́вэ/ n река

road /ро́уд/ n дорога, путь; ~ sign /~ сайн/ дорожный знак

road-map /ро́удмэп/ n карта автомобильных дорог

roadside /ро́удсайд/ n обочина

roadway /ро́удвэй/ n проезжая часть дороги

roast /ро́уст/ n жаркое; vti жарить(ся)

robbery /ро́бэри/ n грабеж

robe /ро́уб/ n мантия, халат

robust /рэба́ст/ adj крепкий; здравый, ясный

rock /рок/ n скала, утес; vti качать(ся), трясти(сь)

rocket /ро́кит/ n ракета

rocking-chair /ро́кингчéэ/ n кресло-качалка

role /ро́ул/ n роль

roll /ро́ул/ n рулон; булочка; vt катить; vi катиться; вращаться; ~ up /~ ап/ свертывать(ся)

roller-skates /ро́улэскэ́йтс/ n pl роликовые коньки

Roman /ро́умэн/ n римлянин; adj римский; католический; латинский; ~ Catholic /~ кэ́сэлик/ католик

romance /рэмэ́нс/ n любовная история, роман; романс

romantic /рэмэ́нтик/ adj романтический

roof /рууф/ n крыша; ~ of the mouth /~ ов зэ ма́ус/ нёбо

room /руум/ n комната; номер (гостиничный); место, пространство; make ~ for /мэйк ~ фо/ освобождать место

rooster /ру́устэ/ n петух

root /руут/ n корень

rope /ро́уп/ n веревка, канат

rot /рот/ n гниение; vi гнить

rotten /ротн/ adj гнилой; дрянной

rouge /рууж/ n румяна; vti румянить(ся)

rough /раф/ adj грубый; шершавый; неотделанный; приблизительный (подсчет); ~ copy /~ кóпи/ черновик

roughly /рáфли/ adv грубо; приблизительно

roulette /рулéт/ n рулетка

round /рáунд/ n круг; шар; обход; (спорт.) раунд; тур; выстрел; adj круглый; ~ sum /~ сам/ кругленькая сумма; adv вокруг

route /руут/ n маршрут, путь; en ~ /ан ~/ по пути

routine /рутúин/ n рутина

row /рáу/ n (разг.) ссора, скандал; vi скандалить

royal /рóйл/ adj королевский

royalty /рóйлти/ n авторский гонорар

rubber /рáбэ/ n каучук; резина; ластик; ~ stamp /~ стэмп/ штамп

rubbish /рáбиш/ n мусор, хлам; вздор

rude /рууд/ adj грубый

rug /раг/ n коврик, плед

ruin /рýин/ n гибель; pl руины; vt губить, разрушать

rule /руул/ n правило; господство, правление; as a ~ /зз э ~/ как правило; vt править, управлять; линовать; vi постановлять; ~ out /~ áут/ исключать

ruler /рýулэ/ n правитель; линейка

ruling /рýулинг/ n постановление; adj господствующий

rumour /рýумэ/ n молва, слух

run /ран/ n бег; пробег; петля на чулке; ход; ряд; in the long ~ /ин зэ лонг ~/ в конечном счете; vt управлять, вести (дела); гнать; vi бегать; бежать; течь; курсировать; работать (о машине); идти (о пьесе); ~

away /~ эвэ́й/ убегать; ~ out /~ а́ут/ выбегать;
кончаться; ~ over /~ о́увэ/ переливаться через край;
давить; ~ through /~ сруу/ бегло просматривать; ~ up
against /~ ап эгэ́йнст/ натыкаться на; ~ away /~ эвэ́й/
убегать

running /ра́нинг/ adj бегущий; текущий; ~ water /~
во́отэ/ проточная вода

runway /ра́нвэй/ n взлетно-посадочная полоса

rural /ру́эрэл/ adj сельский

rush /раш/ n наплыв; натиск; ~ hour /~ а́уэ/ час "пик";
~ order /~ о́рдэ/ срочный заказ; vt торопить; vi мчаться,
бросаться

Russian /рашн/ n русский, русская; русский язык; adj
русский

rust /раст/ n ржавчина; vi ржаветь

ruthless /ру́услис/ adj безжалостный

rye /рай/ n рожь

rye-bread /ра́йбрэд/ n ржаной хлеб

S

sable /сэйбл/ n соболь; соболий мех

sack /сэк/ n мешок; get the ~ /гет зэ ~/ быть
уволенным

sacred /сэ́йкрид/ adj святой, священный

sacrifice /сэ́крифайс/ n жертва; vt жертвовать

sad /сэд/ adj грустный, печальный; be ~ /би ~/ грустить

sadness /сэ́днис/ n грусть, печаль

safe /сэйф/ adj невредимый; безопасный; надежный; n
сейф

safeguard /сэ́йфгард/ n гарантия; охрана; vt гарантировать; охранять

safely /сэ́йфли/ adv благополучно, безопасно

safety /сэ́йфти/ n безопасность

safety pin /сэ́йфтипин/ n английская булавка

sailor /сэ́йлэ/ n матрос, моряк

saint /сэйнт/ n святой

sake /сэйк/ n: for God's ~ /фо годз ~/ ради Бога; for the ~ of /фо зэ ~ ов/ ради (кого-л., чего-л.)

salad /са́лэд/ n салат; ~ bowl /~ ба́ул/ салатница; ~ dressing /~ дре́синг/ заправка к салату

salary /са́лэри/ n жалованье, оклад

sale /сэйл/ n продажа; clearance ~ /кли́эрэнс ~/ распродажа; be for ~ /би фо ~/ продаваться; bill of ~ /бил ов ~/ закладная, купчая

salesgirl /сэ́йлзгёрл/ n продавщица

salesman /сэ́йлзмэн/ n продавец

salmon /са́мэн/ n лосось; семга

saloon /сэлу́ун/ n салон (автобуса, троллейбуса, самолета); бар, пивная

salt /соолт/ n соль; vt солить

salt cellar /со́олтсе́лэ/ n солонка

salty /со́олти/ adj соленый

salvation /сэлвэ́йшн/ n спасение; S. Army /~ а́рми/ Армия спасения

same /сэйм/ adj тот же (самый), такой же; the ~ thing /зэ ~ синг/ одно и то же; all the ~ /оол зэ ~/ все равно sample /caампл/ n образец; vt пробовать

sanction /сэнкшн/ n санкция; vt санкционировать

sand /сэнд/ n песок; pl пляж

sandwich /сэ́нвидж/ n сандвич, бутерброд

sanitary /сэ́нитэри/ adj санитарный

Santa Claus /сэ́нтэкло́оз/ n Дед Мороз

sash window /сэ́швиндоу/ n подъемное окно

satchel /сэ́чел/ n ранец

sateen /сэти́ин/ n сатин

satin /сэ́тин/ n атлас; ~ cloth /~ клос/ блестящий шерстяной материал

satisfaction /сэ́тисфэ́кшн/ n удовлетворение

satisfactory /сэ́тисфэ́ктэри/ adj удовлетворительный

satisfy /сэ́тисфай/ vt удовлетворять

Saturday /сэ́тэди/ n суббота

sauce-boat /со́осбо́ут/ n соусник

saucepan /со́оспэн/ n кастрюля

saucer /со́осэ/ n блюдце

sausage /со́сидж/ n колбаса; сосиски

save /сэйв/ vt спасать, сберегать; prep кроме

savings /сэ́йвингз/ n pl сбережения; ~ bank /~ бэнк/ сберегательный банк

saviour /сэ́йвье/ n спаситель

savour /сэ́йвэ/ n вкус; привкус; аромат; vt смаковать

savoury /сэ́йвэри/ adj вкусный

saw /соо/ n пила; vt пилить

say /сэй/ vt говорить; to ~ nothing of /ту ~ на́синг ов/ не говоря уже о

scaffolding /скэ́фэлдинг/ n леса

scale /скэйл/ n масштаб, шкала; pl весы; on a large ~ /он э лардж ~/ в большом масштабе

scandal /скэндл/ n скандал; позор; злословие

scar /скар/ n рубец, шрам

scarcely /скéэсли/ adv едва

scare /скéэ/ n испуг, паника; vt пугать

scarf /скарф/ n шарф

scarlet /скáрлит/ adj алый

scarlet fever /скáрлитфи́ивэ/ n скарлатина

scatter /скэ́тэ/ vt разбрасывать; рассеивать; vi рассеиваться; расходиться

scene /сиин/ n место действия; (театр.) сцена; зрелище

scenery /си́инэри/ n декорации; пейзаж

scent /сент/ n запах; след; нюх; духи

schedule /шéдьюл/ n расписание; vt составлять расписание

scheme /скиим/ n схема; план; интрига; vi интриговать

scholarship /скóлэшип/ n эрудиция; стипендия

school /скуул/ n школа

school-book /скýулбук/ n учебник

schoolboy /скýулбой/ n школьник

schoolgirl /скýулгёрл/ n школьница

schoolteacher /скýулти́иче/ n учитель(ница)

scientific /сáйенти́фик/ adj научный

scientist /сáйентист/ n ученый

scissors /сы́зэз/ n pl ножницы

sclerosis /склирóусис/ n склероз

scooter /скýутэ/ n мотороллер

score /скор/ n счет; зарубка; метка; два десятка; pl множество

scornful /скóрнфул/ adj презрительный

Scotch /скоч/ adj шотландский; n (разг.) шотландское виски; ~ tape /~ тэйп/ "скотч" (склеивающая лента)

scoundrel /скáундрэл/ n негодяй, подлец

scramble /скрэмбл/ n драка, схватка; vi карабкаться; ~d eggs /~д эгз/ яичница-болтунья

scream /скриим/ n вопль; vi вопить

screen /скриин/n экран; ширма; vt загораживать; демонстрировать на экране; тщательно проверять

screw /скруу/ n винт; vt завинчивать

screwdriver /скрýудрáйвэ/ n отвертка

screw nut /скрýунат/ n гайка

scrupulous /скрýупьюлэс/ adj скрупулезный, добросовестный

sculpture /скáлпче/ n скульптура; vt ваять

seal /сиил/ n печать; пломба; тюлень; морской котик; vt запечатывать, скреплять печатью

seam /сиим/ n шов; шрам

seaman /сúимэн/ n моряк

seamless /сúимлис/ adj без шва

search /сёрч/ n поиски, обыск; vt обыскивать; ~ for /~ фо/ искать

search warrant /сёрчвóрэнт/ n ордер на обыск

seashore /сúишор/ n морской берег

season /сиизн/ n время года, сезон; ~ ticket /~ тúкит/ сезонный билет; vt приправлять (пищу)

seasoning /сúизнинг/ n приправа

seat /сиит/ n сиденье, место; стул; take a ~ /тэйк э ~/ садиться; vt усаживать

second /сэ́кэнд/ adj второй; n секунда

secondary /сэ́кэндэри/ n вторичный; ~ school /~ скуул/ средняя школа

second-hand /сэ́кэндхэ́нд/ adj подержанный

secondly /сэ́кэндли/ adv во-вторых

secrecy /си́икриси/ n секретность

secret /си́икрит/ n секрет; тайна

secretary /сéкретри/ n секретарь, секретарша, министр; S. ~ of State /~ ов стэйт/ госсекретарь (США)

section /секшн/ n отдел; секция; купе

security /сикьюэ́рити/ n безопасность; social ~ /со́ушл ~/ социальное обеспечение; pl ценные бумаги

sedative /сéдэтив/ n успокаивающее средство

see /сии/ vt видеть; понимать; ~ off /~ оф/ провожать; I ~ /ай ~/ понятно; let me ~ /лет ми ~/ дай(те) подумать

seed /сиид/ n семя, зерно; vt сеять

seek /сиик/ vt искать; добиваться

seem /сиим/ vt казаться

seemingly /си́имингли/ adv по-видимому

seize /сииз/ vt хватать, схватывать

seldom /сéлдэм/ adv редко

selection /силéкшн/ n выбор

self /сэлф/ pron сам; себя; свое

self-confidence /сэ́лфкóнфидэнс/ n самоуверенность

self-control /сэ́лфкэнтрóул/ n самообладание

self-government /сэ́лфгáвнмент/ n самоуправление

selfish /сэ́лфиш/ adj эгоистичный

self-made /сэлфмэ́йд/ adj обязанный всем самому себе

self-service /сэ́лфсе́рвис/ n самообслуживание

sell /сэл/ vti продавать(ся); ~ off /~ оф/ распродавать (со скидкой)

seller /сэ́лэ/ n продавец

semi- /сэ́ми/ prefix полу-, наполовину

semicircle /сэ́мисёркл/ n полукруг

semolina /сéмэли́инэ/ n манная крупа

senate /сéнит/ n сенат

senator /сéнэтэ/ n сенатор

send /сенд/ vt посылать, отправлять

senile /сайинайл/ adj старческий

senior /си́инье/ adj старший; n пожилой человек; вышестоящий; студент старшего курса

sensation /сенсэ́йшн/ n ощущение; сенсация

sense /сенс/ n ощущение; чувство; смысл

senseless /сéнслис/ adj бессмысленный, бесчувственный

sensible /сéнсибл/ adj (благо)разумный

sensitive /сéнситив/ adj чувствительный; чуткий

sentence /сéнтэнс/ n приговор; (грам.) предложение; vt приговаривать

sentiment /сéнтимент/ n чувство

separate /сéприт/ adj отдельный; уединенный; /сéпэрэйт/ vt отделять; разлучать; vi расходиться

separation /сéпэрэйшн/ n отделение

September /септэ́мбэ/ n сентябрь

serial /си́эриэл/ adj серийный; n роман, фильм в нескольких частях

series /си́эриз/ n серия, ряд

serious /сиэриэс/ adj серьезный

servant /сёрвэнт/ n слуга, прислуга; civil~ /сивил ~/ государственный служащий

serve /сёрв/ vt служить; подавать (еду); отбывать срок (службы, наказания)

service /сёрвис/ n служба; обслуживание; сервиз; подача; active /эктив ~/ действительная военная служба

serviceman /сёрвисмэн/ n военнослужащий

serviette /сёрвиэт/ n салфетка

session /сэшн/ n сессия; заседание

set /сэт/ n комплект; декорация; сет; сервиз; аппарат; vt ставить; вставлять в оправу; vi садиться (о солнце)

settle /сэтл/ vt поселять; решать; улаживать; оплачивать (счета); ~ down /~ даун/ поселяться

settlement /сэтлмент/ n поселение; расчет

seven /сэвн/ num семь; n семерка

seventeen /сэвнтиин/ num семнадцать

seventeenth /сэвнтиинс/ ord num семнадцатый

seventh /сэвнс/ ord num седьмой; n седьмая часть

seventieth /сэвнтис/ ord num семидесятый

seventy /сэвнти/ num семьдесят

several /сэврл/ adj несколько

severe /сивиэ/ adj строгий, суровый

sew /соу/ vt шить; ~ on /~ он/ пришивать

sewer /съюэ/ n канализационная труба

sewerage /съюэридж/ n канализация

sewing /соуинг/ n шитье

sewing machine /соуингмэшиин/ n швейная машина

sex /сэкс/ n пол, секс

sexual /сэ́кшюэл/ adj половой, сексуальный

shade /шэйд/ n тень; оттенок; абажур

shadow /шэ́доу/ n тень, сумерки; vt затенять, выслеживать

shake /шэйк/ vt трясти; vi сотрясаться, дрожать; vt: ~ hands /~ хэндз/ пожимать руки

shall /шэл/ v: I (we) ~ go /ай (ви) ~ го́у/ я (мы) пойду (пойдем); you (he, she, you, they) ~ go /ю (хи, ши, ю, зэй) ~ го́у/ ты (он, она, вы, они) должен (должен, должна, должны) пойти

shallow /шэ́лоу/ adj мелкий; поверхностный, пустой

sham /шэм/ n подделка

shame /шэйм/ n стыд, позор; ~ on you! /~ он ю/ стыдно!; vt стыдить

shameful /шэ́ймфул/ adj постыдный

shameless /шэ́ймлис/ adj бесстыдный

shampoo /шэмпу́у/ n шампунь; vt мыть голову

shape /шэйп/ n форма; очертание; облик; vt придавать форму

shapeless /шэ́йплис/ adj бесформенный

share /шээ/ n доля; акция; пай; лемех; vt делить; совместно владеть; ~ a room /~ э руум/ жить в одной комнате

shareholder /шэ́эхо́улдэ/ n акционер

sharp /шарп/ adj острый; крутой (поворот); резкий (боль); колкий (замечание); adv точно

shave /шэйв/ vti брить(ся)

shaver /шэ́йвэ/ n бритва

shawl /шоол/ n шаль

she /ши/ pron она; n женщина

shed /шед/ n сарай, навес; vt ронять (листья); проливать (слезы); сбрасывать (одежду)

sheep /шиип/ n овца

sheep-dog /ши́ипдо́г/ n овчарка

sheepish /ши́ипиш/ adj застенчивый

sheepskin /ши́ипскин/ n дубленка

sheet /шиит/ n простыня; лист (бумаги, металла)

shelter /ше́лтэ/ n приют, убежище, укрытие; vt приютить, служить убежищем

shelve /шелв/ vt ставить на полку; откладывать в долгий ящик

sheriff /ше́риф/ n шериф

sherry /ше́ри/ n херес

shift /шифт/ n изменение, смена; vti перемещать(ся)

shine /шайн/ n свет; сияние; блеск; vi блестеть, светить(ся), сиять

shiny /ша́йни/ adj блестящий; лоснящийся

ship /шип/ n корабль, судно

shipment /ши́пмент/ n груз, партия (отправленного товара, погрузка, отправка)

shipper /ши́пэ/ n грузоотправитель

shirt /шёрт/ n рубашка

shiver /ши́вэ/ n дрожь; vi дрожать

shock /шок/ n потрясение, шок; удар; vt потрясать, шокировать

shoe /шуу/ n ботинок; туфля; vt обувать

shoeblack /шу́ублэк/ n чистильщик сапог

shoelace /шу́улэйс/ n шнурок для ботинок

shoepolish /шу́упо́лиш/ n крем для чистки обуви

shoot /шуут/ n росток; состязание в стрельбе; vt стрелять; расстреливать; снимать (фильм); ~ down /~ да́ун/ сбивать

shop /шоп/ n магазин, лавка; цех; vi делать покупки

shop-assistant /шо́пэси́стэнт/ n продавец, продавщица

shopkeeper /шо́пки́ипэ/ n лавочник

shoplifting /шо́пли́фтинг/ n мелкое воровство в магазине

shopper /шо́пэ/ n покупатель

shopping /шо́пинг/ n закупка продуктов; go ~ /го́у ~/ делать покупки

shopwindow /шо́пви́ндоу/ n витрина

shore /шор/ n берег

short /шорт/ adj короткий; низкого роста; I am ~ of money /ай эм ~ ов ма́ни/ у меня не хватает денег; in ~ /ин ~/ вкратце

shortage /шо́ртыдж/ n нехватка, дефицит

shortbread /шо́ртбрэ́д/ n песочное печенье

shorten /шортн/ vti укорачивать(ся), сокращать(ся)

shorthand /шо́ртхэнд/ n стенография; ~ typist /~ та́йпист/ машинистка-стенографистка

shortly /шо́ртли/ adv вскоре

shorts /шортс/ n pl шорты

shortsighted /шо́ртса́йтыд/ adj близорукий; недальновидный

short story /шо́ртсто́ри/ n рассказ

shot /шот/ n выстрел; удар

should /шюд/ v aux: I ~ go /ай ~ гóу/ я должен идти

shoulder /шóулдэ/ n плечо

shout /шáут/ n крик; vi кричать

show /шóу/ n показ; зрелище; киносеанс; спектакль; выставка

showcase /шóукейс/ n витрина

shower /шáуэ/ n ливень; град; душ; vt лить; осыпать; vi литься; сыпаться

shrewd /шрууд/ adj проницательный

shrimp /шримп/ n креветка

shrink /шринк/ vi садиться (об одежде); уменьшаться

shrubbery /шрáбери/ n кустарник

shut /шат/ vti закрывать(ся), затворять(ся); ~ off /~ оф/ выключать (воду и т.д.)

shutter /шáтэ/ n ставень; задвижка; (фото) затвор объектива

shy /шай/ adj застенчивый, робкий

shyness /шáйнис/ n застенчивость

sick /сик/ adj больной; I feel ~ /ай фиил ~/ меня тошнит

sicken /сикн/ vt вызывать тошноту

sick leave /сиклиив/ n отпуск по болезни

sickness /сикнис/ n болезнь, тошнота

side /сайд/ n сторона; бок; борт; ~ by ~ /~ бай ~/ бок о бок

sigh /сай/ n вздох; vi вздыхать

sight /сайт/ n зрение; вид; зрелище; know by ~ /нóу бай ~/ знать в лицо; see the ~s /сии зэ ~с/ осматривать достопримечательности sign /сайн/ n знак; vti подписывать(ся)

signal /сигнл/ n сигнал; vti сигнализировать

signature /сигниче/ n подпись

sign-board /сайнборд/ вывеска

significance /сигнификэнс/ n важность, значение

sign-post /сайнпоуст/ n указательный столб

silence /сайлэнс/ n молчание, тишина; vt заставить замолчать

silencer /сайлэнсэ/ n глушитель

silent /сайлэнт/ adj молчаливый; тихий

silk /силк/ n шелк; adj шелковый

sill /сил/ n подоконник; порог (двери)

silly /сили/ adj глупый

silver /силвэ/ n серебро; vt серебрить; adj серебряный

silver fox /силвэфокс/ n чернобурая лисица

silverware /силвэвэ́э/ n столовое серебро

similar /симилэ/ adj подобный, сходный

similarity /симилэ́рити/ n сходство

simmer /симэ/ vi закипать; кипеть (на медленном огне)

simplify /симплифай/ vt упрощать

simply /симпли/ adv просто

simulate /симьюлэйт/ vt симулировать

simultaneous /симлтэ́йньес/ adj одновременный

since /синс/ adv с тех пор, тому назад; с тех пор как; так как

sincere /синси́э/ adj искренний

sing /синг/ vti петь

singe /синж/ n ожог

singer /си́нгэ/ n певец, певица

single /сингл/ adj один, единственный; отдельный; холостой; ~ bed /~ бед/ односпальная кровать; ~-breasted /~ брéстыд/ однобортный; ~ room /~ рум/ комната на одного человека; ~-ticket /~ тúкит/ билет в один конец

singlet /сúнглит/ n фуфайка

sink /синк/ n (кухонная) раковина; vi погружаться, заходить (о солнце)

sip /сип/ n маленький глоток; vt пить маленькими глотками, потягивать

sir /сёр/ n сэр, господин, сударь

sirloin /сёрлойн/ n филей

sister /сúстэ/ n сестра

sister-in-law /сúстэринлóо/ n невестка, золовка, свояченица

sit /сит/ vi сидеть; ~ down /~ дáун/ садиться

site /сайт/ n местоположение; участок; строительная площадка

situated /сúтьюзэйтыд/ adj расположенный

situation /сúтьюэйшн/ n ситуация; место (работы); расположение

six /сикс/ num шесть

sixteen /сúкстúин/ num шестнадцать

sixteenth /сúкстúинс/ ord num шестнадцатый

sixth /сикс/ ord num шестой; n шестая часть

sixtieth /сúкстис/ ord num шестидесятый

sixty /сúксти/ num шестьдесят

size /сайз/ n размер, величина; объем; формат; номер (перчаток и т.п.)

skate /скейт/ n конек; vi кататься на коньках

skating rink /ске́йтингринк/ n каток

ski /скии/ n лыжа; vi ходить на лыжах

skid /скид/ vi буксовать, скользить; the car ~ed /зэ кар ~ыд/ машину занесло

skill /скил/ n мастерство, умение

skilled /скилд/ adj квалифицированный

skim /ским/ vt снимать (пенки, сливки с молока)

skin /скин/ n кожа; шкура (животного); кожура (фрукта); vt сдирать кожу, шкуру, кожуру

skinny /ски́ни/ adj тощий

skip /скип/ n прыжок; vi скакать

skirt /скёрт/ n юбка

skull /скал/ n череп

sky /скай/ n небо

skyscraper /ска́йскрэ́йпэ/ n небоскреб

slacks /слэкс/ n pl брюки

slander /сла́андэ/ n клевета; vt клеветать

slang /слэнг/ n жаргон

sleep /слиип/ n сон; go to ~ /гóу ту ~/ засыпать; vi спать

sleeper /сли́ипэ/ n спальный вагон

sleeping-draught /сли́ипингдрафт/ n снотворное

sleeping-pills /сли́ипингпилз/ n снотворные таблетки

sleeplessness /сли́иплиснис/ n бессонница

sleepy /сли́ипи/ adj сонный

sleeve /слиив/ n рукав

slice /слайс/ n ломтик, ломоть; vt резать ломтиками

sliding /сла́йдинг/ adj скользящий; ~ door /~ доор/ раздвижная дверь slight /слайт/ adj легкий, незначительный; тонкий; vt третировать, обижать

slightly /слáйтли/ adv слегка

slim /слим/ adj стройный; vi худеть

slip /слип/ n ошибка; лифчик; ~ of the pen /~ ов зэ пен/ описка; ~ of the tongue /~ ов зэ танг/ оговорка

slipper /слúпэ/ n комнатная туфля

slope /слóуп/ n наклон; косогор; откос; vt наклонить; vi иметь наклон

slot machine /слóтмэшúин/ n торговый автомат

slow /слóу/ adj медленный; тупой; the watch is ~ /зэ вотч из ~/ часы отстают

slowly /слóули/ adv медленно

slum /слам/ n трущоба

small /смоол/ adj маленький

small change /смóлчéйндж/ n мелочь

smart /смарт/ adj модный; быстрый; остроумный

smartness /смáртнис/ n нарядность; изящество; ловкость; остроумие

smashing /смáшинг/ adj сокрушительный; (разг.); решительный

smell /смел/ n запах; обоняние; нюх; vt нюхать, почуять; vi пахнуть

smile /смайл/ n улыбка; vi улыбаться

smith /смис/ n кузнец

smoke /смóук/ n дым; vt курить; коптить; vi дымить(ся)

smoker /смóукэ/ n курящий; вагон для курящих

smoking /смóукинг/ n курение; по ~ /нóу ~/ курить воспрещается smooth /смууз/ adj гладкий, ровный, плавный; vt делать ровным

smoothly /смуузли/ adv гладко, плавно

smuggle /смагл/ vt заниматься контрабандой

snack /снэк/ n закуска; ~ bar /~ бар/ закусочная, буфет

snapshot /снэпшот/ n моментальный снимок

sneakers /сниикэз/ n pl тапочки

sneer /сниэ/ n насмешка; vi насмехаться

sneeze /снииз/ n чиханье; vi чихать

snore /снор/ n храп; vi храпеть

snow /сноу/ n снег; vi: it ~s /ит ~з/ идет снег

snowdrop /сноудроп/ n подснежник

snowfall /сноуфол/ n снегопад

snowstorm /сноусторм/ n вьюга, буран

so /соу/ adv так, таким образом; настолько; итак; conj поэтому; ~-called /~ коолд/ так называемый; ~ long! /~ лонг/ пока!; ~ and ~ /~ энд ~/ такой-то; ~~ так себе

soap /соуп/ n мыло; vt намыливать

sober /соубэ/ adj трезвый; vti отрезвлять(ся)

soccer /сокэ/ n футбол

sociable /соушебл/ adj общительный

social /соушл/ adj общественный, социальный; n вечеринка

society /сэсайети/ n общество; светское общество; ассоциация

sock /сок/ n носок

socket /сокит/ n углубление; гнездо; (глазная) впадина; патрон (лампочки); (штепсельная) розетка

soda /соудэ/ n сода; ~ water /~ вуотэ/ содовая вода

sofa /со́уфэ/ n диван, софа

soft /софт/ adj мягкий, тихий (звук); ~ drinks /~ дринкс/ безалкогольные напитки

soften /софн/ vti смягчать(ся)

soldier /со́улдже/ n солдат

solicitor /сэли́ситэ/ n адвокат, стряпчий

solid /со́лид/ adj твердый; солидный; сплошной

solidity /сэли́дити/ n твердость; плотность

solitary /со́литри/ adj одинокий

solution /сэлю́юшн/ n раствор; решение

solve /солв/ vt решать

solvent /со́лвнт/ adj платежеспособный

some /сам/ adj какой-либо, какой-нибудь, какой-то, несколько; indef pron некоторые; одни, другие

somebody (someone) /са́мбэди (са́мван)/ indef pron кто-нибудь, кто-то

somehow /са́мхау/ adv как-нибудь, как-то; почему-то

something /са́мсинг/ indef pron что-либо, что-нибудь, что-то; нечто; кое-что; ~ else /~ элс/ что-то другое

sometime /са́мтайм/ adv когда-нибудь, когда-то, некогда

sometimes /са́мтаймз/ adv иногда

somewhat /са́мвот/ adv слегка, немного

somewhere /са́мвээ/ adv где-нибудь, где-то; куда-нибудь, куда-то

son /сан/ n сын

song /сонг/ n песня

son-in-law /са́нинло́у/ n зять

soon /суун/ adv вскоре, скоро; рано; as ~ as possible /эз ~ эз пóсэбл/ как можно скорее; ~er or later /~э о лэ́йтэ/ рано или поздно

soothe /сууз/ vt успокаивать

sophisticated /сэфи́стикейтыд/ adj утонченный; умудренный опытом

sore /сор/ adj больной; I've got a ~ throat /айв гот э ~ срóут/ у меня болит горло

sorrow /сóроу/ n горе, печаль, скорбь; vi горевать

sorry /сóри/ adj сожалеющий; I am ~ ! /ай эм ~/ простите!, виноват!

sort /сорт/ n сорт; вид; род; vt сортировать

soul /сóул/ n душа; upon my ~ /эпóн май ~/ честное слово

sound /сáунд/ n звук; adj здоровый, крепкий, прочный; safe and ~ /сэйф энд ~/ цел и невредим; vi звучать

soup /сууп/ n суп

soup-plate /сýупплэйт/ n глубокая тарелка

sour /сáуэ/ adj кислый (также перен.); turn ~ /тёрн ~/ прокисать; ~ milk /~ милк/ простокваша

source /соос/ n источник (также перен.)

south /сáус/ n юг; adj южный

southerly /сáзэли/, **southern** /сáзэн/ adj южный

southward /сáусвэд/ adv к югу, на юг

sovereign /сóврин/ adj монарх; соверен (монета); adj суверенный

sovereignty /сóвренти/ n суверенитет

sow /сóу/ vt сеять, засевать

soy-bean /сóйбин/ n соя; соевый боб

spa /спаа/ n курорт

space /спейс/ n пространство; космос; расстояние; промежуток (также о времени); adj космический; ~ rocket /~ рóкит/ космическая ракета

spacious /спэ́йшес/ adj просторный

spade /спейд/ n лопата

spare /спээ/ adj запасной, резервный; ~ time /~ тайм/ свободное время; ~ wheel /~ виил/ запасное колесо; vt щадить; уделять (время)

speak /спиик/ vti говорить

speaker /спи́икэ/ n оратор; диктор (радио)

special /спешл/ adj специальный; особенный; экстренный; ~ delivery /~ дили́ври/ срочная доставка

speciality /спéшиэ́лити/ n специальность

specially /спéшели/ adv специально

specific /списи́фик/ adj специфический

specification /спéсификéйшн/ n спецификация

specify /спéсифай/ vt определять

specimen /спéсимин/ n образец

spectacle /спекткл/ n зрелище; pl очки

spectator /спектэ́йтэ/ n зритель

speculate /спéкьюлэйт/ vi размышлять; спекулировать

speech /спиич/ n речь; make a ~ /мэйк э ~/ произносить речь

speed /спиид/ n скорость; at full ~ /эт фул ~/ на полной скорости; vt ускорять; vi спешить; ~ limit /~ ли́мит/ дозволенная скорость

speeding /спи́идинг/ n превышение скорости

speedometer /спидóмитэ/ n спидометр

speedy /спи́иди/ adj быстрый

spend /спенд/ vt тратить; проводить (время)

spice /спайс/ n пряность

spicy /спа́йси/ adj пряный

spirit /спи́рит/ n дух, привидение; pl спиртные напитки

spite /спайт/ n злоба; in ~ of /ин ~ ов/ вопреки; vt досаждать

splendid /спле́ндид/ adj великолепный

split /сплит/ n расщелина; раскол; vt раскалывать; расщеплять; ~ing headache /~инг хе́дэйк/ дикая головная боль

spoil /спойл/ vt портить; баловать (ребенка)

spokesman /спо́уксмэн/ n представитель

sponge /спандж/ n губка; vt мыть губкой

sponsor /спо́нсэ/ n поручатель, спонсор; vt поддерживать, субсидировать

spontaneous /спонтэ́йньес/ adj самопроизвольный, спонтанный

spool /спуул/ n катушка, шпулька

spoon /спуун/ n ложка

sport /спорт/ n спорт; (разг.) славный малый

spot /спот/ n пятно; on the ~ /он зэ ~/ на месте

sprayer /спрэ́йе/ n пульверизатор

spread /спред/ vti развертывать(ся); распространять(ся); намазывать

spring /спринг/ n весна; прыжок; пружина; рессора; источник; adj весенний; vi прыгать, пружинить

sprinkling /спри́нклинг/ n поливка

sprouts /спра́утс/ n pl брюссельская капуста

spy /спай/ n шпион; vi шпионить

square /сквээ/ n квадрат; площадь; клетка; adj квадратный; ~ foot /~ фут/ квадратный фут

square-built /сквэ́эби́лт/ adj коренастый

squash /сквош/ n давка; сок; игра в мяч (вроде тенниса); vt раздавливать

squeeze /сквииз/ vt сжимать, пожимать (руку); ~ out /~ а́ут/ выжимать

stability /стэби́лити/ n устойчивость

stable /стэйбл/ adj прочный; постоянный; n конюшня, хлев

staff /стааф/ n штат, персонал; (воен.) штаб

stage /стэйдж/ n сцена; стадия, этап; vt инсценировать, ставить

stagnation /стэгнэ́йшн/ n застой

stair /стээ/ n ступенька; pl лестница

staircase /стэ́экейс/ n лестница

stake /стэйк/ n ставка (в игре); (коммерч.) доля капитала; pl приз; be at ~ /би эт ~/ быть поставленным на карту

stall /стоол/ n ларек; (театр.) кресло в партере

stamp /стэмп/ n (почтовая) марка; штемпель; vt ставить печать

stand /стэнд/ n позиция; стоянка; стойка; киоск; остановка; vt ставить; терпеть; vi стоять, находиться; ~ in the way of /~ ин зэ вэй ов/ мешать; ~ up /~ ап/ вставать

standard /стэ́ндэд/ n стандарт; норма; образец; ~ of living /~ ов ли́винг/ жизненный уровень; ~ size /~ сайз/ стандартный размер standing /стэ́ндинг/ n положение, репутация; adj постоянный; ~ committee /~ кэми́ти/ постоянный комитет

standpoint /стэ́ндпойнт/ n точка зрения

star /стар/ n звезда

starch /старч/ n крахмал; vt крахмалить

stare /стээ/ n пристальный взгляд; vi уставиться

starter /ста́ртэ/ n стартер

startle /стартл/ vt пугать; vi вздрагивать

starvation /ставэ́йшн/ n голод; голодание

starve /старв/ vi голодать

state /стэйт/ n государство; штат; состояние; adj государственный; S. Department /~ дипа́ртмент/ Государственный департамент (США); vt заявлять; излагать

statement /стэ́йтмент/ n заявление

statesmen /стэ́йтсмэн/ n государственный деятель

station /стэ́йшн/ n вокзал; станция (радио и т.п.); остановка (автобуса)

stationery /стэ́йшнэри/ n канцелярские товары

stay /стэй/ n пребывание; vi оставаться, гостить

steak /стейк/ n стейк, бифштекс

steal /стиил/ vt воровать, красть

stealing /сти́илинг/ n кража

steam /стиим/ n пар; vt варить на пару

steel /стиил/ n сталь; adj стальной

steering /сти́эринг/ n управление; ~ wheel /~ виил/ руль

step /степ/ n шаг; ступенька; pl стремянка; take ~s /тэйк ~с/ принимать меры; vi шагать stepchild /стéпчайлд/ n пасынок; падчерица

stepfather /стéпфáазэ/ n отчим

stepmother /стéпмáзэ/ n мачеха

sterile /стéрайл/ adj бесплодный; стерильный

stew /стьюю/ n тушеное мясо; vti тушить(ся)

stewardess /стьюóдис/ n (ам.) стюардесса

stick /стик/ n палка, vt втыкать; vi липнуть; ~ to /~ ту/
придерживаться; ~ out /~ áут/ высовывать(ся)

sticking plaster /стúкингплáастэ/ n липкий пластырь

sticky /стúки/ adj клейкий, липкий

still /стил/ adj тихий, неподвижный; adv до сих пор,
еще, однако

stitch /стич/ vt стежок; петля; шов; vt шить; ~ up /~ ап/
зашивать

stock /сток/ n запас; акция; in ~ /ин ~/ в наличии; vt
иметь в продаже; снабжать

stock-broker /стóкбрóукэ/ n биржевой маклер

stock exchange /стóкискчéйндж/ n фондовая биржа

stockholder /стóкхóулдэ/ n акционер

stocking /стóкинг/ n чулок

stock-jobbing /стóкджóбинг/ n биржевые сделки

stomach /стáмэк/ n желудок; живот

stone /стóун/ n камень; косточка (в ягодах); adj
каменный

stool /стуул/ n табуретка

stop /стоп/ n остановка; vt останавливать; прекращать;
пломбировать (зуб)

stopper /стóпэ/ n пробка; затычка

stopping /стóпинг/ n зубная пломба

storage /стóоридж/ n хранение; склад

store /стор/ n запас; магазин; универмаг; vt хранить (на складе), запасать

store-room /стóорум/ n кладовая

storey /стóори/ n этаж

storm /сторм/ n буря, vi бушевать

story /стóори/ n рассказ

story-teller /стóоритэ́лэ/ n рассказчик

stout /стáут/ adj прочный; стойкий; дородный

stove /стóув/ n печка; печь; плита

straight /стрэйт/ adj прямой; adv прямо; ~ away /~ эвэ́й/ сразу

strain /стрэйн/ n напряжение; переутомление; vi напрягаться, переутомляться

strange /стрэйндж/ adj странный; чужой, незнакомый

strategy /стрэ́тиджи/ n стратегия

strawberry /стрóобери/ n земляника, клубника

stream /стриим/ n поток, течение; vi струиться

streamlined /стри́имлайнд/ adj обтекаемый; хорошо налаженный

street /стриит/ n улица

streetcar /стри́иткар/ n трамвай

strength /стренгс/ n сила

strengthen /стрéнгсен/ vti усиливать(ся)

stress /стрес/ n напряжение; vt подчеркивать

stretch /стреч/ n растягивание, протяжение; vt вытягивать; ~ one's legs /~ ванз легз/ разминать ноги

strew /струу/ vt разбрасывать, усыпать

strict /стрикт/ adj строгий

strike /страйк/ n удар; забастовка; vt бить, ударять; vi бастовать; бить (о часах)

striking /стра́йкинг/ adj поразительный

string /стринг/ n веревка; шнурок; ~ of pearls /~ ов пёрлз/ нитка жемчуга; vt нанизывать

strip /стрип/ n полоска; vt сдирать; раздевать; vi раздеваться

striped /страйпт/ adj полосатый

stroke /стро́ук/ n удар; поглаживание (рукой)

strong /стронг/ adj сильный, крепкий; прочный

stronghold /стро́нгхоулд/ n крепость, твердыня, оплот

structure /стра́кче/ n структура; устройство

struggle /страгл/ n борьба; vi бороться

stubborn /ста́бэн/ adj упрямый, упорный

student /стью́юдэнт/ n студент(ка)

study /ста́ди/ n изучение; очерк; этюд; кабинет; vt изучать; vi учиться

stuff /стаф/ n вещество, материал; начинять; засовывать

stuffing /ста́финг/ n начинка

stuffy /ста́фи/ adj душный

stupid /стью́юпид/ adj глупый

stupidity /стьюпи́дити/ n глупость

stupor /стью́юпэ/ n оцепенение

stutter /ста́тэ/ n заикание; vi заикаться

style /стайл/ n стиль, фасон

stylish /ста́йлиш/ adj модный, шикарный

subconscious /сабко́ншес/ adj подсознательный

subdivide /са́бдива́йд/ vt подразделять

subdue /сэбдьюю/ vt подчинять

subject /сáбджикт/ adj подчиненный; подверженный; подвластный; подлежащий; n подданный; предмет, тема; субъект; /сэбджéкт/ vt подчинять; подвергать

sub-let /сáблéт/ vt передавать в субаренду

submit /сэбмúт/ vt представлять (на рассмотрение); vi подчиняться

subordinate /сэбóрднит/ adj подчиненный; /сэбóрдинэйт/ vt подчинять

subpoena /сэбпúинэ/ n повестка в суд; vt вызывать в суд под угрозой штрафа

subscribe /сэбскрáйб/ vt жертвовать деньги; ~ to /~ ту/ подписываться на

subscriber /сэбскрáйбэ/ n подписчик

subsequent /сáбсиквент/ adj последующий

subsidiary /сэбсúдьери/ adj вспомогательный

subsidize /сáбсидайз/ vt субсидировать

subsistence /сэбсúстнс/ n существование; средства к жизни

substantial /сэбстэ́ншл/ adj существенный; питательный

substitute /сáбститьют/ n заместитель, заменитель; vt замещать, заменять

sub-tenant /сáбтэ́нэнт/ n субарендатор

subtract /сэбтрэ́кт/ vt вычитать

suburb /сáбёб/ n пригород

subway /сáбвэй/ n метро

succeed /сэксúид/ vi добиваться, преуспевать; ~ to /~ ту/ наследовать; vt следовать за

success /сэксэ́с/ n удача, успех

successful /сэксэ́сфул/ adj удачный, успешный; преуспевающий

successor /сэксэ́сэ/ n преемник, наследник

such /сач/ adj такой; ~ as /~ эз/ как например

sudden /садн/ adj внезапный

suede /свейд/ n замша

suffer /сáфэ/ vi страдать

sufficient /сэфи́шнт/ adj достаточный

suffrage /сáфридж/ n избирательное право

sugar /шýгэ/ n сахар

sugar-basin /шýгэбéйсин/ n сахарница

suggestion /сэджéсчн/ n предложение

suit /съюют/ n костюм; (юрид.) иск; тяжба; ухаживание; vt устраивать; быть удобным; быть к лицу; vi ладиться; подходить

suitable /съю́ютэбл/ adj подходящий

suit-case /съю́юткейс/ n чемодан

sum /сам/ n сумма, итог; do ~s /ду ~з/ решать задачи; vt: ~ up /~ ап/ подводить итог

summarize /сáмэрайз/ vt резюмировать

summary /сáмэри/ adj суммарный; n резюме

summer /сáмэ/ n лето

summons /сáмэнз/ n вызов (в суд)

sun /сан/ n солнце

sunburn /сáнбён/ n загар; vi греться на солнце

Sunday /сáнди/ n воскресенье

sunflower /сáнфлáуэ/ n подсолнечник

sunrise /сáнрайз/ n восход солнца

sunset /са́нсэт/ n закат

sunshine /са́ншайн/ n солнечный свет

superfluous /съюпёёфлуэс/ adj (из)лишний

superintendent /съюопринтéндэнт/ n управляющий; старший (полицейский) офицер

superior /съюпи́эриэ/ adj высший, превосходящий; n начальник

supermarket /съюопэма́ркит/ n универсам

supervise /съюопэвайз/ vt наблюдать за; руководить; надзирать за

supervision /съюопэви́жн/ n надзор; руководство

supper /са́пэ/ n ужин

supplement /са́плимент/ n дополнение, приложение; vt дополнять

supply /сэпла́й/ n поставка, снабжение; pl запасы, продовольствие; ~ and demand /~ энд дима́анд/ спрос и предложение; vt поставлять, снабжать

support /сэпо́рт/ n поддержка, опора; vt поддерживать; содержать

supporter /сэпо́ртэ/ n сторонник

suppose /сэпбуз/ vt предполагать

suppress /сэпрéс/ vt подавлять; замалчивать (истину)

supreme /съюпри́им/ adj верховный

sure /шу́э/ adj уверенный; верный

surface /сёрфис/ n поверхность

surgeon /сёрджн/ n хирург

surname /сёрнэйм/ n фамилия

surplus /сёрплэс/ adj избыточный; n излишек

surprise /сэпра́йз/ n удивление; неожиданность; сюрприз; vt удивлять

surround /сэра́унд/ vt окружать

surroundings /сэра́ундингз/ n pl окрестности

survive /сэва́йв/ vt оставаться в живых, выживать

suspect /са́спект/ adj подозрительный; /сэспе́кт/ vt подозревать

suspenders /сэспе́ндэз/ n pl подтяжки

suspicious /сэспи́шес/ adj подозрительный

sustenance /са́стинэнс/ n пища; средства к существованию

swab /своб/ n швабра; (мед.) тампон

swaddling clothes /сво́длингкло́увз/ n pl пеленки

swallow /сво́лоу/ n ласточка; глоток; vt глотать

swear /свэ́э/ vi клясться; ругаться; ~ in /~ ин/ приводить к присяге

sweat /свет/ n пот; vi потеть

sweater /све́тэ/ n свитер

sweet /свиит/ adj сладкий; душистый; милый; n конфета, сладкое

sweeten /свиитн/ vt подслащивать

sweetheart /сви́итхарт/ n возлюбленный, дорогой

swelling /све́линг/ n опухоль

swift /свифт/ adj быстрый; ~ car /~ кар/ быстроходный автомобиль

swim /свим/ vi плавать, плыть

swimming /сви́минг/ n плавание; ~ pool /~ пуул/ плавательный бассейн

swindler /сви́ндлэ/ n мошенник, плут

swing /свинг/ n размах, качели; in full ~ /ин фул ~/ в полном разгаре; vti качать(ся), колебать(ся)

swing-door /свингдор/ n вращающаяся дверь

switch /свич/ n прут; (эл.) выключатель; vt переключать; ~ off /~ оф/ выключать; ~ on /~ он/ включать

switchboard /свичборд/ n коммутатор

swollen /своулэн/ adj раздутый

sympathize /симпэсайз/ vi сочувствовать

syringe /сириндж/ n шприц; disposable ~ /диспоузэбл ~/ одноразовый шприц

syrup /сирэп/ n сироп

systematic /систимэтик/ adj систематический

T

table /тэйбл/ n стол; доска; таблица; расписание

table-cloth /тэйблклос/ n скатерть

table-spoon /тэйблспуун/ n столовая ложка

table-ware /тэйблвээ/ n столовая посуда

tablet /тэблит/ n таблетка

tactful /тэктфул/ adj тактичный

tactless /тэктлис/ adj бестактный

tactics /тэктикс/ n тактика

tag /тэг/ n ярлык, этикетка; бирка

tail /тэйл/ n хвост; пола; фалда

tailor /тэйлэ/ n портной

take /тэйк/ vt брать; принимать (ванну, лекарство); занимать (место, время); ~ care of /~ кээр ов/ заботиться о; ~ charge of /~ чардж ов/ брать на себя

ответственность за; ~ off /~ оф/ (vt) снимать; (vi)
взлетать; ~ out /~áут/ вынимать; приглашать (в театр
и т.д.); ~ part in /~ парт ин/ участвовать в; ~ place /~
плэйс/ иметь место; ~ up /~ ап/ браться за

tale /тэйл/ n рассказ, повесть, сказка; tell ~s /тэл ~з/
сплетничать

talk /тоок/ n разговор; pl переговоры; vi говорить

talkative /тóокэтив/ adj болтливый

tall /тоол/ adj высокий

tame /тэйм/ adj ручной, приручённый; vt приручать,
укрощать

tan /тэн/ adj рыжевато-коричневый; n загар; vt дубить;
vi загорать

tap /тэп/ n лёгкий стук; кран; затычка; vt стукать

tape /тэйп/ n лента; тесьма; плёнка; ~ recorder /~
рикóрдэ/ магнитофон

tariff /тэ́риф/ n тариф

tart /тарт/ adj кислый, терпкий; n торт, пирог

task /тааск/ n задача, задание; urgent ~ /ёрджент ~/
неотложное дело

taste /тэйст/ n вкус; ~s differ /~с дúфэ/ о вкусах не
спорят; vt пробовать, отведать; vi иметь вкус

tasteful /тэ́йстфул/ adj сделанный со вкусом

tasteless /тэ́йстлис/ adj безвкусный

tax /тэкс/ n налог; vt облагать налогом

taxable /тэ́ксэбл/ adj подлежащий обложению
налогом

taxation /тэксэ́йшн/ n обложение налогом

tax collector /тэ́кскэлéктэ/ n сборщик налогов

tax-free /тэ́ксфрйи/ adj освобожденный от уплаты налогов

taxi /тэ́кси/ n такси; ~ stand /~ стэнд/ стоянка такси

taxpayer /тэ́кспэ́йе/ n налогоплательщик

tea /тии/ n чай

tea bag /ти́ибэг/ n мешочек с заваркой чая

teach /тиич/ vt учить, преподавать

teacher /ти́ичэ/ n учитель(ница), преподаватель(ница)

teacup /ти́икап/ n чайная чашка

team /тиим/ n команда; бригада;

teapot /ти́ипот/ n чайник для заварки

tear /тээ/ vt рвать, разрывать; vi рваться; ~ apart /~ эпа́рт/ разрывать на части; ~ off /~ оф/ отрывать

tear /ти́э/ n слеза; ~ gas /~ гэс/ слезоточивый газ

tearoom /ти́ирум/ n кафе-кондитерская

tea set /ти́исет/ n чайный сервиз

tea-spoon /ти́испу́ун/ n чайная ложка

teddy bear /тэ́дибэ́э/ n плюшевый медвежонок

tedious /ти́идьес/ adj скучный, неприятный

teenager /ти́инэ́йдже/ n подросток

teens /тиинз/ n pl возраст от 13 до 19 лет; she is still in her ~ /ши из стил ин хэ́ ~/ ей еще нет 20

telephone /тэ́лифоун/ n телефон; ~ booth /~ буус/ телефонная будка; vt звонить по телефону

television /тэ́ливижн/ n телевидение; ~ set /~ сэт/ телевизор

tell /тэл/ vt рассказывать, говорить; приказывать; отличать; vi сказываться (на)

teller /тэ́лэ/ n рассказчик; кассир

temper /тэ́мпэ/ n нрав; настроение; гнев; loose one's ~ /лууз ванз ~/ выходить из себя

temperature /тэ́мпричэ/ n температура

temporary /тэ́мпэрэри/ adj временный

ten /тен/ num десять; n десяток; (карты) десятка

tenancy /тéнэнси/ n аренда, наем

tenant /тéнэнт/ n арендатор; наниматель; съемщик; жилец

tend /тенд/ vt ухаживать за; vi иметь склонность

tendency /тéндэнси/ n тенденция, склонность

tenement /тéнимент/ n арендуемое помещение (имущество, земля, квартира); ~ house /~ хáус/ многоквартирный дом, сдаваемый в аренду

tension /теншн/ n напряжение

tenth /тенс/ ord num десятый; n десятая часть

term /тёрм/ n термин; срок; период; семестр; pl условия; be on good ~s /би он гуд ~з/ быть в хороших отношениях; come to ~s /кам ту ~з/ приходить к соглашению

terminal /тёрминл/ adj конечный; n конечная станция

terminate /тёрминэйт/ vi кончаться, истекать

terrible /тéрэбл/ adj ужасный

territory /тéритри/ n территория; сфера

terror /тéрэ/ n ужас; террор

test /тест/ n испытание; проба; экзамен; ~ tube /~ тьююб/ пробирка; vt испытывать

textbook /тэ́кстбук/ n учебник

textile /тéкстайл/ n текстильное изделие, ткань; adj текстильный

than /зэн/ conj чем; rather ~ /páазэ ~/ скорее чем

thank /сэнк/ vt благодарить; ~ you! /~ ю/ спасибо!

thanks /сэнкс/ n pl благодарность; ~ to /~ ту/ благодаря

that /зэт/ pron тот, та, то, который, кто; conj что, чтобы;
in order ~ /ин óрдэ ~/ для того, чтобы; adv так, до такой
степени

the /зыы/ - полная форма; /зэ/ - редуцированная
форма; определенный артикль, в русском языке
эквивалента не имеет; all ~ better /оол ~ бéтэ/ тем
лучше; ~ more ~ better /~ мор ~ бéтэ/ чем больше, тем
лучше

theater /сúэтэ/ n театр

theft /сефт/ n кража

their /зśе/ adj, theirs /зśез/ poss pron их, свой и т.д.

them /зэм/ pron их, им и т.д.

themselves /зэмсśлвз/ pron себя и т.д., сами и т.д.

then /зэн/ adv тогда, потом, затем

theory /сúэри/ n теория

there /зśе/ adv там, туда; ~ is /~ из/, ~ are /~ аа/ есть

thereafter /зэерáафтэ/ adv с того времени

thereby /зśебáй/ adv тем самым

therefore /зśефо/ adv поэтому

thermometer /сэмóмитэ/ n термометр

thermos /сśрмэс/ n термос

these /зыыз/ adj, pron эти

they /зэй/ pron они

thick /сик/ adj толстый; густой

thicken /сикн/ vti сгущать(ся); утолщать(ся)

thief /сииф/ n вор

thigh /сай/ n бедро

thimble /симбл/ n наперсток

thin /син/ adj тонкий; редкий (о волосах); жидкий; vi худеть, редеть

thing /синг/ n вещь; the only ~ /зэ óунли ~/ единственное

think /синк/ vti думать, мыслить; ~ over /~ óувэ/ обдумывать

thinker /сúнкэ/ n мыслитель

third /сёрд/ ord num третий

thirst /сёрст/ n жажда; vi жаждать; be ~y /би ~и/ хотеть пить

thirteen /сёртúин/ num тринадцать

thirteenth /сёртúинс/ ord num тринадцатый

thirtieth /сёртис/ ord num тридцатый; n тридцатая часть

thirty /сёрти/ num тридцать

this /зыс/ adj, pron этот; эта, это; ~ way /~ вэй/ сюда, вот так

thorough /сáрэ/ adj тщательный, основательный

thoroughfare /сáрэфээ/ n проезд, проход; магистраль

throughly /сáрэли/ adv вполне; тщательно

those /зóуз/ adj, pron те

though /зóу/ conj хотя; несмотря на

thought /соот/ n мысль

thoughtful /сóотфул/ adj задумчивый; заботливый

thousand /сáузэнд/ num, n тысяча

thousandth /сáузэнс/ ord num тысячный; n тысячная часть

thread /сред/ n нитка; нить (также образн.)

threadbare /срéдбээ/ adj потертый; (образн.) избитый

threat /срет/ n угроза

threaten /сретн/ vt угрожать

three /срии/ num три; n тройка

threshold /срéшоулд/ n порог

thrift /срифт/ n бережливость

thrifty /сри́фти/ adj экономный

thriller /сри́лэ/ n сенсационная книга или пьеса; (кино) боевик

thrive /срайв/ vi преуспевать

throat /сро́ут/ n горло

through /сруу/ prep через; сквозь; из-за; adv от начала до конца; I am wet ~ /ай эм вет ~/ я насквозь промок; adj прямой (поезд)

throughout /сруáут/ adv везде; во всех отношениях

throw /сро́у/ n бросок; vt бросать, кидать; метать; ~ aside /~ эсáйд/ отбрасывать; ~ back /~ бэк/ отвергать; ~ off /~ оф/ сбрасывать; свергать; ~ out /~ áут/ выгонять; ~ up /~ ап/ извергать; вскидывать

thumb /сам/ n большой палец (руки)

thunder /сáндэ/ n гром; vi греметь; it ~s /ит ~з/ гром гремит

thunderstorm /сáндэстом/ n гроза

Thursday /сёёзди/ n четверг

thus /зас/ adv так, таким образом

ticket /ти́кит/ n билет; ярлык

ticket-collector /ти́киткэлéктэ/ n контролер

tide /тайд/ n: high ~ /хай ~/ прилив; low ~ /лóу ~/ отлив

tidy /тáйди/ adj опрятный

tie /тай/ n галстук; family ~s /фэ́мили ~з/ семейные узы;
  vt связывать, завязывать; ограничивать

tie-pin /та́йпин/ n булавка для галстука

tiger /та́йгэ/ n тигр

tight /тайт/ adj тугой; тесный

tighten /тайтн/ vti натягивать(ся); сжимать(ся)

tights /тайтс/ n pl трико; колготки

tile /тайл/ n черепица; кафель; ~d floor /~д флор/
  кафельный пол; ~d roof /~д рууф/ черепичная крыша

till /тил/ vt возделывать; prep до; ~ then /~ зэн/ до тех
  пор

timber /ти́мбэ/ n лесоматериал, (строевой) лес

time /тайм/ n время; срок; период; ~ and again /~ энд
  эгэ́йн/ неоднократно; at no ~ /эт но́у ~/ никогда; at the
  same ~ /эт зэ сэйм ~/ в то же время; from ~ to ~ /фром
  ~ ту ~/ время от времени; in ~ /ин ~/ вовремя; have a
  good ~ /хэв э гуд ~/ хорошо проводить время; what ~ is
  it? /вот ~ из ит/ который час?

timetable /та́ймтэ́йбл/ n расписание

timid /ти́мид/ adj робкий

tin /тин/ n олово; жесть; консервная банка

tinfoil /ти́нфойл/ n оловянная фольга

tin-opener /ти́но́упэнэ/ n консервный нож

tiny /та́йни/ adj крошечный

tip /тип/ n верхушка; кончик; чаевые; vt давать на чай

tiptoe /ти́птоу/ n цыпочки; on ~ /он ~/ на цыпочках

tipsy /ти́пси/ adj подвыпивший

tip-top /ти́пто́п/ adv превосходно

tire /та́йе/ n шина

tired /та́йед/ adj усталый

tiresome /та́йесэм/ adj утомительный; надоедливый

tissue /ти́сью/ n ткань; бумажный носовой платок

title /тайтл/ n заглавие; титул; звание; vt называть; озаглавливать

to /ту/ prep в, на, к; ~ and fro /~ энд фро́у/ туда и сюда; a quarter ~ three /э кво́ртэ ~ срии/ без четверти три; ~ my mind /~ май майнд/ по моему мнению; ~ the right /~ зэ райт/ направо; the road ~ New York /зэ ро́уд ~ нью йорк/ дорога в Нью-Йорк; ~ order /~ о́рдэ/ на заказ

toast /то́уст/ n гренок; тост; vt поджа́ри́вать (хлеб); пить за здоровье

toaster /то́устэ/ n тостер

tobacconist /тэбэ́кэнист/ n торговец табачными изделиями

today /туд э́й/ adv сегодня, в наше время

toddler /то́длэ/ n ребенок, начинающий ходить

toe /то́у/ n палец ноги

toffee /то́фи/ n тоффи (конфета типа ириса)

together /тэгэ́зэ/ adv вместе, сообща

toil /тойл/ n тяжелый труд; vi трудиться

toilet /то́йлит/ n туалет, уборная

toilet paper /то́йлитпэ́йпэ/ n туалетная бумага

token /то́укн/ n подарок на память; знак; символ; as a ~ of /эз э ~ ов/ в знак

tolerate /то́лерейт/ vt терпеть, допускать

tolerance /то́лернс/ n терпимость

toll /то́ул/ n пошлина; ~ bridge /~ бридж/ платный мост

tomato /тэма́атоу/ n помидор

tomorrow /тэмо́роу/ adv завтра

ton /тан/ n тонна

tone /то́ун/ n тон

tongs /тонгз/ n pl щипцы; клещи

tongue /танг/ n язык

tonight /тэна́йт/ adv сегодня вечером

tonsilitis /то́нсила́йтис/ n тонзилит; воспаление миндалин

too /туу/ adv также, тоже; слишком

tool /туул/ n инструмент; станок; орудие (также образн.)

tooth /туус/ n (pl teeth) зуб; false teeth /фоолс тиис/ вставные зубы

toothache /ту́усэйк/ n зубная боль

toothbrush /ту́усбраш/ n зубная щетка

toothpaste /ту́успэйст/ n зубная паста

toothpick /ту́успик/ n зубочистка

top /топ/ n верх; верхушка (дерева); вершина (горы); макушка (головы); волчок; ~ secret /~ си́икрит/ совершенно секретно; from ~ to bottom /фром ~ ту бо́тэм/ сверху донизу; on ~ of /он ~ ов/ сверх; adj верхний, высший

topic /то́пик/ n предмет, тема

topical /то́пикэл/ adj актуальный; тематический; ~ question /~ квесчн/ актуальный вопрос

tornado /тонэ́йдоу/ n ураган

total /то́утл/ adj весь, тотальный; n итог

touch /тач/ n прикосновение; контакт; штрих; примесь; чуточка; a ~ of the sun /э ~ ов зэ сан/ легкий солнечный удар; keep in ~ with /киип ин ~ виз/ поддерживать контакт с; vt трогать, касаться

touching /та́чинг/ adj трогательный

touchy /та́чи/ adj обидчивый

tough /таф/ adj жесткий; крепкий; трудный

tour /ту́э/ n поездка, турне; vt совершать турне по

tourist /ту́эрист/ n турист(ка); ~ agency /~ э́йдженси/ бюро путешествий

towards /тэвбо́дз/ prep к, по направлению к; по отношению к; около; для

towel /та́уэл/ n полотенце

tower /та́уэ/ n башня; вышка

town /та́ун/ n город

town hall /та́унхбол/ n ратуша

townsfolk /та́унзфоук/ n горожане

townsman /та́унзмэн/ n горожанин

toy /той/ n игрушка; vi играть

trace /трэйс/ n след; vt прослеживать, калькировать

trade /трэйд/ n торговля; ремесло; профессия; vi торговать

trade-mark /трэ́йдмарк/ n фабричная марка

trader /трэ́йдэ/ n торговец

trade union /трэ́йдъюбюньен/ n профсоюз

tradition /трэди́шн/ n традиция; предание

traffic /трэ́фик/ n движение (любого транспорта); транспорт; торговля; ~ jam /~ джэм/ "пробка"; ~ lights /~ лайтс/ светофор

trailer /трэ́йлэ/ n прицеп

train /трэйн/ n поезд; (спорт.) тренировать

training /трэ́йнинг/ n обучение; тренировка

tranquil /трэ́нквил/ adj спокойный

transaction /трэнзэ́кшн/ n дело, сделка

transcend /трэнсе́нд/ vt переступать пределы

transcript /трэ́нскрипт/ n копия

transfer /трэ́нсфё/ n перенос, перемещение; /трэнсфё́р/ vt переносить, перемещать

transform /трэнсфо́рм/ vt превращать

transformation /трэ́нсфэмейшн/ n превращение

transistor /трэнси́стэ/ n транзистор

transit /трэ́нсит/ n транзит; ~ visa /~ ви́изэ/ транзитная виза

translation /трэнслэ́йшн/ n перевод; трансляция

translator /трэнслэ́йтэ/ n переводчик, переводчица

transmitter /трэнзми́тэ/ n передатчик

transparent /трэнспэ́эрент/ adj прозрачный

transplant /трэнспла́ант/ vt пересаживать

transplantation /трэ́нсплантэйшн/ n трансплантация

transport /трэ́нспот/ n транспорт; /трэнспо́рт/ vt перевозить

trap /трэп/ n ловушка, западня, капкан; vt ловить (в ловушку)

travel /трэ́вл/ n путешествие; vi путешествовать

traveller /трэ́влэ/ n путешественник; ~'s cheque /~з чек/ дорожный чек

treasure /тре́же/ n клад, сокровище; vt ценить, дорожить

treasurer /тре́жрэ/ n казначей

treasury /тре́жри/ n казна; сокровищница

treat /триит/ n угощение; удовольствие; (разг.) очередь платить за угощение; this is my ~ /зыс из май ~/ сегодня я угощаю; vt угощать; (мед.) лечить

treaty /трийти/ n договор

tree /трии/ n дерево; родословная

tremendous /тримéндэс/ adj громадный; потрясающий

tremor /трéмэ/ n дрожь, трепет

trend /тренд/ n направление, тенденция

trespasser /трéспэсэ/ n нарушитель

trial /трáйел/ n испытание, судебный процесс; on ~ /он ~/ под судом

triangle /трáйэнгл/ n треугольник

trick /трик/ n уловка, обман; трюк; vt обманывать

trifle /трайфл/ n мелочь, пустяк

trim /трим/ adj опрятный; vt подрезать; отделывать (платье); подравнивать (волосы)

trimming /трúминг/ n отделка (на платье); приправа (к еде); pl обрезки

trip /трип/ n поездка; экскурсия

triumphant /трайáмфэнт/ adj торжествующий; ликующий

trolley /трóли/ n тележка

troop /трууп/ n отряд; pl войска

tropical /трóпикл/ adj тропический

trouble /трабл/ n забота; хлопоты; беспокойство; беда; неприятность; беспорядки; авария; неисправность; take the ~ /тэйк зэ ~/ брать на себя труд; get into ~ /гет úнту ~/ попадать в беду

trousers /трáузэз/ n pl брюки

truck /трак/ n грузовик

true /труу/ adj подлинный; правильный; верный; ~ copy /~ ко́пи/ точная копия

truly /тру́ули/ adv правдиво, искренне; yours ~ /йооз ~/ искренне ваш (в конце письма)

trunk /транк/ n ствол (дерева); туловище; чемодан; pl трусы; swimming ~s /сви́минг ~с/ плавки

trunk-call /тра́нкко́ол/ n вызов по междугороднему телефону

trust /траст/ n доверие; трест; кредит; vt доверять; поручать; vi надеяться

trustee /трасти́и/ n опекун

trustworthy /тра́ствёзи/ adj надежный

truth /труус/ n истина, правда

truthful /тру́усфул/ adj правдивый

try /трай/ n попытка; испытание; vt испытывать; пробовать; судить; vi пытаться; ~ on /~ он/ примерять (одежду)

tube /тьююб/ n труба; трубка; тюбик

tuberculosis /тьюбёкьюло́усиз/ n туберкулез

Tuesday /тьюю́зди/ n вторник

tuition /тьюи́шш/ n обучение; плата за обучение

tulip /тьюю́лип/ n тюльпан

tumor /тьюю́мэ/ n опухоль; malignant ~ /мэли́гнэнт ~/ злокачественная опухоль

tune /тьююн/ n мелодия

tuner /тьюю́нэ/ n настройщик

tunnel /танл/ n туннель

turkey /тёрки/ n индюк, индюшка

turn /тёрн/ n поворот; очередь; перемена; take a ~ for the better /тэйк э ~ фо зэ бéтэ/ принимать благоприятный оборот; by ~s /бай ~з/ по очереди; vt вращать; поворачивать; заворачивать (за угол); перелицовывать (платье); ~ back /~ бэк/ поворачивать назад; ~ down /~ дáун/ отклонять; ~ inside out /~ инсайд áут/ выворачивать наизнанку; ~ off /~ оф/ закрывать (кран); выключать (свет); ~ on /~ он/ открывать (кран); включать (свет); ~ to /~ ту/ обращаться к; приниматься за; vi появляться, приходить

turning /тёрнинг/ n поворот; перекресток; ~ point /~ пойнт/ поворотный пункт

turnip /тёрнип/ n репа

turtle /тёртл/ n черепаха

turtleneck /тёртлнэк/ n высокий воротник (свитера); свитер с воротником "хомут"

tutor /тьюютэ/ n репетитор; vt обучать, давать уроки

tweed /твиид/ n твид

tweezers /твийиззз/ n pl пинцет

twelfth /твелфс/ ord num двенадцатый

twelve /твелв/ num двенадцать

twentieth /твéнтис/ ord num двадцатый

twenty /твéнти/ num двадцать

twice /твайс/ adv дважды

twin /твин/ n близнец

two /туу/ num два, две; n двойка, двое, пара; put ~ and ~ together /пут ~ энд ~ тэгéзэ/ понять, что к чему

type /тайп/ n тип; класс; род; шрифт; vt печатать на машинке

typewriter /та́йпра́йтэ/ n пишущая машинка
typical /ти́пикл/ adj типичный
typist /та́йпист/ n машинистка
tyre /та́йе/ n шина, покрышка

U

ulcer /а́лсэ/ n язва
ultimate /а́лтимит/ adj конечный; окончательный
umbrella /амбрэ́лэ/ n зонтик
unable /а́нэ́йбл/ adj неспособный; be ~ /би ~/ быть не в
   состоянии
unanimous /юнэ́нимэс/ adj единодушный,
   единогласный
unauthorized /а́но́осэрайзд/ adj неправомочный
unavoidable /а́нэвойдэбл/ adj неизбежный
unbreakable /а́нбрэ́йкэбл/ adj небьющийся
unbutton /анба́тн/ vt расстегивать
uncertain /ансэ́ртн/ adj неуверенный
unchangeable /анче́йнджебл/ adj неизменный
uncle /анкл/ n дядя
uncomfortable /анка́мфэтэбл/ adj неудобный
unconditional /а́нкэнди́шенл/ adj безоговорочный
unconscious /анко́ншес/ adj бессознательный
unconventional /а́нкэнве́ншенл/ adj нешаблонный
uncover /анка́вэ/ vt открывать
undeniable /а́ндина́йебл/ adj неоспоримый
under /а́ндэ/ prep под; ниже; меньше чем; при;
   согласно; ~ the condition /~ зэ кэнди́шн/ при условии
under-age /а́ндэрэ́йдж/ adj несовершеннолетний

undercut /а́ндэкат/ n вырезка (часть туши)

underestimate /а́ндэрэ́стимейт/ vt недооценивать

undergo /а́ндэгоу/ vt подвергаться; испытывать, переносить

undergraduate /а́ндэгра́дьюит/ n студент(ка)

underground /а́ндэграунд/ adj подземный; подпольный; n метрополитен; подполье

underline /а́ндэлайн/ vt подчеркивать

underskirt /а́ндэскёт/ n нижняя юбка

understand /а́ндэстэ́нд/ vt понимать

understanding /а́ндэстэ́ндинг/ n понимание; come to an ~ /кам ту эн ~/ найти общий язык

undertaking /а́ндэтэ́йкинг/ n предприятие; обязательство

underwear /а́ндэвэ́э/ n нижнее белье

undesirable /а́ндиза́йерэбл/ adj нежелательный

undo /анду́у/ vt развязывать; расстегивать

undoubted /анда́утыд/ adj несомненный

undress /андрэ́с/ vti раздевать(ся)

unearned /анёрнд/ adj незаработанный; ~ income /~ и́нкэм/ непроизводственный доход

uneasy /ани́изи/ adj беспокойный; неловкий

uneatable /ани́итэбл/ adj несъедобный

unemployed /а́нимпло́йд/ adj безработный

unemployment /а́нимпло́ймент/ n безработица; ~ benefit /~ бе́нефит/ пособие по безработице

uneven /ани́ивн/ adj неровный; нечетный

unexpected /а́никспе́ктыд/ adj неожиданный

unfair /анфэ́э/ adj несправедливый

unfamiliar /áнфэми́лье/ adj незнакомый

unforeseen /áнфоси́ин/ adj непредвиденный

unfortunately /анфо́рчнитли/ adv к несчастью

unfriendly /анфре́ндли/ adj недружелюбный

unfurnished /анфёрништ/ adj без мебели

ungrateful /ангрэ́йтфул/ adj неблагодарный

ungrounded /áнгра́ундыд/ adj беспочвенный

unhappy /анхэ́пи/ adj несчастливый, несчастный

unhealthy /анхэ́лси/ adj нездоровый

unhurt /áнхёрт/ adj невредимый

uniform /ю́юнифом/ adj единообразный; n форменная одежда

unimportant /áнимпо́ртэнт/ adj неважный

uninsured /áниншу́эд/ adj незастрахованный

unintentional /áнинтэ́ншнл/ adj непреднамеренный

union /ю́юньен/ n союз; объединение

unique /юни́ик/ adj уникальный

unit /ю́юнит/ n единица; воинская часть

united /юна́йтыд/ adj соединенный, объединенный; U. Nations /~ нэ́йшнз/ Организация Объединенных Наций

universal /ю́юнивёрсл/ adj всеобщий; всемирный; универсальный

university /ю́юнивёрсити/ n университет

unjust /áнджа́ст/ adj несправедливый

unkind /анка́йнд/ adj недобрый, злой

unknown /áннóун/ adj неизвестный

unlawful /анло́офул/ adj незаконный

unless /энлéс/ conj если не

unlikely /анлáйкли/ adj маловероятный; adv вряд ли

unlimited /анлúмитыд/ adj безграничный

unlucky /анлáки/ adj несчастливый

unmarried /áнмэ́рид/ adj холостой; незамужняя

unnatural /аннэ́чрл/ adj неестественный, противоестественный

unnecessary /аннэ́сисри/ adj ненужный

unnoticed /аннóутист/ adj незамеченный

unpack /анпэ́к/ vt распаковывать

unpleasant /анплézнт/ adj неприятный

unpopular /анпóпьюлэ/ adj непопулярный

unprofitable /анпрóфитэбл/ adj невыгодный; нерентабельный

unreasonable /анрúизнэбл/ adj безрассудный

unreliable /áнрилáйебл/ adj ненадежный

unselfish /ансэ́лфиш/ adj бескорыстный

unskilled /áнскúлд/ adj неквалифицированный

unsociable /ансóушебл/ adj необщительный

unstable /анстэ́йбл/ adj неустойчивый

until /энтúл/ prep до, до сих (тех) пор; not ~ /нот ~/ не раньше; conj (до тех пор), пока

untrained /áнтрэ́йнд/ adj необученный

unusual /анъю́южуэл/ adj необыкновенный

unwell /анвэ́л/ adj нездоровый; he's ~/хииз ~ / ему нездоровится

unwrap /анрэ́п/ vt развертывать

up /ап/ adj идущий вверх; time is ~ /тайм из ~/ время истекло; adv наверху, вверху; наверх, вверх; ~ to /~

ту/ вплоть до; prep вверх по, вдоль по; ~ the street /~ зэ стриит/ по улице

upbringing /а́пбри́нгинг/ n воспитание

upholster /апхо́улстэ/ vt обивать (мебель)

upon /эпо́н/ prep на; ~ my soul! /~ май со́ул/ клянусь!

upper /а́пэ/ adj верхний, высший; ~ floor /~ флор/ верхний этаж

uppermost /а́пэмоуст/ adj самый верхний; наивысший

upset /апсе́т/ vt опрокидывать; расстраивать; нарушать; огорчать

upside down /а́псайда́ун/ adv вверх дном

upstairs /а́пстэ́эз/ adv наверху, в верхнем этаже

up-to-date /а́птэдэ́йт/ adj современный

uptown /а́птаун/ n жилые кварталы города

upward /а́пвэд/ adj двигающийся вверх, направленный вверх

urban /ёрбэн/ adj городской

urgent /ёрджент/ adj настоятельный; срочный

urine /ю́эрин/ n моча

urn /ёрн/ n урна

us /ас/ pron нас, нам и т.д.

usage /ю́юзидж/ n употребление, обычай

use /ююс/ n польза; употребление, it's no ~ /итс но́у ~/ бесполезно; make ~ of /мэйк ~ ов/ использовать; /ююз/ vt употреблять, пользоваться, применять

used /ююзд/ adj привыкший; подержанный; использованный; get ~ to /гет ~ ту/ привыкать к

useful /ю́юсфул/ adj полезный

usher /а́ше/ n билетер; швейцар

usual /ю́южуэл/ adj обыкновенный, обычный; as ~ /эз
~/ как обычно

utensil /юте́нсл/ n посуда, утварь

utility /юти́лити/ n полезность; public ~s /па́блик ~з/
предприятия общественного пользования

utilize /ю́ютилайз/ vt использовать

utmost /а́тмоуст/ adj предельный; величайший; do one's
~ /ду ванз ~/ делать все возможное

utter /а́тэ/ adj совершенный, абсолютный; vt
произносить, издавать (звук)

utterance /а́тэрэнс/ n высказывание

V

vacancy /вэ́йкэнси/ n вакансия

vacation /вэке́йшн/ n каникулы, отпуск

vaccinate /вэ́ксинэйт/ vt делать прививку

vacuum cleaner /вэ́кьюэмкли́инэ/ n пылесос

vacuum flask /вэ́кьюэмфла́аск/ n термос

vague /вейг/ adj неясный, смутный

vain /вейн/ adj напрасный; тщетный; тщеславный;
самодовольный; in ~ /ин ~/ тщетно

valise /вэли́из/ n саквояж

valuable /вэ́льюэбл/ adj ценный, дорогой

valuables /вэ́льюэблз/ n pl ценности

value /вэ́лью/ n ценность; стоимость; цена; значение; vt
оценивать; дорожить

van /вэн/ n фургон; авангард

vanilla /вэни́лэ/ n ваниль

variaty /вэра́йети/ n разнообразие; ~ show /~ шоу/ варьете

various /вэ́эриэс/ adj различный, разный

varnish /ва́рниш/ n лак; лоск; vt лакировать

vary /вэ́эри/ vti менять(ся); vi отличаться

vast /вааст/ adj громадный; обширный

veal /виил/ n телятина

vegetable /ве́джитбл/ n овощ; adj растительный

vegetarian /ве́джитэ́эриэн/ n вегетарианец

vehicle /виикл/ n перевозочное средство; повозка; автомашина

vein /вейн/ n вена; жила

velocity /вило́сити/ n скорость

velvet /ве́лвит/ n бархат

veneer /вини́э/ n фанера

ventilator /ве́нтилэйтэ/ n вентилятор

venture /ве́нче/ n рискованное предприятие; joint ~ /джойнт ~/ совместное предприятие; vt рисковать; vi отваживаться

verge /вёрдж/ n край; обочина (дороги); on the ~ of /он зэ ~ ов/ на грани; vi: ~ on /~ он/ граничить с

verification /ве́рифике́йшн/ n проверка; подтверждение

verify /ве́рифай/ vt проверять, подтверждать

versed /вёрст/ adj опытный

version /вёршн/ n версия; вариант

vertical /вёртикл/ adj вертикальный

very /ве́ри/ adj настоящий; (тот) самый; adv очень; ~ much /~ мач/ очень много

vet /вет/ n (разг.) ветеринар

veterinary /ве́тринэри/ adj ветеринарный

vibrate /вайбрэ́йт/ vi вибрировать

vicinity /висинити/ n окрестности; соседство; in the ~ of /ин зэ ~ ов/ поблизости

victim /виктим/ n жертва

victor /виктэ/ n победитель

video recorder /видиоурикордэ/ n видеомагнитофон

video tape /видиоутэйп/ n видеолента

view /вьюю/ n вид; мнение; in ~ of /ин ~ ов/ ввиду

viewpoint /вьюпойнт/ n точка зрения

village /вилидж/ n деревня, село

villager /вилиджэ/ n деревенский житель

vinegar /винигэ/ n уксус

vineyard /виньед/ n виноградник

violate /вайелэйт/ vt нарушать (закон); применять насилие

violent /вайелэнт/ adj насильственный; неистовый; сильный

violet /вайелит/ n фиалка; adj фиолетовый; лиловый

virtual /вёртьюэл/ adj фактический

virtuous /вёртьюэс/ adj добродетельный

virus /вайерэс/ n вирус

visa /визэ/ n виза

visibility /визибилити/ n видимость

visible /визэбл/ adj видимый; очевидный

visit /визит/ n визит, посещение; vt посещать

visitor /визитэ/ n гость, посетитель

visual /вижьюэл/ adj наглядный; зрительный

vital /вайтл/ adj жизненно важный, насущный

vocabulary /вэкэбьюлэри/ n словарь, запас слов

vocation /вокейшн/ n призвание; профессия

voice /войс/ n голос

volume /вóльюм/ n том; объем

voluntary /вóлэнтэри/ adj добровольный

volunteer /вóлэнти́э/ n доброволец; vi предлагать (свою помощь, услуги)

vote /вóут/ n голос; голосование; vi голосовать

voter /вóутэ/ n избиратель

voting paper /вóутингпэ́йпэ/ n избирательный бюллетень

voucher /вáуче/ n расписка; квитанция

vow /вáу/ n клятва, обет; vi клясться, давать обет

vulnerable /вáлнэрэбл/ adj уязвимый

W

waffle /вофл/ n вафля

wage(s) /вэйдж(из)/ n заработная плата; vt вести; ~ war /~ вор/ вести войну

waist /вэйст/ n талия

waistcoat /вэ́йскоут/ n жилет

wait /вэйт/ vti ждать

waiter /вэ́йтэ/ n официант

waiting room /вэ́йтингру́м/ n зал ожидания; приемная

waitress /вэ́йтрис/ n официантка

wake /вэйк/ vt будить; vi просыпаться

walk /воок/ n ходьба; походка; прогулка пешком; go for a ~ /гóу фор э ~/ гулять; vi идти; ходить; гулять; ~ about /~ эбáут/ прогуливаться

wall /воол/ n стена

wallpaper /вóолпэ́йпэ/ n обои

wallet /во́лит/ n бумажник

walnut /во́олнэт/ n грецкий орех

want /вонт/ n нужда; недостаток; pl потребности; vt хотеть; нуждаться в; недоставать; wanted /во́нтыд/ требуется... (в объявлениях)

war /вор/ n война; W. Office /~ о́фис/ военное министерство (Англии)

ward /ворд/ n палата (госпиталя); опека; подопечный;

wardrobe /во́рдроуб/ n гардероб

wardship /во́рдшип/ n опека

warehouse /вэ́эхаус/ n склад

wares /вэээ/ n pl изделия, товары

warm /ворм/ adj теплый; сердечный; горячий; I'm ~ /айм ~/ мне тепло

warmth /вормф/ n теплота; сердечность

warning /во́рнинг/ n предупреждение

warrant /во́рэнт/ n ордер; полномочие; гарантия; vt гарантировать

wart /ворт/ n бородавка

wash /вош/ vti мыть(ся); умывать(ся); стирать (одежду); ~ away /эвэ́й/ смывать(ся); ~ up /~ ап/ мыть посуду; n мытье; стирка

washbasin /во́шбейсн/ n умывальная раковина

washing /во́шинг/ n мытье; стирка; белье; ~ machine /~ мэши́ин/ стиральная машина

waste /вэйст/ vt тратить; терять (время); портить; n излишняя трата; отбросы; отходы

waste pipe /вэ́йстпайп/ n сточная труба

watch /воч/ n часы, наблюдение; vt следить за, сторожить; ~ out /~ áут/ берегись!

water /вóотэ/ n вода; vt поливать

waterfall /вóотэфол/ n водопад

watermelon /вóотэмéлэн/ n арбуз

waterproof /вóотэпруф/ adj водонепроницаемый

water supply /вóотэсэплáй/ n водоснабжение

watertight /вóотэтайт/ adj герметический

wave /вэйв/ n волна; vt махать (рукой, платком и т.д.); завивать (волосы)

way /вэй/ n дорога; направление; манера; способ; образ действий; by the ~ /бай зы ~/ кстати; be in the ~ /би ин зы ~/ мешать; make ~ /мэйк ~/ уступать

wayside /вэ́йсайд/ n обочина; adj придорожный

we /вии/ pron мы

weak /виик/ adj слабый; болезненный; ~ point /~ пойнт/ слабое место; ~ tea /~ тии/ жидкий чай

weaken /виикн/ vt ослаблять; vi слабеть

weakness /вийкнис/ n слабость

wealth /вэлф/ n богатство, изобилие

wealthy /вэлфи/ adj богатый

weapon /вэпн/ n оружие

wear /вээ/ n носка; одежда; lady's ~ /лэ́йдиз ~/ женская одежда; vt носить (одежду); ~ out /~ áут/ изнашивать(ся)

weariness /ви́эринис/ n усталость; скука

weather /вэ́зэ/ n погода

weather forecast /вэ́зэфóркаст/ n прогноз погоды

wedding /вéдинг/ n свадьба

wedding dress /вéдингдрэс/ n подвенечное платье

wedding ring /вéдингринг/ n обручальное кольцо

Wednesday /вéнзди/ n среда

week /виик/ n неделя; ~'s wage /~с вэйдж/ недельный заработок

weekday /вúикдэй/ n будний день

weekend /вúикэнд/ n уикэнд

weigh /вей/ vt взвешивать

weight /вейт/ n вес

welcome /вэлкэм/ n приветствие; (радушный) прием; adj желанный; vt приветствовать, (радушно) принимать; ~! добро пожаловать

welfare /вэлфээ/ n благосостояние; пособие по безработице; ~ state /~ стэйт/ государство всеобщего благосостояния

well /вэл/ adj хороший; здоровый; all is ~ /оол из ~/ все в порядке; I'm ~ /айм ~/ я чувствую себя хорошо; adv хорошо; вполне; очень

well-being /вэлбúинг/ n благополучие

well-bred /вэлбрэд/ adj воспитанный

west /вэст/ n запад; adj западный; adv на запад, к западу

western /вэстэрн/ adj западный; n вестерн

wet /вет/ adj мокрый, влажный; ~ fish /~ фиш/ свежая рыба; соленая рыба; "~ paint" /~ пэйнт/ осторожно, окрашено!; ~ through /~ сруу/ промокший до нитки

what /вот/ pron что, сколько, какой; ~ for? /~ фо/ зачем?

whatever /вотэвэ/, whatsoever /вóтсоуэвэ/ adj какой бы ни, любой; pron что бы ни; все, что; ~ he says /~ хи сэз/ что бы он ни говорил

wheat /виит/ n пшеница

wheel /виил/ n колесо; руль; vt катить, везти

wheel-chair /вйилчéэ/ n кресло-каталка

when /вэн/ adv, conj когда

whence /вэнс/ adv откуда

whenever /вэнэ́вэ/ conj когда бы ни; ~ you like /~ ю лайк/ в любое время

where /вээ/ adv, conj где, куда

whereabouts /вэ́эрэба́утс/ adv где, в каких краях; n местонахождение

whereas /вэ́эрэз/ conj тогда как

whereby /вэ́эбай/ adv посредством чего

wherefore /вэ́эфор/ adv для чего; conj по той причине, что

wherein /вээрúн/ adv в чем?

whereupon /вэ́эрэпóн/ conj после чего

wherever /вээрэ́вэ/ conj где бы ни

whether /вэ́зэ/ conj ли; ~ it's true or not /~ итс труу о нот/ правда ли это или нет

which /вич/ pron, conj который; что; adj какой

whichever /вичэ́вэ/ pron какой бы ни, какой угодно

while /ваил/ n время, промежуток времени; for a ~ /фор э ~/ на время

whisker /вúскэ/ n pl бакенбарды; усы; усики (у животных)

whisper /вúспэ/ n шепот; vt шептать

whistle /висл/ n свист; свисток; vi свистеть

white /вайт/ adj белый; седой (о волосах); n белый цвет; белизна; белок (глаза, яйца); turn ~ /тёрн ~/ бледнеть

who /хуу/ pron кто; тот, кто; который

whoever /хуэ́вэ/ pron, conj кто бы ни

whole /хо́ул/ adj весь, целый; n целое; on the ~ /он зэ ~/ в целом

wholesale /хо́улсэйл/ adj оптовая торговля; adv оптом

whom /хуум/ pron кого, которого

whose /хууз/ pron чей, чья, чье, чьи; которого, которой, которых

why /вай/ adv почему; interj ну!

wicked /ви́кид/ adj злой

wide /вайд/ adj широкий; adv повсюду

widespread /ва́йдспрэд/ adj распространенный

widen /вайдн/ vt расширять

widow /ви́доу/ n вдова

widower /ви́доуэ/ n вдовец

width /видф/ n ширина

wife /вайф/ n жена

wild /вайлд/ adj дикий

will /вил/ n воля; сила воли; завещание; vt велеть, хотеть; v aux: служит для образования будущего времени

willingly /ви́лингли/ adv охотно

win /вин/ n выигрыш, победа; vti выигрывать, побеждать

wind /винд/ n ветер

window /ви́ндоу/ n окно

windowsill /ви́ндоусил/ n подоконник

window pane /ви́ндоупэйн/ n оконное стекло

windscreen /ви́нскрин/ n ветровое/переднее стекло; ~ wiper /~ ва́йпэ/ "дворник" windy /ви́нди/ adj ветреный

wine /вайн/ n вино

wineglass /ва́йнглас/ n рюмка

wing /винг/ n крыло; флигель

wink /винк/ vi моргать

winner /ви́нэ/ n победитель

winter /ви́нтэ/ n зима

wipe /вайп/ vt вытирать; стирать

wire /ва́йе/ n проволока; vt телеграфировать

wisdom /ви́здэм/ n мудрость

wise /вайз/ adj мудрый

wish /виш/ n желание; best ~es /бест ~из/ наилучшие пожелания; vti желать; ~ a Happy New Year /~ э хэ́пи нью йее/ поздравлять с Новым Годом

with /виз/ prep с, вместе; у; при

withdraw /виздро́о/ vt отдергивать; брать назад; vi удаляться

withhold /визхо́улд/ vt удерживать

within /визы́н/ prep в, внутри; в пределах; в течение; ~ a year /~ э йее/ в течение года

without /виза́ут/ prep без, вне, за; do ~ /ду ~/ обходиться без; ~ fail /~ фэйл/ непременно

witness /ви́тнис/ n свидетель; свидетельство; vt быть свидетелем; заверять (подпись)

wolf /вулф/ n волк

woman /ву́мэн/ n женщина

womb /вуум/ n (анат.) матка

wonder /ва́ндэ/ n чудо; no ~ /но́у ~/ неудивительно; vi интересоваться

wonderful /ва́ндэфул/ adj чудесный

wood /вуд/ n лес; дерево (материал); дрова

wooden /вудн/ adj деревянный

woodshed /вудшед/ n сарай

wool /вул/ n шерсть

woollen /вулин/ adj шерстяной

word /вёрд/ n слово

work /вёрк/ n работа; труд; произведение; pl завод; out of ~ /áут ов ~/ безработный; vi работать, действовать; выйти, удаться; ~ over /~ óувэ/ перерабатывать

worker /вёркэ/ n рабочий

working day /вёркингдэй/ n рабочий день

workshop /вёркшоп/ n мастерская

world /вёрлд/ n мир, свет

worldwide /вёрлдвайд/ adj всемирный

worry /вáри/ n беспокойство; vi беспокоиться

worse /вёрс/ adj худший; adv хуже

worst /вёрст/ adj наихудший; adv хуже всего

worth /вёрс/ n стоимость; ценность; adj стóящий; be ~ /би ~/ стоить

wound /вуунд/ n рана; vt ранить

wrap /рэп/ vt завертывать; запутывать; ~ it up /~ ит ап/ заверните

wrapper /рэпэ/ n обертка

wrist /рист/ n запястье

wrist watch /риствóч/ n наручные часы

writ /рит/ n повестка

write /райт/ vti писать; ~ down /~ дáун/ записывать; ~ off /~ оф/ вычеркивать

writer /рáйтэ/ n писатель

writing /ра́йтинг/ n писание; in ~ /ин ~/ в письменной форме

writing paper /ра́йтингпэ́йпэ/ n писчая бумага

wrong /ронг/ adj неправильный; не тот; изнаночный; ~ side out /~ сайд а́ут/ наизнанку; ~ side up /~ сайд ап/ вверх дном

wrongly /ро́нгли/ adv неверно

X

xerox /зи́эрокс/ n ксерокс; vt размножать на ксероксе

Xmas /кри́смэс/ n Рождество

X-ray /э́ксрэ́й/ n рентгеновский луч; vt делать рентген

Y

yacht /йот/ n яхта

Yankee /йэ́нки/ n американец, американка; янки; adj американский

yard /ярд/ n двор; склад; ярд (мера)

yarn /ярн/ n пряжа

yawn /йоон/ n зевок; vi зевать

year /йее/ n год; this ~ /зыс ~/ в этом году

yeast /йиист/ n дрожжи

yellow /йе́лоу/ adj желтый

yesterday /йе́стэди/ adv вчера; the day before ~ /зэ дэй бифо́ ~/ позавчера

yet /йет/ adv еще; все еще; as ~ /эз ~/ до сих пор; not ~ /нот ~/ еще нет; conj однако

yield /йиилд/ n урожай; доход; vt приносить (доход, результат и т.п.)

yoghurt /йо́гёт/ n йогурт, простокваша

yolk /йо́ук/ n желток

you /ю́ю/ pron ты, вы

young /янг/ adj молодой; ~ people /~ пиипл/ молодежь

younger /я́нгэ/ adj младший

youngster /я́нгстэ/ n мальчик, юноша

your /йоо/ poss pron твой, ваш

yours /йо́оз/ pron твой, ваш; ~ faithfully /~ фэ́йсфули/ с
   уважением (в конце письма); ~ sincerely /~ синси́зли/
   искренне Ваш

yourself /йосэ́лф/ pron сам, себя (2 л., ед. ч.); you are not
   ~ /ю а нот ~/ ты сам не свой

yourselves /йосэ́лвз/ pron сами, себя (2 л., мн.ч.)

youth /ю́юс/ n молодость, юность; юноша; молодежь

Z

zero /зи́эроу/ n нуль

zip fastener /зи́пфа́аснэ/ n застежка-молния

zone /зо́ун/ n зона

zoo /зуу/ n зоопарк

ГЕОГРАФИЧЕСКИЕ НАЗВАНИЯ

Abu Dhabi /эбу́уда́аби/ г. Абу-Даби

Accra /экра́а/ г. Аккра

Addis Ababa /э́дисэ́бэбэ/ г. Аддис-Абеба

Adriatic Sea /э́йдриэ́тиксйи/ Адриатическое море

Afghanistan /эфгэ́нистэн/ Афганистан

Africa /э́фрикэ/ Африка

Alabama /э́лэбэ́мэ/ Алабама

Alaska /элэ́скэ/ Аляска

Albania /элбэ́йнье/ Албания

Algeria /элджи́эриэ/ Алжир

Algiers /элджи́эз/ г. Алжир

Al Kuwait /элкувэ́йт/ г. Эль-Кувейт

Alma Ata /а́алмээта́а/ г. Алма-Ата

Alps /элпс/ Альпы

Altai /элтэ́ай/ Алтай

Amazon /э́мэзэн/ р. Амазонка

America /эме́рикэ/ Америка

Amman /эма́ан/ г. Амман

Amsterdam /э́мстэдэ́м/ г. Амстердам

Andes /э́ндииз/ Анды

Andorra /эндо́рэ/ Андорра

Angola /энгэ́улэ/ Ангола

Ankara /э́нкэрэ/ г. Анкара

Antarctic Continent /энта́рктикко́нтинент/ Антарктида

Antigua and Barbuda /энти́игээнбарбу́удэ/ Антигуа и
    Барбуда

Apennines /э́пинайнз/ Апеннины

Appalachian Mountains, Appalachians /эпэлэ́йчьен
  ма́унтинз, эпэлэ́йчьенз/ Аппалачские горы,
  Аппалачи

Arabian Sea /эрэ́йбьенси́и/ Аравийское море

Archangel /а́ркéйнджл/ = Arkhangelsk

Arctic Ocean /а́рктикэ́ушн/ Северный Ледовитый океан

Arctic Region /а́рктикри́иджн/ Арктика

Argentina /а́аржентиʹинэ/ Аргентина

Arizona /э́ризэунэ/ Аризона

Arkansas /а́ркэнсо/ Арканзас (река и штат)

Arkhangelsk /арха́ангильск/ г. Архангельск

Armenia /арми́инье/ Армения

Ashkhabad /э́шкэба́ад/ г. Ашхабад

Asia /э́йше/ Азия

Asia Minor /э́йшема́йнэ/ п-ов Малая Азия

Asunción /эсу́нсиэ́ун/ г. Асунсьон

Athens /э́финз/ г. Афины

Atlanta /этлэ́нтэ/ г. Атланта

Atlantic City /этлэ́нтикси́ти/ г. Атлантик-Сити

Atlantic Ocean /этлэ́нтикэ́ушн/ Атлантический океан

Australia /острэ́йлье/ Австралия

Austria /о́стриэ/ Австрия

Azerbaijan /э́зэбайджа́ан/ Азербайджан

Azov, Sea of /си́иэвэ́аазов/ Азовское море

Bab el Mandeb /бэ́белмэ́ндэб/ Баб-эль-Мандебский
  пролив

Bag(h)dad /бэгдэ́д/ г. Багдад

Bahrain, Bahrein /бэрэ́йн/ Бахрейн

Baikal /байка́ал/ оз. Байкал

Baku /баку́у/ г. Баку

Balkan Peninsula /бба́олкэнпини́нсьюлэ/ Балканский п-ов

Baltic Sea /бба́олтикси́и/ Балтийское море

Baltimore /бба́олтимор/ г. Балтимор

Bamako /бама́аку́у/ г. Бамако

Bangkok /бэнгко́к/ г. Бангкок

Bangladesh /ба́нглэдэ́ш/ Бангладеш

Barents Sea /ба́аренцси́и/ Баренцево море

Basra /ба́зрэ/ г. Басра

Beirut /бейру́ут/ г. Бейрут

Belfast /бе́лфаст/ г. Белфаст

Belgium /бе́лджем/ Бельгия

Belgrade /белгрэ́йд/ г. Белград

Bengal, Bay of /ба́йэвбенгба́ол/ Бенгальский залив

Benin /бени́ин, бе́нин/ Бенин

Bering Sea /бе́рингси́и/ Берингово море

Bering Strait /бе́рингстрэ́йт/ Берингов пролив

Berlin /бёли́н/ г. Берлин

Bermuda Islands, Bermudas /бемью́юдэа́йлэндз, бемью́юдэз/ Бермудские о-ва

Bhutan /бута́ан/ Бутан

Biscay, Bay of /ба́йэвбискэ́й/ Бискайский залив

Bishkek /бишке́к/ г. Бишкек

Black Sea /блэ́кси́и/ Черное море

Bogota /бо́гэута́а/ г. Богота

Bolivia /бэли́виэ/ Боливия

Bombay /бомбэ́й/ г. Бомбей

Bonn /бон/ г. Бонн

Borneo /бóрниэу/ о-в Борнео; см. Kalimantan

Bosporus /бóспэрэс/ Босфор

Boston /бóстэн/ г. Бостон

Botswana /ботсвáанэ/ Ботсвана

Brazil /брэзúл/ Бразилия

Brazzaville /брэ́ззэвил/ г. Браззавиль

Britain /бритн/ см. Great Britain

Brunei /брунэ́й/ Бруней

Brussels /браслз/ г. Брюссель

Bucharest /бьюкэрéст/ г. Бухарест

Budapest /бьюдэпéст/ г. Будапешт

Buenos Aires /буэ́нэсáйриз/ г. Буэнос-Айрес

Bulgaria /балгэ́эриэ/ Болгария

Burma /бёрмэ/ Бирма

Burundi /бурýнди/ Бурунди

Byelorussia /бьéлэрáше/ Белоруссия

Cairo /кáйэрэу/ г. Каир

Calcutta /кэлкáтэ/ г. Калькутта

California /кэ́лифóрнье/ Калифорния

Cambridge /кéймбридж/ г. Кембридж

Cameroon /кэ́мерун/ Камерун

Canada /кэ́нэдэ/ Канада

Canberra /кэ́нбэрэ/ г. Канберра

Cape of Good Hope /кéйпэвгýдхэуп/ мыс Доброй Надежды

Cape Town, Capetown /кéйптаун/ г. Кейптаун

Cape Verde Islands /кéйпвёёдáйлэндз/ Острова Зеленого Мыса

Caracas /кэрэ́кэс/ г. Каракас

Caribbean (Sea) /кэ́риби́эн(си́и)/ Карибское море

Carpathian Mountains, Carpathians /карпэ́йфьенма́унтынз, карпэ́йфьенз/ Карпатские горы, Карпаты

Caspian Sea /кэ́спиэнси́и/ Каспийское море

Caucasus, the /ко́окэсэс/ Кавказ

Cayenne /кэйе́н/ г. Кайенна

Central African Republic /сэ́нтрэлэ́фрикэнрипа́блик/ Центральноафриканская Республика

Central America /сэ́нтрэлэмэ́рикэ/ Центральная Америка

Chad /чэд/ Чад

Chad, Lake /лэ́йкчэ́д/ озеро Чад

Channel, the /чэнл/ см. English Channel

Chicago /шика́агэу/ г. Чикаго

Chile /чи́ли/ Чили

China /ча́йнэ/ Китай

Chomolungma /че́умэлу́нгма/ Джомолунгма; см. Everest

Chuckchee Sea /чу́кчиси́и/ Чукотское море

Colombia /кэло́мбиэ/ Колумбия (страна)

Colombo /кэла́мбэу/ г. Коломбо

Colorado /ко́лэра́адэу/ Колорадо

Columbia /кэла́мбиэ/ Колумбия (город и река)

Conakry /ко́нэкри/ г. Конакри

Congo, the /ко́нгэу/ р. Конго

Connecticut /кэнэ́тикет/ Коннектикут

Copenhagen /кэ́упнхэ́йгн/ г. Копенгаген

Corsica /ко́рсикэ/ о-в Корсика

Costa Rica /кóстэри́икэ/ Коста-Рика

Cote d'Ivoire /кэ́утдивуа́ар/ Кот-д'Ивуар

Crete /криит/ о-в Крит

Crimea, the /крайми́э/ Крым

Cuba /кью́юбэ/ Куба

Cumberland /кáмбелэнд/ Камберленд

Cyprus /сáйпрэс/ Кипр

Czechoslovakia /чéкэслэвэ́к이э/ Чехо-Словакия

Dacca /дэ́кэ/ г. Дакка

Dakar /дэ́кэ/ г. Дакар

Damascus /дэмáаскэс/ г. Дамаск

Danube /дэ́ньюб/ р. Дунай

Dardanelles /дáрдэнэ́лз/ пролив Дарданеллы

Dar es Salaam /дáрэссэлáам/ г. Дар-эс-Салам

Delhi /дэ́ли/ г. Дели

Denmark /дэ́нмарк/ Дания

District of Columbia /дíстриктэвкэлáмбиэ/ Округ
Колумбия

Dnieper /дни́ипэ/ р. Днепр

Dniester /дни́истэ/ р. Днестр

Dominican Republic /дэмíникэнрипáблик/
Доминиканская Республика

Don /дон/ р. Дон

Dover, Strait of /стрэ́йтэвдэ́увэ/ Па-де-Кале

Dublin /дáблин/ г. Дублин

Dushanbe /дьюшáамбэ/ г. Душанбе

Ecuador /э́квэдóр/ Эквадор

Edinburgh /э́динбэрэ/ г. Эдинбург

Egypt /и́иджипт/ Египет

Elbe /элб/ р. Эльба

Elbrus, Elbruz /элбру́уз/ Эльбрус

El Salvador /элса́лвэдор/ Сальвадор

England /и́нглэнд/ Англия

English Channel /и́нглишчэ́нл/ Ла-Манш

Equatorial Guinea /э́квэто́ориэлги́ни/ Экваториальная
  Гвинея

Estonia /эсто́унье/ Эстония

Ethiopia /и́ифиэ́упье/ Эфиопия

Eton /иитн/ г. Итон

Euphrates /юфрэ́йтиз/ р. Евфрат

Europe /ю́эрэп/ Европа

Everest /э́верест/ Эверест

Falkland Islands /фо́оклэнда́йлэндз/ Фолклендские о-ва

Federal Republic of Germany /фе́дерл
  рипа́бликэвджёрмэни/ Федеративная Республика
  Германия, ФРГ

Finland /фи́нлэнд/ Финляндия

Florence /фло́рэнс/ г. Флоренция

Florida /фло́ридэ/ Флорида

Formosa /фомэ́усэ/ Формоза; см. Taiwan

France /фраанс/ Франция

Gabon, Gaboon /гэбо́н, гэбу́ун/ Габон

Gambia /гэ́мбиэ/ Гамбия

Ganges /гэ́нджиз/ р. Ганг

Geneva /джини́ивэ/ г. Женева

Genoa /дже́нэуэ/ г. Генуя

Georgetown /джо́джтаун/ г. Джорджтаун

Georgia I /джо́оджье/ Джорджия (штат США)

Georgia II /джо́оджье/ Грузия

Germany /джёрмэни/ Германия

Ghana /га́анэ/ Гана

Gibraltar /джибро́олтэ/ Гибралтар

Glasgow /гла́асгэу/ г. Глазго

Gobi, the /гэ́уби/ Гоби

Great Britain /грэ́йтбри́тн/ Великобритания

Greece /гриис/ Греция

Greenland /гри́инлэнд/ Гренландия

Guadeloupe /гва́адэлу́уп/ Гваделупа

Guatemala /гвэ́тима́алэ/ Гватемала

Guinea /ги́ни/ Гвинея

Guinea-Bissau /ги́нибиса́у/ Гвинея-Бисау

Guyana /гайа́анэ/ Гайана

Hague, The /хейг/ г. Гаага

Haiti /хе́ити/ Гаити

Hamburg /хэ́мбёрг/ г. Гамбург

Hanoi /хэно́й/ г. Ханой

Havana /хэвэ́нэ/ г. Гавана

Havre /хаавр/ г. Гавр

Hawaii /хава́йи/ Гавайи (острова и штат)

Helsinki /хе́лсинки/ г. Хельсинки

Himalaya(s), the /хи́мэлэ́йе(з)/ Гималаи, Гималайские
  горы

Hindustan /хи́ндуста́ан/ п-ов Индостан

Hiroshima /хиро́шимэ/ г. Хиросима

Ho Chi Minh /хэ́учи́ими́н/ г. Хошимин

Holland /хо́лэнд/ Голландия; см. Netherlands

Hollywood /хо́ливуд/ г. Голливуд

Honduras /хондьо́эрэс/ Гондурас

Hong Kong /хонко́нг/ Гонконг

Horn, Cape /ке́йпхо́рн/ мыс Горн

Houston /хью́юстэн/ г. Хьюстон

Hudson /хадсн/ р. Гудзон

Hudson Bay /ха́дснбэ́й/ Гудзонов залив

Hungary /ха́нгэри/ Венгрия

Iceland /а́йслэнд/ Исландия

Idaho /а́йдэхэу/ Айдахо

Illinois /и́лино́й/ Иллинойс

India /и́ндье/ Индия

Indiana /и́нди́э́нэ/ Индиана

Indian Ocean /и́ндьенэ́ушн/ Индийский океан

Indonesia /и́ндэни́изье/ Индонезия

Iowa /а́йэуэ/ Айова

Iran /ира́ан/ Иран

Iraq /ира́ак/ Ирак

Ireland /а́йэлэнд/ Ирландия

Israel /и́зрэйл/ Израиль

Istanbul /и́стэнбу́ул/ г. Стамбул

Italy /и́тэли/ Италия

Jaffa /джэ́фэ/ г. Яффа

Jakarta /джекáртэ/ г. Джакарта

Jamaica /джемэ́йкэ/ Ямайка

Japan /джепэ́н/ Япония

Java /джáавэ/ о-в Ява

Jerusalem /джерýусэлем/ г. Иерусалим

Jibuti /джибýути/ г. Джибути

Jidda /джи́дэ/ г. Джидда

Johannesburg /джехэ́нисбёрг/ г. Йоханнесбург

Jordan /джоодн/ 1) Йордания 2) р. Йордан

Kabul /кообл/ г. Кабул

Kamchatka /кэмчэ́ткэ/ п-ов Камчатка

Kansas /кэ́нзэс/ Канзас

Karachi /кэрáачи/ г. Карачи

Katmandu /кáатмандýу/ г. Катманду

Kattegat /кэ́тигэ́т/ пролив Каттегат

Kazakhstan /кáазахстáн/ Казахстан

Kent /кент/ Кент

Kentucky /кентáки/ Кентукки

Kenya /кéнье/ Кения

Kiev /ки́иеф/ г. Киев

Kilimanjaro /ки́лимэнджáарэу/ Килиманджаро (гора)

Kinshasa /киншáасэ/ г. Киншаса

Kirghizstan /кеги́зстан/ Кыргызстан

Kishinev /ки́шинёф/ г. Кишинёв

Klondike /клóндайк/ Клондайк

Korea /кори́иэ/ Корея

Kuril(e) Islands /кури́илáйлэндз/ Курильские о-ва

Kuwait /кувэ́йт/ Кувейт

Kyoto /киэ́утэу/ г. Киото

Lahore /лэхо́р/ г. Лахор
Laos /ла́уз/ Лаос
Latvia /лэ́твиэ/ Латвия
Lebanon /ле́бэнэн/ Ливан
Leipzig /ла́йпзиг/ г. Лейпциг
Leningrad /ле́нингрэд/ г. Ленинград; см. St. Petersburg
Lesotho /лэсэ́утэу/ Лесото
Lhasa /ла́асэ/ г. Лхаса
Liberia /лайби́риэ/ Либерия
Libya /ли́биэ/ Ливия
Liechtenstein /ли́ктэнстайн/ Лихтенштейн
Lima /ли́имэ/ г. Лима
Lisbon /ли́збэн/ г. Лис(с)абон
Lithuania /ли́туэ́йнье/ Литва
Liverpool /ли́вэпул/ г. Ливерпул(ь)
Loire /луа́а/ р. Луара
London /ла́ндэн/ г. Лондон
Los Angeles /лосэ́нджилиз/ г. Лос-Анджелес
Louisiana /луи́изиэ́нэ/ Луизиана
Luanda /луэ́ндэ/ г. Луанда
Lusaka /луса́акэ/ г. Лусака
Luxembourg /ла́ксэмбег/ г. Люксембург

Madagascar /мэ́дэгэ́скэ/ Мадагаскар
Madrid /мэдри́д/ г. Мадрид
Magellan, Strait of /стрэ́йтэвмэге́лэн/ Магелланов пролив
Maine /мэйн/ Мэн (штат США)

Malaysia /мэлэ́йзиэ/ Малайзия

Malta /мо́лтэ/ Мальта

Managua /мэна́агвэ/ г. Манагуа

Manchester /мэ́нчистэ/ г. Манчестер

Manhattan /мэнхэ́тн/ Манхаттан

Manila /мэни́лэ/ г. Манила

Manitoba /мэ́нитэ́убэ/ Манитоба

Maputo /мэпу́утэу/ г. Мапуту

Marseilles /масэ́йлз/ г. Марсель

Martinique /ма́ртини́ик/ о-в Мартиника

Maryland /мэ́эрилэнд/ Мэриленд

Massachusetts /мэ́сэчу́уситс/ Массачусетс

Mauritania /мо́орите́йнье/ Мавритания

Mauritius /мэри́шес/ Маврикий

Mecca /ме́кэ/ г. Мекка

Mediterranean Sea /ме́дитэрэ́йньенси́и/ Средиземное
  море

Melanesia /ме́лэни́изье/ Меланезия

Mexico /ме́ксикэу/ Мексика

Mexico (City) /ме́ксикэу (си́ти)/ г. Мехико

Miami /майэ́ми/ г. Майами

Michigan /ми́шигэн/ Мичиган

Michigan, Lake /лэ́йкми́шигэн/ оз. Мичиган

Milan /милэ́н/ г. Милан

Milwaukee /милво́оки/ г. Милуоки

Minnesota /ми́нисбутэ/ Миннесота

Minsk /минск/ г. Минск

Mississippi /ми́сиси́пи/ Миссисипи (река и штат)

Missouri /мизу́эри/ Миссури (река и штат)

Moldova /молдо́ва/ Молдова

Monaco /мо́нэкоу/ Монако

Mongolia /монго́улье/ Монголия

Montreal /мо́нрио́л/ г. Монреаль

Morocco /мэро́коу/ Марокко

Moscow /мо́скоу/ г. Москва

Mozambique /мо́узэмби́ик/ Мозамбик

Munich /мью́юник/ г. Мюнхен

Nairobi /на́йэро́уби/ г. Найроби

Namibia /нэ́мибье/ Намибия

Naples /нэ́йплз/ г. Неаполь

Nauru /нау́уру/ Науру

N'Djamena /нджаме́нэ/ г. Нджамена

Nebraska /нибрэ́скэ/ Небраска

Nepal /нипо́л/ Непал

Netherlands /нэ́зелэндз/ Нидерланды

Neva /нэ́йвэ/ р. Нева

Nevada /нева́адэ/ Невада

New Guinea /нью́югу́ни/ Новая Гвинея

New Orleans /нью́юо́рлиэнз/ г. Новый Орлеан

New York /нью́юйо́рк/ Нью-Йорк (город и штат)

New Zealand /нью́юзи́илэнд/ Новая Зеландия

Niagara /найэ́гэрэ/ р. Ниагара

Niagara Falls /найэ́гэрэфо́олз/ Ниагарский водопад

Nicaragua /ни́кэрэ́гьюэ/ Никарагуа

Nice /ниис/ г. Ницца

Nigeria /найджи́риэ/ Нигерия

Nile /найл/ р. Нил

North America /нóосэмéрикэ/ Северная Америка
North Carolina /нóоскэ́рэлáйнэ/ Северная Каролина
North Dakota /нóосдэкóутэ/ Северная Дакота
North Pole /нóоспóул/ Северный полюс
North Sea /нóоссúи/ Северное море
Norway /нóовэй/ Норвегия
Noumea /нумэ́йе/ г. Нумеа
Nuremberg, Nurnberg /ньюэрэмбёг,   ньюю́рнбэрх/
   г. Нюрнберг

Oakland /óуклэнд/ г. Окленд
Oceania /óушиэ́йнье/ Океания
Ohio /оихáйэу/ Огайо
Oklahoma /óуклэхóумэ/ Оклахома
Oman /оумáан/ Оман
Oregon /óригэн/ Орегон
Oslo /óзлоу/ г. Осло
Oxford /óксфэд/ г. Оксфорд

Pacific Ocean /пэсúфикóушен/ Тихий океан
Pakistan /пáакистáан/ Пакистан
Palestine /пэ́листайн/ Палестина
Panama /пэ́немáа/ Панама
Panama Canal /пэ́немáакэнэ́л/ Панамский канал
Papua New Guinea /пэ́пьюэньюгúни/ Папуа — Новая
   Гвинея
Paraguay /пэ́рэгвай/ Парагвай
Paris /пэ́рис/ г. Париж
Pearl Harbor /пёёлхáабэ/ Пирл-Харбор

Peking /пики́нг/ г. Пекин

Pennsylvania /пе́нсилвэ́йнье/ Пенсильвания

Persian Gulf /пёёшнга́лф/ Персидский залив

Peru /пэру́у/ Перу

Philadelphia /фи́лэде́лфье/ г. Филадельфия

Philippines /фи́липинз/ Филиппины

Poland /по́улэнд/ Польша

Portugal /по́отьюгэл/ Португалия

Prague /пра́аг/ г. Прага

Pretoria /прито́ориэ/ г. Претория

Puerto Rico /пвёёто́ури́икоу/ Пуэрто-Рико

Pyongyang /пьёнгйа́нг/ г. Пхеньян

Pyrenees /пи́рэни́из/ Пиренеи

Quebec /квибе́к/ Квебек

Red Sea /рэ́дси́и/ Красное море

Republic of South Africa /рипа́бликэвса́усэ́фрикэ/
   Южно-Африканская Республика, ЮАР

Reykjavik /ре́йкьевик/ г. Рейкьявик

Rhine /ра́йн/ р. Рейн

Rio de Janeiro /ри́иоудэджени́эроу/ г. Рио-де-Жанейро

Rocky Mts /ро́кима́унтинз/ Скалистые горы

Romania /румэ́йнье/ Румыния

Rome /ро́ум/ г. Рим

Russia /ра́ше/ Россия

Sahara /сэха́арэ/ Сахара

Sakhalin /сэ́кэли́ин/ о-в Сахалин

Samoa /сэмбуэ/ о-ва Самоа

San Francisco /сэнфрэнси́скоу/ г. Сан-Франциско

San Salvador /сэнса́лвэдо/ г. Сан-Сальвадор

Santiago /сэ́нтиа́гоу/ г. Сантьяго

Santo Domingo /сэ́нтэдоуми́нгоу/ г. Санто-Доминго

Sao Paulo /са́унпа́улу/ г. Сан-Паулу

Sao Tomé and Principe /са́унтэмэ́йэнпри́нсипэ/ Сан-Томе и Принсипи

Saudi Arabia /са́удиэрэ́йбье/ Саудовская Аравия

Scotland /ско́тлэнд/ Шотландия

Seine /сэйн/ р. Сена

Senegal /се́ниго́ол/ Сенегал

Seoul /со́ул/ г. Сеул

Sevastopol /сива́сто́пэл/ г. Севастополь

Shanghai /шэнгха́й/ г. Шанхай

Siberia /сайби́эриэ/ Сибирь

Sicily /си́сили/ о-в Сицилия

Singapore /си́нгэпо́/ Сингапур

Sofia /со́уфье/ г. София

Somalia /соума́алье/ Сомали

South America /са́усэмэ́рикэ/ Южная Америка

South Carolina /са́уска̀рэла́йнэ/ Южная Каролина

South Dakota /са́усдэко́утэ/ Южная Дакота

South Korea /са́ускэри́иэ/ Южная Корея

South Pole /са́успо́ул/ Южный полюс

Spain /спэйн/ Испания

Sri Lanka /срила́нкэ/ Шри-Ланка

Stockholm /сто́кхоум/ г. Стокгольм

St. Petersburg /сэнпи́итэзбёг/ г. Санкт-Петербург

Sudan, the /судáан/ Судан

Suez Canal /сýизкс́нэл/ Суэцкий канал

Swaziland /свáазилэнд/ Свазиленд

Sweden /свиидн/ Швеция

Switzerland /свйтсэлэнд/ Швейцария

Sydney /сйдни/ г. Сидней

Syria /сйриэ/ Сирия

Tadjikistan /таджйкистáан/ Таджикистан

Taiwan /тайвэ́н/ о-в Тайвань

Tanzania /тэ́нзэнйэ/ Танзания

Tashkent /тэшкéнт/ г. Ташкент

Tatarstan /тáтарстáн/ Татарстан

Tbilisi /тбилйси/ г. Тбилиси

Teh(e)ran /тиэрáан/ г. Тегеран

Tel Aviv /тéлевйив/ г. Тель-Авив

Tennessee /тэ́нэсйи/ Теннесси

Texas /тэ́ксэс/ Техас

Thailand /тáйлэнд/ Таиланд

Thames /тэмз/ р. Темза

Tibet /тибéт/ Тибет

Tokyo /тóукьоу/ г. Токио

Toronto /тэрóнтоу/ г. Торонто

Trinidad and Tobago /трйнидэдэнтэбэ́йгоу/ Тринидад и
  Тобаго

Tunis /тьююнис/ г. Тунис

Tunisia /тьюнйзиэ/ Тунис

Turkey /тёёки/ Турция

Turkmenistan /тёкменистáан/ Туркменистан

Uganda /югэ́ндэ/ Уганда

Ukraine, the /юкрэ́йн/ Украина

Ulan Bator /у́уланба́атэ/ г. Улан-Батор

Ulster /а́лстэ/ Ольстер

United Arab Emirates /юна́йтыдэ́рэбэми́эритс/ Объединенные Арабские Эмираты

United Kingdom of Great Britain and Northern Ireland /юна́йткди́нгдэмэвгрэ́йтбри́тэнэннóозэна́йэлэнд/ Соединенное Королевство Великобритании и Северной Ирландии

United States of America, USA /юна́йтыдстэ́йтсэвэмéрикэ, ю́ю́эсэ́й/ Соединенные Штаты Америки, США

Urals, the /ю́эрэлз/ Урал

Uruguay /у́ругвай/ Уругвай

Utah /ю́юта/ Юта

Uzbekistan /у́збекиста́ан/ Узбекистан

Vatican /вэ́тикэн/ Ватикан

Venezuela /вéнезвэ́йлэ/ Венесуэла

Venice /вéнис/ г. Венеция

Vermont /вэмóнт/ Вермонт

Victoria /виктóориэ/ г. Виктория

Vietnam /вьéтнэ́м/ Вьетнам

Virginia /вэджи́нье/ Виргиния

Vistula /ви́стьюлэ/ р. Висла

Vladivostok /влэ́дивóсток/ г. Владивосток

Volga /вóлгэ/ р. Волга

Wales /вэйлз/ Уэльс

Warsaw /вóосо/ г. Варшава

Washington /вóшингтон/ Вашингтон (город и штат)

Western Samoa /вéстэнсэмбуэ/ Западное Самоа

West Virginia /вéствэджúнье/ Западная Виргиния

White Sea /вáйтсúи/ Белое море

Wisconsin /вискóнсин/ Висконсин

Wyoming /вайóуминг/ Вайоминг

Yellow Sea /йэ́лоусúи/ Желтое море

Yemen /йэ́мен/ Йемен

Yerevan /йэ́ревáан/ г. Ереван

Yugoslavia /ю́югоуслáавье/ Югославия

Zaire /зайэр/ Заир

Zambia /зэ́мбиэ/ Замбия

Zanzibar /зэ́нзибáа/ о-в Занзибар

Zimbabwe /зимбáабви/ Зимбабве

Zurich /зы́оэрик/ г. Цюрих

ТАБЛИЦЫ МЕР И ВЕСОВ

1. Меры длины

русское наимен.	сантиметр (см)	метр (м)
англ. наимен.	centimetre	metre
1 см =		
1 м =	100	
1 км =		1000
1 дюйм =	2,54	
1 фут =	30,5	0,3
1 ярд =	91	0,9
1 миля =		1609

километр (км)	дюйм	фут	ярд	миля
kilometre	inch In.	foot Ft.	yard	mile
	0,39			
	39,4	3,28	1,09	
			1094	0,6
	12			
	36	3		
1,6			1760	

2. Меры веса

русское наимен.	грамм (г)	кило- грамм (кг)	тонна (т)	унция	фунт
англ. наимен.	gram (gr.)	kilogram (kg.)	tonne	ounce Oz.	pound Lb.
1 г =				0,035	
1 кг.	1000				2,2
1 т =		1000			2204,6
1 унция=	28,3				
1 фунт=	454	0,45		16	

3. Меры емкости жидких тел

русское наимен.	литр (л)	пинта	галлон
англ. наимен.	litre	pint	gallon Gal.
1 л =		1,76	0,22
1 пинта =	0,57		
1 галлон =	4,54	8	

4. Важнейшие единицы мер, применяемых в сельском хозяйстве

Меры земельной площади

русское наимен.	кв. метр (кв. м)	гектар (га)	акр
англ. наимен.	sq.metre	hectare	acre
1 га =	10 000		2,47
1 акр =	4000	0,4	

HIPPOCRENE FOREIGN LANGUAGE DICTIONARIES
Modern • Up-to-Date
Easy-to-Use • Practical

Albanian-English Standard Dictionary
0744   ISBN 0-87052-077-6 $14.95 pb

English-Albanian Dictionary
0518   ISBN 0-7818-0021-8 $14.95 pb

Armenian-English/English-Armenian Concise Dictionary
0490   ISBN 0-7818-0150-8 $11.95 pb

Armenian Dictionary in Transliteration (Western)
0059   ISBN 0-7818-0207-5 $9.95 pb

English-Azerbaijani/Azerbaijani-English
0096   ISBN 0-7818-0244-X $11.95 pb

Bulgarian-English/English-Bulgarian Practical Dictionary
0331   ISBN 0-87052-145-4 $11.95 pb

Byelorussian-English/English-Byelorussian Concise Dictionary
1050   ISBN 0-87052-114-4 $9.95 pb

Czech-English/English-Czech Concise Dictionary
0276 ISBN 0-87052-981-1 $11.95 pb

Danish-English/English-Danish Practical Dictionary
0198 ISBN 0-87052-823-8 $14.95 pb

Dutch-English/English-Dutch Concise Dictionary
0606 ISBN 0-87052-910-2 $11.95 pb

Estonian-English/English-Estonian Concise Dictionary
1010 ISBN 0-87052-081-4 $11.95 pb

Finnish-English/English-Finnish Concise Dictionary
0142 ISBN 0-87052-813-0 $9.95 pb

Georgian-English/English-Georgian Concise Dictionary
1059 ISBN 0-87052-121-7 $8.95 pb

English-Hungarian/Hungarian-English Dictionary
2039 ISBN 0-88254-986-3 $11.95 hc

Hungarian-English/English-Hungarian Concise Dictionary
0254 ISBN 0-87052-891-2 $8.95 pb

Icelandic-English/English-Icelandic Concise Dictionary
0147 ISBN 0-87052-801-7 $8.95 pb

Kurdish-English/English-Kurdish Dictionary
0218 ISBN 0-7818-0246-6 $11.95

Latvian-English/English-Latvian Dictionary
0194 ISBN 0-7818-0059-5 $14.95 pb

Lithuanian-English/English-Lithuanian Concise Dictionary
0489 ISBN 0-7818-0151-6 $11.95 pb

Norwegian-English/English-Norwegian Dictionary
(Revised Edition)
0202 ISBN 0-7818-0199-0 $11.95 pb

Polish-English/English-Polish Concise Dictionary
0268 ISBN 0-7818-0133-8 $8.95 pb

Polish-English/English-Polish Practical Dictionary
0450 ISBN 0-7818-0085-4 $11.95 pb

Polish-English/English-Polish Standard Dictionary
0665 ISBN 0-87052-882-3 $22.50 hc

Polish-English/English-Polish Standard Dictionary
0207 ISBN 0-7818-0183-4 $16.95 pb

Romanian-English/English-Romanian Dictionary
0488 ISBN 0-87052-986-2 $19.95 pb

Russian-English/English-Russian Standard Dictionary with Business Terms
0440 ISBN 0-7818-0280-6 $16.95 pb

English-Russian Standard Dictionary
1025   ISBN 0-87052-100-4 $11.95 pb

Russian-English Standard Dictionary
0578   ISBN 0-87052-964-1 $11.95 pb

Slovak-English/English-Slovak Concise Dictionary
1052   ISBN 0-87052-115-2 $9.95 pb

Ukrainian-English/English Ukrainian Practical Dictionary,
Revised
0343   ISBN 0-7818-0306-3 $11.95 pb

Ukrainian-English Standard Dictionary
0006   ISBN 0-7818-0189-3 $14.95 pb

Uzbek-English/English-Uzbek
0004   ISBN 0-7818-0165-6 $11.95 pb